# ECONOMIC ANALYSIS FOR EDUCATIONAL PLANNING

# ECONOMIC ANALYSIS FOR EDUCATIONAL PLANNING:
Resource Allocation in Nonmarket Systems

edited by KARL A. FOX
with contributions by
Karl A. Fox
Jati K. Sengupta
T. Krishna Kumar
Bikas C. Sanyal

The Johns Hopkins University Press
Baltimore and London

Copyright © 1972 by The Johns Hopkins University Press
All rights reserved
Manufactured in the United States of America

The Johns Hopkins University Press, Baltimore, Maryland 21218
The Johns Hopkins University Press Ltd., London

Library of Congress Catalog Card Number 70-175453
ISBN 0-8018-1292-5

# Contents

Preface................................................................. ix

CHAPTER 1. INTRODUCTION TO NONMARKET SYSTEMS.......... 1
    *Karl A. Fox*

  General remarks....................................................... 1
  Types of nonmarket systems and their behavior....................... 3
  Decisions for nonmarket systems and the theory of economic policy...... 3
  Systems analysis for market and nonmarket systems................... 12
  The plan of the book................................................. 16

CHAPTER 2. QUANTITATIVE ANALYSIS OF NONMARKET SYSTEMS. 19
    *Jati K. Sengupta*

  General remarks....................................................... 19
  Analyzing nonmarket systems by competitive and noncompetitive rules... 21
  Framework of mixed systems........................................ 24
  Resource allocation in educational systems.......................... 30

CHAPTER 3. QUANTITATIVE MODELS OF PLANNING FOR
             EDUCATIONAL SYSTEMS............................. 36
    *Jati K. Sengupta*

  General remarks....................................................... 36
  Objectives and constraints in modeling educational systems............ 38
  Current mathematical models of educational systems: A brief appraisal of
    selected models.................................................... 50
  Economic theory relevant for educational planning.................... 69
  Methods of macroeconomic planning for educational systems........... 73

CHAPTER 4. RESOURCE ALLOCATION PROCESSES IN LINEAR
             STATIC MODELS...................................... 80
    *T. Krishna Kumar*

  Introductory remarks................................................. 80
  Price-guided allocation in competitive and planned systems............ 83
  Decentralization of decisions using decomposition techniques.......... 92
  Organizational and game-theoretic approaches to resource allocation...... 115

CHAPTER 5. RESOURCE ALLOCATION PROCESSES IN NONLINEAR
AND DYNAMIC MODELS............................. 117
T. Krishna Kumar

Introductory remarks.............................................. 117
Price-guided allocation in imperfectly competitive models............... 120
Decomposition methods in nonlinear and dynamic models.............. 122
Economic implications of applying decomposition techniques to educational
and other systems................................................ 141

CHAPTER 6. ECONOMIC PROBLEMS OF RESOURCE ALLOCATION
IN NONMARKET SYSTEMS........................... 148
Jati K. Sengupta

General remarks.................................................. 148
Problems of imputation in benefit-cost analysis for public goods.......... 150
Aggregation, disaggregation, and consistency problems of policymaking... 187
The indivisibility problem and suboptimization....................... 210
Implications of second-best policies and partial optimization............ 216

CHAPTER 7. THE SYSTEMS APPROACH TO RESOURCE
ALLOCATION IN EDUCATIONAL PLANNING........... 224
Bikas C. Sanyal

Objectives of a systems approach.................................... 224
A systems analysis framework for educational systems.................. 225
Activity analysis, state space, and scheduling models................... 238
Simulation techniques in educational planning........................ 251

CHAPTER 8. SOME EMPIRICAL PROBLEMS INVOLVED IN
SPECIFYING QUANTITATIVE MODELS FOR
EDUCATIONAL PLANNING........................... 258
Karl A. Fox

Illustrative model for a small college................................. 258
Comparing workloads and performance among departments within a
university...................................................... 267
Comparisons among universities..................................... 276
Workload, cost, and quality estimates for a given department........... 284
Problems of aggregation........................................... 294

CHAPTER 9. OBJECTIVE FUNCTIONS AND OPTIMIZATION MODELS
FOR INSTITUTIONS OF HIGHER EDUCATION.......... 296
Karl A. Fox

Educational institutions in a multicounty functional economic area
framework..................................................... 296
Optimization models for university planning.......................... 307
National salary differentials for scientists within and among scientific fields. 314
Correlates of quality in graduate education........................... 320
Some elements of practical modeling for university departments.......... 323

CONTENTS vii

CHAPTER 10. THE AREAS OF POTENTIAL APPLICATION............ 340
Karl A. Fox

Extending economic analysis to nonmarket systems.................... 340
Optimization models at many levels................................. 342
Concluding remarks................................................ 345

References................................................................ 347

Author Index............................................................. 367

Subject Index............................................................ 371

## Tables

|  | | Page |
|---|---|---|
| 4.1 | Some characteristics of departments A, B, and C...................... | 101 |
| 4.2 | Complete model of departments A, B, and C with department-specific and joint college-level restrictions.................................... | 102–105 |
| 4.3 | A model of decentralized decisionmaking (Dantzig–Wolfe) applied to a college planning model: Values of key magnitudes at successive iterations or communication phases between the college dean and department chairmen.......................................................... | 107 |
| 6.1 | Basic data of the $Y$-subdepartment model........................... | 158 |
| 6.2 | Optimal solutions of $Y$-subdepartment activity models: A, B, C, D, and E............................................. 162, 164, 166, 168, | 169 |
| 6.3 | Goal programming: Basic model..................................... | 184 |
| 6.4 | Goal programming: Solutions to the three linear programs.............. | 189 |
| 6.5 | Goal programming: Solutions in the parametric case................... | 189 |
| 7.1 | Activity analysis model of a university department: The simplified simplex tableau............................................................ | 235 |
| 7.2 | Activity analysis model of a university department: Degree activities.... | 242 |
| 8.1 | Publication styles in different disciplines, based on responses by senior scholars to the Cartter–American Council on Education Survey of Graduate Education in the United States, April 1964........................ | 289 |
| 8.2 | Publication styles in major groups of disciplines based on responses by senior scholars in April 1964: (A) Actual responses and (B) actual responses adjusted for differences in percentages of time spent on research and writing | 290 |
| 9.1 | Importance of selected characteristics in explaining variation in professional salaries. All professions, 1966 National Register.................. | 315 |
| 9.2 | Net relationships between professional salaries and employer-experience characteristics: All professions, 1966 National Register................. | 316 |
| 9.3 | Net relationships between professional salaries and specified characteristics: All professions, 1966 National Register............................. | 317 |
| 9.4 | Correlates of quality in graduate education in the United States: Attributes and performance measures as of 1963–64 to 1967–68.................... | 321 |

|  |  | Page |
|---|---|---|
| 9.5 | Number of graduate faculty members per department, fall 1966 | 322 |
| 9.6 | Preliminary estimates of 1972–73 output levels and input requirements for X-department programs: Approximation I | 324–327 |
| 9.7 | Some implications of the gross benefit figures per student quarter ascribed to the resident instruction program | 334 |
| 9.8 | Component $S$ of $X$-department: Planned activities and budget restrictions for 1970–71 | 336–337 |

# Figures

|  |  | Page |
|---|---|---|
| 1.1 | The theory of economic policy | 4 |
| 1.2 | Condensed flow diagram of the Brookings econometric model | 14 |
| 2.1 | The decisionmaking system of a university | 34 |
| 3.1 | Education, manpower, and interindustry accounts | 42 |
| 3.2 | Terminal flows and internal states identified in the model of an educational institution as a "black box" | 47 |
| 4.1 | A set of extreme points and alternative subproblem constraints | 97 |
| 7.1 | General systems approach to education | 228 |
| 7.2 | A systems model for a university | 244 |
| 7.3 | Objectives of a university | 250 |
| 7.4 | General flow chart of the university cost simulation model | 254 |
| 7.5 | Instruction and instructional support model | 256 |
| 8.1 | Rated quality of economics faculty, by percent of respondents providing ratings | 278 |
| 8.2 | Relationship of rated quality of graduate faculty to index of publications, 71 economics departments | 279 |
| 9.1 | Distribution of town population sizes in the Fort Dodge area | 299 |
| 9.2 | Fifty-mile commuting distances from the central business districts of Iowa SMSA central cities | 300 |
| 9.3 | Fifty-mile commuting distances from the central business districts of all FEA (including SMSA) central cities in or near Iowa | 301 |
| 9.4 | Commuting fields of central cities | 302–303 |
| 9.5 | Functional economic areas of the United States | 304–305 |
| 9.6 | Estimated 1968–69 national salary structure for economists employed by educational institutions on an 11–12 month basis | 319 |

# Preface

This book has the following objectives:

1. To bring together those concepts from economic theory, mathematical programming, and systems analysis that seem most likely to be useful in the quantitative planning of educational systems;

2. To summarize and illustrate the application of these concepts to components of educational systems, particularly systems of higher education; and

3. To suggest the applicability of these concepts to other nonmarket systems.

Part of the motivation for this book comes from needs felt by the editor in connection with his role as head of a large and complex university department from 1955 down to the present. This role has kept him continuously involved with a College of Agriculture, a College of Sciences and Humanities, a Graduate College, an Agricultural Experiment Station, a Cooperative Extension Service, and two centers which link economics with other disciplines. The outputs desired by these various administrative units are different. However, each consumes resources which are partly interchangeable, and this raises the question of a consistent rationale for resource allocation.

It is conceivable that each functional component of a university might arrive at an optimal internal allocation of its resources without attempting to measure the quantities and "prices" of its outputs. Thus, a perceptive extension administrator might interpret feedback from his various clienteles as indicating that certain activities should be reduced and others expanded. The question of how much could be answered recursively over a series of years, with each year's feedback indicating whether the planned adjustments had gone too far or not far enough. A system of curriculum committees might arrive at optimal adjustments in the undergraduate program, and a wise graduate dean might arrive at optimal adjustments in degree requirements and admissions policies, without using quantitative information of any sort. Finally, an astute president might make an optimal allocation of his flexible resources among the various colleges and professional schools by an intuitive balancing of pressures and impressions. The resulting pattern of resource allocation might be Pareto-optimal, in the sense that no member of the university community could be made better off without making at least one other member worse off.

This is, no doubt, a solution "devoutly to be wished"; it is the nonmarket analog of general economic equilibrium under perfect competition. However, the theoretical possibility of a general economic equilibrium depends on a number of assumptions, such as: (1) that each producer knows the market price of every output he produces or could produce and every input he uses or could use; (2) that each producer has perfect knowledge of his production function and can readily determine (and implement) his optimal production response to any given vector of output and input prices, his object being to maximize net revenue; (3) that each consumer has a utility function and a budget constraint and can readily determine (and implement) his optimal consumption response to any given vector of prices for consumer goods; (4) that there are no indivisibilities, externalities, or economies of scale; and (5) that no one producer or consumer is large enough (in economic size) to have a perceptible effect on the price of any output or input.

These assumptions are not fully met in any real economy and it is unlikely that their equivalents are fully met in any real university. Nevertheless, there are enough market-like signals originating both inside and outside of a university so that good verbal communication among administrators, faculty members, and students might lead to an allocation of resources the optimality of which could not be refuted.

But such a conclusion requires faith on the part of members of the university community and also on the part of legislators, donors, parents, and other support groups. In the face of competition for legislative appropriations and of criticisms from within the university community, this faith is bound to be challenged, and it may become necessary to specify what outputs are being produced under the current allocation of resources and to indicate what outputs would be produced under various alternative allocations.

I have believed for some years that these questions of resource allocation could be clarified by the careful measurement of inputs, outputs, and transformation functions and by the use of an internally consistent system of prices within the university, whether or not these prices could be derived unequivocally from phenomena discernible in the larger society. Useful models of university departments would therefore be optimization models with explicit, quantitative objective functions.

During 1961–64 I talked about optimization models with various faculty members in the economics department and wrote up voluminous notes. One of these faculty members, Donald L. Winkelmann, was the first in our group to implement an activity analysis model of a (hypothetical) department. He presented his model at the Midwest Economic Association meetings in April 1965; it was a "teacher assignment" model using estimates of the effectiveness of each faculty member in each of a number of courses.

For various periods during 1965–67, Yakir Plessner, Francis McCamley, and Balder von Hohenbalken worked with me to implement various kinds of optimization models based on data for the teaching and research components of the economics department. In the summer of 1966, Plessner completed a four-year dynamic programming model, using an objective function which included teaching outputs with market-like prices and research outputs to which no prices were assigned. As the department chairman transferred successive units of resources from teaching to research, the value of the objective function declined; at some point the chairman would decide that the next increment of research would not be worth its opportunity cost to the teaching program. The allocation of resources between teaching and research at that point would be optimal *as viewed by the chairman*.

During 1966–67, von Hohenbalken developed "An economic policy model to maximize the excellence of an academic department," using a target and instrument approach in the tradition of Tinbergen's theory of economic policy. The von Hohenbalken manuscript has not been published.

McCamley completed his dissertation on "Activity analysis models of educational institutions" in 1967. McCamley used decomposition (decentralization) techniques in a static linear programming framework to model the interaction among three (hypothetical) department chairmen and a college dean in arriving at an optimal allocation of the dean's "central" resources among the departments. In addition, each department had specialized resources which could be used only for its own activities.

McCamley's dissertation, a report by Fox, McCamley, and Plessner on "Formulation of management science models for selected problems of college administration," and an article by Plessner, Fox, and Sanyal "On the allocation of resources in a university department" are listed in the References.

In 1967 Jati K. Sengupta also became interested in the quantitative planning of educational systems. Fox and Sengupta were joined by Bikas C. Sanyal (1967–October 1969), D. K. Bose (September 1967–May 1968), and T. Krishna Kumar (January 1968–July 1969); the group met frequently during 1967–69.

Quantitative models for educational planning were practically nonexistent prior to 1962. The rate of publication of such models increased rapidly after 1964; the state of the literature as of 1967 is reflected in an article by Fox and Sengupta on "The specification of econometric models for planning educational systems: An appraisal of alternative approaches." Another article by Sengupta and Fox on "A computable approach to optimal growth of an academic department" was submitted for publication in February 1968, but appeared with some delay (January 1970).

As we began writing the present book (in 1969), we decided that several branches of economic theory were relevant to economic analysis and policy for nonmarket systems. Some of the topics were as old as Pareto; others have figured prominently in the economic theory of socialism, in the "new public finance" of Buchanan and Tullock, in welfare economics, in the theory of economic policy, and in the theory and recent practice of central planning in socialist countries.

Chapters 2, 3, 4, 5, 6, and 7 are based on the branches of economic theory just mentioned, plus the specialized literatures on quantitative planning of educational systems and on mathematical programming techniques. Chapter 1 uses the Tinbergen–Theil theory of economic policy to link objective functions for nonmarket systems with the familiar cardinal and ordinal objective functions of firms and consumers. Chapter 8 deals with the empirical problems involved in specifying quantitative models of university departments and colleges. Chapter 9 discusses practical methods for specifying optimization models and objective functions for a university and its components, using published data of various sorts in addition to the university's own information system. Chapter 10 discusses the prospects for applying quantitative models to university planning in the near future.

The book is a co-operative product. We wrote within the framework of an agreed-upon outline and influenced each other through group discussions and through coauthorship of working papers and articles which underlie portions of some chapters. The principal author of each chapter is listed in the Contents and at the beginning of the chapters.

Readers who are primarily interested in empirical studies of universities and/or in departmental planning should begin with Chapters 8, 9, and 10. The examples presented there suggest that many issues which arise at the department and subdepartment levels can be clarified with the aid of small-scale optimization models; these can be used in a participatory context. Further reflection will indicate, however, that problems of planning and resource allocation at the level of an entire university call for all the help that economic theory can give and for sophisticated computational techniques. At this stage, the empirically oriented reader may be motivated to study Chapters 1 through 7.

Readers with a strong interest in economic theory and in educational planning at an advanced level should proceed consecutively from Chapter 1 through Chapter 10.

All four of the contributors wish to express their gratitude to the National Science Foundation for supporting most of the research upon which this book is based.

Several former students at Iowa State University have contributed to the shaping of this book. Yakir Plessner, now at Hebrew University, and Francis McCamley, now at the University of Missouri, conceptualized and implemented some highly informative models of university departments; some of their methods and results are described in Chapters 3, 6, and 7. Gene Gruver, now at the University of Pittsburgh, wrote the part of Chapter 6 which deals with goal programming and efficiency in decision models for educational institutions, corrected many errors in the first draft of the entire manuscript and checked most of the references.

Juanita Adams deserves special credit for her excellent work on a difficult manuscript. Her resourcefulness in interpreting our handwriting, reproducing our equations, and progressively reducing typographical errors saved us much time. Gloria Wiener also helped on the final typing of some sections. Shirley Cheatum edited and typed the final list of references.

The titles and affiliations of the authors of this book are as follows:

Karl A. Fox, Distinguished Professor and Head, Department of Economics, Iowa State University, Ames, Iowa.
Jati K. Sengupta, Professor of Economics and Statistics, Iowa State University, Ames, Iowa.
T. Krishna Kumar, Assistant Professor of Economics and Statistics, Florida State University, Tallahassee, Florida.
Bikas C. Sanyal, International Institute for Educational Planning, Paris, France.

KARL A. FOX

*Ames, Iowa*
*August 4, 1971*

# ECONOMIC ANALYSIS FOR EDUCATIONAL PLANNING

CHAPTER 1

# Introduction to Nonmarket Systems

*Karl A. Fox*

**General remarks**

Market prices play a central role in economic theory. This theory can be stated most elegantly for the case of perfect competition, in which each firm sells all of its outputs and buys all of its variable inputs at explicit market prices over which the firm has no control. As early as 1897, and more fully in 1909, Pareto (see References) developed the postulates of perfect competition into a theory of general equilibrium for all producers and consumers in an economic system.

Under stated assumptions, general economic equilibrium is characterized by an optimal allocation of resources among firms and an optimal combination of resources within firms. Given constant technology, a particular general equilibrium pattern of inputs and outputs for each firm and for the economy as a whole will continue so long as their relative prices are unchanged. Conversely, any change in relative market prices will in general lead to a change in the pattern of production.

Although any real economy contains many departures from perfect competition, economic theory still enables us to say a good deal about the efficient allocation of resources within a real firm. For example, it gives us a criterion for comparing alternative techniques for producing a given product in terms of their respective dollar costs, and it enables us to compare the profitability of alternative products or groups of products which a firm could produce with a given set of inputs.

Examples of nonmarket institutions include schools, government agencies, political parties, churches, and various voluntary associations.

It seems intuitively clear that some of the concepts we apply to business firms are also applicable to nonmarket institutions. A nonmarket institution, like a firm, transforms inputs into outputs. Some quantitative measures of inputs and outputs are often recorded, and so in most cases are monetary receipts and expenditures. If we can identify and measure the outputs of, say, a post office, we can compare alternative techniques for producing these outputs in terms of their money costs. Even in an institution such as a church, in which some of the labor may be donated, we can compare the man-hour requirements of alternative ways of achieving certain of its outputs.

We can also study the obverse of this question: Can a post office, a school, or a church increase its outputs from a given set of resources? If we could assure ourselves that the quality of the outputs did not change, we should be able to estimate a production possibilities frontier for a nonmarket institution as readily as for a business firm. It should be noted, however, that, unless we were willing to assign relative weights or "prices" to units of different kinds of outputs, we could not say that one combination of outputs was larger than another unless at least one kind of output was greater and no kind of output was smaller than in the alternative situation.

The policymakers for nonmarket institutions, to the extent that they know the resource costs of alternative outputs, often make decisions which imply judgments as to the relative values or prices per unit of the alternative outputs. Also, many nonmarket institutions consciously compete with others of their kind. Different churches in a town may compete for membership and financial support. Universities may compete with one another for promising undergraduate or graduate students and promising or productive faculty members. The terms "promising" and "productive" imply a criterion or objective function on the part of the officials of a university by which they judge that the acquisition of certain faculty members and certain students would be of advantage to the university.

Finally, nonmarket institutions of a given kind may compete for personnel both with market institutions and with other kinds of nonmarket institutions. Universities, government agencies, and business firms in a metropolitan area may compete on equal salary terms for secretaries, clerks, and maintenance workers. Universities, government agencies, and private firms may also compete for scientists with Ph.D. degrees. Both market and nonmarket institutions evidently make judgments that the acquisition of certain types of employees will be to their advantage. However, the market institution gets its income from the sale of outputs (and appreciation of assets); the public university gets its income partly from student fees, partly from legislative appropriations, and partly from grants and contracts; the government agency may derive its income exclusively from funds appropriated by a city council, state legislature, or national congress.

Thus, there are tantalizing analogies between nonmarket and market institutions. We propose to apply economic theory and quantitative techniques—particularly optimization techniques—to educational planning in an explicit fashion which is still (as of 1971) relatively new in the nonmarket sectors of our society.

## Types of nonmarket systems and their behavior

The conventional analysis of market systems by economists is based on three essential postulates: (1) the incentive of profit (or utility) maximization; (2) the allocative role of market prices which are explicit signals for exchange; and (3) the possibility of output (or resource) adjustment through price signals and profit incentives. We have already referred to the power of these postulates, with realistic modifications, in appraising the performance of business firms.

In our opinion there is no complete and satisfactory economic theory as yet for determining optimal allocation of resources in a nonmarket framework. By a nonmarket system or framework is meant any of the following three categories at least: (a) a quasi market in which noneconomic quantities such as nonprice and nonprofit variables are as important as the price and the profit variables of a market system; (b) an internal or divisionalized market in which the exchanges and the allocations are hypothetical, but are intended to simulate the behavior of an actual market system in which the behavior relations of the participants are specified in certain economic forms; and (c) an organizational system in which the rules of organizational behavior and functioning evolve out of several factors, e.g., the political-cum-institutional framework, value systems and experiences of the active participants, and the information flows available to the organization.

## Decisions for nonmarket systems and the theory of economic policy

In some respects, Jan Tinbergen's theory of economic policy offers a bridge between the analysis of market and nonmarket institutions.

Tinbergen (1939) was the first person to construct an econometric model of a national economy. Later, Tinbergen's series of books on the

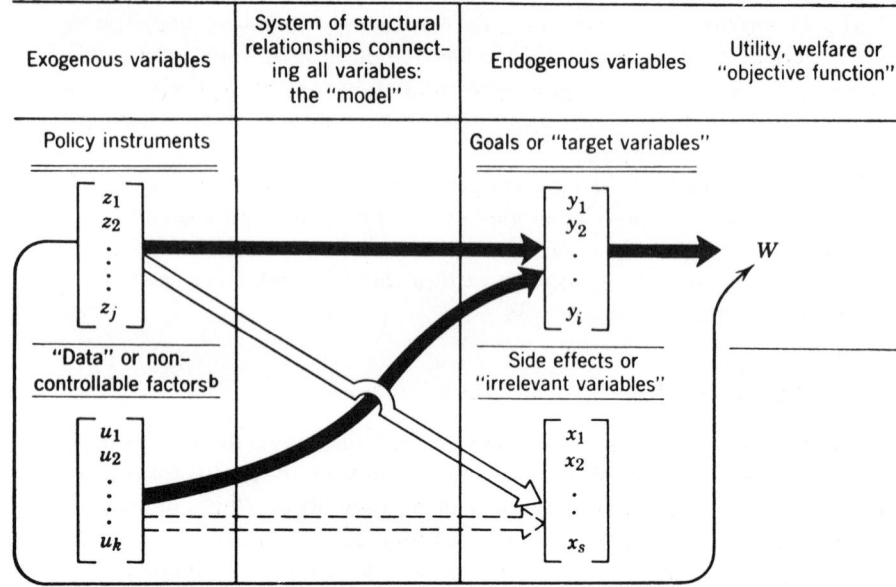

[a] Classification of variables based on J. Tinbergen.
[b] Not subject to control by the policy maker or level of government that sets the goals and uses the policy instruments in question.

**Fig. 1.1. The theory of economic policy.**

theory of economic policy (1952, 1954, 1956) supplied a bold new interpretation of the relationship of econometric models to the practical formulation of economic policies. For these contributions, Jan Tinbergen (jointly with Ragnar Frisch) received the first Nobel prize in economics in 1969.

Tinbergen's theory of economic policy can be summarized in terms of Figure 1.1.* The three basic ingredients of his quantitative economic policy model are as follows: a welfare function $W$ of the policymaker, which is a function of $I$ target variables $y_i$ and $J$ instrument variables $z_j$; a quantitative model $M$, which sets up statistical or empirical relationships essentially between the $I$ target variables and the $J$ instrument variables; and a set of boundary conditions or constraints on the target, the irrelevant and the instrument variables. The policy model may be a fixed target or a flexible target model; in the former, $W$ contains fixed target values, but in the latter, such target values are chosen as will optimize the welfare function $W$.

* Fig. 1.1 and most of the following section are excerpted from Fox, Sengupta, and Thorbecke (1966).

The model $M$ specifies the set of quantitative relations among the variables. Such relations in their original form, as distinct from the "reduced form," are called structural relations, and their coefficients are called structural coefficients. These structural relations may be divided into three groups: behavioral, technical, and definitional. The most important equations are the behavioral ones, which contain essentially quantitative theories and hypotheses about empirical economic behavior, for example, demand or supply relations or the reactions of economic groups to risk and uncertainty.

The variables of the model $M$ may be classified into four different types, the target variables $y_i$, which are to be purposefully (though indirectly) influenced by the policymaker; the instrument variables $z_j$, which are the means available to the policymaker; the data $u_k$, which are not subject to control by the policymaker, and the irrelevant variables $x_s$, which are side effects in which the policymaker is not interested.

If for ad hoc reasons we regard some economic variables $x_s$ as irrelevant for a given policy decision, we can in most cases eliminate them from a complete model by algebraic means, leaving a set of equations containing only policy instruments and targets (plus the effects of strictly noncontrollable variables). Figure 1.1 may help to clarify the classification of variables in the Tinbergen-type policy model. The random components of the policy model are not explicit in the diagram. Furthermore, the light arrow running from the instrument vector to the welfare function $W$ probably understates the importance of this connection, because a cost imputation on the basis of either shadow prices or direct monetary expenditure can, in most cases, be made for the instrument variables used by a policymaker. In any case, the welfare function $W$ can incorporate as elements instrument variables in addition to the target variables as such.

Assuming linearity and eliminating the vector $x$ of irrelevant variables, an economic policy model may be very simply specified in terms of three systems of equations:

Optimize $W = a'y + b'z$ (preference function) \hfill (1)

under the conditions:

$Ay = Bz + Cu$ (the model $M$), and \hfill (2)

$$\left.\begin{array}{l} y_{\min} \leq y \leq y_{\max} \\ z_{\min} \leq z \leq z_{\max} \end{array}\right\} \text{ (boundary conditions),} \tag{3}$$

where $A$, $B$, and $C$ are matrices of coefficients of appropriate orders and $y$, $z$, and $u$ are appropriate column vectors of targets, instruments, and data.

Since for the policy problem our unknown is the vector $z$ of instruments, we solve for $z$ from equation (2):

$$Bz = Ay - Cu. \tag{4}$$

If the matrix $B$ has constant elements and is square and nonsingular, the inverse of $B$ exists and hence the vector of instruments $z$ can be uniquely solved from equation (4) by premultiplying both sides by $B^{-1}$, i.e.:

$$z = (B^{-1}A)y - (B^{-1}C)u = Gy + Hu. \tag{5}$$

The nature of the dependence of $z$ upon $y$ is associated with different types of structures of the matrices $B$ and $A$:

i) If $B$ and $A$ are strictly diagonal matrices, then to each target there corresponds one and only one instrument and vice versa. There is no simultaneity in the relationship between the instruments and the targets. The practical implication would be that the policymaker could pursue each target with a single highly specific instrument. Or, he could afford to assign responsibility for each target and its unique instrument to a different cabinet officer or agency head without providing any mechanism for co-ordination or even communication among these officials!

ii) If the matrices $B$ and $A$ are strictly triangular and of similar dimensionality, the policy model given by equation (4) is called recursive (or correspondingly consecutive). In this case we have a "pure causal chain" model, to use a concept developed by Wold in his theory of estimation. The two-way simultaneity of relations between the vectors $z$ and $y$ (i.e., $z$ affecting $y$ and $y$ affecting $z$) can be reduced to a unilateral dependence.

We must emphasize that $z$ and $y$ are vectors:

$$z = \begin{bmatrix} z_1 \\ z_2 \\ \cdot \\ \cdot \\ \cdot \\ z_J \end{bmatrix}, \quad y = \begin{bmatrix} y_1 \\ y_2 \\ \cdot \\ \cdot \\ \cdot \\ y_I \end{bmatrix}.$$

Even if most of the $z_j$'s were unilaterally dependent on certain of the $y_i$'s, the vectors $z$ and $y$ would be interdependent (or show two-way simultaneity) if any one (or more) of the $y_i$'s depended on one or more of the $z_j$'s.

If the matrices $A$ and $B$ are strictly triangular, the first element $z_1$ of the vector $z$ will depend only on the single element $y_1$ of vector $y$ and other data ($u$). The second element $z_2$ will depend on $z_1$, $y_1$, $y_2$ and other data, but since $z_1$ has already been solved in terms of $y_1$, we have $z_2$ depending only on $y_1$, $y_2$, and not on any $y_i$ higher than $i = 2$. Apart from the advantages of this pattern for statistical estimation, such a strictly recursive model allows a very simple policy interpretation. Specifically, if each equation were assigned to a different policymaker, the system of equations would specify a hierarchy such that a policymaker in a given position need not look at the instruments selected by those who are below his position in the hierarchy of equations in order to determine his own optimal policy.

iii) If many of the elements of the matrices $B$ and $A$ are zero (which sometimes occurs in practice in input-output models and in investment planning), it may happen that such matrices are quasi-diagonal or block-diagonal rather than strictly diagonal. This means that each matrix contains square submatrices which, after appropriate arrangement of rows and columns, form blocks on the principal diagonal, the off-diagonal elements being zero.

In this case of a block-diagonal policy model, the over-all model could be split (or decomposed) into two or more independent parts, depending on the number of blocks in the block-diagonal form. A centralized plan (model) could thus be decentralized into "relatively independent" subplans (submodels) which would permit efficient decentralized decision-making.

iv) Again, if the matrices $B$ and $A$ are quasi-triangular or block-triangular, i.e., triangular in blocks of submatrices, the set of instruments corresponding to any given block can be solved for without any knowledge of other instruments belonging to blocks which are lower in the hierarchy. In this case the over-all central plan (or model) could be split into separate unilaterally dependent plans (or models).

So far we have assumed implicitly, if not explicitly, that we are discussing a fixed-target policy model; we may presume that some welfare function $W$ lies behind the selection of target values, but $W$ itself is not specified. In fact, however, a Tinbergen-type policy model may be fixed, flexible, random, or mixed. In the flexible case we select the instruments to optimize the welfare function $W$ subject to the conditions of the model. In the random case we optimize the expected value (or some appropriate deterministic equivalent such as the variance or the probability that $W$ takes a particular value or falls within a particular confidence interval) of the preference function. The randomness in the model may enter either through errors of statistical estimation of the model $M$ from past observational data or because the targets set may have random components (or intervals within which random variation will be tolerated). A model is mixed when some targets are fixed, some are flexible, and still others are random. Various other combinations are possible, e.g., some targets may be allowed to take only integral values, some may be continuous except at some "jump points," etc.

The concept of "efficiency" used in the theory of economic policy is also important. This concept is applicable to a flexible target policy model and also to the random and mixed cases. Suppose for simplicity we write the welfare function $W$ as a scalar function of the target variables, the instruments and random terms $(v)$; that is,

$$W = W(y_1, y_2, \ldots, y_I; z_1, z_2, \ldots, z_J, v)$$

after appropriate substitutions through the model. Then, assuming differentiability and other regularity conditions, we may state that the optimum set of instruments would be given by solving the following set of $J$ partial differential equations which are the necessary conditions for an extremum (optimum):

$$\frac{\partial W}{\partial z_j} = \sum_{i=1}^{I} \frac{\partial W}{\partial y_i} \frac{\partial y_i}{\partial z_j} + \frac{\partial W}{\partial z_j} = 0, j = 1, 2, \ldots, J, \tag{6}$$

provided the random term $v$ is identically zero and the second-order condition for a maximum or minimum is fulfilled. The term $(\partial y_i/\partial z_j)$ expresses the effectiveness of the instrument $z_j$ in inducing a change in the value of the target $y_i$ when all other instruments are kept constant. Hence the term $\Sigma_{i=1}^{I}(\partial W/\partial y_i)(\partial y_i/\partial z_j)$ expresses the sum of all marginal (partial) effects upon $W$ of a unit change in $z_j$ acting indirectly through the target variables $y_i$. The direct effect of the instrument $z_j$ upon $W$ is specified by the term $\partial W/\partial z_j$.

These efficiency indicators, which are partial measures of impact of the use of instruments, may be used to construct numerical tables to indicate the rates of substitution between different instruments. It should be noted that these indicators are not in terms of elasticities, hence comparisons of the effectiveness of different instruments are not free from the units in which these instruments are measured.

The logical structure of Figure 1.1 can be adapted to the situation of a business firm. If the firm is operating under perfect competition, the target variables may be identified as the firm's various outputs; the instruments may be identified as the firm's various inputs; the model will consist of a set of activities available to the firm for transforming inputs into outputs; the objective function $W$ will consist of the algebraic sum of each output weighted by its market price and each input weighted by its unit cost; the noncontrollable factors could be exogenous shifts in the demand curves for the firm's products or the supply curves for its inputs; and the side effects or irrelevant variables could include (among other things) air and water pollutants for which the firm was not required to pay penalties.

Note also that Figure 1.1 could be enriched to represent the situation of a business firm operating under various kinds of market imperfections and holding certain goals in addition to the short-run maximization of profits. Thus, the objective function of the firm could include the achievement of certain levels of production capacity at specified future times; a certain share of the total market for the kinds of outputs it produces; a certain level of inventories; or a certain level of cash reserves. Alternatively, these goals could be included in the model as constraints, so that the objective function as such was concerned only with the maximization of net revenue (subject to these constraints).

The inclusion of other target variables in the objective function, in addition to profit, presents us with a mixed situation. For example, if we seek to maximize an objective function which includes both net revenue and market share, we are forced, implicitly or explicitly, to assign a dollar value to a unit change in market share. If the objective of increasing market share competes with the objective of maximizing net revenue after a certain point, the opportunity cost of a one percent further increase in market share may be identified as the reduction in net revenue which this effort will require.

This situation is similar to one which Plessner, Fox, and Sanyal (1968) depicted in their dynamic programming model of a university department. The outputs of the department's teaching program (in terms of graduates with B.S., M.S., and Ph.D. degrees) were assigned dollar values equal to the discounted present values of the expected net increases in lifetime earnings resulting from the completion of these degrees. Such calculations have become familiar through the publications of T. W. Schultz (1963), Gary Becker (1964), and others. The authors did not feel that they could assign dollar values to the department's research outputs, although research competed with teaching for faculty time. They hypothesized a department chairman who was not satisfied with a zero level of research, but who approached a (subjective) optimal allocation of resources by transferring successive units of faculty time from teaching to research until the last increment of research time was viewed as barely worth its opportunity cost to the teaching program. This implicitly set a dollar value on the last unit of research time *as viewed by the chairman*, though perhaps by no one else.

The specification of objective functions in the theory of economic policy involves essentially the same problem that confronts us in specifying objective functions for universities and other nonmarket institutions, i.e., the absence of generally recognized prices for all or many of the outputs. Van Eijk and Sandee (1959), analyzing the context of economic policy in the Netherlands as of 1956, decided that against a 100 million guilder balance of payments surplus $E - M$ could be set 400 million guilders of government expenditure $x_G$, or 500 million guilders of investment $i$, or a 2 percent increase in real wages $w_R$, or a 1.33 percent decrease in consumer prices $p_c$, or an 0.5 percent increase in employment $a$, or a 200 million guilder surplus $S_G$ of government receipts over government expenditures. These were marginal rates of substitution or "barter terms of trade" among the six variables listed; from these a linear objective function could be written as:

$$W = 1.0(E - M) + 0.25x_G + 0.20i + 5.0w_R - 7.5p_c + 0.20a \\ + 0.50S_G + \text{constant}, \qquad (7)$$

subject to specified upper and lower limits within which the targets (and implicitly the instruments) could be varied. Theil (1964) specified quadratic objective functions representing (1) the trade unionist position, (2) the employer position, and (3) a neutral position and worked out the implications of each for optimal time paths of the same set of target and instrument variables in the Netherlands over a three-year horizon, using the same 40-equation model of the Dutch economy to link target and instrument variables in all cases. On one level, the barter terms of trade could be discussed as matters of taste or intuition, with different policymakers bringing to bear their own judgments and experiences as tempered by recent political platforms and by the public and private statements of persons wielding political or intellectual influence. On another level, they suggest the need for further clarification as to who is hurt (or helped), how, and how much by a unit change in each national aggregative variable.

*Ordinal versus cardinal objective functions in the theory of economic policy*

Theil (1961) drew a very specific analogy between the theory of economic policy and the theory of consumption. He pointed out that ordinal utility was sufficient in principle to lead the policymaker to select the optimal set of values of the instrument variables (according to his own preference ordering, of course). Theil's model is essentially:

$$\max W = f(x,y) \qquad x:m.1 \qquad (8)$$
$$y:n.1$$

## INTRODUCTION TO NONMARKET SYSTEMS

subject to:

$$Qy = Rx + s, \qquad Q:n.n \qquad (9)$$
$$R:n.m$$
$$s:n.1$$

where $x$ is a vector of $m$ instruments, $y$ is a vector of $n$ targets, $Q$ is a matrix with scalar numbers on the diagonal and zeros elsewhere, $R$ is a matrix of coefficients specifying the effects of the instruments on values of the (normalized) targets $q_i y_i$, and $s$ is a vector of constants (each $s_i$ is a linear combination of the data variables, whose values are regarded as predetermined constants during the optimization period, and any constant term in the equation expressing $y_i$ as a function of the instruments and data). The $y_i$ may be expressed in different units, such as per capita disposable income (in dollars), total employment (millions of workers), the consumer price index (1957–59 = 100), and so on; the diagonal elements in $Q$, $q_i(i = 1,2,\ldots,n)$ may be thought of as analogous to prices per unit of $y_i$, in that each unit of $y_i$ uses up $q_i$ units of the restriction imposed (or resource provided) by the $i$th equation.

The income constraint of consumption theory is here replaced by the set of $n$ reduced-form equations derived from the econometric model (i.e., those equations which express the target variables as functions of the instruments and data after the vector of irrelevant variables has been eliminated from the original structural system). To impose the present constraint set we write:

$$\max W - \lambda'(Qy - Rx - s), \qquad (10)$$

where $\lambda$ is a column vector of $n$ Lagrangean multipliers. Maximization leads to:

$$\frac{\partial W}{\partial x} + R'\lambda = 0 \qquad (11)$$

and

$$\frac{\partial W}{\partial y} - Q'\lambda = 0, \qquad (12)$$

where $\partial W/\partial x$ and $\partial W/\partial y$ are column vectors of the marginal welfare contributions or "utilities" of the instruments and the target variables, respectively.

For clarity, we may write typical individual rows of the vectors of first derivatives as:

$$\frac{\partial W}{\partial x_j} + (\lambda_1 r_{1j} + \lambda_2 r_{2j} + \ldots + \lambda_n r_{nj}) = 0, j = 1, 2, \ldots, m \qquad (13)$$

and

$$\frac{\partial W}{\partial y_i} - \lambda_i q_i = 0, \qquad\qquad i = 1, 2, \ldots, n. \qquad (14)$$

If $W$ has been given a cardinal specification, each $\partial W/\partial x_j$ will be a cardinal number and each $\lambda_i$ will be the shadow price of the $i$th equation, in units of $W$, at the optimal solution. If $W$ has been given an ordinal specification, the ratio of the marginal utilities of any two instruments $x_j$ and $x_k$ can be expressed as:

$$\frac{\partial W/\partial x_j}{\partial W/\partial x_k} = \frac{(\lambda_1 r_{1j} + \lambda_2 r_{2j} + \ldots + \lambda_n r_{nj})}{(\lambda_1 r_{1k} + \lambda_2 r_{2k} + \ldots + \lambda_n r_{nk})}. \qquad (15)$$

This ratio will not be affected if we multiply both numerator and denominator by the same scalar $k$ (say) where $k$ is any real number whatsoever.

### Systems analysis for market and nonmarket systems

The systems with which we will be concerned in this book can be represented (on a formal level) as sets of equations which describe how inputs into the system are transformed into outputs from the system. Some of these systems are dynamic in the sense that future values of some variables are dependent upon current and past values of the same and/or other variables. Dynamic systems may be driven by exogenous variables—for example, a public school system must adapt to exogenous rates of growth of the school-age population.

A dynamic system to which no formal objective function is adjoined may be used to simulate the effects of different time patterns of exogenous variables and the effects of deliberate changes in parameters, such as student-faculty ratios or tuition fees, upon the time paths of all variables in the system. If the real system (a university, say) is adequately represented by the set of equations, it will simulate all important effects (direct and indirect, simultaneous and cumulative) of the exogenous variables and parameter changes upon the endogenous variables, and provide valuable insights as to how the system works.

Presumably a series of simulations, each reflecting different values of certain instruments or parameters, will help an administrator in choosing the one particular set of policies he will put into effect. A choice is made, and the administrator evidently regards it as the *best* choice within the array of alternatives he has seen fit to examine. Though the simulation mode eschews explicit objective functions, it requires administrators to act as though they were guided by implicit ones.

An optimizing system is guided by an explicit objective function. As a rule, one particular set of values of the policy instruments or parameters will optimize this objective function and all other sets will be suboptimal. However, if an administrator is uncertain about the relative prices of different outputs or the relative penalties for falling a little short of different targets, he may test the sensitivity of the optimal solution to variations in specified prices or weights—i.e., to variations in the objective function. Thus, in actual practice simulation and optimization models are both open to intuitive judgment and intervention.

Figure 1.1 *with* the objective function $W$ has the logical structure of an optimization model; *without* the objective function it would have the logical structure of a simulation model.

Figure 1.2 is a condensed flow diagram of the Brookings quarterly econometric model of the United States (Duesenberry et al. 1965, pp. 24–25). It is designed to simulate the behavior of the economy in response to exogenous factors, including various kinds of policy interventions. The model consists of about 150 behavior equations and a large number of definitional equations and accounting identities (e.g., the gross national product must equal the sum of its components). In fact, the model contains, and simulates changes in, all major elements in the national income and product accounts as well as many wage, price, employment, and production variables. In principle, it could be converted to a policy model by adjoining an objective function. We may note in passing that the model proved to be approximately block-triangular or *block-recursive*, as in Case (iv) of the preceding section.

We include Figure 1.2 here because it represents a success story in the development of economics which may perhaps be replicated for the social sciences as a whole. Cumulative work on national income and product accounts in the United States began in the 1920s. The first major time series on the U.S. national income and its components was published by Simon Kuznets (1937). Keynes's *General Theory of Employment, Interest and Money* (1936) provided a theoretical model for full employment policy which attached great significance to the quantitative interrelationships among the national income and its components (consumption, savings, investment), the level of employment, and the rate of interest. Shortly thereafter, Tinbergen constructed an econometric model of the United States (1939) using Kuznets's national income measures and other economic time series. Leontief's first empirical applications of

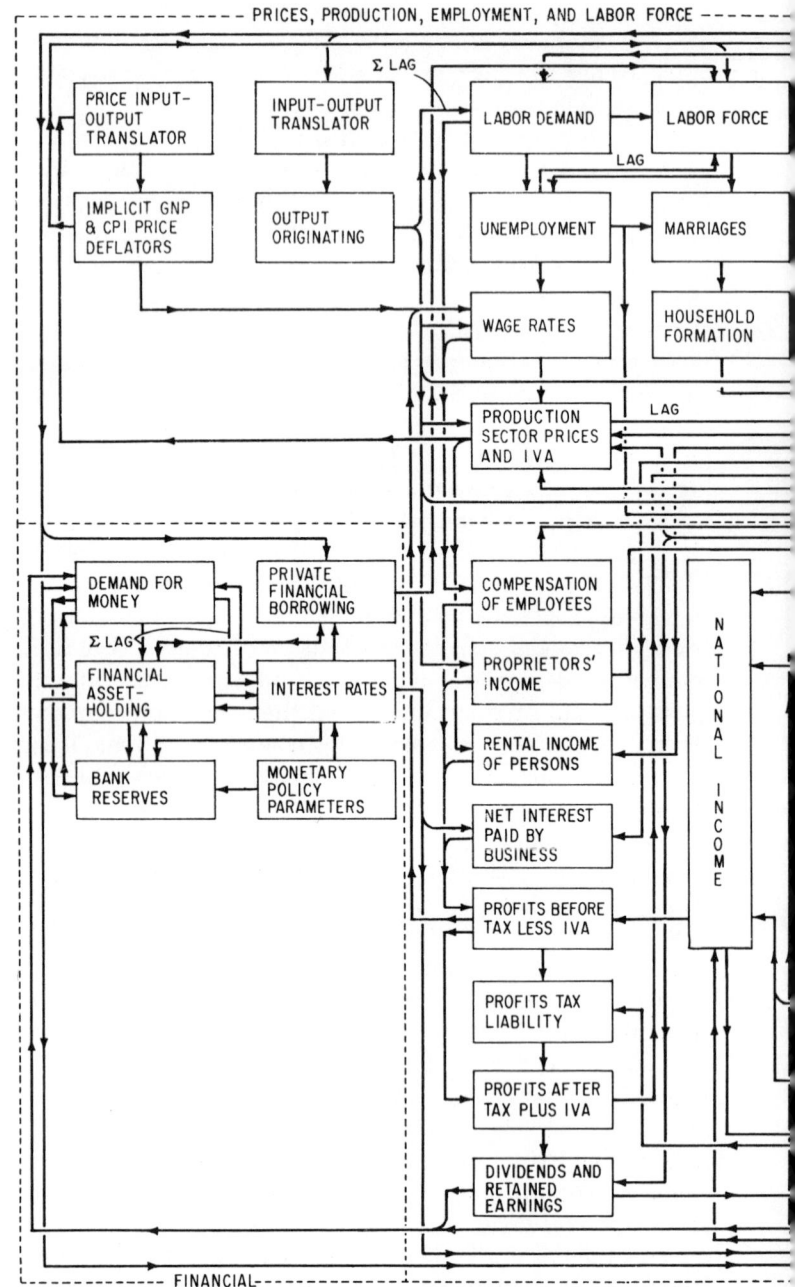

Fig. 1.2. Condensed flow diagram of the Brookings econometric model. Source: Duesenberry, Fromm, Klein, and Kuh (1965), pp. 24–25.

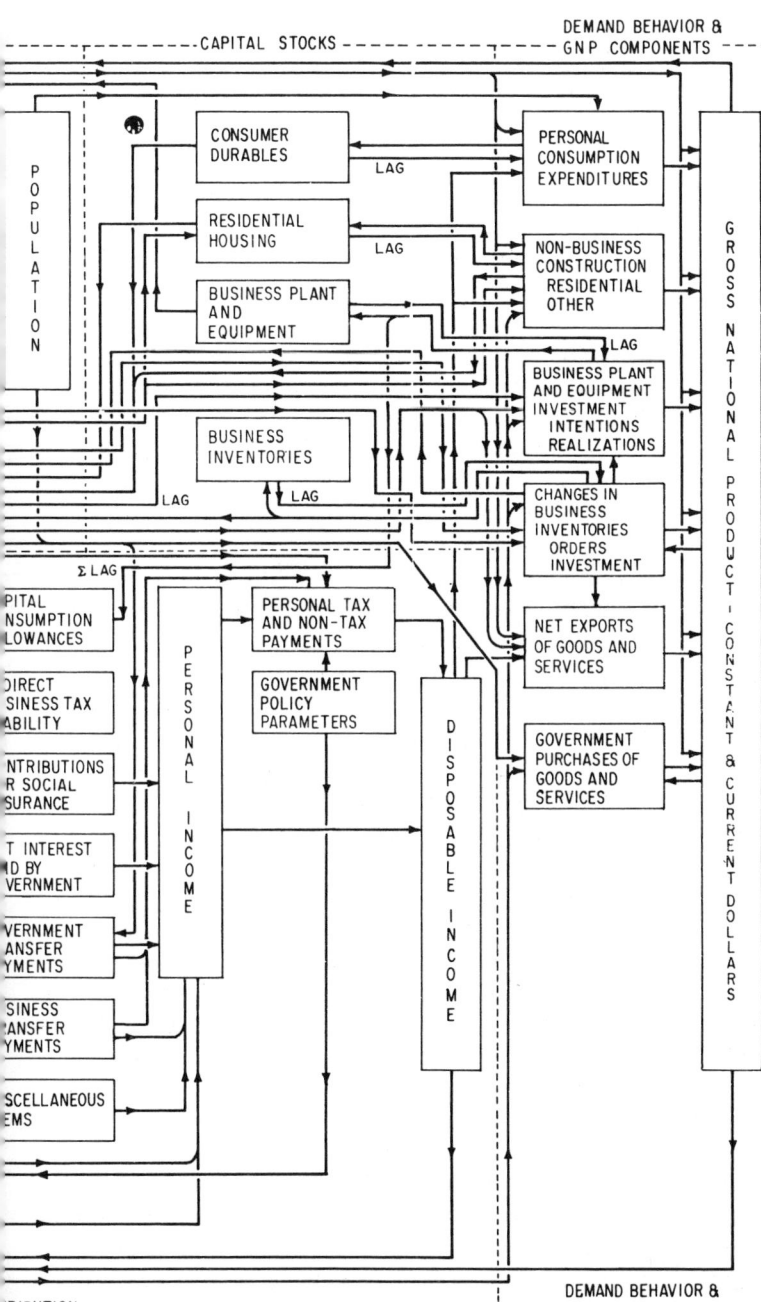

input-output analysis, which depended on an exhaustive sectoral breakdown of the gross national product and on dollar estimates of all intersectoral flows, were also made in the late 1930s (1941). All of these contributions, plus much subsequent elaboration and refinement, were prerequisite to the Brookings quarterly econometric model, which was constructed by a team of fifteen or twenty distinguished economists during 1961–63. The utility of each successive improvement in modeling the economic system gave impetus to improvements in the collection and organization of the relevant economic data.

Drawing on the same theory and methodology, income and product accounts and economic models have been developed at subnational levels, including individual metropolitan areas and multicounty functional economic areas. The economy is an important component of the social system of any geographically bounded community, and the first empirical models of complete social systems may be developed for relatively small areas (e.g., a small town and its trade area or perhaps a functional economic area).

The relation of an educational system to the surrounding society may also be conceptualized first for a small community containing a single school. Roger Barker (1968) has provided basic data which might be used in such a conceptualization. From there on, principles of aggregation and of central place hierarchies which have been used in purely economic models might be adapted to the modeling of educational systems and their surrounding societies for successively larger communities. The functional economic area turns out to be a particularly important level for such modeling, as it provides an appropriate setting for community colleges and for continuing education facilities and programs, as well as for the secondary and primary schools which serve smaller subareas.

A model of the entire educational system and the surrounding society at the national level must somehow accommodate the phenomena reflected in Figure 1.2 in addition to many others of a sociological and psychological nature.

**The plan of the book**

Chapter 1 serves as an introduction to all the remaining chapters.

Chapter 2 describes three types of models which depart in various ways from the economists' model of perfect competition, namely: (1) a quasi-market model; (2) an internal market model; and (3) an organizational model. A number of problems of resource allocation in a nonmarket framework are discussed, including those posed by public goods as distinct from private goods; simulation objectives of modeling as distinct from optimization objectives; choice of first-best as distinct from second-best policies; and problems of resource allocation through price guidance rather than output guidance.

Chapter 3 deals specifically with quantitative models of planning for educational systems at the national level and at the level of a university and its departments. Current mathematical models of educational systems are reviewed, and certain topics in the economic theory relevant to educational planning are discussed. These topics include welfare economics and discretionary behavior, pricing theory for multiproduct firms, and the theory of optimal growth. Chapters 2 and 3 were written by Jati K. Sengupta.

Chapters 4 and 5 are based on a longer manuscript prepared for this book by T. Krishna Kumar. In our practical work on departmental planning we have made extensive use of price-guided allocation rules and of decomposition (decentralization) techniques which imply an internal or divisionalized market for the allocable central resources of a university. The decomposition method of Dantzig and Wolfe and the two-level planning method of Kornai and Lipták are given particular attention in Chapter 4. Generalizations of these two methods to nonlinear and dynamic models are presented in Chapter 5.

Chapter 6, by Jati K. Sengupta, emphasizes the economic problems of resource allocation in nonmarket systems. These include (among others) problems of imputation in benefit-cost analysis for public goods; problems of aggregation, disaggregation, and consistency; the problem of indivisible resources; and the implications of second-best policies and partial optimization. The section in Chapter 6 on goal programming was contributed by Gene Gruver.

Chapter 7 is based on an initial draft by Bikas C. Sanyal. It presents a general systems approach to educational planning and reviews a number of models developed at Michigan State University, the University of California, Iowa State University, and other institutions.

Chapter 8 deals with the empirical problems involved in specifying quantitative models of university departments and colleges. Chapter 9 discusses objective functions and optimization models for a university and its component units on a practical, operational level. It presents optimization models of a specific department for use in medium-range (five-year) and short-term (year-to-year) planning. The rationales for the input and output prices, and hence for the departmental objective function, are explicitly stated. Recent quantitative studies of national salary structures for scientists (by Melichar) and of correlates of quality in graduate education (by the National Science Board) are summarized and interpreted as indicating that phenomena of concern to individual departments can also be measured at the level of national aggregates and averages. Chapter 10 discusses the prospects for application of quantitative models to educational planning in the near future and suggests a comprehensive measure (the gross social product) which would incorporate inputs and outputs of all market and nonmarket systems, including educational systems.

Readers primarily interested in empirical studies of universities or in departmental planning should begin with Chapters 8, 9, and 10 and then return to Chapters 2 through 7. Readers with a strong interest in economic theory and in educational planning at an advanced level should proceed consecutively from Chapter 2 through Chapter 10.

CHAPTER 2

# Quantitative Analysis of Nonmarket Systems

*Jati K. Sengupta*

**General remarks**

The conventional analysis of market systems by economists is based on three essential postulates: (1) the incentive of profit (or utility) maximization; (2) the allocative role of market prices which are explicit signals for exchange; and (3) the possibility of output (or resource) adjustment through price signals and profit incentives. The first postulate helps to define not only a scale for comparing alternative solutions (i.e., a common denominator) provided by the market *tâtonnement* but also an associated system of shadow prices (i.e., Lagrange multipliers associated with resource constraints) which will support the allocation system. The second postulate requires that market prices should play their optimizing resource allocative roles. The third postulate specifies that resource adjustments and output variations are possible within the market framework, so that the price signals and profit incentives would under certain conditions lead to successive adjustments until an equilibrium state is reached.

The competitive model places very specific interpretations and/or restrictions on the above three postulates. First, it requires that resources (inputs or outputs) are all divisible, so that the profit for producers and utility for consumers can be exactly computed, quantified, and apportioned; also, there should be no saturation of goods and services at any feasible solution level. Second, it requires that the decisionmakers (producers and consumers) must be price-takers so that the rule of anonymity (or universality) of prices must hold; in particular, for any given type of output there should be only one price, if it is not a free good. (This also requires that the volumes of demand and output by any one consumer and producer respectively must be so small as to have no effect on the market price for the good.) Third, it requires relative to the third postulate that the household indifference maps and firm production possibility sets are convex and the market allocation preserves the consistency between consumption bundles and production in the sense that aggregate production plus initial resources must equal aggregate consumption demands.

Also implicit in the competitive model are the two crucial assumptions emphasized by Arrow (1969) that all prices can be known by all individuals with no costs of information or transaction and that the market process of charging prices does not consume extra resources. Under these assumptions and certain regularity conditions we get the fundamental theorem of welfare economics that a competitive equilibrium allocation of resources is Pareto-optimal and that any Pareto-optimal allocation can be achieved as a competitive equilibrium solution by a suitable reallocation of initial resources. (Note that any feasible allocation is defined to be Pareto-optimal if there does not exist any other feasible allocation which makes at least one person better off without making anyone worse off.)

A quasi-market model, differentiated in some respects from a perfectly competitive model, explicitly allows more weight to nonprice variables and nonprofit goals, and, what is more important, it allows rules of exchange both in and out of equilibrium (i.e., these rules of exchange are sometimes called non*tâtonnement,* since *tâtonnement*-type exchanges are all hypothetical [Hahn, Negishi 1962]). Non*tâtonnement* rules of exchange need not be price-guided; as a matter of fact, methods of planning resource allocation without using shadow prices have been analyzed recently in relation to some actual experiences of central planning, and these are discussed in some detail in Chapter 6.

The organizational model of behavior is at the other extreme from a market model. In its polar characteristics it represents a nonmarket economy in which (a) nonprice variables, nonprofit goals, and nondivisible resources (inputs and outputs) are prominently present; (b) non*tâtonnement* exchanges and resource transfers are very important due to transaction and information costs; (c) price signals and output quotas may be replaced by other organizational procedures, e.g., other methods of internalizing externalities in interdivision interdependence (Davis, Kamien 1969); and (d) solutions may be attempted by central directives and informal organizational procedures.

## Analyzing nonmarket systems by competitive and noncompetitive rules

We will argue, in our discussion of various resource allocation processes for educational systems in Chapters 4–6, that an educational system provides a case in which the characteristics of an internal market are present to a significant degree. Although organizational behavior rules and budgetary procedures are evolved in most institutions of higher education, there exists, in our opinion, a significant area of internal decisionmaking within universities in which price-guided allocation rules, appropriately modified by other rules necessary in cases of market failure, will still apply and fruitful empirical applications can be devised. It is in this context and spirit that our discussion of various linear and nonlinear methods of decentralization of resource allocation decisions is highly relevant to planning for educational systems.

By noncompetitive rules of resource allocation we mean that some of the important ingredients of a competitive market model may fail to hold. For instance, (a) the prices administered by the center may contain imputed and monopolistically determined elements (Nikaido 1964; Sengupta 1971a); (b) the marginal cost-pricing rules may be modified by other directives in order to incorporate nonmarket elements of externalities, benefits, and costs; and (c) the various sources of market failure due to the presence of indivisibility of resources in various forms, the case of unpaid for externalities in production (and also consumption), and the case of public goods of certain types (e.g., bridges) with very high initial fixed costs and negligible or very small marginal costs, may lead to replacement of the market framework by other organizational procedures in order to avoid large amounts of communication, transactions, and exclusion costs (Arrow 1969).

The theory and experience of central planning as it developed in the socialist countries provide very interesting insights into methods of over-all resource allocation for the whole economy, in which profit-oriented producers are replaced by plant managers, prices are administered by the center along with various taxes and transfers, and targets or norms are utilized along with directives and price signals (i.e., premium and penalty payments for over- or under-fulfillment of production targets). In a sense, these planning experiences (Ward 1960; Montias 1960; Feinstein 1967) have emphasized (in striking contrast to theoretical beliefs) the difficulties of insuring Pareto-type optimality conditions in the real world through an internal market mechanism which is analogous to but distinct from the functioning of an explicit market as visualized in the models of Pareto, Walras, and Marshall.

It is true, as Lange (1967) and others have strongly emphasized, that the central planning board could, in principle, always act as a competitive market, but now the electronic computer can simulate the workings of the competitive market in a more efficient manner. The market process with its *tâtonnements* or trial and error methods may appear old fashioned, particularly regarding computing efficiency, now that the computer has achieved a significant degree of speed and capability.

Simulating a competitive market mechanism may be an interesting learning device, sometimes a very costly one also if the proper algorithms and computer languages are not applied. However, it may be quite difficult to implement in realistic situations the Pareto-efficiency conditions of resource allocation for investment and other resources, particularly when the incentives of the plant managers are not the same as those of private producers, when shadow prices may be very unlike the private market prices, in that the former may conceal inefficiency through administrative and central directions and target fixation, and when consumer preferences may be at best underemphasized in the practice and ideology of central planning.

The experiences with supplementing producer prices by means of premium and penalty payments for producer-managers in Poland (Montias 1960) and Yugoslavia (Ward 1960) have shown very clearly how these signals may fail to reflect the actual pattern of scarcity of resources due to communication gaps between objectives perceived by the center and by the individual producers and the difficulty of co-ordination through price variations alone. Also, the objective of fixing a price on the basis of costs to include only marginal costs is not very easy to implement in an institutional framework in which the demand elements in price setting are not explicitly emphasized and the scheme of planned incentives or disincentives (i.e., the output bonus in Poland [Montias 1960]) for each producer-manager is much more difficult to monitor and implement since the quality factor may be sacrificed in order to overfulfill quantity targets.

For economies having a mixed framework (i.e., one in which a large public sector co-exists with a very important private market sector), as do many developing economies, it has generally been felt that the private market sector has failed in most cases to generate the requisite supplies of overhead capital and basic capital formation that are so essential to stimulate over-all economic growth, and to improve the distribution of market power, income, and property so as to accelerate the process of industrialization and growth. The public sector's role in planning new investment, in reallocating old investment along socially desirable lines (i.e., developing depressed regions and basic overheads), and in providing socially desirable guidelines of growth for the private sector is now explicitly recognized in the literature on economic planning and development for less developed economies; this implicitly ignores the fact that public enterprises may develop inefficiency in resource utilization, so long as administrative prices, central control, and budgetary support guarantee their permanence. Similarly, mere replacement of private monopoly elements in production, marketing, and consumer services by public control and regulation may not improve the efficiency of resource allocation; there are definite needs for developing a method of efficiency pricing appropriate for the public sector enterprises. However, the latter job is very difficult to perform, monitor, and implement.

If we define a public good after Steiner (1969) as any publicly induced or provided collective good, where collective goods (which may be either consumption goods or durable goods having investment goods elements) arise whenever some segment of the public is collectively prepared to pay for a different bundle of goods and services than the unhampered conditions of a private market will produce, then it appears that most of the education sector, including institutions of secondary and higher education which are publicly provided or supported through federal, state, or local finance, can be characterized as a provider of services which have aspects of collective goods that are publicly supported. In less developed economies, where growth considerations are more important, the redistribution role of the education sector in equalizing economic opportunities and potential income earning capacities is explicitly recognized, since skill-formation of the appropriate kind may be a source of disguised savings potential for inducing a higher growth rate. In the United States and other developed countries, where the total expenditure on education is quite large, it is explicitly recognized (Schultz 1963; Becker 1964; Weisbrod 1964) that a part of such expenditure may be considered as investment in human capital, much like the expenditure on durable goods. The income redistributive roles of publicly supported elementary and secondary education have also been explicitly analyzed and compared with those of privately supported schools (Mincer 1958; Becker et al. 1966; Hansen 1963, 1969).

These studies suggest among other things that, unlike private market goods (i.e., privately supplied noncollective goods), educational service as a publicly provided collective good must have (a) various characteristics of nonmarket returns and costs (e.g., social overhead aspects); (b) various sources of externalities (e.g., benefits of research diffused in other sectors) in the technology of production, consumption, and distribution; and (c) a mechanism for avoiding (or correcting) various market imperfections such as high information costs, elements of monopoly power, and high transaction costs associated with any method of directly charging potential buyers. These characteristics of market failure indicate that analysis of the noncompetitive elements of the educational system is as important as that of the competitive elements associated with an internal market structure. This is the theme of our discussion of resource allocation processes and mechanisms for the educational system in Chapters 3-7.

## Framework of mixed systems

The economic analysis of that part of the resource allocation process in a mixed framework which lends itself to decisionmaking through quantitative policy models raises a number of difficult problems of fundamental importance, not all of which will be discussed in this book. We consider the following aspects of the general problem of resource allocation in a nonmarket framework:

A. Problems posed by public goods as distinct from private goods;
B. Simulation objectives of modeling as distinct from optimization objectives;
C. Choice of first-best as distinct from second-best policies; and
D. Problems of resource allocation through price guidance rather than output guidance.

*Public vs. private goods*

The definition of public goods (Steiner 1969) referred to before has considerable flexibility in that it specifies characteristics or attributes that may apply to particular aspects of a good. Public education may thus have some aspects of a public good if it has both quantitative and qualitative differences from privately produced education and if it has collective demands from some segment of the public. Steiner has distinguished three types of public goods: (1) those arising from intrinsic or technical characteristics of specific goods that result in externalities which are not incorporated effectively in the market; (2) those arising from imperfections in market mechanisms; and (3) those arising not from specific goods and services but from environmental aspects. The two basic characteristics of public goods are that nonconsumers of such goods cannot be separated from potential or actual consumers (i.e., high exclusion costs) and that consumption by one person does not reduce the consumption opportunities of others.

The view that education is completely a public good has two very serious implications for educational resource planning. First, as a public good the production of education and knowledge is intended for social and collective needs which are completely outside the private market and its cost-return calculations. Second, the potential net benefits of education as a publicly supported collective good may be more important than the direct monetary returns and market benefits. However, such arguments are only partly valid for the education sector. As Blaug (1968a) has emphasized: "Education is not a pure 'public good' because its economic benefits are largely personal and divisible: below the statutory leaving age, it is possible to buy more education and above the statutory age the number of places in higher education are rationed out in accordance with examination results. It follows that there is nothing in the nature of education as an economic service that prevents meaningful comparison of its financial costs and benefits" (Blaug 1968b, p. 249).

Also, decisionmaking in a university system has several levels at which a process of sorting qualified students intended for higher education is in effect. Decisions regarding the allocation of teaching resources between different courses in undergraduate and graduate instruction, the allocation of budgetary funds between different activities, and the most appropriate size of computer and library facilities (widely used by other sectors of the university) all provide situations in which there are various constraints, and any consistent prescription of a policy has to impute shadow prices whether explicit or implicit. Under appropriate circumstances these shadow prices can be used to simulate the workings of a competitive market. It is this view of education as a quasi-public good which has led us to analyze the various competitive shadow price-guided rules in university systems in Chapters 4–7.

*Simulation vs. optimization*

The systems analysts who approach the problem of modeling an educational system (e.g., a university system) from a very pragmatic viewpoint are most reluctant to assume any optimizing objective function, which is not directly observable; rather they are concerned with specifying the interrelationships between the various subsystems with their observed cost or return components and then with simulating the behavior of the system through parameter variations in the models. The generation of alternative profiles of system behavior under alternative presumptions about policy variables, parameters, and constraints is supposed to afford insights into the predictive usefulness of the model and into the various interdependence effects subsisting in its various parts. Simulation studies could, of course, be very general in incorporating the effects of randomness and other unforeseen situations; however, in application to educational models (Keeney et al. 1967; Weathersby 1967; Lave et al. 1968; Hartley 1968) two basic types have been frequently adopted: first, the cost components of a university system have been compared in various ways to develop schemes of program budgeting measures of cost effectiveness; and second, a method of updating the system parameters from data on past performance has been frequently employed to obtain realistic simulated solutions (Alper 1968; Zemach 1968; Armitage et al. 1970) on the basis of which a policymaker may avoid decisions which may be economically or otherwise undesirable.

Two types of implicit optimization cannot, however, be avoided in such simulation studies. First, the past performance and data provide the systems analysts with a structure for modeling the system, but since they consider consistent and feasible solutions only, it implies that consistency and feasibility are highly desirable; implicitly, this provides the case for suboptimization, since less feasible and less consistent policies are not preferred. Second, the generation of simulated data representing probable system behavior is intended for the policymaker to use and take a decision. In a sense, the simulated data are only helpful if by using them the policymaker can arrive at a better decision than would otherwise be possible. This end use of the simulated data suggests very clearly that if, as in the theory of economic policy (Tinbergen 1954; Theil 1964; Fox et al. 1966), the objective function of the policymaker is explicitly introduced as an ordering device, policy simulations will be more effective and useful. For instance, if the policymaker has any notion of desired performance of the system, the simulated model may be used to compute, under both pessimistic and optimistic assumptions about other exogenous factors, the values of the control variables required to achieve the desired state (e.g., such values of the control variables may be too expensive or otherwise undesirable, etc.). We have considered empirical and theoretical analyses of optimization through the activity analysis models for university systems in this spirit, i.e., the requirement of consistency among multiple policymakers and the implicit costing of policy constraints for attaining the desired levels of system behavior. In our view, simulation and suboptimization are more complementary than competitive.

*First-best vs. second-best policies*

An optimizing policy model for an educational system, formulated for instance in linear or nonlinear programming terms (e.g., an activity analysis model), may have special problems in completely characterizing the best solution (vector) whenever the constraints or the parameters of the objective function are not exactly known. So long as most production of education and training is outside the working of private market mechanisms, the elements of nonmarket returns and costs are very important; also important are the various externalities involved. In other words, it is not possible to restrict the benefits of education only to those who have paid for it in terms of student time and tuition costs; similar is the case with the contributions of research outputs. Since however it is not always possible to know beforehand the exact nature of additional constraints (or constraint modifications) which may be forthcoming, one can allow for it by adopting a safety-first approach through policies which are satisficing rather than optimizing, i.e., in a sense suboptimal policies are chosen rather than the optimal. The reasons for selecting suboptimal or second-best policies may be several, and this sometimes leads to various concepts of second-best. In Chapter 6 we distinguish between five basic types of second-best policies and their relevance for resource planning in the education sector.

It may be useful to refer here to one type of second-best policy (Lipsey and Lancaster 1956–57) which is closely related to the Pareto-optimality criterion of resource allocation. Consider an activity analysis model (e.g., it may represent the resource allocation process of an educational system [Sengupta and Fox 1969]), where we maximize a scalar real-valued differentiable (concave) function (which may represent the objective function of a policymaker):

$$f(x) = f(x_1, x_2, \ldots, x_n) \tag{1}$$

of $n$ variables $x_j$, subject to some constraints which may be represented in one form by:

$$g(x) = g(x_1, x_2, \ldots, x_n) = 0, \tag{2}$$

where $g$ is a real valued differentiable function of the activities or variables $x_j$. With more than one constraint, the number of such equations as (2) would increase. For this simple case of one constraint, the first-order conditions of a Pareto optimum may be easily derived by using the Lagrange multiplier $\lambda$ for (2) as:

$$f_{x_i} - \lambda g_{x_i} = 0, \, i = 1, \ldots, n, \tag{3}$$

where the subscript $x_i$ denotes the partial derivatives with respect to $x_i$. Solving for the Lagrange multiplier $\lambda$ and using it, the Pareto conditions can be rewritten as:

$$(f_{x_i}/f_{x_n}) - (g_{x_i}/g_{x_n}) = 0; \, i = 1, \ldots, n-1. \tag{4}$$

If (1) is interpreted as a utility function and (2) as a transformation function, then (4) states the familiar result that, at the optimum, marginal rates of substitution in consumption must equal those in production. The solution vector here satisfying (4) represents the first-best, provided the sufficiency conditions for a maximum also hold.

Lipsey and Lancaster (1956-57) then construct a second-best problem by adjoining an additional constraint in the form:

$$(f_{x_1}/f_{x_n}) = k \cdot (g_{x_1}/g_{x_n}); k \neq 1, \tag{5}$$

a parameter which because of $k \neq 1$ violates one of the Pareto conditions in (4). Now assume that the functions $f(x)$ and $g(x)$ in (1) and (2) are separable in components (i.e., $f(x) = f_1(x_1) + f_2(x_2) + \ldots + f_n(x_n)$ and that we maximize (1) subject to (2) and (5). The necessary conditions for an optimum would now be:

$$0 = f_{x_i} - \lambda g_{x_i} - \mu \cdot \left[ \frac{f_{x_n} f_{x_1 x_i} - f_{x_1} f_{x_n x_i}}{(f_{x_n})^2} - k \cdot \frac{g_{x_n} g_{x_1 x_i} - g_{x_1} g_{x_n x_i}}{(g_{x_n})^2} \right] \tag{6}$$

where

$$f_{x_i x_j} = \frac{\partial^2 f}{\partial x_i \, \partial x_j}, \; i = 1, 2, \ldots, n, \text{ and}$$

$\mu$ = Lagrange multiplier for (5).

Note that by the assumption of separability of $f(x)$ and $g(x)$ we have:

$$f_{x_i x_j} = 0 = g_{x_i x_j}, \text{ for all } i \neq j. \tag{7}$$

Using this in (6) we obtain:

$$f_{x_i} - \lambda g_{x_i} = 0; i = 2, \ldots, n - 1. \tag{8}$$

This equation is identical with the Pareto-optimality condition (3) in the first-best solution, except for the first and $n$th commodity. In other words, the necessary condition of optimality (6) for the second-best solution leads to the same identical Pareto-optimal conditions as in the first best for all commodities except two, the first and the $n$th commodities. Hence, only for these two commodities are special methods (e.g., corrective mechanisms through lump sum transfers, tax subsidy schemes, etc.) necessary to obtain Pareto-optimality conditions; for all other commodities, separability of the function $f(x)$, $g(x)$ (which implies the absence of externalities of some sort) is sufficient to guarantee the Pareto-optimality conditions of a first-best policy. Davis and Whinston (1965) argue that separability in terms of decision units (e.g., consumers and producers) is quite possible and of some practical relevance, provided that there is no externality in the system through production technology.

Two points, however, may be noted. First, the additional constraint (5) which violates one of the Pareto conditions (4) is taken in such a form that the value of $k \neq 1$ is assumed fixed and known; this would by implication fix a particular value of $\lambda$ different from that given in (3). This means that the parameter $k$ in equation (6) cannot be treated as a constant fixed beforehand. Second, the postulate of separability (7), when interpreted in terms of decision units, develops in effect a method of incorporating decision rules of consumers and producers expressed as functions of the Lagrange multipliers. Since Lagrange multipliers are in general unknown until the optimal value is reached, this procedure appears to be asking more than may be feasible. Also, if the Lagrange multipliers are used not at their optimal values (i.e., provisional dual prices as they are called in decomposition algorithms [Sengupta and Fox 1969]), then shadow prices may not be stable and may not satisfy the rule of anonymity for decision units. We will discuss this question and other forms of second-best policies in Chapter 6.

*Price vs. quantity guidance*

Resource allocation methods guided by marginal cost pricing (when marginal costs reflect the true scarcity of resources) or by shadow pricing rules (when the policy constraints impose implicit costs on the system) are essentially based on the postulates of a competitive market model. For large-scale programming models such price-guided allocation rules, which are frequently suggested in various types of decomposition algorithms (Sengupta and Fox 1969), may be very slow, nonmonotonic, and expensive, if such prices are to be attained through trial-and-error methods, simulating the *tâtonnement* processes of a competitive market. If there are transaction costs and information costs associated with each step of the trial-and-error method, then the whole process of correct price guidance may be very uneconomic. This has sometimes been characterized as a case of market failure, and this can arise even when the trial-and-error process simulates the market. Decision units have limited computing capacities and the sensitivity of the solution to errors may not always be very small, even in linear programming problems (Kornai and Lipták 1965). This has led to the supplementing of price-guided allocation rules by output quotas and other direct methods of output guidance.

Allocation methods not using shadow prices have also been suggested as consistent methods of planning. These methods may have some merit in policy models in the form of integer programming problems, where convergence of the decomposition methods of price guidance may be very, very slow, apart from other difficulties due to the nonconvexity of the feasible set of nonnegative integer points. Our discussions of price-guided and output-guided resource allocation methods in Chapters 4–6 emphasize the complementarity between the two methods.

**Resource allocation in educational systems**

As a nonmarket system the education sector has a number of characteristics which are very similar in some respects to the goods and services flowing through the cash nexus of a market economy.

First, its outputs (production of degrees, skills, and research) have definite monetary returns determined by market factors of demand and supply, although the nonmonetary returns are not limited to those who have paid tuition and received degrees after satisfying the requirements; similarly most of the inputs to the educational sector (e.g., faculty and supporting staff; flow of services from capital resources, such as building space and equipment; and composite overhead resources, such as the library and the computer) have definite monetary costs largely determined by the prevailing market conditions, although some inputs such as student time and community support of research and instruction have nonmarket cost elements which may be difficult to evaluate.

Second, the budgets available to the education sector (e.g., a university system) through state support and other direct means provide definite limits and constraints within which the resources allocable among several departments and activities have to be utilized. A severe budget cut is known to lead to a decline in the quality and standard of education, and through the national market operation the faculty may have a high degree of mobility. This framework is very similar to the decisionmaking problem of a multiproduct firm. Much like a multi-product firm, the university system has to plan for the growth of its departments under the assumption that the trend of the demand vector is adequately forecast and very likely to be realized. Uncertainty of sales here takes the form of uncertainty in demand for places in the various component fields. Also, the problems of contraction due to a fall in demand are much more difficult than those of expansion, since the bulk of the direct costs of the university system tend to be inflexible and independent of the services (i.e., the divergence between potential output and actual realized output tends to be the wider, the greater the fall in demand).

Third, there exist significant elements of joint production (e.g., between graduate teaching and research, graduate and undergraduate teaching, joint teaching in two or more departments [James 1969] etc.) in the educational system, and there is also some indivisibility of resources in the sense, for example, that half of a faculty member could not be hired for graduate teaching. It is an important economic question with important policy implications as to how such joint costs are to be allocated between different resources, fixed, semifixed, and variable, and to what extent the interdependence between activities at various levels of a university system can be internalized through a process of internal pricing in an internal or quasi-market framework. Our empirical applications to resource allocation in university systems are intended to analyze such issues, which appear in our opinion to be basically similar to the resource allocation decisions of a multiproduct firm.

However, the education sector, unlike a market economy, produces a quasi-public good which has various nonmarket returns, costs, and externalities; its objective may be much different from profit maximization, the quality of the services and goods produced may be as much if not more important than the quantity, and the prices of the various resources (e.g., faculty inputs) may contain distinct nonmonetary elements (e.g., the prestige of belonging, esteem from students and colleagues, the quality of community environment) which are never measured by a market economy through its cash nexus.

*The education sector in the over-all economy*

In Chapter 3 we discuss in some detail the various formulations of models for the educational sector in the national economy. Basically these models discuss either the need for adapting education to the needs of over-all growth of the national economy or the importance of imputing growth in productivity to the skills and educational attainments of the factor labor.

Two other important points may be emphasized in this connection; first, the income redistributive effects of investment in the education sector; and second, the accounting and economic implications of potential output feasible in the education sector. The redistributive role of education financed through public support has been strongly emphasized in economic planning for less developed economies; it has also been analyzed (Hansen 1969; Windham 1969; Hansen and Weisbrod 1969) with respect to the school system and higher education in the United States and other developed economies. The critics (Balogh and Streeten 1968) who complain about the monopoly (and noncompetitive) elements in the educational system tend to overlook the regressive tendency of the public education system as a redistributive mechanism (i.e., the monetary returns to high-income groups may tend to be higher than those to low-income groups from a given level of educational attainments, because of the noncompetitive elements prevailing in institutional markets). Suppose, however, that we have an economy under a central planning board, which considers the problem of reducing the inequality of income distribution to a desirable level. There are various possible alternatives and combinations of policy which may achieve this objective (e.g., tax and fiscal policies, redistribution through education and through other social services which have a built-in element of progressive income distribution, etc.); however, we have to adjoin the constraint that the over-all growth of the economy should be affected either very little or not at all. Note that this hypothetical policy problem assumes two stages of national policy, with the methods of increasing national income (i.e., growth) at the first stage and with reducing the inequality of income distribution at the second stage. It should be emphasized also that the conditions of Pareto optimality may not be optimal from a social welfare viewpoint in a framework which includes significant inequality of income distribution.

The formulation of this type of policy problem (Fox et al. 1966) is admittedly very partial, since it does not incorporate adequately the other roles of the education sector besides the income redistribution role. However, if the redistributive effect is jointly produced with other effects (such as generation of skills) by the educational sector and the former is considered desirable by the central planner, then one may consider the implicit costs of generating a given degree of redistribution through public education and compare them with those obtained by other means. The idea of developing a policy of negative income tax and associating it with the income redistributive role of education may have some validity in terms of the other joint effects of education (Southwick and Zionts 1969).

The second aspect of valuation of the potential output and capacity of the education sector raises such questions as how to measure it and what would be its relation with GNP and other measures computed annually. One view of the problem (Fox 1970) is to develop an aggregative measure, such as the gross social product (GSP), which would have GNP embedded in it (however the nonmarket returns and possibly costs associated with GSP have to be valued in some consistent accounting fashion). Its implications for economic growth, welfare, and efficiency in decisionmaking are worth exploring, since, in the national balance sheet over a period, it is no doubt true that much of the potential output gets realized into actual output if the economy is growing at a desirable rate. (For instance, the historical experience of countries such as Japan, which have high growth rates, suggests very high expenditure on the education sector and its growth.) A second view is to use, along with others, such measures as potential output of the education sector along with potential outputs of other sectors which have significant nonmarket components (e.g., government departments, social services) in the process of allocation of resources and budgets for such sectors. Since the diffusion of research knowledge and technological know-how is a time-consuming process, such a method would give appropriate weight to investment for research and development (R & D). In private corporations the initial investments for R & D in, say, developing new products or new technology are very likely to contain some such potential expected return components.

*Allocation in systems of higher education*

The resource allocation processes in higher education, which are discussed in detail in both theoretical and empirical terms in later chapters (i.e., Chapters 3–8) comprise basically three aspects of the problem: (1) the allocation of composite resources (e.g., computer time, joint teaching in two or more departments) through communication between different decision levels using various methods of decomposition and price-guided allocation; (2) the activity analysis models available for resource allocation within a university system, specifying the technological and other interdependence of production in activity analysis terms (for instance, a capital good is considered in terms of a flow of services and the resource allocation problem of an academic department in a university is posed as a current decision problem regarding the optimal use of the flow of services from capital, both physical and human); and (3) the problems of growth of the various components of the university system, particularly when there are aspects of "public goods" in education and research.

As an illustration of the economic problems of internal decisionmaking in a university system, the following flow diagram (Fig. 2.1), by Brink (1966), may be helpful as a descriptive device. This diagram identifies twenty-five decision points in the decisionmaking system of a university, of which seven are outside and eighteen are inside. First, suppose it is possible to model the basis of decisionmaking at these eighteen inside points; this would then define the submodels. Co-ordination of these various submodels is needed for efficiency and economy of time costs.

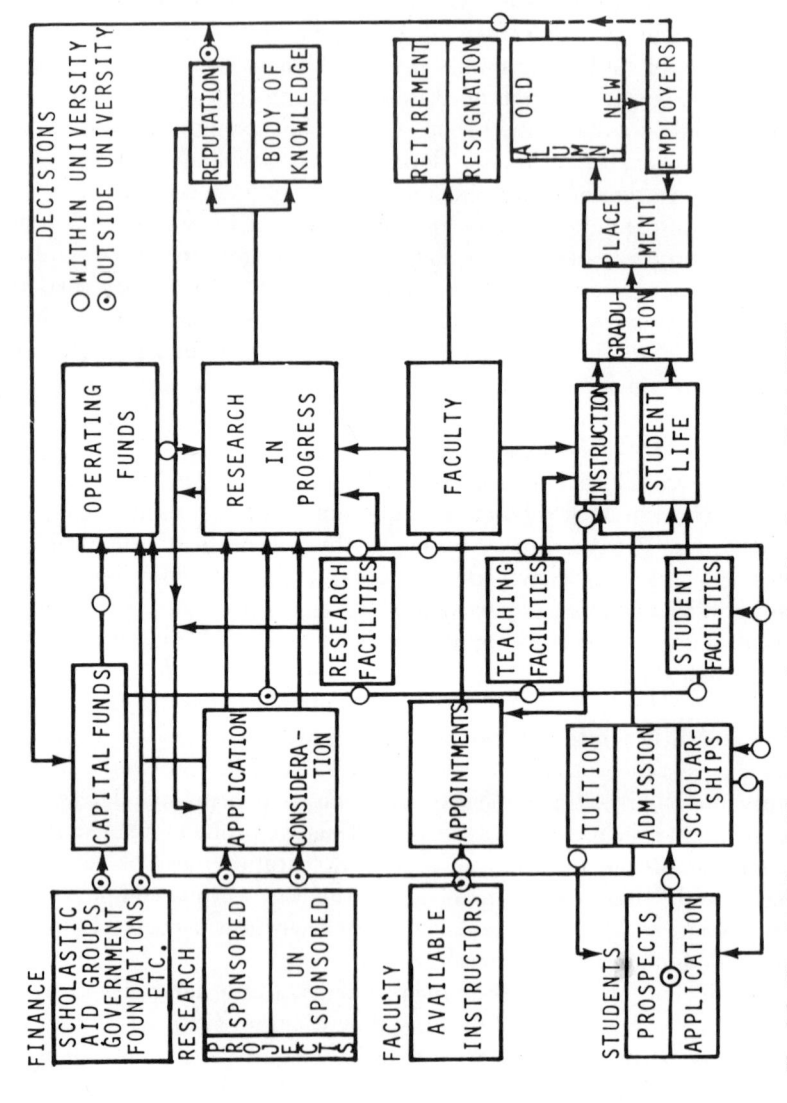

**Fig. 2.1.** The decisionmaking system of a university. Source: Brink (1966).

This framework is suitable for applying decomposition techniques, provided a central policymaker uses a definite objective function to be optimized. Second, consider the subsystem represented by the faculty and its allocation among various activities, such as graduate teaching; undergraduate teaching; research, both inside and outside; thesis supervision; and administrative work. How can we model the situation in which the allocation of faculty man-hours is considered to be the most desirable and appropriate to the needs? The various activity analysis models which we discuss in later chapters attempt to provide some tentative if not exact answers to questions of this sort.

Third, consider the case of long-range planning for the expansion of capacity of the university system, since it is expected that in the next decade the student enrollment is going to increase substantially. Questions regarding the optimal size of a university system and, for that matter, the optimal size of an academic department within such a system cannot be settled entirely inside the system, since through provision of capital funds the external decisionmakers (the state or federal government and the community) may substantially affect the decisions regarding the long-range expansion of a university system. However, it is essential that there be an exchange of information (i.e., a dialogue) regarding the views held by the inside and outside decisionmakers and their objective bases. In our opinion the formulation of a policy model for a university system, which merely quantifies the judgment estimates of the decisionmakers about the various flows in Figure 2.1, would be very helpful in making this two-way dialogue more meaningful and cooperative. Models should never replace the need for human judgment and social responsibility; they only provide a framework in terms of which alternative states of the systems can be appraised, weighed, and sometimes ranked by one or multiple policymakers. It is in this spirit that we discuss the various formulations of educational models for planning.

CHAPTER 3

# Quantitative Models of Planning for Educational Systems

*Jati K. Sengupta*

### General remarks

It is only very recently that the question "Can educational systems be modeled?" has been seriously posed as a problem in resource allocation by educational researchers, systems analysts, and economists. The present annual expenditure of resources on education (both public and nonpublic) in the United States, for example, is roughly of the order of $50 billion, and over the next ten years it is expected to exceed $65 billion, if educational expenditure grows at the conservative rate of 3 percent per year. Expenditure of resources on higher education would be about $18 billion. These figures do not include estimates of current income forgone while attending school. It follows that the economics of resource utilization in educational systems is of great importance for the national economy, not to speak of its intertemporal effects and consequences.

The role of the education sector in the over-all economy, its linkages with other sectors by its input requirements and output provisions and the characteristics of the production and distribution processes associated with it present some challenging problems for an economist interested in the theory and application of optimal growth, for an educational researcher interested in analyzing the significant decision processes in educational systems, and for a systems analyst-cum-operations researcher interested in modeling alternative budgeting procedures and structural forms for the interrelationships existing in educational systems. At the level of a particular university which is directly involved in allocating educational resources for higher education, two basic considerations arise: the question of appropriate pricing for the resources currently available to the system in the short run and the question of distribution of effects of decisions by multiple decisionmakers in the long run. Pricing here reflects the efficiency, or otherwise, of the current utilization of educational resources, whereas distribution refers to sharing of responsibility in resource allocation, co-ordination, and control through nonpricing rules and guidelines, such that consistency in decisionmaking among multiple policymakers may be attained or approximated. Whereas pricing rules attempt to characterize optimality of resource allocation under the assumptions of a perfectly competitive market system (e.g., Pareto-optimal allocation), the distribution rules seek to specify the need for consistency in policymaking by pointing out situations (e.g., indivisibility of some resource, lack of an explicit market system, etc.) in which there is market failure and, hence, the pricing rules are neither operative nor optimal.

Economists are naturally most interested in pricing rules for various market structures, but it is only recently that they have become aware of the problems of developing a resource-allocative pricing process for resources which are internal to an organization but demanded by several of its divisions. Unlike market prices, these interim or internal prices (Sengupta and Fox 1969) are not in financial units of external markets but in implicit units of marginal contribution to the objective function of the organization. These internal prices have been variously termed and utilized in planning procedures. The detailed description, analysis, and appraisal of these methods and their application to educational resource allocation problems are discussed in Chapters 4 and 5.

Unlike the economists and their interest in rules of efficiency pricing, the systems analysts, operations researchers, and experts on administrative behavior have emphasized the need for alternative forms of modeling of educational systems, their objectives, and structures as the first steps toward understanding the various aspects of decisionmaking processes in such systems. Consistency rather than optimality and also the use of nonprice strategies and rules of co-ordination rather than purely pricing considerations are some of the basic implications of this emphasis. Simulation methods for analyzing alternative modeling structures are frequently emphasized in this approach, due to the fact that several parts of the model may be only incompletely known (e.g., the net prices of the objective function, the opportunity cost of research vis-à-vis graduate teaching, the implicit cost of transfer of teaching activities between certain courses, etc.). The theoretical and empirical implications of some of these questions are discussed in detail in relation to university education systems in Chapters 6 and 7.

The purpose of this chapter is to discuss briefly the economic background of the general problems of resource allocation at different levels and the various analytical attempts recently made to model educational systems and their resource utilization processes.

**Objectives and constraints in modeling educational systems**

As in the theory of economic policy (Tinbergen 1956; Fox et al. 1966; Stone 1963), the basic ingredients for modeling an educational system derive first from the identification of the various objectives and goals of the system and second from an investigation into the constraints and interdependencies among various factors and relationships in the system. If models are intended for policy application or analyzing policy implications, then the goals and objectives provide an optimizing criterion in terms of which the unknown variables of the policy problem, the educational resources and expenditures, have to be solved for or optimized. At the national level this is analogous to considering targets such as full employment, price stability, balance of payments equilibrium, etc., which can be approached by varying instruments, such as government expenditure, tax rates, and even subsidies to exports.

In models in which policy application or implication is not directly intended, the goals and objectives may remain implicit rather than explicit. For instance, the notion of balanced growth leads under some assumptions, to a manpower requirements approach (Parnes 1964; Hollister 1968; Poignant 1967; Harbison and Myers 1964; Correa 1963; Wolff 1965) for the education sector, i.e., the requirements for skilled manpower in various sectors of the economy resulting from its equilibrium growth must be met by appropriate resource and expenditure planning in the education sector; otherwise, the discrepancies in manpower demand and supply would generate various types of imbalances (shortages) which might retard the growth of the economy.

These two approaches, the policy approach and the forecasting approach, have been most frequently attempted in models of educational systems at the national level.

*National level: education sector*

Models of the education sector at the national level, which are not directly related to the policy approach, may be broadly classified into three groups: (1) an input-output framework (LeVasseur 1968) with education and noneducation sectors; (2) a framework for estimating the costs and returns associated with investment in human capital, and thereby providing an implicit measure of performance of the education sector in relation to other sectors; and (3) a cost analysis of deviations from the desired goals and norms set by national policymakers for the education sector, where such deviations may be due to various causes, e.g., uncertainty in forecasting, developments in other sectors resulting in resource shortages, etc.

A. *Input-output analysis.* Input-output analysis in national models of economic planning and development in general has proved a very useful tool for economists, and its various applications (Fox et al. 1966) in both static and dynamic frameworks have included such diverse fields as interregional and spatial models and various types of social and national accounting (Stone 1955; Stone and Brown 1962). Its use in educational models at the national level is dependent on the success with which a sector called "education" can be defined in its interrelationships with other sectors. At least four different types of treatment of the education sector in a national input-output framework are available in the literature:

(1) The education sector is outside the interacting network of a two-way input-output table, since it provides autonomous inputs, such as labor and skills, in the form of human capital; hence, the employment aspect is determined in this view either outside the interacting relations between the industrial sectors or through the growth requirements of the over-all economy (Johansen 1960).

(2) The education sector is just like other interacting sectors in that it has definite outputs, such as skilled labor and human capital, that are used by other noneducation sectors, and it has definite input requirements from other sectors in the form of current and capital resources (e.g., equipment, construction, and manpower needs of educational institutions). However, the growth of the noneducation sectors is assumed to be more important, and therefore models in this group (Correa 1963; Tinbergen et al. 1965) emphasize the need for quantitative adaptation of education to economic growth.

(3) The education sector is of equal importance with other interacting sectors of an economy, since an inappropriate supply structure of its two major outputs, the services of labor and human capital (including technical skills and on-the-job training facilities), that are required by other sectors may seriously affect the growth of other sectors. In some underdeveloped countries the employment objective

may be as important as the productivity objective, and the central planners would be ill-advised to consider the education sector as a residual. Adapting economic growth to the needs of the education sector through agri-business and other service industries in the rural sectors is sometimes argued on this basis in development policies for less developed countries with labor surpluses. Similar arguments are sometimes advanced in less developed countries for modifying or adapting the latest technology of the advanced economies to labor-intensive forms rather than importing highly capital-intensive advanced technology. In some models of investment planning (Fox et al. 1966; Mahalanobis 1955; Frisch 1960) in which the employment objective is emphasized equally with other growth and output objectives, the education sector's contribution is subsumed in the service industries sector which includes medical, education, and other training facilities.

(4) The links between education, manpower, and national economic policy should be viewed in this approach along with the links between technological change, improved physical capital, and national economic policy in the design of an appropriate medium-term and long-run policy of growth and stabilization for an economy. Attempts to integrate social accounting and demographic studies with the conventional input-output analysis (LeVasseur 1968), to investigate the quantitative and qualitative factors associated with human and physical capital (Stone 1965; Walden 1964), and to look into the various market and nonmarket returns (and costs) from investment in human capital (Weisbrod 1962; Hansen 1963; Moser and Layard 1964; Denison 1962; Vaizey 1964) have been emphasized in the literature.

A few comments may now be made about some of the important limitations of the above approaches, particularly from the viewpoint of empirical and sometimes policy applications. The first approach, developed as an outgrowth of traditional input-output models, neglected the dynamic implications of the existence of the education sector through skill generation and investment in human capital. The neo-classical tradition of considering growth of the labor force as exogenous to the model may be permissible in aggregative models of growth, but in a disaggregative framework this may be very misleading, particularly in situations in which technological change is not of the neutral type.

The second approach views the education sector as the supplier of various services, e.g., manpower and skills to meet the needs of growth in the whole economy. It is based on the assumption that the structure of the economy can be forecast or projected on a perspective plan basis, and from there the requirements from the education sector can be estimated on the basis of fixed coefficients relating manpower requirements to over-all growth. The fact that supply can at times create its own demand is neglected in this approach. Also the dynamic role of research and the diffusion of knowledge and inventive activity are seriously underemphasized in this approach. Another basic weakness of this type of requirement approach is that its projected requirements usually do not allow explicitly for changes in relative prices which may seriously alter the forecasts.

The third approach presents the basic difficulty of quantifying concepts such as capital-output ratio and gestation period for the education sector, in which some of the services and goods (e.g., research, teaching activity, etc.) may contain intangible and quality factors not easily evaluable; also, the estimates of capital-output ratios for these services may be too unstable to be useful in projection and equilibrium analysis.

The fourth approach is in a sense most satisfactory as a general structural approach. Figure 3.1, taken from LeVasseur (1968), will serve as a convenient illustration of this type of model. The mathematical relationships underlying the flow diagram have been systematized in a model called GAME (global accounts for manpower and education) model, which prescribes a very general structure which may be easily modified for special needs and situations. The GAME model, which is also represented by a large-scale computer program, basically utilizes three tools to develop an integrated approach, i.e., a systems analysis technique known as the industrial dynamics approach (Forrester 1961) for a simulation analysis, an iterative method for checking consistency through the input-output table applicable to the interacting sectors, and a method of social accounts which sometimes can incorporate the various quality factors and nonmonetized elements through budgeting procedures.

With reference to the flow diagram in Figure 3.1, two points should be emphasized. First, the manpower demands by industry are not considered explicitly as investment in some form of capital, since the interaction between two forms of capital, physical and nonphysical, is not explicitly considered. Second, the coefficients relating capital investment for the education sector to industrial sector production may be very difficult to construct due to definitional and aggregation problems, and the stability of manpower requirement coefficients may be of a very different order than the interindustry input-output coefficients. Due to the fact that potential outputs are not always realized, the use of an

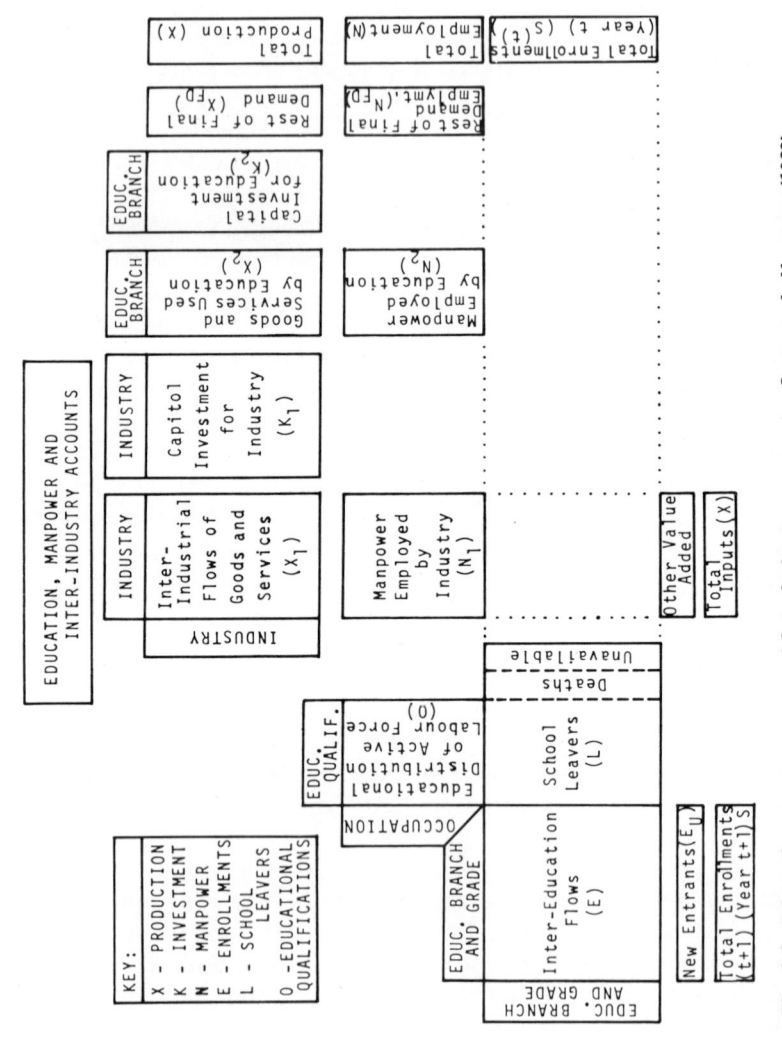

Fig. 3.1. Education, manpower, and interindustry accounts. Source: LeVasseur (1968).

input-output table with other flows, as in Figure 3.1, tends to underestimate sometimes the contributions of services and quality factors associated with skilled manpower. Like technology acting on capital, the education sector acts on the manpower to improve its general, technical, and social skills, and the interindustry flows must have some means of incorporating such phenomena.

B. *Cost-benefit analysis.* Assuming that the education sector acts as a catalytic agent for initiating and spreading inventive activity and knowledge through skilled manpower and research services, the contribution of this sector can be assessed through the costs and returns associated with its production of knowledge and skills.

The social benefits (or costs) from the activity of the education sector include more than market returns, due to several facts (Weisbrod 1962), i.e. (a) the nonmarket returns in the form of psychic income and cultural satisfaction; (b) nonmarket returns to the family and community through interaction and diffusion of knowledge; (c) the option value of being able to pursue a higher level of education or research (i.e., "the option value approach attributes to investment in one level of schooling a portion of the additional return over cost which can be obtained from further education—specifically, that portion which is in excess of the opportunity cost rate of return" [Weisbrod 1962]); and (d) the external benefits of research activity done in the education sector.

The returns to the education sector may be measured in several ways, of which two deserve special mention. First, the return may be estimated through the contribution of that part of labor input in the aggregate production function which represents the attainments due to on-the-job training and schooling. Assuming an aggregate production function with constant returns to scale with homogenous inputs called aggregate labor and aggregate capital, and the other usual assumptions of the neoclassical models of growth, Denison (1964) estimated that over the period 1929–57 the education sector contributed about 23 percent of the growth in total national income and about 42 percent of the growth in per capita income in the United States. T. W. Schultz (1961a, b) and Becker (1964) explicitly allowed the value of student time as a labor input into the educational process, and their estimates show that earnings forgone as a measure of inputs accounted for over half of the total costs of secondary and higher education in the United States (i.e., according to Schultz's estimates, total investment in human capital formation in schools rose from 9 to 34 percent of total investments in physical capital formation; Becker (1964) extended the forgone income hypothesis to on-the-job training and on-the-job investment in own human-capital formation; Mincer (1962) estimated that there are substantial investments in on-the-job training and learning in the United States, and there is a substantial increase in those investments).

Two basic criticisms of this rate of return approach have been leveled. First, the residual method of imputing the residual growth of output not accounted for by the growth of physical capital and the volume of labor to the attainments of education and on-the-job training is questioned due to its assumption (Balogh 1967) of an aggregative production function with constant returns to scale as in Denison's approach. However, this criticism would have far less validity in the disaggregative context of specific industries or sectors. It may be difficult to separate the consumption and investment components of total expenditure on education, and there may be some noncompetitive elements in the educational system, but there is no doubt that the rising levels of education have made a significant contribution to productivity in agriculture, manufacturing, and other industries and that the markets for professional and skilled manpower reflect a substantial degree of competition. Measurement difficulties do not obviate the fact that increases in skill and knowledge are still the main keys to economic growth.

Second, there is the method of computing the average discounted lifetime earnings stream due to extra education or training. As Blaug (1965) has observed: "We cannot simply multiply the cost of education by the rate of return to education to obtain a measure of education's contribution to national income. The calculated yield of investment in education depends upon the age pattern of an average differential lifetime earnings stream; it would have to be age-specific to be the type of coefficient which can derive the contribution of an investment to national income, once the cost of the investment is known" (pp. 241–42). The main objection to this approach is that a view of the future pattern of earnings has to be assumed or projected to compute the present value, although that view may be substantially altered by later developments. Also, this method may not very well capture the rate of return from the various research and extension activities performed in university systems the returns to which are diffused and not easily internalized. However, there is no doubt that as an approximate measure these net return estimates are probably as good as can be expected in this situation. One possible check on these estimates is to use the internal rate of return method (Hansen 1963) to compute the return to total resource investment in primary and secondary school education and higher education. Empirical evidence suggests that such alternative computations tend to indicate a similar characteristic, i.e., a high rate of return to resource investment in schooling.

C. *Decision analysis and goal programming.*\* If educational requirements can be specified at the national level as quantitative goals or targets, just like the goals of full employment or desired rate of economic growth, then the trend of current expenditure on the education sector can be appraised as a means to attain the desired targets. The efficiency of alternative means of attaining the desired goals may then be evaluated on the basis of the theory of economic policy (Fox et al. 1966). Further, the implicit costs associated with alternative decision rules for varying the means in order to attain the desired goals may be evaluated, using decision models presented by Theil (1964). Such computations of implicit costs or losses through deviations from desired goals are useful to policymakers in planning the scale of educational growth in an economy (MacDonald 1964). Also, the short-run and long-run problems can be usefully separated for purposes of analysis; in the short run, problems of deviation from the trend would be considered, but in the long run the problems of increasing (or decreasing) trend rates of expansion (or contraction) would be analyzed.

D. *Policy implications and optimization.* The policy model formulation of the education sector at the national level adds two additional features to the models thus far considered. First, it explicitly introduces objective functions (i.e., social welfare functions) for the whole economy, including the education sector, and allows optimization in some form or another. Second, it considers some of the budgetary and fiscal constraints and other limitations due to which over-all optimization may be restricted to the choice of suboptimal or second-best policies.

So far as the objective function is concerned, two alternative ways of optimization have been introduced for the education sector. First, the demands imposed on the education sector in the form of manpower requirements resulting from optimal growth of an economy implicitly introduce an objective for the education sector, since the optimal growth of the economy is visualized in terms of maximization of a discounted sum of GNP. The studies by Jean Benard (1967) on French data and by Irma Adelman (1966) on Argentine data are illustrative of this approach. Second, the explicit introduction of an objective function for the education sector, e.g., maximization of the excess of total benefits over costs

---

\* An empirical illustration of goal programming and related methods is given in Chapter 6 under the title: "Goal programming and efficiency in models for educational institutions."

of education in order to compute the optimum manpower requirements, treating the inputs into the education sector from the rest of the economy as exogenously determined, offers another more important approach. The empirical application of such an approach has been considered by Samuel Bowles (1967), using data for northern Nigeria.

The framework of the above optimization models has been one of linear programming, which has the advantage that its shadow prices whenever they are nonnegative provide measures of implicit costs associated with various policy constraints and budgetary restraints. When such constraints prevent the attainment of an over-all optimum, and therefore a first-best, policy, we have to consider second-best or suboptimal situations. The implications of such second-best policies in relation to planning for the education sector are discussed in Chapter 6.

Note, however, that the optimization framework requires that (like GNP) the education sector must have an aggregate output measure (i.e., educational output component of GNP) over which optimization has to be quantified. The framework of neo-classical growth models with its concept of an aggregate production function provides one basis for such a construction, although the index number and aggregation problems are serious stumbling blocks here. Once the analogy with the neo-classical growth model is conceived, it is possible to incorporate the effects of learning experiences (e.g., learning by doing introduced through the aggregate production function [Sheshinski 1967]) and the optimal course of inventive activity (Shell 1967) over time, although returns from research activity may be far more difficult to quantify or impute.

*University level: academic departments*

The problems of resource allocation and investment in higher education, particularly at the university level, have perhaps all the characteristics of the national level problems except that decisionmaking in a university system represents much more prominently a partial equilibrium framework with potentially more active roles for price variables.

Since there appears to be a considerable degree of skepticism about quantifying the objectives and goals of a university system, systems analysts (Keeney et al. 1967; Judy 1969) developed university-wide models on the basis of various input and output flows and their observed cost components; then, they applied simulation techniques by varying the estimates of several parameters which are very crucial to the system behavior but not always stable. The following flow diagram (Fig. 3.2) taken from Keeney et al. (1967) is illustrative of the general model

QUANTITATIVE MODELS OF PLANNING 47

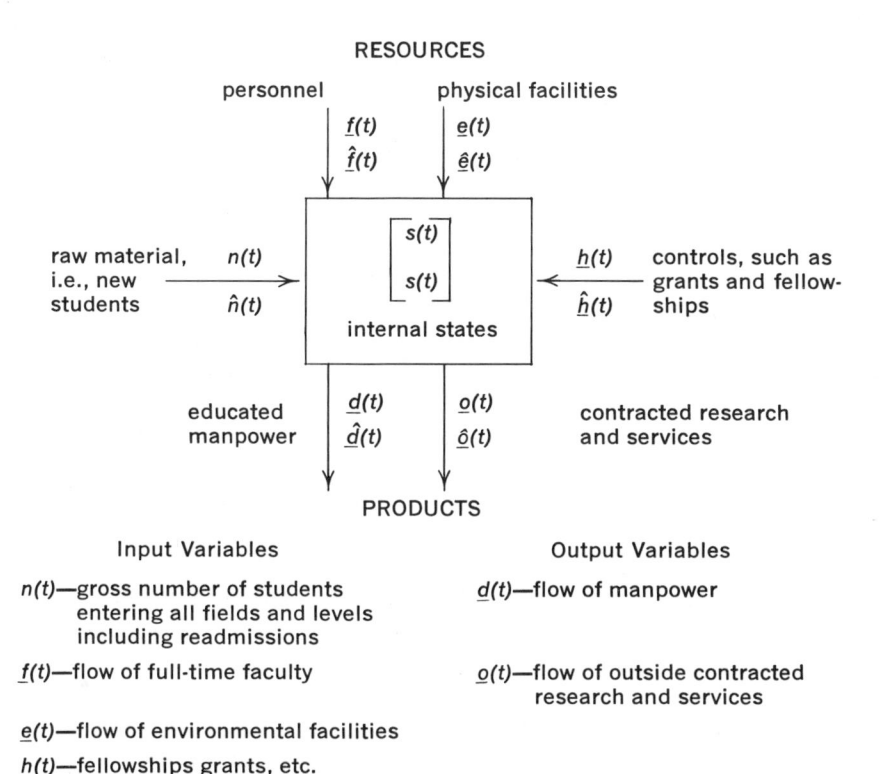

```
                           RESOURCES
            personnel          physical facilities
                    f(t)              e(t)
                    f̂(t)              ê(t)
                     ↓                ↓
                   ┌─────────────────────┐
raw material,  n(t)│       [s(t)]        │ h(t)    controls, such as
i.e., new      ───→│        s(t)         │←─────   grants and fellow-
students       n̂(t)│                     │ ĥ(t)    ships
                   │   internal states   │
                   └─────────────────────┘
                          d(t)   o(t)
              educated    d̂(t)   ô(t)    contracted research
              manpower     ↓      ↓      and services
                           PRODUCTS
```

Input Variables                    Output Variables

n(t)—gross number of students      d(t)—flow of manpower
entering all fields and levels
including readmissions

f(t)—flow of full-time faculty     o(t)—flow of outside contracted
                                          research and services

e(t)—flow of environmental facilities

h(t)—fellowships grants, etc.

**Fig. 3.2. Terminal flows and internal states identified in the model of an educational institution as a "black box." Source: Keeney, Koenig, and Zemach (1967).**

structure, its classification of control and state variables and the costs associated with various flows recursively interrelated over time. (Note that in Figure 3.2 the notation $\hat{x}$ is used to indicate accounting costs associated with a flow of type $x$ where, for example, $x$ may be the costs associated with grants and fellowships.)

The systems model has three sources of implicit optimization which are, of course, not explicitly considered. First, the identification of various decision levels in university systems and the assumptions about mutual consistency of the various decisionmakers imply a type of vector optimization, although some qualitative and subjective elements may be involved in the concepts of "activity," "input," or "output" used by different policymakers. However, those parts of the input and output of a university system which are directly measurable (e.g., cost of education and returns from additional skills) could provide the benchmark for comparing other components of inputs and outputs. As a matter of fact, this situation is suitable for suboptimization, if not complete optimization, and the techniques of decomposition which analyze the value of central co-ordination along with divisional decentralization are certainly applicable here. Even the implicit costs of inconsistency can be broadly appraised in such a partial optimization framework. (This view is discussed in detail in Chapters 4 and 5, where various pricing and decision-theoretic implications of decomposition techniques are considered.)

Second, the direct costs of education only reflect a part of the total costs and benefits of education. We have already seen in earlier sections that there are various nonmarket elements of benefits from schooling and university training, and unless costs reflect the net economic cost of all resources involved in the university system it is not possible to evaluate and appraise the relative efficiency of resource utilization in the university system.

Third, even in the system equations of a systems model of higher education (Keeney et al. 1967) there is the concept of balance and equilibrium which suggests that the policymakers' notions of desired levels and requirements (e.g., a desired level of the student-teacher ratio, a desired expansion of a certain department, a desired rate of growth of faculty salaries, etc.) are very important in such a framework. In the language of goal programming, preassigning desired levels may only reflect attempts at suboptimization or second-best policies. Reasons for such choice of second-best policies may be due to lack of precise information about the interdependence of policies and other uncertainties associated with communication gaps and lags, etc.

This view is clearly emphasized by the analysis of decisionmaking in a typical university system by Brink (1966), from whose study we have reproduced Figure 2.1 (see Chapter 2, page 34). The various feedback relations shown in Figure 2.1 are partly derived from empirical information flows based on University of Pennsylvania data and partly from what is believed to be the logical structuring of interrelationships between various decision points. Between the four subsystems (finance, research, faculty, and students) there are twenty-five decision points identified in Figure 2.1, of which seven are outside and eighteen inside the university system. The relative efficiency of utilization of resources involved in the inside decisionmaking process of a university cannot be appraised, unless modeling for a university explicitly recognizes its multiversity character and identifies goals which can be suboptimized, if not optimized. If the approach of Schultz and Becker is followed, so that a part of the expenditure in the university system can be identified as the investment component of total investment in human capital, then the rate of return provides a broad measure of evaluation.

Another fruitful line of approach in our opinion is to consider the problem of resource allocation in a university department from the standpoint of department chairmen, deans, and other active policymakers in the system. This view (Fox et al. 1967; Plessner et al. 1968; Fox and Sengupta 1968; Sengupta and Fox 1970; Fox et al. 1969) will be discussed in detail, both theoretically and empirically, in later chapters. It may only be pointed out at this stage that our policy framework of optimization and suboptimization includes three different facets, i.e. (a) the interaction between policymakers, e.g., the department chairman and the dean, analyzed through decomposition techniques assuming a net returns concept based on discounted value of lifetime earnings from additional skills and degrees; (b) the resource allocation processes of a multiproduct firm which operates under various internal and external constraints, some of which may be noncompetitive; and (c) the need for consistency and aggregation, due to several probabilistic factors associated with external points of decisionmaking outside the university.

In other specific areas of decisionmaking within the university, other types of optimization techniques have been applied, such as program budgeting methods (O.E.C.D. 1968) for long-range planning and budgeting, and scheduling techniques (Schotta and Schotta 1967) in course and instructional media planning.

*School system: secondary education*

Although we will not discuss in any detail the problems of allocation of resources involved in primary and secondary school systems, it must be pointed out that they have attracted substantial amounts of analytical and empirical attention (O.E.C.D. 1969) in such various aspects as cost and budgeting procedures, estimation of returns from schooling, optimal class size and instructional media, economies of scale in school size, and comparison of returns from investment in private and public schools.

From a policy viewpoint two aspects of the resource investment process in the school system deserve in our opinion much more intensive economic analysis than has been attempted so far in the existing literature. First, concern with the incidence of resource investment and expenditure in the school system on such social and ceonomic goals as equalizing educational opportunities and reducing income disparities suggests that income-redistribution effects are implicit if not explicit in the public school system financed by state support. To what extent educational policies should incorporate such goals, when fiscal policies and other methods may be available to the state, and how the cost-benefit analysis for the education sector would be modified due to this objective needs more analysis and empirical investigation. Second, the methodological problem of quantifying an output measure in index number terms reflecting the performance of various school systems may be usefully analyzed through the following empirical inquiries: e.g. (a) To what extent do differences in school expenditures or costs reflect differences in quality of education? (b) To what extent are there economies or diseconomies of scale in the various phases of school operation? (c) To what degree can the various implicit costs and external returns from schooling in terms of income forgone be internalized to develop a procedure for efficiency costing and budgeting rather than pure accounting calculations? Some of these questions (Froomkin 1968; Williams 1963; Riew 1966; Hansen 1970) are only beginning to be investigated.

### Current mathematical models of educational systems: A brief appraisal of selected models

An educational system can be defined at various levels, at the national level, at the level of a particular university, and at the level of a particular department or discipline in a specific university. At each level there arise fundamental problems of planning which are no less interesting and important than those of national economic planning which are usually discussed in the context of economic growth models and policymaking (Fox et al. 1966; Theil 1964). The process of planning an educational system at any level is understood here to include any or all of the following aspects:

a) an analysis of basic variables, both quantitative and qualitative, characterizing an educational system;

b) an analysis of the over-all goal and its components;

c) a prognosis of the trend of growth (or decline) and its structural aspects characterizing the evolution of an educational system over time;

d) the implications for planning of the uncertain components in evaluation of demand and supply, price and cost or intangible aspects.

In this section, we present a critical survey of some of the most important models for planning an educational system which have been proposed so far and outline the requirements of a more satisfactory model. In our survey we emphasize in particular (a) the operational and hence mostly quantitative aspects of the models, meaning thereby that qualitative variables, insofar as they occur, are assumed to be measurable by index numbers, scores or payoff values partly based on subjective judgment and partly on other indicative variables which are quantitative; (b) their usefulness in the design and application of policies, e.g., the various aspects of optimization and suboptimization considered in the models; and (c) the nature of their analysis of the dynamic elements of the problem of planning an educational system.

In the final analysis, of course, any model is restricted to a particular framework of assumptions and constraints, purposes at hand and approximations at large. However, we still believe that the specification of alternative logical structures (i.e., a set of consistent and flexible relationships between the most relevant variables characterizing an educational system) through alternative econometric models helps to a considerable degree in affording an insight into the possible interdependence of effects (and costs?) of alternative policies, the probable area of in-optimal decisionmaking, and even the need for trading off one subgoal for another in view of the final effect on the over-all goal or objective of the system.

We do not deny the role of subjective judgment in these evaluations of potential efficiency but we suggest that any clarification of the logical structure of decisionmaking at different levels of an educational system in terms of a network of a policy model would help considerably in narrowing down the areas of difference in alternative subjective evaluations.

*Aggregative models: Input-output type analysis*

The aggregative models of educational systems at the national level may be classified into at least four different groups, the common link apparently provided by the specification of a production function whereby education provides the skills and manpower for over-all economic growth measured in terms of real output trends:

- A. models with few sectors (usually two sectors) with national output as an exogenous variable (Tinbergen and Bos 1965; Sengupta and Tintner 1963);
- B. models with several sectors based on open-dynamic input-output models (Stone 1965; Smith and Armitage 1967);
- C. programming models with investment in education as a component of aggregate national investment (Adelman 1966; Moser and Redfern 1965a, b);

D. recursive models with specific variables relating to a particular component of the over-all educational system (Stoikov 1964; Intriligator and Smith 1966; Bolt et al. 1964), e.g., the allocation of scientific personnel between teaching, research, and other work or the investment needs of a planned change in the scale of higher education in an economy to attain a desired level of formation of skills of appropriate types.

Perhaps the simplest model in category A is specified by means of a one-input production function and an equilibrium relation for the growth of labor force with a certain education level (e.g., a third-level or a secondary-level education). Denote by $N_t$ the stock of labor force with a given education level, by $Y_t$ the total volume of real income or production of a given economy, by $m_t$ the number of those who have entered the labor force within the previous six years (for example) and by $n_t$ the total number of students at that given education level attending classes, then the basic model (Tinbergen and Bos 1965) is as follows:

$$N_t = a_1 Y_t + a_2 n_t; \quad \text{(production function)} \tag{1}$$

$$N_t = (1 - d_1)N_{t-1} + m_t; \quad \text{(growth of labor force)} \tag{2}$$

$$m_t = g n_{t-1}; \quad \text{(supply of labor).} \tag{3}$$

Here $d_1$ represents drop-out rates (assumed to be an estimated constant) due to retirement, death, and other factors, and the coefficient $g$ represents a factor of proportionality between $m_t$, the gross increase in the stock of manpower $N_t$ during the last six years, and $n_{t-1}$ (i.e., the total number of students attending classes at that education level during period $t - 1$).

Equation (1) says that the labor force with a given education level consists of those currently employed in production (assumed proportional in numbers to the volume of national output) and of those teaching at that level of education (assumed proportional to the current number of students). Since the model has one degree of freedom (Fox et al. 1966), one can close the model by postulating an exogenously determined relation. For example, if real national output is growing at a rate of $r$ percent per year, then the requirement of a balanced growth of student population at the given education level is specified from the system as:

$$n_t = (g/a_2)n_{t-1} + Y_0(1 + r)^{t-1}(1 - d_1 - a_1 - a_1 r), \tag{4}$$

given the initial levels $n_0$, $Y_0$ and $N_0$ at $t = 0$. Here the balanced growth concept is one of regular growth of the skill formation through student training parallel to the desired growth of the economy in terms of real output. If the balanced growth rate specified by (4) is not satisfied, then we have either insufficient or excessive supply in relation to the requirement level over time.

There is another interesting way of closing the model if one introduces cost of training, i.e., investment cost of skill formation $c_t$, which is assumed, for simplicity, to be linearly proportional to the number of students trained, e.g.:

$$c_t = in_t; \ (i = \text{constant of proportionality}), \tag{5}$$

then by combining (1) through (3) with (5):

$$Y_t = (1 - d_1)Y_{t-1} + (a_2 + g)c_{t-1}/(a_1 i) - a_2 c_t/a_1 i. \tag{6}$$

By means of this relation (6) and given the initial values $Y_0$, $c_0$ and $N_0$ one can derive a partial optimum rate of growth of investment cost of skill formation by maximizing the end-period income level with a planning horizon of, say, a decade or so (or maximizing the sum total of incomes over the given planning horizon). The rate of investment cost (and hence the rate of growth of skill formation) so computed is called partially optimum, because the model does not incorporate in a basic sense the rest of the economy and the investment activity therein. Further, it has only one input in the production function and it does not include other technological constraints due to the interdependence of the education sector with the rest of the economy and the restrictions imposed by the over-all fiscal capacity of the economy.

Two obvious lines of extension of the above model are readily apparent. First, the production function in the model could be generalized to incorporate curvilinear relationships, the result of capital and technology, which may be determined outside the model, but their restrictions must remain implicit behind the partial equilibrium setup of this education model. Second, the various types of education generating different types of skills could be distinguished, along with an appropriate breakdown of the over-all national economy (and its output) into "sectors," so that the student population and labor force could be conceived as vectors, where each component of the vector may be age-specific and skill-specific.

The second line of extension is basically equivalent to the multisectoral model of the educational system developed by Stone (1965), which may be viewed as a typical model in category B. In this model, the educational system is defined to be a system of connected processes and the model includes all forms of education, training, and retraining. The flow equation of the system is basically similar to that of an open-dynamic input-output model, in that a given year's activity levels expressed in terms of students are shown as functions of future vectors of graduate leavers who are potential entrants to the labor force.

As in the input-output model, this type of formulation enables us to calculate the requirements for activity levels in the educational system corresponding to a desired rate of change in the structure of output and in the structure of skill formation. Let the column vector $s_t$ denote the stock of students of specified age groups in various levels (or processes) of education at the beginning of year $t$ and $\hat{h}$ be a diagonal matrix of age-specific survival rates, then $\hat{h}s_t$ denotes the surviving student population at the beginning of year $t$. Out of this a proportion (i.e., $\hat{p}\hat{h}s_t$ where $\hat{p}$ is a diagonal matrix with proportions in the diagonal) continues in the system from one education level (or process) to another and the remaining (i.e., $(I - \hat{p})\hat{h}s_t$ which is denoted as $g_t$) are graduate leavers at the end of year $t$. It is assumed that the numbers of students who stay in the various processes can be expressed in terms of next year's initial stock of students, i.e.,

$$\hat{p}\hat{h}s_t = Js_{t+1}, \tag{7}$$

where $J$ denotes a matrix with ones in the diagonal immediately above the leading diagonal and zeros everywhere else (since the matrix $\hat{p}$ can be interpreted to denote the probability that a surviving student who was in process [level] $j$ this year will be found in process [level] $j + 1$ next year). Hence it follows that:

$$\hat{h}s_t = Js_{t+1} + g_t, \tag{8}$$

where $g_t = (I - \hat{p})\hat{h}s_t$ which implies that

$$s_t = (\hat{h}^{-1}J)s_t + (\hat{h}^{-1}J)\Delta s_t + \hat{h}^{-1}g_t, \tag{9}$$

where $\Delta s_t = s_{t+1} - s_t$ and $I$ = identity matrix. The equation (9) which shows the recursive relationship between present numbers of students in different processes (or levels) and the future numbers of graduate leavers from the different processes is basically similar to the flow equation of an open-dynamic input-output model in which the output levels are the elements of vector $s_t$ and the final products are the elements of $\hat{h}^{-1}g_t$.

According to this interpretation, the input structure behind the output vector $s_t$ has now to be introduced. Denote by $X$ a matrix whose rows relate to different economic inputs (e.g., number of teachers of different skill groups, building space, research equipment, etc.) and whose columns refer to different educational levels or processes (e.g., secondary level, undergraduate college level, graduate level, Ph.D. level, postdoctoral research, etc.). Then by dividing the elements in each column by the corresponding activity levels, we obtain a coefficient matrix $U$, i.e.:

$$U = X\hat{s}_t^{-1}, \tag{10}$$

where $\hat{s}_t$ denotes a diagonal matrix whose diagonal elements are composed of the corresponding elements of the vector $s_t$. Any changes in the elements of the coefficient matrix $U$ reflect changes in the structure (qualitative or quantitative) of economic inputs into various educational processes. Thus the "technology" of the educational system is reflected in the coefficient matrices $U$ and $\hat{h}^{-1}J$ where the latter reflects mainly the changes in the normal time to complete different learning processes at different levels. Denoting the vector of row sums of matrix $X$ by $x_t$, one could compute the required supply of economic inputs corresponding to any preassigned level of output vector $s_t$, i.e.,

$$x_t = U s_t. \tag{11}$$

As in the model of category A discussed before, our model now can be closed in several ways. First of all, assume that the structure of growth of $s_t$ is solved from (9) and plugged into (11) to compute the vector of required input levels $x_t$; then by comparing the existing supply of input structure with the required one, we may find the deficiency or otherwise of the present supply and estimate its consequences (e.g., a deficient supply system has to be reflected in any of the following: a lowering of standards, a postponement of the present rate of improvement, and so on). The evaluation of consequences for the over-all output or income components may be facilitated by postulating an impact relation, e.g.:

$$\bar{y}_t = \bar{y}_{t-1} + R v_{t-1}, \tag{12}$$

$$v_t = C x_t + b, \tag{13}$$

where $\bar{y}_t$ is a vector of those components of national output which are relevant, $v_t$ is a vector of cost components associated with the structure of inputs $x_t$, and the matrices $R$, $C$, and vector $b$ are constants the estimates of which are assumed to be known. In this setup any deficient supply of input structure would be reflected in its effects on the components of national output $\bar{y}_t$, since the matrix $R$ represents the output-creating effects of investment in education. A second way of closing the model is to introduce social welfare functions, e.g., minimize:*

* Note that the specification of the welfare function (15) would include cumulative disutility functions $\int_o^t - U(v_t, y_t) dt$, which are assumed in Ramsay-type optimal growth theory (Sheshinski 1967; Shell 1967).

either : $(w'v_T + \bar{w}'\bar{y}_T)$ (14)

or: $W(v_0, v_1, v_2, \ldots, v_T; \bar{y}_0, \bar{y}_1, \ldots, \bar{y}_T)$ (15)

and determine the optimal levels of $x_t$ and $\bar{y}_t$ subject to the constraints:

$$\bar{y}_t \geq \bar{y}_{t-1} + Rv_{t-1}, \tag{16}$$

$$s_t \geq (\hat{h}^{-1}J)s_t + (\hat{h}^{-1}J)\Delta s_t + \hat{h}^{-1}g_t, \tag{17}$$

$$x_t = Us_t;\ v_t = Cx_t + b;\ s_t, x_t, v_t, \bar{y}_t \geq 0, \tag{18}$$

where $w$ and $\bar{w}$ are vectors of non-negative weights for the terminal cost, $W(\cdot)$ indicates a weighted combination of the components of $v_t$ and $\bar{y}_t$, and $T$ is the end-year of the planning horizon.* Note that the objective function (15) can be viewed as the net contribution of the education sector to national income over time, the contribution being evaluated by the returns from investment in human capital as in Schultz (1961) and Bowles (1967).

Another interesting aspect of the model presented by relations (9) through (11) is that it allows a decomposition of the over-all system into subsystems, for each of which a demand-supply analysis and, for that matter, the conditions for equilibrium growth can be specified. Suppose we consider the teaching input into the educational processes and partition the matrix $U$ of (10) to define a submatrix $A$ taking only the set of rows relating to teachers in the various educational processes. Then the demand for teachers $D_t$ can be presumed to depend mainly on the activity levels of different educational processes measured by the size of student population, i.e.:

$$D_{t+1} = As_{t+1}. \tag{19}$$

Further, the supply of teachers $S_{t+1}$ could be related to the number of the existing stock $S_t$ of teachers who remain active and the number of graduate leavers (B.S. through Ph.D.'s) who enter into teaching careers, i.e.:

$$S_{t+1} = (I - \hat{d})S_t + Bg_t;\ I = \text{identity matrix}, \tag{20}$$

where $\hat{d}$ is a diagonal matrix whose diagonal elements refer to the wastage rates of different kinds of teachers and the elements of the matrix $B$ denote the proportion of different kinds of graduates taking up teaching as

---

* This type of closing is quite conventional in the theory of linear dynamic input-output models characterizing an intertemporally optimal path of capital accumulation (Solow 1959), although other types of closure are easily conceivable (Johansen 1960; Lange 1960).

a career. Again, if the estimated supply computed from (20) tends to be deficient in relation to estimated demand from (19), then several policy alternatives (e.g., increasing the prospects of return in teaching occupations, decreasing the intensity of demand for teachers at undergraduate levels by changes in curricula or methods of teaching, or lowering of standards, etc.) have to be conceived to reduce the gap between demand and supply.

Two comments are in order about the model in category B presented above. First, although the flow equation of an open-dynamic input-output model provides a very close analogy to the basic equations derived in (9) through (11), there is some need in the latter system to distinguish between capacity variables and current account variables. For instance, the development of a good faculty in one department of a university has at least two effects: It raises the quality of teaching and research training provided to its students, so that the current rate of formation of skills in students is increased, and it stimulates further improvement and professional development within the faculty itself through mutual interaction among faculty members in the given department and in other related departments and through the development of teamwork in research. An appropriate stock of faculty members engaged in teaching and research is essential for maintaining a given level of educational output, but for upgrading the level of educational performance (e.g., upgrading the professional excellence of an academic department) a far more essential factor may be the catalytic role played by a few eminent or highly creative faculty members in providing the core of an improved environment in which accelerated research output and professional growth are easily achievable. Similarly it is essential to recognize the role of external benefits to other departments when a given department such as Mathematics attains a higher level of excellence and thereby acquires the potential for giving better training to students of other departments. Other aspects of external benefits and nonmarket returns are emphasized by Weisbrod (1962), Mincer (1962), and others.

The identification of indivisible elements in the variables characterizing an educational system is a task of primary importance which needs to be carefully performed before the scale effects (i.e., the economies and diseconomies) of the over-all evolution of an educational system can be incorporated in the above-type linear dynamic difference equations. A closely related aspect is the evaluation of implicit costs of activities, such as research and educational administration, which cannot most appropriately be fitted into the strait-jackets of demand and supply because of the lack of a so-called common denominator, price. Hence, decomposition with respect to such activities has to be treated, at the least, at a level different from the rest.*

Second, the sequential aspects of educational policies affecting the educational system and its quality of excellence need to be incorporated into the model structure in a basic sense; in other words, the implicit opportunity costs of alternative educational policies pursued by multiple policymakers and their sequential effects over time are not amenable to analysis within the confines of the aggregative model above. The degree to which the elements of the matrices $\hat{p}$, $\hat{s}_t$, $R$, $A$, and $B$ are amenable to influence through deliberate policies pursued by policymakers at different stages is a subject of considerable importance in educational planning. Further, it must be noted that most of these coefficients are average estimates with a margin of uncertainty around them, and therefore it is all the more necessary to emphasize the role of adaptive and/or self-correcting decision rules.

Even at the aggregative level, the dynamic input-output type model in category B can be easily extended to incorporate the details of investment planning in the education sector and in the rest of the economy, viewing the total allocable investible resource at any period as having two outlets, one of which is the education sector and the other is the rest of the economy. This viewpoint readily takes us into models of category C.

A model in this category (Adelman 1966) uses a dynamic programming approach with a planning horizon of a decade or more, with investment in education optimized simultaneously with investment in real capital for different sectors of the economy. The optimal time patterns of production, imports, and exports for each of the several sectors of the economy are also determined concurrently. An appropriate objective function, e.g., the maximization of the economy's rate of growth (i.e., maximization of the discounted sum of GNP over the given horizon) is set up and optimized subject to a set of linear constraints of several types: (a) Constraints for the educational system specifying the initial supply of teachers, the supply of school buildings, etc. along with the technological conditions for the transformation of students at a given level (undergraduate) to a higher level (graduate) whenever feasible; (b) sociocultural constraints stipulating that the enrollments in each type of school are nondecreasing through time; (c) labor force change equations which

* The concept of decomposition of an over-all model into several submodels has different variants of interpretation, e.g. (a) a method of two-level planning by linking the submodel solutions through a two-facet objective function in each submodel, of which one facet reflects the external effects of the submodel on the other sectors; (b) a method of allocating resources on the basis of suboptimal solutions; and (c) a recursive linking of submodels. These are discussed in detail in Chapters 4–6.

stipulate the differential productivity contributions of graduates and dropouts from schools and colleges of a given type to the supply of labor of a particular skill (it is to be noted that these equations provide the principal link between the educational system and the productive sectors of the economy); (d) constraints for the productive sectors of the economy specifying the technological conditions of production and investment and limiting the economy's use of primary resources to available stocks of productive capacity (by sector), manpower (by skill), and foreign exchange and saving; and (e) a set of behavioral constraints about certain minimum levels of domestic consumption and the maximum absorptive capacity of investment in each sector. Finally, the terminal requirement is that the sectoral investment in the last period of the planning horizon must at least cover that period's depreciation charges.

The optimal solution of such a model specifies the optimal levels of two sets of decision variables: (1) For the noneducational part, the optimal sectoral levels of domestic production, imports, fixed capital formation, net foreign capital inflow, etc.; and (2) for the educational system, the optimal number of graduates and dropouts in each time period to be allocated to a particular type of employment (i.e., labor of a given skill or retention within the school either as a student or as a teacher).

About the relative usefulness of such a type of formulation, two claims are generally made. First, the shadow prices of various labor skills and other resources computed from the linear programming model are taken to provide some indication about the desirable direction of change in the pattern of education and training facilities of different types through implicit calculations of the marginal social benefit from investment in education. For instance, the differences between the shadow prices of graduates of various types and their respective average earnings may provide some broad and notional estimate of the role of market incentives and prospective returns. Second, it is a mark of great flexibility that this type of model allows for the simultaneous computation of an optimal pattern of growth in the economy and an optimal pattern of enrollment and resource use in the educational system. The demands for skilled and educated labor are generated endogenously and in a sense recursively by the optimal pattern of economic and educational growth.

However, it is perhaps necessary to mention the need for cautious interpretation of this type of model. First of all, the shadow prices are strongly conditioned by the way the coefficients of the objective function and of the restraints are set up, e.g., the estimates of relative productivity coefficients of labor with various levels of education are very crucial in determining the shadow prices. Also, they should not be interpreted as market prices measured in financial units of account. To that extent the statistical sensitivity to errors in specification or estimation presents quite a complicated problem. Second, the linearity of the coefficient structure generally prevents any variation in the marginal rates of substitution between different education and skill levels and this means that the substitution rates between different component-goals in the over-all goal of the central objective function are fixed once for all for the not-too-short planning horizon. This could be relaxed by postulating nonlinear, maybe up to quadratic, relations with changes in relative marginal rates of substitution. This would also facilitate the analysis of sensitivity of the optimal solutions of the linear program. Third, a very important difficulty with the programming formulation is that the optimal solutions are not available in an analytic form, such as the regression of a set of dependent variables on the set of independent variables, and hence the extrapolation of optimal solutions beyond the period considered or with slightly altered or added constraints is fraught with great problems. One way in which the problems could be tackled is to compute not only the optimal solution but also the second-best and third-best basic feasible solutions, which could be utilized when the coefficients in the objective function (for instance) reflecting relative marginal productivities are subject to revision and updating. The second-best and third-best solutions may provide an indication of the range of variation of the optimal solution (i.e., the first-best solution) when the coefficients of the objective function are liable to small perturbations. Also, the objectives of the education sector, differentiated from the objectives of growth and productivity, are not separately analyzed in this study. To this extent the education sector is required to adapt to the needs of economic growth which may be largely determined by other sectors (Benard 1967; Bowles 1967). Also, the redistributive role of education through equalizing educational opportunities and reducing sources of income disparity, which may be highly important in underdeveloped countries and even developed economies (Froomkin 1968; Hansen 1970), is completely neglected in this type of analysis. The implicit costs of policy constraints and various monopolistic elements in investment processes for human capital require more intensive analysis both theoretically and empirically.

In a somewhat specific and more or less analytic (or predictive) approach, the models in category D deal with a particular component of the over-all educational system (implicitly, in a partial equilibrium set-up) and analyze the impact of variation in some of the coefficients on the relevant endogenous variables of the system. An interesting problem at this level is the allocation of scientific effort between teaching and research in relation to the needs of prospective growth of an economy. This has been considered by Stoikov (1964) and others.

Denote by $S_t$ the total volume of scientific personnel in an economy engaged in teaching or research in period $t$, out of which $R_t$ denotes those who are engaged in research and $E_t$ represents the rest, those who are engaged in teaching. The growth of total scientific personnel ($S_t$) and total number of teachers ($E_t$) are assumed to be explained as follows:

$$S_{t+1} - S_t = gE_t - hS_t, \qquad (21)$$

$$E_{t+1} - E_t = agE_t - hE_t, \qquad (22)$$

and

$$S_t = R_t + E_t, \qquad (23)$$

where $g$ is the number of students trained per scientist-year of teaching, $h$ is the rate of exit and dropout of scientists from the profession per year due to retirement and other causes, assumed to be the same for both teaching and research personnel, and $a$ is the fraction of graduating scientists entering teaching as a career. Define by $Q_t$ the quantum of research effort with a finite planning horizon $[0, T]$ measured by the sum total of research scientist man-years for the entire planning horizon, then the policy problem posed is: How should the newly trained scientists be allocated between teaching and research, i.e., what should be the most appropriate or optimal value of the ratio $a$?

From equations (21) through (23) one could solve for $R_t$ and $Q_T$ as:

$$R_t = (1-h)^t \left( R_0 - \frac{1-a}{a} \cdot E_0 \right) + \frac{(1-a)E_0}{a} \cdot (1 + ag - h)^t, \qquad (24)$$

$$Q_T = \sum_0^T R_t = \frac{(1-h)^{T+1} - 1}{h} \left( \frac{(1-a)E_0}{a} - R_0 \right) \qquad (25)$$

$$+ \frac{(1-a)E_0}{a} \cdot \frac{(1 + ag - h)^{T+1} - 1}{ag - h},$$

where the subscript zero indicates initial values. One way to analyze the problem is to vary the ratio $a$ along with plausible values of other coefficients for an economy, observe the effect on the quantum of research effort with alternative durations of the finite planning horizon, and then decide taxonomically on the most reasonably appropriate value of $a$ which very nearly maximizes in an approximate sense the variable $Q_T$. If the actual value of $a$ deviates far from the approximately optimal value so computed, then appropriate policy measures (e.g., appropriate emphasis on the incentives and prospects in teaching and research, etc.) need be conceived so as to minimize the gap between the two ratios.

It may appear that this model is very specific and simplistic, but this need not be true. First of all, the competitive relation between teaching and research postulated by the basic equations of the model may be easily modified to allow for ranges of complementarity. Similarly, the exogenous role of needs of economic growth can be very easily incorporated by postulating the relative marginal contribution of research effort to the total real output of the national economy. Second, the activities of teaching and research could be further disaggregated into different levels and fields, so that $E_t$, $R_t$, $S_t$ could be interpreted as vectors, and, likewise, the coefficient $a$ could be interpreted as a suitably defined matrix, the elements of which could provide the decision variables to be optimally determined. Further, the costs of allocation, training, and research, along with the constraints of the noneducation sector, could be incorporated as secondary boundary conditions. Third, this type of formulation is suitable for deriving linear decision rules with a quadratic preference function of the policymaker, provided the desired levels and values can be preassigned by the policymaker (Theil 1964) and that the decision rules have a sequential character of self-correction in the face of uncertainty in data, represented by equational errors.

A recursive framework of supply and demand relations, analytically and estimation-wise more general than that of Stoikov and others, has been proposed by Fox (1966b). In this set-up, if the U.S. National Register of Scientific and Technical Personnel data for different years are fully comparable, the changes in the number $q_i$ and average salary $p_i$ of scientists in specialty $i$ ($i = 1, 2, \ldots, m$) ought to follow some kind of "cobweb" model, i.e.:

$$\text{demand function: } p_i(t) = a_i + b_i q_i(t) + c_i y(t) + u_i(t), \tag{26}$$

$$\text{supply function: } q_i(t) = \alpha_i + \beta_i p_i(t-1) + \gamma_i z(t) + v_i(t), \tag{27}$$

$$(i = 1, 2, \ldots, m),$$

where the variable $y$ is a demand factor and the variable $z$ is a supply factor which in practice might include lagged salaries for several previous periods rather than one only, and the variables $u_i(t)$, $v_i(t)$ are the equational error terms concerning which the usual assumptions about the statistical distribution are required for estimation purposes (Radner and Miller 1970).

Some aspects of the flexibility of this type of model are worth emphasizing at this stage. First, the demand factor $y(t)$, the supply factor $z(t)$ and the definition of specialty could be given a more generalized interpretation, provided of course the conditions of econometric identification of the above model are not violated. For instance, the demand factor $y(t)$ could be related to the trend of growth of prospective student population, to the relative attractiveness or otherwise of different specialties, and so on. Similarly, the specialty category $i$ may refer to the different subcategories of a discipline, economics for example. The supply factor $z(t)$ may likewise be broadly interpreted to include national policies (e.g., specific budget provisions directed toward increasing the supply of scientists of specialty category $i$) and/or improved salary standards, etc. These generalizations could in principle be grafted through partial submodels allowing for interactions between subcategories of a given specialty category $i$, whenever it is feasible and operational to do so. Second, the aspects of stabilization and optimization (Sengupta and Fox 1969) could be easily built into the above framework by defining appropriate policies in terms of the policy variables $y$ and $z$. For instance, if $z(t)$ represents policies about improved relative salary standards, say, and the above cobweb-type model generates cobweb-type fluctuations, then in some cases an appropriate selection of values for the policy variable $z(t)$ may help to reduce those fluctuations. Again, if there is a demand-supply gap, an analysis of losses (in terms of potential losses of national income) can be made. By introducing a quadratic or other form of disutility function (as a function of the potential loss) it is sometimes possible to define an intertemporal path of values of the policy variable $z(t)$ (or a combination of $y(t)$ and $z(t)$) which would be optimal in the sense of minimizing the cumulative sum of potential loss over time (Fox et al. 1966; Theil 1964).

*Component analysis and probabilistic models*

An approach which in a sense has close relations with the input-output type of analysis (except perhaps its flow equations) seeks to determine and specify the factors and components of private demand for education and how to plan for provision of places in colleges and universities in different branches when this demand is partly probabilistic. This approach may be called component analysis, since it emphasizes the role of components and factor items explaining the pattern and structure of private demand for education.

From the economic concept of a demand function, it may be postulated that the private demand for extra education beyond the compulsory statutory age is a function of the price of extra education appropriately defined. Since extra education can be viewed partly as a consumer good and partly as an investment good, the concept of an appropriate price of extra education must have two facets, i.e., a comparison of the costs (outlay for additional years in schooling) and returns (present value of extra lifetime earnings after tax associated with extra education, using as a discount rate the yield of the best alternative investment opportunity) appropriately viewed. For instance, Blaug (1966) has attempted to define the equilibrium demand price of education $p$ in terms of the ratio of the internal rate of return on investment in education $r_e$ and the average yield of equities and debentures $r_b$, by postulating that the private demand curve for extra education is a positive function of the internal rate of return on investment in education and a negative function of the average yield of equities and debentures.

The internal rate of return approach as distinct from the present value approach is here adopted as the criterion for evaluating net return from investment in education because of its simplicity of calculation in this framework. The internal rate of return on investment in education is that rate at which the present value of the extra lifetime earnings from extra education equals the cost of staying at school, i.e.:

$$\sum_{t=18}^{65} [(-C_t + kE_t)/(1 + r_e)^t] = 0, \tag{28}$$

where

$C_t$ = costs of staying in school to complete different degrees;

$E_t$ = earnings differential associated with extra education and extra degrees;

$k$ = a constant $(0 < k < 1)$ reflecting that part of extra lifetime earnings which can be attributed explicitly and implicitly to extra education alone;

$t$ = age at which costs are incurred or the earnings received; and

$r_e$ = internal rate of return on investment in education.

There are two basic questions which can be raised about the concept of a demand function for education approximated through rates of return and cost. First, the costs of staying in school from a private viewpoint are likely to be very different from the total public costs, and, similarly, the computation of returns from extra education depends to a large degree on the elasticity of substitution between different skills and the market opportunity of transferability between jobs. Second, the concept of equilibrium price implicit in the above approach needs clarification with respect to the assumption regarding the supply side. If the quality of supply of education (i.e., supply of teaching, research and other services so as to generate skills among students) is any way reflected in the public costs of providing education of the requisite type, then the degree of indivisibility of the inputs to education, the extent of specificity of the quality of teaching, and the type of research attitude determine to a significant degree the elasticity of public costs of providing quality education, and then some implicit evaluation of the cost components and the quality of educational inputs seems called for. Further, there is the statistical problem of identification of the specific ways in which differential prospects of discounted returns offer explanation for the trend in the structure of private demand for education at different levels and for places in different departments of a university.

The presence of a margin of uncertainty in predicting the pattern and intensity of private demand for education at a certain level has led certain authors (Alper and Smith 1967; Alper 1966) to formulate probabilistic models of optimal supply under conditions of uncertainty. Probabilistic considerations have generally been introduced in this connection in two different ways. First, in the input-output model developed by Stone (1965) and analyzed before, the demand for places in colleges or universities is represented as a multistage stochastic process, a branching process of a type which has been applied very successfully in explaining the spread of epidemics. Hence, in this approach the volume of demand for places in the university at a given stage depends partly on the number of those who have already entered the places and partly on the number of those who have not entered. A second approach (Alper 1966; Alper and Smith 1967) which appears to be more operational, treats the problem of provision of places in a sector of education to satisfy an unknown social demand as an optimal control problem by considering the possibility of trading off a slight deterioration (improvement) in present performance of the existing educational system for the gain in (cost of) information about unknown parameters (like the social or potential demand) in order that better decisions can be made in the future.

Let $u$ be the number of places to be made available in a specific sector of education, say electrical engineering, $n$ be the unknown number of potential entrants (i.e., social demand) and $x$ be the actual number of students occupying the places in any given time, i.e.:

$$x = \min\,(u,n). \tag{29}$$

It is assumed that the cost of providing a place ($c(u)$) is the same whether occupied or not, and the total benefit derived by a student actually occupying a place is assumed to be a constant $b$ per unit; hence, the total costs may be written as:

$$C = u - b \min (u,n), \qquad (30)$$

where the cost $c(u)$ is assumed proportional to $u$, i.e., $c(u) = mu$ and the unit of $c(u)$ is so chosen that $m = 1$.

Clearly one should require $b > 1$, i.e., benefits outweigh costs, as otherwise no places should be provided at all. If the potential social demand is known with certainty, the optimal problem is very simple: Choose $u = n$ in order to minimize $C$ defined in (30). However, $n$ is not exactly known and the decisionmaker's a priori knowledge can only formulate a probability density function of $n$, $f(n)$ say, within a certain range $N \leq n \leq M$; the problem is then to choose a value for the control variable $u$ so as to minimize the expected value of costs defined in (30), the expectation being taken over the prior distribution $f(n)$. It can be shown that the optimal value of $u$ denoted as $u^*$ is a solution to the equation:

$$1/b = \int_{u*}^{M} f(n)dn \qquad (31)$$

and the corresponding minimal value of expected cost is:

$$EC^* = -b \int_{N}^{u*} nf(n)dn. \qquad (32)$$

When successive stages are available to observe the effects of selecting a particular $u$, one has to optimize the expected value of future costs by balancing the expected costs at the next stage against the benefit of additional information gained by narrowing the range of possible values of $n$ by using dynamic programming; thus, a sequential optimum policy can be specified when through successive stages the feasible policy tends to converge to optimality.

Two economic implications of the above result are worth emphasizing. First, the uncertainty in demand for places is much like the uncertainty in sales for a firm selling in a private market, and in this respect the university system is much like a large-scale multiproduct firm, like which it develops a policy of safety-reserves and flexibility in faculty capacity in order to take care of temporary deviations from equilibrium trend. Second, the net benefits (or costs associated with $x$ and $u$ in [30]) considered in the above approach do not include various external and nonmarket returns and social aspects, not to speak of the investment component of expenditures on human capital (Weisbrod 1962; Schultz 1961a). If there are economies (or diseconomies) of scale in expansion (or contraction), these total costs and returns must also reflect the influence of uncertainty in the long run in building capacity of departments too small in case of economies (or too large in case of diseconomies). Especially important are the expansion and diversification of departments, such as computer science, which offer common services to various other departments in the university system.

*Microanalysis and the disaggregative approach*

Although the general techniques and methodology of the aggregative approach would retain much of their validity and usefulness in a microanalytic context, when for example the optimization problem is discussed as a problem of resource allocation within a university or a specific department, the empirical framework of a microeconomic decision unit is likely to have several advantages. This is so for several reasons. First of all, since the aggregation difficulties are much less in this specific context, the coefficients of the model in terms of explicit or implicit prices and costs, the specific constraints of budget, manpower, faculty time available for research, etc. and most important, perhaps, the identification of sources of interaction between decisionmakers at different levels, are likely to be much more meaningful and representative in the specification of policies directed toward various goals. Second, the evolution of a university or a specific department provides some indication of the various facets of effects of alternative policies pursued by policymakers at different levels. Similarly, a cross-section or time series comparison of two universities or two departments is likely to suggest interesting insights about the quality of performance and/or excellence. However, there is one major bottleneck in the microanalytic approach: The generalization from the case history of one university or one department may be very misleading unless all the peculiarities of the specific case are explicitly recognized and taken into account.

Perhaps the simplest problem in the microanalytic approach which has received early attention is the problem of allocation of available faculty time to teaching various classes and doing research of different types so as to maximize the present net imputed value (i.e., the implied revenue) of the department's output, under a plausible set of restrictions regarding the available limitations of teaching and research man-hours and other resources and facilities. At the static level, a transportation type or personnel assignment type of programming model (e.g., assigning faculty to different courses) offers a good starting point.

A more generalized version of this type of programming model for determining optimal resource allocation within academic departments has been considered by Plessner, Fox, and Sanyal (1968), in which the activities are much more detailed (e.g., these include transfer of faculty time from graduate to undergraduate teaching, or research, or administration; budget constraints and salaries; office space; different levels of students; etc.) and the evaluation of net returns from extra degrees (M.S., Ph.D.) through estimates of extra lifetime earnings appropriately discounted is made much more specific. Further, the model is allowed to operate for more than one year to analyze the impact of additions to existing faculty and changes in time allocation.

It may be of some importance to mention some of the difficulties in the above formulation. First of all, there is a basic difficulty in the linear programming approach to the extent that linearity assumes the constancy of marginal rates of substitution between different activities. At least a quadratic transformation surface is worth attempting. One consequence of relaxing the linearity assumption would be, perhaps, that the relation between teaching and research could vary within different ranges. Second, there is some need to incorporate a distinction between fixed resources and relatively flexible resources. Only a part of the total fixed resources affects the short-run evaluation of the department; the rest helps mainly in building the potential capacity of a department, the effects of which are felt in the long run. From this viewpoint, the interaction beween researchers, the building of a cluster of research teams (viz., research is much like an epidemic, it affects many) is quite important to the specification of a model. In other words, an interaction between the short-run and the long-run aspects of optimization should be specifically introduced into the model. Third, although the presumption of the department chairman as a single policymaker is very helpful in specifying a scalar objective function to be optimized, it is also necessary to incorporate satisficing behavior and the presence of multiple policymakers with preference functions not always reducible to a common denominator. Consistent solutions of the satisficing behavior for each policymaker are still feasible in some cases and these are discussed in Chapters 6–7 (see also Fox et al. 1969).

A somewhat different type of approach, along the line of Theil's treatment of decision rules (1964), has been adopted by von Hohenbalken and Fox (1967) to formalize a policy model for an academic department to maximize its excellence, defined in some sense by an appropriate choice of instrument variables such as salaries, teaching load, research facilities, etc. From the ratings of relative quality of departments in groups of leading universities (Cartter 1965) one formulates a sort of desired standard of excellence (measured for example by the number and quality of Ph.D.'s granted, the number of eminent professors, the volume and quality of publications) which any given department might aspire to reach through its use of resources and instruments. Taking the desired values as a reference level, a quadratic cost function is set up and optimized by the choice of instrument variables. The effects of instrument variables on the endogenous variables of the system may be analyzed through regression equations estimated from cross-section data on a number of departments in the relevant discipline that head the list in Cartter's report (1966). The coefficients of the quadratic cost function setup are either subjectively built up or estimated on the basis of data for one or two individual departments. However, it should be mentioned that this model is entirely static; hence the sequential aspects of a policy evolving through time cannot be analyzed. Further, the assignment of desired levels of the variables connoting excellence is somewhat arbitrary and no trade-off of one desired level for another is considered in the model. The fact that the desired levels may be easier to achieve for some variables than for others has not been considered.

Moreover, the usual difficulty with a quadratic cost or disutility function, that it attaches equal weights to deviations from the standard level whether they are positive or negative, may perhaps be avoided by suitable provision of lower bounds on some of the basic and more fundamental activities and by the addition of a parametric set of values for the desired levels of excellence. In a dynamic model, this of course calls for suitably updating the desired levels of excellence over time.

At the level of a university having several departments, the above set of approaches is still conceivable; the only new type of consideration that should enter into the optimization process is provided by the decomposition algorithms which are most suitable for multiple policymakers with a central co-ordination. McCamley (1967) and others (Weathersby 1967; Lee 1969) have constructed in this line activity models of resource allocation for a university, for a small college, and for a large department within a university, where in each case there are multiple decisionmakers with some co-ordination at the center. An analysis, appraisal, and extension of some of these decomposition methods is presented in Chapters 4–6.

**Economic theory relevant for educational planning**

In this section we describe very briefly some of the basic methods of economic theory which are relevant for educational planning at the national and university levels. In our view the characteristics of resources involved in education are such that it is impossible to apply a standard economic model which is well defined in economy theory. From the standpoint of quantitative policymaking based on models for an educational system, three basic economic questions are frequently emphasized in our approach in the book. First, a criterion of optimality of resource allocation, known in economic theory as the Pareto optimality (or efficiency) criterion, is frequently used as a standard for comparing alternative allocation patterns for resources invested in the educational system. However, since the elements of indivisibility of some resources and of noncompetitive behavior tend to violate some of the conditions of Pareto optimality, we need to analyze the various situations in which competitive market solutions may fail and the second-best policies may have to be adopted. This part of the theory is closely related to welfare economics and the analysis of optimizing and discretionary behavior. Second, a representative academic department in a university, though operating under several specified and nonspecified goals, represents in much of its short- and long-run resource allocation decisions the optimizing behavior of a multiproduct firm operating under uncertainty insofar as sales and output prices are concerned. There are national markets for negotiating the average prices of degree outputs, although they may not satisfy all the requirements of a perfectly competitive system. Long-run planning for expansion of an academic department must allow for the expected market tendencies in the educational sector. Similarly in the short run, the allocation of various resources, such as faculty man hours, research funds, and administrative support, some of which may have different degrees of specificity and nontransferability, presents a decision problem in which alternative costs may be calculated for alternative feasible allocations. This framework is analogous to that of a multiproduct firm and its resource allocation decisions. Third, the sources of growth of the educational system, the university, or the education sector may be largely traced to three sets of factors which also provide the main key to the over-all economic growth of an economy, viz., the manpower requirements and demands for places due to growth in other sectors, changes in technology, including the technology of producing skills and diffusing the knowledge which fructifies productivity (i.e., learning by doing), and the existence of social overheads and other facilities of organizational structure which permit desirable resource transfers through market incentives and organizational goals. This aspect of educational planning is very similar to the models of aggregate economic growth.

## Welfare economics and discretionary behavior

The implications of various marginal conditions of Pareto optimality applied to resource allocation problems of an educational system comprising various subsystems are discussed in Chapters 4–6, particularly under the following decision situations:

a) when there is no external market to internalize the various interdependencies of the different subsystems in the production of teaching and research and other joint activities;

b) when there is a system of co-ordination at the center (e.g., the dean of a college acts as a co-ordinator for the academic department heads) through methods of internal pricing through shadow prices;

c) when there are multiple policymakers who arrive at a consistent method of policymaking by weighing goals and the means to achieve them; and

d) when additional and sometimes unforeseen constraints tend to violate the Pareto-optimality conditions, necessitating that the policymaker adopt second-best or third-best policies.

Identifying the decision levels in the university system (Simon 1967) where the various resource allocation decisions are made, and modeling its structure, would enable one to understand and appraise the various welfare implications of feasible decisions. The basic tasks of welfare economics-based educational planning would be to explore the various nonmarket elements of externalities, benefits, and costs in the objectives, input-output relations, and resources invested in the educational system. It is only very recently (Kershaw and Mood 1970; Mood and Stoller 1967; James 1969) that some of these questions have been seriously posed by economists and management scientists.

## Pricing theory for multiproduct firms

The activity analysis models of resource allocation in educational systems (e.g., in universities) discussed in Chapters 4–7 are basically oriented as policy models for multiproduct firm behavior. Apart from simulating the implications of imputing a net price for all outputs of an academic department (which is only an indirect estimate of net returns reflecting both market and nonmarket elements), the three main decision situations explored in this respect relate to the following:

a) the existence of fixed and semifixed resources in educational systems which because of nondivisibility to a degree may give rise to an element of nonconvexity in the otherwise convex production possibility set over which the resource allocation system in the educational framework may define a solution (the question of quasi rents and shadow prices for semifixed resources which may be required under conditions of increase in enrollment is also discussed in this connection in Chapter 6);

b) the presence of price uncertainty associated with the expected return from the outputs produced in the educational system, only part of which are internalized to the university system; and

c) the problem of allocation of joint costs between activities under static and dynamic conditions, when some of the goods (such as research of certain types) have high fixed costs but very negligible marginal costs.

*Theory of optimal growth*

Optimal growth in neo-classical models presumes an aggregate production function involving aggregate inputs and technological change and a social welfare functional (e.g., discounted sum of instantaneous utility functions defined over outputs) which distinguishes consumption needs from those of investment or capital accumulation. For an educational system, including a university system, such a type of characterization is possible under two conditions. First, we must have a measure of performance for the educational system, preferably in terms of a concept of aggregate output much like GNP. Second, the different goals and objectives of the system must be specified in quantitative terms so that its implicit costs and/or returns can be evaluated. Fox (1970) has argued regarding the first that to evaluate all inputs and outputs (both economic and noneconomic) of the higher education system in a consistent manner, we need a measure which may be called the "gross social product" or GSP, which has the GNP embedded in it. He suggests approaching this product measure of higher education through a generalization of consumption theory (i.e., equating marginal contributions in alternative behavior settings). A very similar case can be built on the Schultz–Becker theory of treating a part of all expenditure on the education system as investment in human capital, as important as investment in physical capital.

The setting of goals for purposes of optimization or suboptimization is not so difficult if we follow the tradition of neo-classical growth models, in which stationary solutions at their infinite horizon, steady-state levels are considered. In the educational system it is of great practical importance that the goals be distinctively identified and translated into a quantitative form so that they can be operationally useful for policy-making purposes in the short- and medium-term planning horizon. In discussing the various problems of resource allocation in higher education, Kershaw and Mood (1970) have referred to its six major outputs as identified by the Public Policy Research Organization, from which output-based goals can be discerned and possibly quantified. The six major outputs of higher education identified are:

a) classification of youths into differentiated products (i.e., those allowed entry into higher education are distinguished from those who are not);
b) occupational training;
c) research;
d) organization of knowledge and its diffusion;
e) general education; and
f) services through research, consulting, and other nonacademic activities.

On the surface, the outputs of type (b), (c), and (f) appear to have economic or market values, at least in part, and for the remaining ones an imputing process could be developed in principle (e.g., the option value of continuing higher education after the B.S. degree may be indirectly estimated through relative incomes forgone [Weisbrod 1962], and this would provide a broad measure of the output of type [a]). This is not to deny that there exist many difficult problems of quantifying such goals through returns and costs. Our intention is only to indicate that in principle the economist's model of neo-classical optimal growth can be developed for application to the growth problems of an educational system.

## Methods of macroeconomic planning for educational systems

Insofar as their growth aspects are concerned, the aggregative models of educational systems have adopted three interrelated approaches:

First, the growth of the education sector has been related to the important structural variables characterizing over-all national growth, such as population growth and demographic evolution, manpower and skill requirements, expenditures on research and training, and investment-cum-growth requirements of the rest of the economy.

Second, a system analysis approach has been developed at a more dynamic level for the input and output components of an educational system which is defined to be a system of connected processes, including all forms of education, training, and retraining. This approach, like the first, is designed to make predictions about the growth of different components of the educational system that are required in equilibrium, given the growth rates of exogenous factors such as the potential number of students, economic growth for the rest of the economy, changes in earnings differentials for different skill groups, and the like. Simulation methods have frequently been adopted in this approach to analyze the effects of variations of the parameters on the set of feasible solutions.

Third, an optimization approach has been developed, mostly on the lines of control theory applications, which seeks to specify an optimal intertemporal growth path of strategic variables, such as the number of scientists engaged in teaching when the objective function imputes either a measure of social benefits as a source of value of educational outputs or a measure of contribution to the sectoral and national levels of real output.

When we consider a single academic department (the analysis can sometimes be extended to a cluster of departments) and its problems of expansion over time, it appears that the policymakers responsible for it are also in need of a meaningful concept of optimal growth. It is possible to develop the above three approaches used in aggregative models of educational systems with appropriate modifications so that they are suitable for the context of a single academic department. If we consider that the goal of an academic department is to make the best possible use of its resources over time, the lines of modification should incorporate, for the sake of realism and practicality if you will, some of the following considerations, most of which are considered very important in the theories of growth applied at the sectoral or the firm level:

a) The decomposition aspects of decisionmaking, which presume the existence of multiple decisionmakers in a university, require an analysis of the whole process of imputing appropriate marginal productivity contributions at various levels of decentralization.

b) Insofar as growth involves an intertemporal comparison of alternative feasible time paths measured by appropriate performance variables, the intertemporal allocation aspects (e.g., through variation of budgets for teaching and research over time, changing the allocation of faculty time among different activities, or planning for additional investment of resources in certain new lines of teaching or research) should have clear time-orientation regarding short-term and long-term objectives. In the short-run analysis, which could be very detailed, as in the activity analysis approach (and the prediction of exogenous variables may be fairly precise in this framework), it may be necessary to impose bounds on the system in terms of maximum permissible growth (determined by capacity of the system) and minimum growth (determined by the conditions of minimal rates of student inflow over time, etc.). In the long- and medium-term analysis, the expansion of capacity itself has to be analyzed, and there is some need here to identify the concept of capacity with quantitative and operational precision as far as possible. Two important factors appear to be relevant in this context, as the various models of capacity expansion for the firm (Manne 1967; Sengupta and Sen 1969) serve to point out: (i) the element of economies or diseconomies of scale of expansion in capacity and its implications, and (ii) the set of other elements such as the exogenous rate of discounting over time, the cost of obtaining funds for expansion, and the limited rate of growth of maximum total demand which provide definite limits to the possibility of unlimited expansion of the academic department as a firm.

c) The optimality aspects in the concept of optimal growth, which generally presume the existence of a set of feasible solutions defined by the restrictions and the conditions of the mathematical model, require some of the following analyses:

i) the objective function which is optimized in the model should be viewed not only as a scalar payoff function but also as a vector, the different components of which provide alternative subgoals, not all of which could be brought to a common denominator. The latter view of the objective function, which leads to a vector optimization problem and which has close similarity with the decomposition aspects of decision-making referred to before, contributes ample flexibility to the otherwise rigid structure of a linear (or quadratic) programming problem based on a scalar payoff function;

ii) even when a scalar objective function is considered for specifying an optimality ordering among the set of feasible solutions, satisficing behavior in terms of second-best, third-best and/or other consistent but suboptimal solutions (Sengupta 1966a, b; Aris 1963) should be incorporated in the objective function, so that the alternative possibilities of trade-off between subgoals are explicitly allowed for; and further

iii) the problems of specification of the scalar objective function can be considerably facilitated by incorporating facets of the objective function which preassign a set of desired levels of targets or norms for some or all of the important variables in the model. The preassigned targets or norms should initially be viewed in terms of the outlook of the decision-maker of the academic department, although these may have to be revised as the implicit costs of achieving these norms become known. If the objective function can be set up as a quadratic function in terms of deviations of the activity variables from their desired values, and the model used is linear, this approach leads to linear optimal decision rules, which under certain conditions have desirable statistical properties (Theil 1964).

**d)** Last but not the least important is the analysis of probabilistic aspects of the growth problem, which may be generated from different sources, such as the time rate of arrival of new students in specified fields, the estimate of imputed cost of faculty time committed in a particular course, and even the forecast trend in the over-all budget provision for a given academic department.

Our analysis of growth planning for educational systems, discussed in Chapters 5 and 6, specifically considers three types of decision situations:

a) problems of balanced and equilibrium growth which optimize the scale of expansion;

b) selection of optimal control variables which optimize a performance cost measure over time for the educational system; and

c) problems of dynamic decomposition of an over-all policy into subsystem policies appropriately co-ordinated by the center.

In order to illustrate these situations, consider one of the simplest formulations, i.e., an activity analysis model of an academic department (which may have subdepartments). This may be written as:

$$\text{maximize } z(t) = c'(t)x(t) \quad c(t), x(t): n \cdot 1 \tag{33}$$

under the restrictions $\quad A: m \cdot n$

$$Ax(t) \leq b(t); x(t) \geq 0; \quad b(t): m \cdot 1$$

where $x(t)$ is the activity vector which may depend on time in some sense to be described later, $b(t)$ is the vector of *fixed* resources, and $c(t)$ is the vector of net returns, in the sense that its typical element $c_j(t)$ may be expressed as the excess of gross return per unit ($p_j(t)$) over the total *variable* costs (i.e., $\sum_k \bar{p}_{kj}(t) b_{kj}(t)$, where $b_{kj}(t)$ is the variable resource requirement per unit of activity $x_j(t)$ and $\bar{p}_{kj}$ its cost). It is now only necessary to identify the activities and various resources of an academic department within the linear programming framework (33).

First, it is essential to make a distinction between resources which are relatively fixed and those which are relatively variable within the planning horizon for which the model is designed. Within a horizon not exceeding four years, perhaps, the following resources may be considered as more or less fixed: building space, equipment and fixed physical facilities, stock of existing faculty in different fields (and to a certain extent the expected increase in that stock), actual (and to a certain extent potential) stock of student-instructors, and committed parts of budget grants and outside research contracts (and to a certain extent expected changes in those grants and contracts) in different fields. Some of the common resources which are more or less variable, and the costs of which are incorporated in computing the $c_j$ coefficients, are indirect labor in the form of secretarial staff and the cost of materials required for research, teaching, and other activities. The components of the activity vector $x(t)$ may comprise teaching at various levels (undergraduate and graduate), research in different fields and of different types (outside support, departmental support, or otherwise), other activities such as extension work, management of the department or laboratories, or even outside consulting work. Once the variable costs are known, estimates of the $c_j(t)$ coefficients may be built up in several different ways, e.g., (i) by computing net returns from extra degrees (M.S., Ph.D.) through estimates of extra lifetime earnings appropriately discounted; (ii) by adding a mark-up on the total cost of producing an extra degree (just like the full-cost pricing principle) with possible variations in mark-up to reflect the quality of records of the degree recipients and their associated earnings potentials; and (iii) by a combination of the first two methods with some additional imputation of returns of activities, such as independent research.

However, even in the standard form (33) the linear programming structure cannot be very flexible and operational unless several features are built into the model. First, the model will gain increased degrees of flexibility if additional dummy activities are defined to allow substitution possibilities, such as transfer of faculty time from teaching to research, transfer of teaching loads between faculty members (similarly on the resource side, the transfer of budget allocations between different components may be introduced). Second, the model should be allowed to incorporate the activities defined for more than a year (e.g., about three to four years likely to give a representative average picture), and similarly for the resource vector; it is for this reason that the time index $t$ is used as an argument in the program (33). If the program is built to incorporate restrictions and activities defined over a four-year period, say, the objective function may be suitably updated so as to refer to either the maximization of the end-of-four-year period net return or the sum total of net (discounted) returns over a given planning horizon. Third, the substitution possibilities between the different components of the resource vector $b(t)$ itself may be introduced, in the sense that any additional discretionary budget may be spent for different combinations of fixed resources. Another way of analyzing substitution possibilities, but in terms of the activities, is to redefine any component $\Delta b_i(t)$ of the increment vector $\Delta b(t)$ as $\Delta b_i(t) = \sum_{j=1}^{n} \Delta b_i(t) u_{ij}$, where $j$ denotes the number of activities and the $u_{ij}$ are non-negative allocation proportions. This latter approach, known as the active approach of decomposition, may be used to redefine the new level of the resource vector as $b(t) + \Delta b(u,t)$, where $u$ represents the matrix $(u_{ij})$. Note that the matrix $u$ introduces additional control variables which may be varied with purpose by the policymaker. Further, it may be shown that the allocation matrix $u$ serves to decompose the over-all linear program into separable subprograms linked through a decomposition algorithm of the Dantzig and Wolfe type.

The linear programming framework (33) may however be generalized along more interesting lines, useful for wider applicability. First, the model (33) does not explicitly show the implications of additional demands for the academic department; neither does it show the consequences of departures from desired values or standards of specific output-like activities. One simple way to introduce this is to adjoin to the objective function of model (33) another facet reflecting the cost of departures from desired values. Second, after running the linear program (33) with given resource estimates, the policymaker may be interested in planning calculations of the following type: Suppose he anticipates an additional discretionary budget $B_0$ over the coming year, which may be spent for augmenting the resources $\Delta b_i(t)$ at unit costs $k_i$, then how does the structure of the old optimal solution change as a function of the anticipated budget $B_0$? Let $\bar{b}_i(t) = b_i(t) + \Delta b_i(t)$ $(i = 1, \ldots, m)$, then the structure of the original problem is specified as a function of $B_0$ by solving the following linear programming problem:

$$\text{maximize } z(t) = \sum_{j=1}^{n} c_j(t) x_j(t) \tag{34a}$$

under the restrictions

$$\sum_{j=1}^{n} a_{ij} x_j(t) + x_{n+1}(t) \leq \bar{b}_i(t), \tag{34b}$$

$$\sum_{i=1}^{m} \sum_{j=1}^{n} k_i(a_{ij} x_j(t) + x_{n+i}(t)) \geq \sum_{i=1}^{m} k_i \bar{b}_i(t) - B_0, \tag{34c}$$

all $x_j(t) \geq 0$, \hfill (34d)

where $x_{n+1}(t)$ is the slack (or auxiliary) variable of the initial linear program. If a solution is available for $B_0 = 0$ (i.e., $\bar{b}_i(t) = b_i(t)$), then the set of new optimal solutions can be generated as a function of the anticipated budget $B_0$, provided estimates of $k_i$ and $\bar{b}_i(t)$ are available.

One final remark may be made about the programming framework considered so far. In a basic sense the framework retains the static outlook of the theory of the firm, since the distinction between fixed and variable resources is more or less maintained. However, if it could be assumed that the initial state from which we started was one of equilibrium, in the sense that we were concerned only with flow variables, so that the increments of stock variables entered as data of the problem, then the following type of growth programming structure could be proposed:

$$\text{maximize} \sum_{j=1}^{n} [\gamma_j(t)\Delta x_j - w_j(\Delta x_j - \Delta x_j^*)^2] \tag{35a}$$

under the restrictions

$$\sum_{j=1}^{n} b_{ij}\Delta x_j \leq \beta_i(t-1); i = 1, \ldots, m \tag{35b}$$

$$\Delta x_j = x_j(t) - x_j(t-1) \geq 0. \tag{35c}$$

Here $\Delta x_j$ denotes the growth of the $j$th activity (if decay is also to be allowed, the non-negativity requirement for $\Delta x_j$ should be dropped), $\beta_i(t-1)$ denotes the availability of both flow resources, such as variable cost, and the incremental stock resources, such as the addition to the stock of existing faculty, the $b_{ij}$ are input coefficients, the $\gamma_j(t)$ are estimates of net return associated with the growth activity $\Delta x_j$, and the $w_j$ are non-negative weights assigned to the deviation of actual growth from the desired growth $\Delta x_j^*$ of activity $j$.

Note that this growth programming model presumes in its specification that resources are available at the end of period $(t-1)$ to be used for augmenting the structure of activities in the next year. If the "production process of education" takes more time, this could be easily incorporated in the model. Similarly, the objective function could be interpreted as an intertemporal discounted sum of net benefits over costs.

CHAPTER 4

# Resource Allocation Processes in Linear Static Models

T. Krishna Kumar

**Introductory remarks**

The allocation of resources has been central to economic theory and practice for a long time. As early as 1897, and more completely in 1909, Pareto defined an economic optimum by the requirement that there should not exist any other allocation of resources which makes at least one person better off without making anybody worse off. In the static framework of a competitive market system this leads, under certain simplifying assumptions, to a set of marginal rules for the optimum allocation of scarce resources among alternative uses. These rules of Pareto-optimal allocations have been generalized in recent times in several directions; also, the recent resurgence of neo-classical conditions in the specification of equilibrium and optimum growth theory (Morishima 1964) has emphasized the central role of competitive prices interpreted as either explicit market prices or implicit imputed (i.e., shadow) prices.

Theory apart, history has recorded two alternative, and sometimes polar, methods of allocating economic resources for achieving the goals of an optimum régime. The first emphasizes the individual motives of profit and utility maximization and uses the competitive decentralized market as a model of resource allocation (Feinstein 1967). The second emphasizes the social ownership of means of production and technology and uses the model of socialist central planning for resource allocation. Whereas the first method uses the price signals in the markets, the second uses a set of administrative norms or directives to determine the allocation of quantities. Recent times have seen the mixture of these two polar methods in different ways, e.g., the emergence of mixed economies in developing countries with public and private sectors, the use of market prices and incentives in some areas of socialist central planning (Lange 1958; Sik 1967) and the emphasis on public goods and social needs in some areas of capitalistic economies (Samuelson 1969; Davis and Whinston 1967) in which private markets do not exist.

A most significant and important factor that has emerged recently is the electronic computer. The computer has profound significance for the determination of resource allocation and the optimum economic régime. On the one hand, it provides a reproducible method of interaction between the information flows and the decisionmakers in complex systems, as exemplified by the so-called decomposition techniques of mathematical programming; on the other, it makes the distinction between the market system and the central planning board quite thin, and possibly irrelevant in a technical sense. The trial-and-error method of the competitive market appears to simulate (Lange 1967) and be simulated by the iterative method of successive adjustment done by an electronic computer. Neither the rules of price guidance of the Pareto-type framework nor the directives of input-output quota allocations under central planning appear to have incorporated the basic implications of a computer simulating the behavior of a group of decisionmakers or agents. As yet there is no satisfactory criterion for comparing alternative ways of information processing and exchange and the economics of information is still in a formative stage.

It is our view that there is no complete and satisfactory economic theory, as yet, for determining optimal allocation of resources in a nonmarket framework. By a nonmarket system or framework is meant any of the following three categories at least: (a) a quasi market in which noneconomic quantities such as nonprice and nonprofit variables are as important as the price and the profit variables of a market system; (b) an internal or divisionalized market, in which the exchanges and the allocations are hypothetical, but are intended to simulate the behavior of an actual market system in which the behavior relations of the participants are specified in certain economic forms; and (c) an organizational system, in which the rules of organizational behavior and functioning evolve out of several factors, e.g., the political-cum-institutional framework, value systems and experiences of the active participants, and the information flows available to the organization. We will concern ourselves here only with the resource allocation decisions of those types of organizations which are directly or indirectly involved in the administration of scarce resources for satisfying effective demands, e.g., public enterprises or local governments, the planning boards in socialist countries, and the boards responsible for the financing of public school and state university systems.

It is interesting to note that the three categories of nonmarket systems distinguished above have associated with them separate theories of behavior, sometimes overlapping but for the most part leading to noncompetitive specialization among three types of disciplines: economics, computation theory, and organization-cum-decision sciences. Economists have long been concerned with quasi markets in their different facets, e.g., imperfections and monopolistic elements in a competitive market, motives and goals other than profit maximization, and even allocation rules which are discretionary and non*tâtonnement*. The computation scientists have found out in the last two decades that the so-called Lagrange multipliers can be profitably used to decompose a large-scale problem in linear (and sometimes nonlinear) programming into a set of small subproblems, each of which can be solved in a certain sequential way until the over-all problem is solved. Such a sequential process of computation (Sengupta and Fox 1969), otherwise known as a decomposition technique, allows the over-all system-optimization problem to be simulated and decomposed into smaller suboptimization problems. If the decision levels can be institutionally distinguished as, for example, in a large corporation with multiple divisions or a central planning agency co-ordinating the investment decisions of several production sectors, then the decomposition technique merely illustrates the method of optimal decentralization. In cases in which the decision levels cannot be identified so naturally, the decomposition techniques assume a more important role, and they tend to impute a simulated market and its workings. If there are interdependencies in resource allocation, such methods may be very valuable in showing an optimizing direction and the possibilities of informational economies through several types of decentralized subdivisions of the over-all decision.

Organization theory (Simon 1959) and the related behavior sciences emphasize very strongly the nonmarket aspects of decisionmaking in the behavior of economic or other organizations; in particular, the structure and hierarchy of organization, the information flows within the system, and the functional characteristics (Balderston 1964) of the system occupy a far more important place in this theory than do the exchanges prevailing in a market internal or external.

In this chapter and the next we will present these three alternative bases of resource allocation, emphasizing in particular their economic considerations and contexts. These methods, we believe, are potentially applicable to an educational system comprising institutions of higher education, some of the major outputs and inputs of which can be identified or imputed. The educational system, viewed as a part of the nonmarket system, has in our view a definite and very important problem of allocation of resources (e.g., capital, both physical and human, and the current account budgetary funds), which has both static and dynamic implications. In its static framework, the conditions of Pareto optimality and the mathematical programming techniques of decomposition have great relevance.

## Price-guided allocation in competitive and planned systems

The premise that a static system of perfect competition can attain (under simplifying assumptions which exclude externalities, indivisibilities, and imperfections) static efficiency in allocation of resources in the sense of Pareto optimality has sometimes been interpreted to mean that such an allocation should be sought after in a quasi market or even under central planning in a socialist economy. Such interpretations ignore several important considerations of the real economic world, e.g. (a) the income distribution effects resulting from such allocations may not be desirable; (b) the competitive pricing rule tends to break down in decreasing-cost industries and in the cases of collective and public goods; (c) there are other cases of market failure due to externalities and the breakdown of some of the competitive assumptions; and (d) the dynamic efficiency considerations related to the growth of the competitive system are almost completely neglected.

The significance of these exceptions to the Pareto-optimal allocation framework can be appraised better if we recapitulate the assumptions of the Pareto model, which are as follows:

i) There exists a preference-ordering satisfying a set of continuity and consistency assumptions for each of the consumers in the system; the preference-ordering of each consumer is independent of the preference-ordering of any other consumer (i.e., there are no external economies or diseconomies of consumption);

ii) each producer in the system is guided in his decisions about the level of production and the composition of inputs by a profit motive; the technology of each producer is independent of the technology of any other producer (i.e., there are no external economies or diseconomies of production);

iii) both the factor and the product markets are perfectly competitive in the sense that no individual can have a perceptible effect on the market price (for each commodity, it is assumed that there are infinitely many producers and consumers);

iv) all the goods are perfectly divisible;

v) each consumer and each producer has perfect information and there are no uncertainties;

vi) the time perspective in which the alternative welfares are compared is limited to a period that corresponds to the short-run equilibrium period of the producers (assumed to be the same for all producers); and

vii) in the entire domain of alternative allocations that are evaluated, diminishing returns and diminishing marginal rates of transformation and substitution prevail;

viii) each consumer consumes all commodities and each producer produces all commodities (this assumption is implicit in assuming an interior maximum).

A movement from a position which does not satisfy the Pareto-equilibrium conditions to a position of Pareto equilibrium involves a change in the income distribution. One important criticism of the Pareto-equilibrium conditions is that Pareto optimality does not imply welfare maximization, as the system does not incorporate any way of ordering the different income distributions. The question of a desirable or equitable income distribution has to be imposed on the system. One partial answer to this question of equitable income distribution is to seek for a Pareto-optimal income redistribution. A convenient device is to assume that each consumer preference ordering depends not just on the levels of different commodities acquired or consumed but also on the resulting income. The producers' preferences are scaled not by profits alone but by profits and other nonmarket transfers. With these modifications in preference-orderings the usual rules of Pareto optimality give rise to the so-called "compensation principle" of welfare economics proposed by Kaldor (1939), Hicks (1939), Scitovsky (1941), and Bator (1957, 1958).

The arguments that lead to Pareto-optimality conditions can be sketched very briefly: Consider a consumer in a competitive economy under the above assumptions; he is assumed to maximize his ordinal utility subject to a budget constraint. From this behavioristic assumption, it follows that he attempts to consume any two commodities in such quantities that the marginal rate of substitution between them is equal to their price ratio. In a perfectly competitive economy, for any other consumer who consumes the same two commodities the marginal rate of substitution will equal the same price ratio (assumption iii). Thus the marginal rates of substitution between two commodities are the same for all consumers. This result holds for all pairs of commodities. Under the assumption (vii) it further follows that these first-order conditions are sufficient to ensure that the resulting allocation of commodities between consumers is a global optimum.

Similarly, in the case of producers each producer will attempt to acquire any two resources in such quantities that the ratio of their marginal value products is equal to their price ratio. Since this ratio of prices for the two resources is the same for all producers (assumption iii), it follows that the marginal rate of technical substitution (i.e., the ratio of marginal value products) between any two resources is the same for all producers. Under assumption (vii), it further follows that these first-order conditions are also sufficient for an optimal distribution of resources among the producers.

Under a given technology for a producer, any given composition of resources determines a set of alternative output compositions. The locus of all such output bundles is called his transformation function. Under perfect competition, the producer would choose that particular output composition on the transformation function for which the marginal rate of transformation between any two commodities equals their price ratio.

One fundamental limitation of this analysis is the very restrictive assumption (viii) required for an interior maximum. Lerner (1944) and Kuznets (1948) deal with this by replacing the equalities between marginal rates of substitution by inequalities. A rigorous extension of the classical result of Pareto to the case in which assumption (viii) is dropped is made by Arrow (1951). He replaces assumption (viii) by the requirement that all quantities produced and consumed must be non-negative. Arrow establishes the Pareto efficiency of the competitive price system using the elements of convex set theory (concave programming). Under this modified framework, if the marginal rate of substitution of $x_2$ for $x_1$ for an individual is less than their price ratio, he does not consume the second commodity (i.e., $x_2 = 0$).

As Debreu (1959) indicated, Arrow's analysis of competitive equilibrium and welfare propositions can be assumed to include the case of any finite horizon, short or long, provided other assumptions hold for the economy. The device proposed is to regard the same commodity at different periods as different commodities. The attainment of a global optimum is assured by the assumption of nonincreasing returns and diminishing marginal rates of substitution (the case in which assumption [vii] is modified to include constant returns is investigated by Koopmans [1957]).

A very important question of economic policy arises in the competitive Pareto-model, if one has to allow a definite role to the government or the public for corrective fiscal and income distribution policy. Two suggestions are available in the theoretical literature.

One view postulates that the Pareto model is inappropriate in such a dynamic framework, in which the goal of the public sector is to maintain a steady and continuous growth of real income through corrective actions. This view is an extension (Kaldor 1956; Robinson 1964) of the Keynesian-type model in its emphasis on corrective fiscal and other direct public policies rather than indirect policies and price mechanisms. This view is opposed to the neo-classical models of growth which are having a modern resurgence (Solow 1956; Arrow and Kurz 1970), because the latter assume the existence of aggregate production functions with the associated marginal productivities of capital and labor which may be related to implicit prices, such as the shadow rates of interest and real wages as if in a competitive market economy.

A second view considers the role of the government sector in terms of additional constraints in an otherwise competitive Pareto framework and asks whether new Pareto-optimal marginal rules can be found under the added constraints. This approach is currently referred to as the theory of the second best, although it is implicit in the "general rationing" idea advocated by Lerner (1944) and in the idea of a commodity-wise levy in a mixed economy considered by Boiteux (1956) and Corlett and Hague (1953–54). The theory of second best advocated by Lipsey and Lancaster (1956–57) has been discussed in recent times from several angles, which appear to raise grave doubts as to the desirability of seeking policies to enforce Pareto-like conditions under the added constraints.*

A related problem which arises in this connection is that there is no method available for comparing Pareto-efficient resource allocations under two alternative sets of preferences. It follows, therefore, that if the Pareto-optimality conditions hold for an economic system in which there is no actual explicit market, the optimal allocations in the Pareto sense and the associated shadow prices must be interpreted properly. One interpretation is that these shadow prices are such that they would sustain the optimal allocation of resources if there existed a competitive market system. Note that the latter market is hypothetical and imputed. In many respects it is identical with the concept of an internal or

* The divergences between private and social benefits (and costs) in the presence of externalities were pointed out very clearly by Pigou (1932) and some of these externalities can be interpreted as additional constraints on an otherwise competitive market system.

divisionalized market described before. This identification is easily discernible in price-guided allocation rules in models of central planning in socialist countries and in those of divisionalized firms in corporate business organizations in private enterprise economies.

A centrally planned economy or system, of course, differs from a competitive market economy in several ways. One important difference is that the entrepreneurs, with their profit-maximization motives, are replaced in a planned system by a set of managers who may sometimes lack clear-cut incentives or meaningful goals. Theoretical models for the working of such a centrally planned system were developed by Barone (1938) and Lange and Taylor (1938) in the thirties. The role of the state or the central planning board in these models is to co-ordinate by successive adjustments of the price vector (i.e., Walrasian adjustment, suggested by Barone) and/or the aggregate excess demand vector (i.e., a combination of the Walrasian and Marshallian type adjustments suggested by Lange) the competitive game to be played by the set of households and the set of managers. Under certain assumptions this leads to very simple rules of price (or quantity) adjustment, given an arbitrary start. For example, the state may follow the rule of raising (lowering) the price of any commodity if it finds that total demand at the arbitrary or trial price exceeds (falls short of) total supply. Such processes are known to converge under appropriate conditions (e.g., under the assumptions [i], [iv], and [v–viii] of the Pareto model), although it might take quite some time, depending on the speed of convergence. In his more recent writings Lange (1958, 1967) has emphasized the necessity and feasibility (due to the capabilities of electronic computers) of introducing a large area of decentralized decisionmaking in a centrally planned economy. He proposes that the central authorities of the state determine only the basic proportions and directions of the economy and achieve desirable resource allocations and transfer between sectors less through administrative commands and more through economic means, such as financial and other incentives.

*Alternative adjustment rules: Policy implications*

It must be apparent now that the price adjustment mechanisms for centrally planned systems envisaged in the models of Barone, Lange, Lerner, and others have a great deal in common with the competitive price mechanism and the Pareto-equilibrium framework.

However, some important differences and similarities between such planned economy rules and the competitive price and output adjustments are worth emphasizing at this point. First, in this case of central planning assumed to operate under a social welfare function, the private marginal rates of substitution (and private marginal benefits) prevailing in a private enterprise competitive situation are replaced by the social marginal rate of substitution (and social marginal benefits) evaluated in terms of the social welfare function. Second, the Lange–Lerner model assumes an ideal income distribution (i.e., equalitarian distribution) in the sense of an equal marginal utility of income to all individuals; also the objective function considered by Lerner is a simple addition of individual utilities. Under these conditions, as Negishi (1960) has shown, the Kuhn–Tucker (1950) theorem on vector optimality implies a scalar objective (utility) function, which may be viewed as the sum of individual utilities (i.e., the coefficients of individual utilities in the scalar objective function may in fact be viewed as the reciprocals of the marginal utilities of income). The connection with Pareto optimality, which characterizes a vector optimality situation (see Debreu [1959]), is now immediate. Third, if the social welfare function is operationally interpreted in terms of Tinbergen's theory (Tinbergen 1954; Fox, Sengupta, and Thorbecke 1966) of economic policy, then the Lange–Lerner type rules of pricing and output adjustment may be very closely related to decentralization of economic decisions in a mixed-economy framework of planning.

These marginal conditions and rules may also be directly compared with Pigou's welfare economics (1932), which postulated in a competitive model an economic welfare function which depended on two arguments: the national dividend (national income) and a measure of income distribution. A partial ordering was defined in this function as follows: Any improvement in national dividend (income distribution) without worsening (reducing) income distribution (national dividend) is supposed to be an improvement in the social welfare. The economic allocation problem for the economy with a given income distribution is to determine the rules for production, exchange, and investment over a finite horizon in such a way that the long-run social welfare is a maximum.

Under certain assumptions (e.g., that investment decisions are made optimally so as to maximize the long-run social welfare), the Pigouvian welfare optimization problem can be decomposed into two stages. In the first stage, national dividend is maximized, subject to a given distribution of income, and in the second stage, income inequality (i.e., a distributional measure) is reduced (i.e., improved) subject to a given national dividend. Pigou emphasized very strongly that even in solving the first-stage problem under very simplifying assumptions (e.g., no joint costs, no indivisibilities) divergences between private and social costs and benefits would arise and hence rules of adjustment would be needed by which the market prices in an otherwise perfectly competitive model were corrected so that the resulting resource allocations would maximize the national dividend. On the consumption side, the correction measures may take several forms, e.g. (a) imposition by the state (society) of an over-all net social cost or benefit with each bundle of consumption on each consumer; (b) correcting all the prices for the consumer by appropriate taxes; (c) correcting the income available to consumers by direct taxes, such as those on property and income; or (d) correcting both prices and income by appropriate corrective taxes on prices and income. Similar corrective measures on the production side applied to firms can also be conceived.

The most important operational difficulty in the set of corrective measures arises from the theory of economic policy. So long as the social welfare function is not identified with the objective of a definite set of decisionmakers, the corrective measures cannot be more than marginal and in the small; otherwise they would affect the income distribution and we have to evaluate a change in social welfare which is nonmarginal and in the large. However, two important contributions of the Pigouvian model were to emphasize the divergences between private and social welfare, even under a competitive market framework, and the need for appropriate corrective measures.* Recent economic discussion on industrial pollution and external diseconomies of private production, on the imbalance in supply of public goods (e.g., recreation services, health, and education) relative to those of private goods, and on the needs for public goods serve to illustrate this point very clearly.

*Market prices, internal prices, and the theory of second best*

Apart from the role of the public sector in initiating corrective measures, there are important pathological situations in real economic life which call for public (or state) allocation of economic resources. First, there is the case of collective goods (or public goods) for which there are definite social needs, but which, under ordinary market conditions, private enterprise would not find it profitable to produce. Similar is the case of commodities for which the effective market price will be usually less than the minimum average variable cost and the marginal cost

---

* Note that these corrective measures applied to "correct prices" appear basically similar to the decomposition techniques of decentralization guided by a sequence of interim shadow prices. The latter are discussed in some detail on pages 92–115.

pricing rule will fail to cover the overheads and a part of variable costs. There has been some argument in the past by Hotelling (1938) and others defending the marginal cost pricing rule by combining it with an additional policy of covering the overheads and losses by general taxation. However, the recent discussions on the issue of public goods have emphasized the importance of identifying the different aspects of externalities involved before an appropriate price policy can be deemed to be the preferred one.

Second, the public sector need not have the same objectives as a private monopoly and to the that extent the role of even the public sector enterprises (such as electricity and transport in some countries) may not be purely profit-oriented. In past discussions on the welfare implications of securing ideal output when the elements of monopoly power are present, the monopoly elements have been invariably interpreted as distortions of the Pareto-optimality conditions of a competitive model (see Kahn [1935], Lerner [1934], and Little [1957]). However, in the case of the public sector, monopoly distortions may not be necessary, since the losses from following the marginal cost pricing rule and the overheads may be covered by general and direct taxation or lump-sum transfers. In practice, the latter may not be neutral or small-scale relative to the competitive rule. A partial answer to this problem, at least at the theoretical level, is to reinterpret the objective of the public sector as one of balancing the budget (or optimizing its level in some sense) subject to a set of tolerance limits or constraints on the prices for public goods and the tax rates.

Third, pricing policies in a partial equilibrium framework, especially for public utilities or nationalized enterprises, have sometimes been subjected to a two-part tariff rule, one part reflecting the marginal cost pricing principle and the other covering overheads or the needs for expansion. One interesting illustration is the pricing rule for nonstorable goods or services produced by public utilities having cyclical or periodic demand; this is commonly referred to as "peak load pricing" (see Boiteux [1949 and 1960], Steiner [1957], and Hirshleifer [1958]). Also, it is of great interest to note that a two-part pricing rule has been explored as an appropriate policy for some of the firms under a socialist planned economy; Kornai and Lipták (1962) have suggested that this approach easily generalizes to decomposition rules of linear and nonlinear programming.

The case in which marginal cost pricing leads to a deficit in the public sector enterprise but the latter has a legal obligation to balance its budget has been discussed by Boiteux (1956) in a somewhat general setting as follows: Perfect competition is assumed among firms in the private sector and among consumers, and the policy problem posed is to determine optimum decision rules in some sense for the enterprises in the public sector that are consistent with the decisions made by consumers and the firms in the private sector, and also with the additional restriction that each public sector enterprise should balance its budget. In this framework of two sectors, two optimal sets of rules are derived, i.e., in the private competitive sector the marginal costs and marginal productivities are equated to market prices, while in the public sector, comprising either a single or several firms, the same equalities hold with respect to a set of shadow prices which must be such that each public enterprise breaks even, i.e., balances its budget. Note that the shadow prices for the output of the public sector need not correspond with the market prices; in fact, the difference between the shadow price and the market price of good $i$ (produced by the public sector firm) may be interpreted as a "toll" (or tax) levied by the public firm on good $i$ in order to bring about equality between marginal costs and productivities on the one hand and market prices, net of taxes, on the other hand.

Two characteristics of the rule of equating marginal costs to a set of shadow prices in the public sector firms must be emphasized. First, this formulation brings out explicitly the fact that all profits (or losses) of public sector firms are automatically redistributed among consumers, so that the consumers' total income (which includes transfer payments and shares of profits of the private and public firms) contains transfer payments (e.g., an amount $r_k$ for the $k$th consumer) and these transfer payments are compensations, by including which we would derive the compensated or modified demand function for the public firm's output of the $i$th good. This means that if the rules of distribution of profits (or losses) of the two sectors among consumers are preassigned and the transfer payments are dispensed with, then the optimal tolls referred to before would simply become proportional to profit-maximizing tolls, i.e., to the tolls which would be charged by a private monopolist under these conditions. Second, the set of optimal tolls and the set of transfer payments are solved for simultaneously in this approach. This means that the optimal tolls, which in effect allow the public sector firms to follow the rule of shadow prices in their input and output policies, must be consistent with the scheme of transfers which the consumers take into account in their budget constraints and in maximizing their respective utility functions. There still remains, of course, a basic difference between the two situations, in one of which transfer payments (compensations) are actually paid and in the other of which they are only hypothetical.

The former involves generating a market clearing process with Pareto-optimal properties, whereas the latter implies that consumers may in fact have flexible demand schedules different from the compensated ones.*

The divergences between shadow prices and market prices and the various policy measures which should be applied to reduce them may be interpreted in a different context, i.e., the possibility of decentralized decisionmaking within a corporation or a large divisionalized firm, which has its objective function with facets for different divisions. This leads to questions of appropriate decomposition of the over-all optimization model of the firm into its different divisions (note that in the general equilibrium of a Pareto-optimal model, the over-all optimum can be decomposed [i.e., decentralized] into consumers' and producers' optima).

## Decentralization of decisions using decomposition techniques

There are different ways of looking at the techniques of decomposition; of these, the decentralization of decisions is perhaps the most appealing to an economist. The invisible hand glorified in the competitive system of Adam Smith (1937) is a classic example of decomposition, in which the competitive market prices serve under certain assumptions as the means for decomposing a large decision problem into consumers' and producers' decisions with their separate objective functions. One aspect common to all decomposition techniques is the use of a mechanism by which the market (or a system) moves to an equilibrium position from a nonequilibrium one. Two common methods of market adjustment discussed in economic theory are the Walrasian *tâtonnement* through successive price revisions and the Marshallian output adjustment through successive revisions of demand and supply. The former assumes that in nonequilibrium situations excess demand (supply) tends to raise (lower) the market price, whereas the latter postulates that when out of equilibrium the demand price tends to exceed (fall short of) the supply price thus leading to increased (decreased) supply.

Arrow and Hurwicz (1960), Arrow et al. (1958), and Uzawa (1961) have extensively studied the Walrasian *tâtonnement* process in the competitive framework as a mechanism for generating successive approximations, through decentralized decisions, to the problem of optimal resource

---

* Note that the idea of optimal tolls related to the transfer payments is closely related to Lindahl's theory of public expenditure, where the distribution ratio of tax burden among the groups within the community plays a role similar to that of prices in the adjustment between supply and demand (Johansen 1965, chap. 6).

allocation. They showed in a very general nonlinear (concave) programming framework that the equilibrium (i.e., price and quantity equilibrium) in a competitive model may be interpreted as an optimum. The Lagrange multipliers of the nonlinear program may then be interpreted as implicit (or shadow) prices which could be used to decompose the over-all problem into two sets of subproblems, one for the consumers and the other for the firms. Also, they defined a gradient method of successive price revision which is one useful form of specification of the Walrasian *tâtonnement* process. However, since the concept of a dual nonlinear program corresponding to a primal one is more general, one could suggest other types of decomposition rules as computation methods. For example, the analogy of primal and dual methods of computation (e.g., primal and dual simplex in linear programming) of the optimal solution of a programming problem suggests two types of decomposition and decentralization processes which may be termed as the shadow price-guided resource allocation and the resource-directive allocation. The first characterizes a *tâtonnement* process of the Walrasian type, whereas the second specifies a Marshallian type output adjustment mentioned before.

The shadow price-guided processes of resource allocation in a competitive equilibrium model have also been interpreted by Koopmans (1951) in two interesting ways, e.g., one is the imputation of a policymaker at each level of decisionmaking (i.e., a custodian for each commodity market, a manager for each production process, the consumers and the helmsman at the center) and the second is the characterization of the optimum in terms of the vector objective functions.

Note that the latter (which is sometimes called "efficiency" to distinguish it from optimality) is in fact implied by the Pareto-optimality conditions, as we indicated before. Under this generalized framework, the shadow prices may be related not only to scalar optimality but also to vector optimality or efficiency,* and their applications to intertemporal problems of resource allocation (e.g., in problems of optimal growth under a Ramsay-type objective function) are easily conceived.

Now we leave the domain of the over-all economy and its model of competitive equilibrium and consider specific situations of partial equilibrium. For instance, we may have the allocation problem of a large corporation (multiproduct firm, system) having several interdependent divisions (interrelated products, subsystems), and the decision problem is to develop an optimal pricing rule for the intermediate or internal

* These various types of decomposition and decentralization processes and their computational and economic implications are discussed in some detail in Chapter 2 of Sengupta and Fox (1969).

products and other interdependent activities. Even in such situations it turns out that the over-all decision problem can be decomposed into parts or subproblems, under suitable assumptions, of course, and the Lagrange multipliers can be used to develop a shadow price-guided allocation much like the Walrasian *tâtonnement* or other processes of adjustment. Also if a manager for each activity or group of activities (or division) can be imputed, the over-all decision being the responsibility of the center (i.e., the helmsman), one can use the decomposition method to decentralize the decisionmaking processes for different policymakers.

In realistic economic situations, there are at least three basic motivations for seeking such a decentralized method of decisionmaking. First, economy of information and the avoidance of costs due to recognition lags may be secured by having the center perform only a co-ordinating function, with the divisions (or their managers) taking the responsibility for detailed tasks of optimal resource allocation. Second, the decision models of complex systems or institutions, such as universities, can never be complete and exact once and for all, like the design of a machine, and hence the organizational system must provide scope for new information and knowledge, updating of the old, and possibly some organizational slacks for research into new areas which may be quite remote from the present-day habits and traditions. In some of the applied models of investment planning (Malinvaud 1967), economists have long been concerned with the means of providing some flexibility to over-all policymaking, because the relations (e.g., production function, demand function in a specific form, etc.) of the economic model are not exact but behavioristic. In recent years engineers have also joined behavioral scientists in realizing the need for decomposition methods as the following passage by Kulikowski, a Polish electrical engineer, shows:

> Optimum control of large scale, complex systems, which consist of many dynamic and interacting subsystems, represents an important and at the same time difficult problem for the control engineer. This situation is partly due to the fact that the existing optimization theories usually deal with isolated, simple systems and the available controllers or computers are frequently designed or programmed for single, simple processes.
>
> As a result there exists a growing interest in the so-called *multi-level control* of complex systems. Kulikowski (1966, p. 157).

Electrical engineers are developing automatic controllers in which a higher-level controller *modifies* the performances of lower-level controllers to achieve the best over-all performance (Mesarovic 1960; Pearson 1966; Kulikowski 1966).

A third motivation for decentralization of decisions using decomposition techniques in some form is to show that in organizations with multilevel controls and hierarchy, the implicit or shadow prices are really dependent on several factors, i.e., the levels of decisionmaking distinguished, the weights in the over-all objective function, the types of resource interdependence, and, above all, the characteristics of convergence to an optimal or equilibrium solution. The rule of marginal cost pricing is, in effect, conditioned by all these factors in an organizational system, apart from the fact that there may be several intangible and qualitative factors involved in the model formulation.

We now consider some decomposition methods in the linear programming framework to illustrate its uses for decentralized decisionmaking in a partial equilibrium setting.

*Decomposition method of Dantzig and Wolfe (1960)*

Consider a large linear programming (LP) problem in which the coefficient matrix in the constraints is partitioned into nonzero blocks $A_j$ and $B_j$ with a corresponding partition of the resource vector such that some resources are specific to the $j$th subproblem, whereas others are like overheads required by all activities. The over-all program may be formulated as follows: Determine an $n_j$ element column vector $x_j (j = 1, \ldots, n)$ which:

$$\text{maximizes } \sum_{j=1}^{n} c_j' x_j \tag{1a}$$

under the restrictions $\quad c_j : n_j \cdot 1$

$$\sum_{j=1}^{n} A_j x_j = b, \qquad A_j : m \cdot n_j \tag{1b}$$

$$B_j x_j = b_j \text{ (all } j = 1, \ldots, n), \, B_j : m_j \cdot n_j \tag{1c}$$

$$x_j \geq 0 \text{ (all } j). \qquad b_j : m_j \cdot 1 \tag{1d}$$

This is an LP problem in

$$\sum_{j=1}^{n} n_j$$

variables subject to

$$m + \sum_j m_j$$

constraints. Note that the constraints (c) are subprogram constraints specific to $x_j$ only, whereas (b) denotes a set of $m$ joint constraints. An actual formulation of a problem involving linear inequalities can be converted into a form with linear equalities such as those that appear in (1) by introducing a set of costless disposal activities.

Now assume for simplicity that the subprogram constraints (c) define a convex set:

$$S_j = \{x_j | x_j \geq 0, B_j x_j = b_j\} \tag{2}$$

which is bounded for each $j = 1, \ldots, n$. For a given $j$, let the set of extreme points of the convex polyhedron $S_j$ be $W_j = \{x_{j1}, x_{j2}, \ldots, x_{jr_j}\}$; then define:

$$P_{jk} = A_j x_{jk} \text{ and } c_{jk} = c'_j x_{jk} \text{ for } k = 1, 2, \ldots, r_j. \tag{3}$$

Now the extremal problem equivalent to the original LP problem is to determine the decision variables $s_{jk}$ ($j = 1, \ldots, n$; $k = 1, \ldots, r_j$) which:

$$\text{maximize } \sum_j \sum_k c_{jk} s_{jk} \tag{4a}$$

under the restrictions

$$\sum_j \sum_k P_{jk} s_{jk} = b \text{ ($m$ constraints)}, \tag{4b}$$

$$\sum_k s_{jk} = 1 \text{ ($n$ constraints)}, \tag{4c}$$

$$s_{jk} \geq 0 \text{ all } j = 1, 2, \ldots, n, \text{ and } k = 1, 2, \ldots, r_j. \tag{4d}$$

To prove the equivalence, note that any point $x_j$ of the set $S_j$ may be written as a convex combination of its extreme points, i.e., $\sum_k x_{jk} s_{jk}$ where $s_{jk} = \{s_{j1}, s_{j2}, \ldots, s_{jr_j}\}$ would satisfy the weight conditions (c) and (d). Then (4b) is equivalent to (1b) and (4a) is equivalent to (1a) in view of (3).

We may note that the set of extreme points $W_j = \{x_{j1}, \ldots, x_{jr_j}\}$ provides full information on the subproblem constraints; i.e., about the set of constraints that are specific to $x_j$ only.

Suppose one set of subproblem constraints can be represented by the area bounded by the lines $OA$, $BC$, $CD$, $DE$, and $EO$ which represent the subproblem constraints (Fig. 4.1). Suppose that we initially know that only points $O$, $A$, and $B$ are feasible and that the feasible region is a convex polyhedral set. Then we can optimize under the condition that the subproblem solution should lie somewhere in region I given by $OABO$. If we get additional information that point $C$ is also feasible, then we can improve our decision by optimizing under the condition that the subproblem solution should lie somewhere in region II given by $OABCO$.

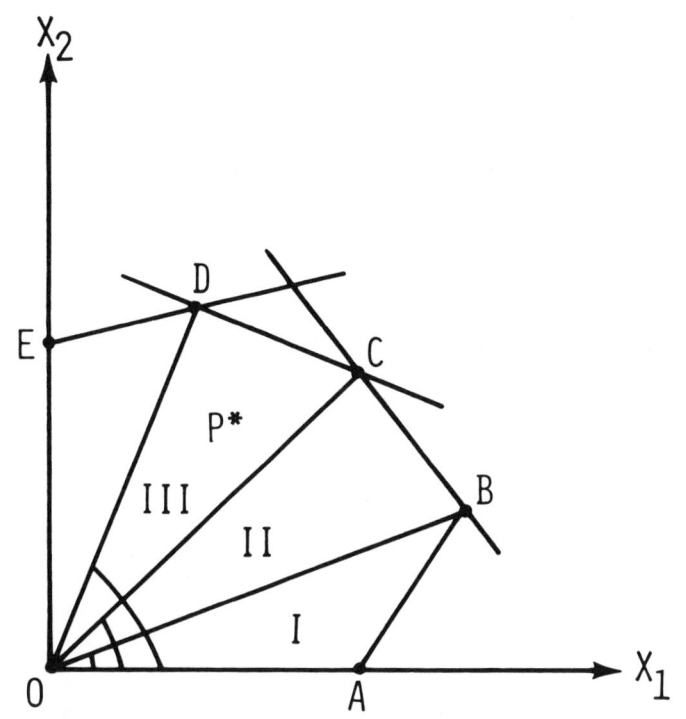

Fig. 4.1. A set of extreme points and alternative subproblem constraints.

Although full information on the subproblem constraints is provided by all the extreme points, a knowledge of only a few of these extreme points could be sufficient to determine the optimal solution.

Suppose that the over-all optimal solution is obtained when the subproblem solution is $P$ in region III. If we know through successive approximations that $O$, $A$, $B$, and $C$ are feasible, our information is not yet adequate, but once we know that in addition $D$ is feasible, our information is sufficient to determine the optimal policy. Given that $O$, $A$, $B$, $C$, and $D$ are feasible, the additional information that $E$ also is feasible is superfluous. Similarly, given that $O$, $C$, and $D$ are feasible, the information that any other extreme point is feasible is superfluous.

The extremal problem (4) has $m + n$ constraints excluding the nonnegativity constraints. Assuming that initially we have enough information about the subproblem extreme points to enable us to pick $m + n$ linearly independent columns, problem (4) has a basic feasible solution. Associated with this basic feasible solution there exists a set of $y(m \times 1)$ and $\bar{y}(n \times 1)$ such that (see Dantzig [1963, pp. 196–97]):

$$y'P_{jk} + \bar{y}_j = c_{jk} \quad \text{for } s_{jk} \text{ in the basis,} \tag{5}$$

i.e.,

$$y'A_j x_{jk} + \bar{y}_j = c'_j x_{jk}. \tag{6}$$

Consider the original problem (1):

$$\text{maximize } \sum_{j=1}^n c'_j x_j + y'(b - \sum_{j=1}^n A_j x_j)$$

$$\text{subject to } x_j \geq 0; \; B_j x_j = b_j \quad (\text{for all } j = 1, \ldots, n),$$

assuming $y$ is the right or optimal dual vector associated with the first $m$ joint constraints. If $y$ is given a priori, the above decision problem takes the form:

$$\text{maximize } \sum_{j=1}^n (c_j - A'_j y)' x_j, \tag{7}$$

subject to $x_j \geq 0$; $B_j x_j = b_j$ for all $j = 1, \ldots, n$, which decomposes into $n$ subproblems:

$$\text{maximize } (c_j - A'_j y)' x_j \tag{8a}$$

$$\text{subject to } x_j \geq 0; \; B_j x_j = b_j. \tag{8b}$$

Now consider the case in which $y$ in the formulation is the simplex multiplier obtained from the first basic feasible solution of the extremal problem. Notice that the optimal solutions of the $n$ subproblems (8) are extreme points of the corresponding subproblem constraints. We may consider the following alternatives:

*Case (i):* In the set of extreme points given by the $n$ subproblems there is no element that is not already included in the initial basis of the extremal problem. In this case the original basis is optimal. To prove this, assume the contrary, i.e., that the original basic feasible solution is not optimal. Then there exists at least one $x_{jk}$ such that the simplex evaluator or the relative cost factor (see Dantzig [1963, p. 196]) in the extremal problem:

$$c_{jk} - y'P_{jk} - \bar{y}_j > 0, \text{ i.e., } c'_j x_{jk} - y'A_j x_{jk} - \bar{y}_j > 0.$$

Since $c'_j x_{jk} - y'A_j x_{jk}$ is maximized in each of the $n$ subproblems and since $\bar{y}_j$ is a constant, this $x_{jk}$ should have been generated by one of the $n$ subproblems (note that the $c'_j x_{jk} - y'A_j x_{jk}$ provided initially is suboptimal because then it was only equal to $\bar{y}_j$). This $x_{jk}$ cannot be one of those included in the original basis, since it violates condition (6).

*Case (ii):* All the extreme points that solve the $n$ subproblems denoted respectively by $x_j(1)$ where (1) refers to the first iteration, are such that $c'_j x_j(1) - y' A_j x_j(1) - \bar{y}_j \leq 0$. In this case also the original basic feasible solution is optimal. The proof is similar to the proof of case (i) and hence it is omitted.

*Case (iii):* $\max_j c'_j x_j(1) - y' A_j x_j(1) - \bar{y}_j > 0$.

Suppose that $c'_r x_r(1) - y' A_r x_r(1) - \bar{y}_r = \max_j c' x_j(1) - y' A_j x_j(1) - \bar{y}_j$.

In this case the value of the extremal problem can be improved by introducing $x_r(1)$ into the basis. This is done through one simplex iteration. The column that goes out of the basis is given by the usual simplex computation applied to the extremal problem.

Under case (iii) we obtain a new basic feasible solution with a new set of simplex multipliers. Using these new simplex multipliers associated with the first $m$ joint constraints as $y$, we can define the second iteration of the $n$ subproblems (8). We can continue this approach until we end up with a situation falling into case (i) or case (ii).

From iteration to iteration the value of the extremal problem is improved. In cases of degeneracy one can use the methods of lexicographic ordering or perturbation to assure oneself that the same basis is not repeated. Since the number of extreme points for each of the $n$ subproblems is assumed finite, the iterations converge to the optimum in a finite number of steps. Once the optimal solution $(s_{jk}^*)$ is obtained for the extremal problem we can write the optimal solution to the original problem as:

$$x_j^* = \sum_k s_{jk}^* x_{jk}. \tag{9}$$

What the above decomposition method shows is that there are economies in replacing a complex linear decision problem by a set of decentralized decision problems and a central co-ordinating problem. Although Dantzig and Wolfe developed the method—called a decomposition algorithm—as a computational device they noted its implications for decentralized decisions.*

A. *Application to an educational model.* To illustrate these implications we shall consider a linear programming model for a college with three departments, departments A, B, and C.† Department A has

---

* Koopmans (1951) and Gale (1960) noted the decentralization aspects within a competitive economy with linear (homogeneous) models of production.
† This example is taken from Fox et al. (1967).

thirteen activities, the levels of which are denoted by $x_{Aj}(j = 1, \ldots, 13)$, as follows:

$x_{A1}$, $x_{A2}$ and $x_{A3}$ are the activity levels which correspond to the research activities.

$x_{A4}$ = the number of M.S. degrees per year awarded to students providing their own support.

$x_{A5}$ = the number of M.S. degrees per year awarded to students who obtain financial support by working as research assistants.

$x_{A6}$ = the number of M.S. degrees per year awarded to students who obtain financial support by working as teaching assistants.

$x_{A7}$ = the number of undergraduate sections per year taught solely by faculty members.

$x_{A8}$ = the number of undergraduate sections per year taught jointly by faculty members and graduate teaching assistants.

$x_{A9}$ = the number of graduate sections taught per year.

$x_{A10}$ = the number of units (section equivalents) of faculty time devoted to thesis supervision.

$x_{A11}$, $x_{A12}$, and $x_{A13}$ are the activity levels for the various types of faculty time allocations among research, graduate teaching, and undergraduate teaching.

Department B has eleven activities, the levels of which are denoted by $x_{Bj}(j = 1, \ldots, 11)$:

$x_{B1}$ and $x_{B2}$ are the activity levels for the research activities.

$x_{B3}$ = the number of M.S. degrees per year awarded to students providing their own support.

$x_{B4}$ = the number of M.S. degrees per year awarded to students who are also teaching assistants.

$x_{B5}$, $x_{B6}$, and $x_{B7}$ are the numbers of each of the various types of sections taught per year.

$x_{B8}$ = the number of units (section equivalents) of faculty time devoted to thesis supervision.

$x_{B9}$, $x_{B10}$, and $x_{B11}$ are the activity levels for the faculty time allocation activities (allocations among research, graduate teaching, and undergraduate teaching).

Department C has thirteen activities the levels of which are denoted by $X_{Cj}(j = 1, \ldots, 13)$:

$x_{C1}$, $x_{C2}$, and $x_{C3}$ are the activity levels for the research activities.

$x_{C4}$ = the number of M.S. degrees per year awarded to students providing their own support.

$x_{C5}$ = the number of M.S. degrees per year awarded to students who are also research assistants.

$x_{C6}$ = the number of M.S. degrees per year awarded to students who are also teaching assistants.

$x_{C7}$, $x_{C8}$, and $x_{C9}$ are the numbers of each of the various types of sections taught.

$x_{C10}$ = the number of units (section equivalents) of faculty time per year devoted to thesis supervision.

$x_{C11}$, $x_{C12}$, and $x_{C13}$ are the activity levels for the faculty time allocation activities (allocations among research, graduate teaching, and undergraduate teaching).

Table 4.1 describes the characteristics of the three departments. Table 4.2 describes all the activities of the college; the first three rows

Table 4.1. Some characteristics of departments A, B, and C

| Item | Department A | Department B | Department C |
|---|---|---|---|
| Number of faculty members—[a] | 5.5 | 8.5 | 7.5 |
| Undergraduate teaching required (number of student courses) | 1,850 | 2,750 | 2,250 |
| Graduate service teaching required (number of student courses) | determined by college dean | | 210 |
| Research budget ($'s) | 50,000 | 20,000 | 45,000 |
| Faculty salaries ($'s) | 11,000 | 10,000 | 12,000 |
| Undergraduate class sizes | | | |
| Faculty instructors | 35 | 30 | 40 |
| Both faculty and graduate student instructors | 30 | 25 | 35 |
| Graduate class sizes | 24 | 15 | 18 |
| Thesis class sizes | 6.5 | 7.0 | 7.5 |
| Teaching assistant salaries ($'s) | 2,800 | 2,600 | 2,750 |
| Research assistant salaries ($'s) | 2,750 | — | 2,700 |
| Number of inputs supplied by teaching assistants (sections taught per year) | 5 | 5 | 6 |
| Number of years required to obtain M.S. degree | 2 | 2 | 2 |
| Number of courses taken to obtain M.S. degree | | | |
| in: Department A | 10 | 3 | 4 |
| in: Department B | 3 | 10 | 0 |
| in: Department C | 0 | 0 | 9 |
| Thesis credits | 3 | 3 | 3 |
| Objective function weights: | | | |
| Research publications | 2.50 | 2.00 | 3.00 |
| M.S. degrees | 1.50 | 1.75 | 2.00 |

[a] Each department is assumed to have an integral number of faculty members, one of whom devotes half of his time to administrative functions.

Table 4.2. Complete model of departments A, B, and C with department-specific and joint college-level restrictions

*Department A activities:*

| Row number | 5.00 A1 | 3.75 A2 | 2.75 A3 | 1.50 A4 | 1.50 A5 | 1.50 A6 | A7 | A8 | A9 | A10 | A11 | A12 | A13 |
|---|---|---|---|---|---|---|---|---|---|---|---|---|---|
| 1 |  |  |  | 10 | 10 | 10 |  |  | −24 |  | 7.4 | 7.4 |  |
| 2 |  |  |  | 3 | 3 | 3 |  |  |  |  |  |  |  |
| 3 | 3 |  |  |  |  | 5.6 |  |  |  |  |  |  |  |
| 4 | 3 | 1 | 1 |  | −2 |  |  |  |  |  |  |  |  |
| 5 | 1 | 1 | 1 |  |  |  |  |  |  |  | −⅓ | −⅓ | −1 |
| 6 | 3,000 | 1,500 | 750 |  | 5,500 |  |  |  |  |  | 3,600 | 3,600 | 11,000 |
| 7 |  |  |  |  |  |  | −35 | −30 |  |  |  |  |  |
| 8 |  |  |  | 3 | 3 | 3 | 1 | 0.5 |  | −6.5 | −6 | −4 |  |
| 9 |  |  |  |  |  |  |  | 0.5 | 1 | 1 | −2 | −4 |  |
| 10 |  |  |  |  |  | −10 |  |  |  |  |  |  |  |
| 11 |  |  |  |  |  |  |  |  |  |  | 1 | 1 | 1 |
| 12 |  |  |  | 1 |  |  |  |  |  |  |  |  |  |
| 13 |  |  |  |  |  |  |  |  |  |  |  |  |  |

Rows 1–3: College level restrictions
Rows 4–13: Department A restrictions
Rows 14–22: Department B restrictions
Rows 23–33: Department C restrictions

102

Table 4.2. (continued)

| | Row number | 2.10 B1 | 2.40 B2 | 1.75 B3 | 1.75 B4 | B5 | B6 | B7 | B8 | B9 | B10 | B11 |
|---|---|---|---|---|---|---|---|---|---|---|---|---|
| | | | | | | | | | | ($c_{Bj}$'s) | | |
| College level restrictions | 1 | | | | | | | | | | | |
| | 2 | | | 3 | 3 | | | | | | | |
| | 3 | | | 10 | 10 | | | −15 | | 8.5 | 8.5 | |
| | | | | | 5.2 | | | | | | | |
| Department A restrictions | 4 | | | | | | | | | | | |
| | 5 | | | | | | | | | | | |
| | 6 | | | | | | | | | | | |
| | 7 | | | | | | | | | | | |
| | 8 | | | | | | | | | | | |
| | 9 | | | | | | | | | | | |
| | 10 | | | | | | | | | | | |
| | 11 | | | | | | | | | | | |
| | 12 | | | | | | | | | | | |
| | 13 | | | | | | | | | | | |
| Department B restrictions | 14 | 1 | 1 | | | | | | | | | |
| | 15 | 1,000 | 2,600 | | | | | | | −0.15 | −0.15 | −1 |
| | 16 | | | | | | | | | 1,500 | 1,500 | 10,000 |
| | 17 | | | 3 | 3 | −30 | −25 | | | | | |
| | 18 | | | | | 1 | 0.6 | 1 | −7 | −8.5 | −6.0 | |
| | 19 | | | | | | | | | −1.5 | −4.0 | |
| | 20 | | | | −10 | | 0.4 | | | | | |
| | 21 | | | 1 | | | | | | | | |
| | 22 | | | | | | | | 1 | 1 | 1 | 1 |
| Department C restrictions | 23 | | | | | | | | | | | |
| | 24 | | | | | | | | | | | |
| | 25 | | | | | | | | | | | |
| | 26 | | | | | | | | | | | |
| | 27 | | | | | | | | | | | |
| | 28 | | | | | | | | | | | |
| | 29 | | | | | | | | | | | |
| | 30 | | | | | | | | | | | |
| | 31 | | | | | | | | | | | |
| | 32 | | | | | | | | | | | |
| | 33 | | | | | | | | | | | |

103

Table 4.2. (continued)

|  | Row number | 5.40 C1 | 4.75 C2 | 3.00 C3 | 2.00 C4 | 2.00 C5 | 2.00 C6 | C7 | C8 | C9 | C10 | C11 | C12 | C13 |
|---|---|---|---|---|---|---|---|---|---|---|---|---|---|---|
| College level restrictions | 1 2 3 |  |  |  | 4 | 4 | 4 5.5 | | | | | 9.0 | 9.0 | |
|  | | | | | | | 4 | | | | | | | |
| Department A restrictions | 4 5 6 7 8 9 10 11 12 13 | | | | | | | | | | | | | |
| Department B restrictions | 14 15 16 17 18 19 20 21 22 | | | | | −2 5,400 | | −40 | −35 0.7 0.3 | −18 1 | | | | |
| Department C restrictions | 23 24 25 26 27 28 29 30 31 32 33 | 3 1 3,000 | 2 1 1,750 | 1 500 | 9 3 | 9 3 −12 | 9 3 | 1 | | 1 | −7.5 1 | −0.25 3,000 −7 −2 1 | −0.25 3,000 −5 −4 1 | −1 12,000 1 |

*(cc<sub>i</sub>'s)* Department C activities:

Table 4.2. *(concluded)*

| | Row number | | Department restrictions b Vector | College restrictions |
|---|---|---|---|---|
| College level restrictions | 1<br>2<br>3 | ≤<br>≤<br>≤ | | 0<br>0<br>220 |
| Department A restrictions | 4<br>5<br>6<br>7<br>8<br>9<br>10<br>11<br>12<br>13 | ≤<br>≤<br>≤<br>≤<br>≤<br>≤<br>≤<br>≤<br>≤<br>≤ | 0<br>0<br>40,000<br>−1,850<br>0<br>0<br>0<br>0<br>5.5<br>2.0 | |
| Department B restrictions | 14<br>15<br>16<br>17<br>18<br>19<br>20<br>21<br>22 | ≤<br>≤<br>≤<br>≤<br>≤<br>≤<br>≤<br>≤<br>≤ | 0<br>20,000<br>−2,750<br>0<br>0<br>0<br>0<br>8.5<br>1.0 | |
| Department C restrictions | 23<br>24<br>25<br>26<br>27<br>28<br>29<br>30<br>31<br>32<br>33 | ≤<br>≤<br>≤<br>≤<br>≤<br>≤<br>≤<br>≤<br>≤<br>≤<br>≤ | 0<br>0<br>45,000<br>−2,250<br>−210<br>0<br>0<br>0<br>0<br>7.5<br>3.0 | |

105

refer to the joint constraints that involve activities from more than one department. For example, row 1 sets a constraint on the number of graduate sections taught per year in department A. The planning problem facing the college has 37 activities and 33 constraints. If a single college dean were to plan for all the three departments he should *acquire* all the data presented in Tables 4.1 and 4.2 and then solve an LP problem with $\binom{70}{33}$ (i.e., number of combinations of 33 columns selected from 70 columns) basic solutions. (It would be a sizable and difficult task for a dean to obtain all the information needed to formulate this problem on a realistic scale, with several or many large departments.)

We shall consider partitioning this problem into one central executive or restricted master problem and three departmental problems. We assume that there is one department chairman for each of the department problems and one dean of the college to co-ordinate and guide the departmental chairmen. The dean could himself be a member of an echelon within a hierarchy of university administrators, so that university planning would be multilevel planning (or multilevel control; see Mesarovic [1960]). We shall, however, restrict ourselves here to a two-level planning example with the college dean setting the rules for (co-ordinated) action.

Table 4.3 shows the iterative steps of the Dantzig–Wolfe decomposition method (which is, of course, different from the gradient or other methods) applied to the college planning model just described: Iterations 1 and 2 correspond to phase I of the simplex method applied to the college dean's restricted master problem. Iteration 1, for example, has in its basis the auxiliary variables associated with the first joint constraints and the auxiliary variables associated with the three convex combination constraints such as (4c), one for each department.

Rows 1, 2, and 3 give the simplex multipliers $y$ which are also called "provisional dual prices" by Baumol and Fabian (1964), associated with the first three joint constraints of the restricted master problem. Rows 4, 5, and 6 give the provisional dual prices $\bar{y}_A$, $\bar{y}_B$, $\bar{y}_C$ associated with the convex combination constraints such as (4c). We assume that the college dean communicates the provisional dual prices of the first three joint resources to the three department chairmen. The department chairmen under these provisional prices solve their respective departmental problems which were laid down under (8). After solving these departmental problems, the department chairmen communicate to the dean their specific requirements for the joint resources.

As we mentioned earlier, in this type of information gathering, the dean should compare the benefit of new information with the cost of ob-

Table 4.3. A model of decentralized decisionmaking (Dantzig–Wolfe) applied to a college planning model: Values of key magnitudes at successive iterations or communication phases between the college dean and department chairmen

| Variable | Phase I 1 | Phase I 2 | 3 | 4 | 5 | 6 | 7 | 8 | 9 | 10 | 11 |
|---|---|---|---|---|---|---|---|---|---|---|---|
| | | | | | COLLEGE | | | | | | |
| Provisional prices × 1,000 | | | | | | | | | | | |
| Resource 1 | 1,000.00 | 0.00 | 9.94 | 17.64 | 143.35 | 80.90 | 33.54 | 59.12 | 46.44 | 59.44 | 59.25 |
| Resource 2 | 1,000.00 | 0.00 | 0.00 | 0.00 | 102.66 | 48.40 | 10.54 | 95.73 | 75.48 | 82.39 | 82.39 |
| Resource 3 | 0.00 | 10.51 | 0.00 | 869.66 | 3,558.78 | 243.18 | 300.96 | 1,567.98 | 1,210.66 | 1,451.21 | 1,446.37 |
| Opportunity cost of additional information: | | | | | | | | | | | |
| Dept. A | −1.00 | −0.61 | 7.12 | −41.36 | −166.63 | 12.84 | 6.63 | −63.32 | −44.13 | −56.25 | −56.03 |
| Dept. B | −1.00 | −1.00 | 7.57 | −75.26 | −310.90 | 6.21 | −14.59 | −118.82 | −88.60 | −109.59 | −108.96 |
| Dept. C | −1.00 | −0.74 | 3.15 | −55.12 | −235.98 | 5.56 | 2.81 | −89.54 | −63.16 | −80.83 | −80.47 |
| Value of objective funct. | −198.00 | −0.04 | 17.04 | 18.17 | 46.15 | 53.66 | 57.17 | 57.54 | 58.06 | 58.36 | 58.37 |
| | | | | Department A problem | | | | | | | |
| Contribution to central objective funct.: | | | | | | | | | | | |
| Net | 241.76 | −0.58 | 49.02 | −25.87 | −161.18 | 18.53 | 8.15 | −62.97 | −43.99 | −56.25 | −56.03 |
| Gross | 0.00 | 0.00 | 51.88 | 20.76 | 13.95 | 17.74 | 20.74 | 17.38 | 20.38 | 20.74 | 17.74 |
| Central resource require.: | | | | | | | | | | | |
| Resource 1 | −251.01 | 50.83 | 285.28 | −82.23 | −159.84 | −194.33 | −152.17 | −133.58 | −91.43 | −152.17 | −194.33 |
| Resource 2 | 9.25 | 15.25 | 85.58 | 23.40 | 12.36 | 17.32 | 23.32 | 16.10 | 22.10 | 23.32 | 17.32 |
| Resource 3 | 57.97 | 55.29 | 174.19 | 55.29 | 55.29 | 57.97 | 57.97 | 55.29 | 55.29 | 57.97 | 57.97 |
| | | | | Department B problem | | | | | | | |
| Contribution to central objective funct.: | | | | | | | | | | | |
| Net | 199.51 | −0.93 | 79.31 | −64.31 | −296.16 | −2.43 | −13.12 | −118.45 | −88.23 | −109.53 | −108.96 |
| Gross | 0.00 | 0.00 | 80.64 | 13.27 | 11.52 | 12.51 | 13.27 | 11.51 | 13.26 | 12.32 | 12.32 |
| Central resource require.: | | | | | | | | | | | |
| Resource 1 | 13.20 | 16.20 | 133.00 | 16.20 | 13.20 | 16.20 | 16.20 | 13.20 | 16.20 | 14.59 | 14.59 |
| Resource 2 | −212.71 | 54.00 | 443.33 | 54.00 | −102.42 | −196.29 | 85.99 | −157.60 | −141.17 | −103.08 | −103.08 |
| Resource 3 | 95.13 | 88.88 | 297.58 | 88.88 | 88.88 | 95.13 | 88.88 | 92.01 | 92.01 | 89.22 | 89.22 |
| | | | | Department C problem | | | | | | | |
| Contribution to central objective funct.: | | | | | | | | | | | |
| Net | −2.14 | −0.70 | −33.72 | −37.81 | −228.00 | 5.99 | 2.81 | −89.21 | −63.16 | −80.83 | −80.48 |
| Gross | 0.00 | 0.00 | 34.20 | 25.58 | 11.19 | 32.64 | 25.58 | 25.21 | 25.21 | 24.21 | 25.21 |
| Central resource require.: | | | | | | | | | | | |
| Resource 1 | 2.14 | 6.43 | 48.15 | 30.12 | 6.43 | 44.25 | 30.12 | 28.43 | 28.43 | 28.43 | 28.43 |
| Resource 2 | 0.00 | 0.00 | 0.00 | 0.00 | 0.00 | 0.00 | 0.00 | 0.00 | 0.00 | 0.00 | 0.00 |
| Resource 3 | 70.45 | 66.95 | 101.73 | 72.28 | 66.95 | 94.90 | 72.28 | 71.90 | 71.90 | 71.90 | 71.90 |

taining it. How do we measure the cost of obtaining new information? At any iteration the constraint (4c) of the restricted master problem must be a convex combination of the extreme points provided by the department up to that iteration. A marginal violation of the constraint for any department, viz., $\sum_k s_{jk} > 1$ implies that we are letting the departmental solution go beyond the convex polyhedral set defined by the already available extreme points of that department. The opportunity cost of obtaining marginal information may be represented by the shadow price or provisional dual price associated with the constraint $\sum s_{jk} = 1$. Rows 4, 5, and 6 in Table 4.3 provide this information. It should be noted that these provisional prices are again only approximations to the actual costs of information.* For instance, we expect that the true cost of acquiring additional information (i.e., the true marginal benefit of new information) must decline as we acquire more and more information. This is not reflected in Table 4.3 because our figures are only estimates of the true costs based on the existing information at any iteration.

At iteration 4, to consider a specific situation, the dean finds an optimal solution for the restricted master problem and sets prices 17.64, 0, and 869.66 for the three joint resources. Further, given the information available at iteration 4, estimated costs of obtaining more information for departments A, B, and C are given by $-41.36$, $-75.26$, and $-55.12$. Under iteration 4's provisional prices for the three joint resources, the three departments solve their respective problems and communicate to the dean their new requirements of the three joint resources and their net contribution to the college objective function, viz., $(c_j - A_j'y)'x_j$ (for $j = A, B, C$). These net contributions and the costs of new information are only estimates of the true benefits and costs based on the information available at iteration 4. The college dean accepts all the new information for which the benefits are more than costs. The dean stops asking for new information when the net benefit is less than the cost, as in iteration 10 for department A and in iteration 11 for departments B and C.

In the above presentation, in the absence of any knowledge as to the cost of additional information, i.e., the marginal cost of information, we have taken the marginal benefit of going beyond the currently available feasible region as its estimate. In an actual planning problem, if the college dean has a priori estimates of the costs of acquiring additional

* Note that all costs of processing information or transmitting it between levels, i.e., costs of computational services due to the complexity of submodels, are ignored in the estimates provided by the provisional dual prices.

information these estimates should replace the $\bar{y}_A$, $\bar{y}_B$, and $\bar{y}_C$ of our earlier analysis. It is of course implicit that these costs and benefits should be evaluated in terms of a common denominator, say a monetary unit (dollars). The estimates $\bar{y}_A$, $\bar{y}_B$, and $\bar{y}_C$ are measured in the same units as are the net benefits to the college.

We have implicitly assumed so far that the college dean and each department chairman act as a team and that the department chairmen act only as subordinates to the dean, who sets the "rules of action"—such as (i) gather the adequate information; (ii) choose that action which maximizes the net benefit to the college; and (iii) communicate your requirements for the joint resources. In an actual organization we may, of course, have deviations from this assumption of team decision. It is quite likely that the department chairmen, while trying to co-operate with the dean, will be influenced by their own preferences and those of faculty members in the departments which they represent. In this case there may be conflict of interest between the department chairmen and the dean; if so, the problem can be decomposed into three two-person non-co-operative or co-operative games, where within each game each player acquires more and more information on the pure strategies of the other player. We will not go into this game-theoretic approach here.

Our aim in this example is to display the logic of decentralized decisionmaking and not to endorse a highly artificial means of communication between deans and chairmen. Difficulties of communication arise partly because neither deans nor chairmen have accurate measures of what is being produced and how much it is worth. A linear programming framework encourages us to organize our information about class sizes, staffing patterns, degrees granted, and research publications in a systematic way so that the existing input-output structure of a department may be understood by both chairman and dean. It is obvious (though more so to a dean than to a chairman) that some stipulated total amount of college-level resources must be allocated among the constituent departments; it is not obvious, in the absence of an explicit objective function, why one allocation pattern is better than another.

A set of provisional prices for outputs could clarify the latter question, and the sensitivity of optimal allocations to reasonable variations in relative prices could also be examined in a somewhat generalized and aggregated model of a college. Chairmen and dean would gain increased insight into the properties of the college as a system and into the approximate costs and values of its inputs and outputs. The *idea* of an objective function to be optimized would probably improve the decisions of the chairmen and the dean, whether or not formal computations were used.

The scope for various types of gamesmanship would be substantially reduced.

*Two-level planning method of Kornai and Lipták*

The decomposition algorithm of Dantzig and Wolfe achieves optimal allocation of the joint resources through a price mechanism—quoting a different price for each of the joint resources at different iterations until the over-all optimal solution is obtained. The two-level planning procedure of Kornai and Lipták (1965) achieves the over-all optimal solution through a quota mechanism—offering different amounts of the joint resources at different iterations.

Consider the following problem:

maximize $c'x$

subject to $Ax \leq b;\ x \geq 0$.

Suppose that this problem can be rewritten as problem (10) below, taking into account the near block-diagonality of the matrix $A$ after perhaps rearranging a few rows and columns:

$$\text{maximize } \sum_{j=1}^{n} c'_j x_j \tag{10a}$$

$$\text{subject to } \sum_{j=1}^{n} \bar{A}_j x_j \leq \bar{b}, \tag{10b}$$

$$B_j x_j \leq b_j \quad \text{for } j = 1, \ldots, n, \tag{10c}$$

$$x_j \geq 0 \quad \text{for } j = 1, \ldots, n, \tag{10d}$$

where $\bar{A}_j = m \cdot n_j$; $x_j : n_j \cdot 1$; $\bar{b} : m \cdot 1$; $B_j = m_j \cdot n_j$; $b_j : m_j \cdot 1$. The first $m$ resources are a set of $m$ joint resources and the $m$ rows represented by $\bar{A}_j$ are the linking rows, whereas the other resources are partitioned into nonoverlapping sets ($n$ in number) of specific subproblem resources. The above problem termed "the OCI problem" (overall central information problem) by Kornai and Lipták can also be written as:

$$\text{maximize } \sum_{j=1}^{n} c'_j x_j \tag{11a}$$

$$\text{subject to } \sum_{j=1}^{n} A_j x_j \leq b; \quad \left( b = \begin{pmatrix} \bar{b} \\ b_1 \\ \vdots \\ \vdots \\ b_n \end{pmatrix} \right) \tag{11b}$$

# RESOURCE ALLOCATION IN LINEAR STATIC MODELS

and $\quad x_j \geq 0 \quad$ for $j = 1, \ldots, n,$ (11c)

where

$$A_j = \begin{pmatrix} \bar{A}_j \\ \vdots \\ B_j \end{pmatrix};$$

$\bar{A}_j$ occupies the first $m$ rows, rows $m + 1$ to

$$m + \sum_{i=1}^{j-1} m_i$$

have zeroes, rows

$$m + \sum_{i=1}^{j-1} m_i + 1$$

to

$$m + \sum_{i=1}^{j} m_i$$

have elements of $B_j$ and rows

$$m + \sum_{i=1}^{j} m_i + 1$$

to

$$m + \sum_{j=1}^{n} m_j$$

have zeroes. $A_j$ is therefore a

$$\left( m + \sum_{j=1}^{n} m_j \right) \cdot n_j$$

matrix.

The dual of the above problem can be written as:

$\quad$ minimize $b'y$ $\qquad$ (12a)

$\quad$ subject to $A'_j y \geq c_j \quad$ for $j = 1, \ldots, n;$ $\qquad$ (12b)

$\quad$ and $\quad y \geq 0.$ $\qquad$ (12c)

Suppose we partition the vector $b$ into $n$ vectors $U_j$, such that

$$\sum_{j=1}^{n} U_j = b,$$

where $U_j$ represents the allocation of the resources to the $j$th subproblem. Now define a quantity $U$:

$$U = \begin{pmatrix} U_1 \\ \vdots \\ U_n \end{pmatrix};$$

where each $U_j$ is a

$$\left(m + \sum_{j=1}^{n} m_j\right) \cdot 1$$

vector composed of the allocation vectors $U_j$. Once a specific $U$ is chosen, the subproblems (called the sector programming problems by Kornai and Lipták) can be written as:

| maximize $c'_j x_j$ | | (13a) |
|---|---|---|
| subject to $A_j x_j \leq U_j$, | (primal) | (13b) |
| and $\quad x_j \geq 0$; | (for $j = 1, \ldots, n$). | (13c) |

and

| minimize $U'_j y_j$, | | (14a) |
|---|---|---|
| subject to $A'_j y_j \geq c_j$, | (dual) | (14b) |
| and $\quad y_j \geq 0$ | (for $j = 1, \ldots, n$). | (14c) |

Two programs are thus defined: the OCI program (11 and 12), and the sector programs (13 and 14). We call any partitioning of $b$ into $n$ sector allocations represented by $U$ a "central program."

Let $X_j(U)$ denote the set of all feasible sectoral output programs (i.e., the primal feasible set of sector $j$ under $U$), with $X_j^*(U)$ denoting the set of optimal output programs; similarly, let $Y_j$ and $Y_j^*(U)$ denote respectively the set of feasible and optimal price programs for sector $j$. Note that the sets of feasible price programs do not depend on the central program $(U)$, and it is only the sets of optimal price programs that depend on the central program. Let $Y$ denote the set of all feasible price programs of the OCI problem (12).

We shall assume that there exists an optimal solution to the OCI problem. Then from the duality theorem of linear programming it follows that:

$Y \neq \phi$ ($\phi$ is an empty set).

An examination of the feasible regions of the price problems shows that

$Y = Y_1 \cap Y_2 \neq \phi$.

Hence $Y_1 \neq \phi$ and $Y_2 \neq \phi$; i.e., each division has at least one feasible price program.

Instead of choosing any central program $U$, such that it is a partition of $b$, we would like to choose those central programs that provide feasible sectoral output programs. The sectoral output problems will have a feasible solution if and only if the corresponding sectoral price problems have optimal solutions.

Any central program that generates a feasible output program for the OCI problem is called a "feasible central program." Under certain conditions it can be shown that for any feasible central program $U$, the $n$ sectors have optimal solutions.

Let $\phi_j(\bar{u}) = \max c'_j x_j = \min \bar{u}'_j y_j$

$$x_j \epsilon X_j(\bar{u}) \quad y_j \epsilon Y_j.$$

The over-all optimum of the OCI problem can be written as:

$$\phi(\bar{u}) = \sum_{j=1}^{n} \phi_j(\bar{u}) = \sum_{j=1}^{n} \min U'_j y_j \text{ subject to } y_j \epsilon Y_j. \tag{15}$$

It can be seen that $\phi(u)$ is a continuous and concave function, being the lower envelope of a finite number of linear functions.

The two-level planning problem equivalent to the original OCI problem takes the following form:

1. Determine (at the center) a feasible central program that yields an over-all optimum to the over-all problem, i.e., solve the concave programming problem:

$$\text{maximize } \phi(U) = \sum_{j=1}^{n} \phi_j(U) \tag{16a}$$

$$\text{subject to } U \epsilon U^*, \tag{16b}$$

where $U^*$ is a convex polyhedral set that generates all the feasible output programs of the OCI problem.

2. Given $U^*$, the optimal central program, determined at level 1 above, determine the optimal divisional programs $X_j^*(U) (j = 1, \ldots, n)$. Then the $X_j^*(U^*)$ constitute the optimal output programs for the OCI problem.

The determination of $\phi(U)$ is not an easy task, however, as it is equivalent to solving $n$ linear programming problems parametrically. Kornai and Lipták reduce the two-level planning problem to a problem of solving a polyhedral game by methods of fictitious play (Robinson 1951).

In economic terms what Kornai and Lipták suggest is the following:

First, the center arbitrarily allocates the resources to the sectors. Then the sectors supply the center the demand prices for the resources depending on their marginal productivities. The center would then find a reallocation of the resources that it expects to give the maximum returns for the resources if the sectors maintain the prices (or marginal productivities) quoted to the center. When the center reallocates the resources, the sectors no longer maintain the same prices for the resources. They communicate a new set of prices to the center (a set of prices that minimizes the cost of the resources). The center again determines a new allocation that would maximize the returns for the resources under these new prices quoted by the sectors. This procedure continues until we reach a situation in which neither player can increase his pay-off.

The above method for solving a polyhedral game assumes that the game is regular—i.e., corresponding to each strategy of one player the other player has a counter strategy. We assumed that $U \in U^*$, the set of all feasible central programs, i.e., the central programs which generate the feasible programs of the OCI problem. Hence the strategy set $U^*$ is regular. Similarly, the strategy set $Y$ of the second player is regular or evaluable only if corresponding to each $y \in Y$ there exists a counter strategy $U \in U^*$.

As Kornai and Lipták (1965, p. 155) comment, the construction of the polyhedral set $U^*$ and the assurance that all $y \in Y$ are regular or evaluable are hard to come by for any given practical situation. For example, the college model treated in the previous section cannot easily be decomposed into a two-level planning problem of the type developed by Kornai and Lipták.

However, Kornai and Lipták note that in the special case in which the elements in the matrices $A_j$ and the resource vector $b$ are all nonnegative numbers (which was not the case in our college model of the previous section), the set of evaluable central programs $U^*$ can be represented just by the partitioning condition of resource $b$; i.e.:

$$U^* = \left\{ U = \begin{pmatrix} U_1 \\ \vdots \\ U_n \end{pmatrix} \middle| \sum_{j=1}^{n} U_j = b \right\}.$$

Further, it also follows that each $y \in Y$ is evaluable in this case and the problem leads to a workable polyhedral game.

*Critical comments on the two methods*

While the theoretical development of the two-level planning method is quite interesting in itself, we believe that in solving large planning problems the method of Dantzig and Wolfe is better than the method of two-level planning. Note the process of information gathering (the coefficient generation property) of the Dantzig–Wolfe method which is absent in the Kornai–Lipták method. The communication process between the center and sectors terminates in a finite number of steps. This is not true in the case of the Kornai–Lipták method. The Dantzig–Wolfe method has a monotonicity property which is again absent in the Kornai–Lipták method.

What is sometimes more important is the point that the Dantzig–Wolfe method can incorporate the case of a quadratic objective function far more easily than can the other method. However, the Kornai–Lipták method attacks a more general situation in the sense that it does not require the resources to be distinguished as central and sectoral; also its game-theoretic solution indicates the possibilities of collusion and other bargaining situations, if there are reasons to believe that the successive revisions of policy by the center are either too slow or are likely to be truncated.

## Organizational and game-theoretic approaches of resource allocation

The two decomposition techniques discussed above in the LP framework have been applied not only to problems of national planning but also to the multiproduct firm. The latter case, in which the firm sells in an otherwise competitive market although its internal resources are transferred between its divisions by means of accounting or internal prices, is frequently referred to as the theory of the divisionalized firm (Arrow 1959; Dean 1955; Hirshleifer 1957). In this theory the resource-using decisions of different divisions are made consistent with the overall objective function of the firm by means of a set of administered prices for those resources which are shared by more than one division.

Two cases of administered prices may be clearly distinguished. First, the output of one division may be one of the inputs to another division of the firm, necessitating an internal transaction if the other division has no option to buy that input from outside. Second, there may be some common resources required by several divisions which the firm as a whole may buy and then allocate between divisions. In these two cases, the prices at which the transactions take place may be called internal prices or transfer prices. Usually these prices do not have any direct relation to the corresponding market prices. However, these could be easily related to the decomposition and decentralized processes we have discussed before and they can be used to co-ordinate, control, and evaluate the production performance of the various divisions of a corporation-type firm (Gordon 1964; Ijiri 1965).

From an organizational standpoint (Shubik 1962) the decision problem of a divisionalized firm may be viewed as a team-decision problem in which there are two or more decision variables, and these different decisions are *made* to depend on different aspects of the environment (in our case, in fact, each divisional decision is made by a divisional manager, but all managers are supposed, under a central co-ordination scheme, to maximize jointly a single firm's pay-off). Team-decision problems of this type are analyzed by Marschak (1955) using a game-theoretic approach and by Radner (1962) using a Bayes's decision-theoretic approach. Following Shubik (1961, 1962), we can solve this team-decision problem using the theory of $n$-person co-operative games.

According to von Neumann and Morgenstern[*] (1953), the $n$-person co-operative game can be solved using the concept of a (superadditive) characteristic function. Here all players act in such a way as to maximize jointly the firm's profits and then use their bargaining power as represented by (or derived from) the characteristic function itself to arrive at a fair imputation of the profits.

A somewhat different type of use of a game-theoretic model of resource allocation arises when the objective functions or the net pay-offs are only partially known. The nature, availability, and costs of information flows become very critical in such a framework. Also, the imputation schemes and their stability become dependent on the way in which lack of information at each stage of the game entails costs through expected losses defined in the system (Radstrom 1964). Some of these considerations (Fox et al. 1969) will be referred to in more detail in Chapter 6.

---

[*] For an excellent summary and critical appraisal of game theory and decision theory the reader may refer to the book by Luce and Raiffa (1957).

CHAPTER 5

# Resource Allocation Processes in Nonlinear and Dynamic Models

*T. Krishna Kumar*

**Introductory remarks**

The static framework of decentralization using decomposition techniques is much more general than it might have appeared from our analysis in Chapter 4. Although from a computational and operational viewpoint a linear (or linearized) and static formulation is sometimes preferable, economic realism demands that we indicate the domains of operational applicability of the decomposition techniques to generalized situations of nonlinear and dynamic models, at least partially. As a matter of fact, a competitive equilibrium model in its general form, which characterizes Pareto efficiency, is nonlinear, although Koopmans (1951) considered a linear activity analysis type formulation to characterize its shadow price-guided allocation mechanism (see also Plessner 1967). The Arrow–Hurwicz formulation (1960), however, emphasized the nonlinear programming framework, although their gradient method of successive price revision (which is comparable to the Walrasian *tâtonnement* process) is sometimes interpreted in terms of linearized equations for showing the characteristics of convergence to equilibrium values.*

Three basic reasons may be cited for introducing some nonlinearities (e.g., quadratic functions) into the linear decomposition techniques. First, the simple cases of imperfect competition, with demand curves

---

* The computational and economic meaning of several types of decomposition methods (e.g., methods of Dantzig and Wolfe, Kornai and Lipták, Arrow and Hurwicz, Koopmans, and others) are discussed in some detail in Chapter 2 of Sengupta and Fox (1969).

having less than infinite elasticity, cannot be included unless we define at least a quadratic objective function of the firm (in the more general case the interaction between multicommodity demand and supply may have to be admitted, provided these are not associated with significant indivisibilities or other peculiarities). Second, whenever decomposition techniques are thought of as being applied to a large-scale system (or corporation) having subsystems (or divisions), it is tacitly assumed that the objective function of the system (or corporation) is completely quantifiable. This, of course, is hardly the case, due to various intangible elements involved (e.g., goals other than profits, subjective estimates of intrafirm transfers, market goodwill, etc.). For the allocation of resources within an educational system (e.g., university) which involves both physical and human capital, the inputs and outputs which may have to be valued at imputed accounting costs and prices are much more extensive. In these cases the linear activity analysis or programming models of decomposition should only be considered as first approximations,* which may further be tested through introducing nonlinearities with respect to their sensitivity, substitution between activities, and the implicit costs of linearized specification. This view is all the more important if there is a margin of uncertainty or errors in the model in its parameters or constraints. Third, the theory of economic policy developed by Tinbergen (1952, 1956) and Theil (1961, 1964) showed that in some situations the policymakers' notions of desired values of targets and instruments are sufficient to construct a tentative loss function in terms of quadratic deviations from the desired values and, since the desired quantities can be parametrically varied, this scheme of calculation offers valuable insights into the policymaking problem, apart from providing a benchmark for comparison. It is known that if there are random residual errors in the model, then under certain additional assumptions this quadratic loss function approach becomes very similar to the least squares method of estimation (also in discrete time dynamic models it satisfies a certainty equivalence theorem as shown by Theil [1961, 1964]). Although loss functions other than in a quadratic form are conceivable, the essential point of the loss function approach is that it provides a method of simulating the behavior of policymakers who have to make decisions anyway in situations where some of the input and output variables (e.g., research activity for an educational system administrator) do not have any tangible market prices.

* Distinguishing between the economic and noneconomic parts of the policymakers' objective function, a systematic parametric procedure for estimating the contribution of research outputs in a university department has been analyzed by Plessner, Fox, and Sanyal (1968).

The threefold aspects of nonlinearity mentioned above are particularly important for what we have called the quasi-market and the divisionalized firm-type systems, where we have the partial equilibrium set-up of a mixed system comprising market (i.e., nonhypothetical exchange) and nonmarket (i.e., internal, and sometimes hypothetical, exchange) characteristics. The educational system (e.g., a university system) represents in our view these mixed characteristics (i.e., use of nonprice variables and imputations for some of its internal inputs and outputs and also the internal exchanges and accounting practices in lieu of explicit market adjustments) in a most significant manner. An academic department in a university may be thought to be very similar to a multiproduct firm, producing various research and degree outputs with inputs such as faculty, budgets, and other supporting facilities for both current and capital account activities. Its objective function may comprise various goals which may be conveniently partitioned into two parts, economic and extra-economic. The economic part may be formulated in several ways, of which two are worth emphasizing:

a) The capitalized value of expected lifetime earnings of students who graduate from the department in all its programs less the departmental costs; and

b) The setting of goals in terms of desirable levels of activities and outputs and then considering the implicit cost of deviations from the goal or the desired level (here the goal setting function of the policymaker must be derived from the trends in demand, supply and price structures of various skills in national markets).

Note that this multiproduct firm operates in an industry comprising the national market for various professional skills. The objective function (a) above is based on the assumption that forecasts of earnings of future graduates and degree-recipients for the given department could be made from observing the national market behavior in the past and the present (note that this is very similar to a perfectly competitive market assumption); the second objective function (b) assumes that conscious goal-setting by policymaking authority and planning for resource allocations and diversification accordingly may avoid some of the losses due to imperfect adjustment of the multiproduct firm to the over-all needs of the industry. (Note that this is very similar to the quota-allocation methods used in central planning.)* It is in this context that we now present the decomposition techniques under imperfectly competitive systems which are potentially applicable to the different levels of decisionmaking of an

* A multiproduct firm model under conditions of central planning in a socialist economy is discussed along these lines in Kornai and Lipták (1962).

educational system as a multiproduct firm within a broad industry framework.

## Price-guided allocation in imperfectly competitive models

Now consider a system (e.g., a multiproduct firm, a multidivision corporation) producing $n$ products with $m$ resources. Let $x_1, \ldots, x_n$ be the amounts of the products produced and $c_1, \ldots, c_m$ be the amounts of resources initially available. Let $g_i(x_1, \ldots, x_n)$ be the amount of resource $i$ required to produce $x_1, \ldots, x_n$. Let the pay-off of producing $x_1, \ldots, x_n$ be given by a function $f(x_1, \ldots, x_n)$. The decision problem can now be written as:

$$\text{maximize} \quad f(x_1, \ldots, x_n) \tag{1a}$$
$$x_1 \ldots x_n$$

$$\text{subject to } g_i(x_1, \ldots, x_n) \leq c_i \quad \text{for } i = 1, \ldots, m, \tag{1b}$$

$$\text{and } x_j \geq 0 \text{ for } j = 1, \ldots, n. \tag{1c}$$

If we assume that the marginal net benefit or pay-off is nonincreasing then $f(x_1, \ldots, x_n)$ will be a concave function. If diminishing returns prevail in production then $g_i(x_1, \ldots, x_n)$ will be convex. Suppose that there exists a meaningful nontrivial solution to the problem that does not use all the $m$ resources (this is the Slater condition assumed in place of the Kuhn–Tucker constraint qualification). Following the treatment of Balinski and Baumol (1968) we can now formulate the following dual problem:

$$\text{minimize } \alpha(x,v) = \sum_{i=1}^{m} c_i v_i + [f(x) - \Sigma v_i g_i(x)]$$
$$+ \sum_{j=1}^{n} x_j \left[ \sum_{i=1}^{m} v_i \frac{\partial g_i}{\partial x_j} - \frac{\partial f}{\partial x_j} \right] \tag{2a}$$

$$\text{subject to } \sum_{i=1}^{m} v_i \frac{\partial g_i}{\partial x_j} \geq \frac{\partial f}{\partial x_j} \quad \text{for } j = 1, 2, \ldots, n \tag{2b}$$

$$\text{and } v_i \geq 0 \quad \text{for } i = 1, 2, \ldots, m, \tag{2c}$$

where $x = (x_1, \ldots, x_n)$.

*Nonlinear Duality Theorem:* If there exists an optimal solution $x^*$ for (1) then there exists an imputation of costs $v^*$, such that $(x^*, v^*)$ solves (2). Further $\alpha(x^*, v^*) = f(x^*)$.

The proof of this theorem follows directly from the saddle point theorem of Kuhn and Tucker if we notice the following points:

i) the primal slacks can be written as

$$s_i = c_i - g_i(x);$$

ii) the dual slacks can be written as

$$l_j = \sum_{i=1}^{m} v_i \frac{\partial g_i}{\partial x_j} - \frac{\partial f}{\partial x_j} \text{; and}$$

iii) the Lagrangean associated with problem (1) can be written as

$$L(x,v) = f(x) + \sum_{i=1}^{m} v_i(c_i - g_i(x)),$$

where $v_i$ denotes the Lagrange multipliers. The Kuhn–Tucker necessary and sufficient conditions yield for $j = 1, \ldots, n$ and $i = 1, \ldots, m$:

$$\left(\frac{\partial L}{\partial x_j}\right)^* = \left(\frac{\partial f}{\partial x_j}\right)^* - \Sigma v_i^* \left(\frac{\partial g_i}{\partial x_j}\right)^* \leq 0 \text{ and } x_j \geq 0, \tag{3a}$$

$$x_j^* \left(\frac{\partial L}{\partial x_j}\right)^* = x_j^* \left[\left(\frac{\partial f}{\partial x_j}\right)^* - \Sigma v_i^* \left(\frac{\partial g_i}{\partial x_j}\right)^*\right] = 0, \tag{3b}$$

$$\left(\frac{\partial L}{\partial v_i}\right)^* = (c_i - g_i(x^*)) \geq 0 \text{ and } v_i^* \geq 0, \tag{3c}$$

and

$$v_i^* \left(\frac{\partial L}{\partial v_i}\right)^* = v_i^*[c_i - g_i(x^*)] = 0. \tag{3d}$$

The above conditions can be rewritten in terms of the primal-dual variables and their slacks:

$$l_j^* \geq 0 \text{ and } x_j^* \geq 0, \tag{4a}$$

$$l_j^* x_j^* = 0, \tag{4b}$$

$$s_i^* \geq 0 \text{ and } v_i^* \geq 0, \tag{4c}$$

and

$$s_i^* v_i^* = 0. \tag{4d}$$

It can be easily seen that $\alpha(x^*,v^*) = L(x^*,v^*)$, since from the complementary slackness condition (4b) above it follows that $\alpha(x^*,v^*) = L(x^*,v^*)$ and condition (4d) that $L(x^*,v^*) = f(x^*)$, so that $\alpha(x^*,v^*) = L(x^*,v^*) = f(x^*)$.

The terms in (2a) can be given the following interpretation:

The first term $\Sigma c_i v_i$ is the imputed value of all the resources. The second term denotes the economic rent (the total return less the imputed cost of the resources used). The third term denotes the opportunity cost of producing unprofitable products.

An economic interpretation of the duality can be given. (i) The imputation $v = (v_1, \ldots, v_m)$ must be such that it imputes all the net benefits or pay-off to the $m$ resources and to the unused capacity (as economic rent). This follows from the duality relation $f(x^*) = \alpha(x^*,v^*)$. (ii) The imputation must be such that the imputed value of the resources is a minimum. This is implied by the first term of (2a). (iii) The imputation must be such that it imputes a zero value to any unused resource. Conditions (ii) and (iii) follow from the minimization of the first and second terms of (2a). (iv) The opportunity cost of producing an unprofitable product must be a minimum. This follows from the last term of (2a). This duality interpretation provides the basic logical framework for extending the linear decomposition methods so as to include substitution and interdependence effects.

### Decomposition methods in nonlinear and dynamic models

Now consider the details of the price-guided allocation mechanism of decomposition in the framework of Dantzig and Wolfe (1960) who in fact suggested an extension of their decomposition technique for LP problems to nonlinear programming problems as well. Their procedure involves solving a set of nonlinear subproblems in a sequential fashion, but this procedure may not always terminate in a finite number of steps. Taking advantage of the finite iterative calculations advanced for the quadratic programming problem, van de Panne and Whinston (1964) suggested a simpler quadratic decomposition technique that terminates in a finite number of steps and in which each subproblem is an LP problem.

To illustrate the algorithm we shall consider a (quadratic) programming problem that has, say, $n$ functionally identifiable sectors, sector $j$ being in charge of an output vector $x_j$.

We shall describe the problem as:

$$\text{maximize } c'x - \tfrac{1}{2}x'Cx \tag{5a}$$

$$\text{subject to } \sum_{j=1}^{n} A_j x_j = b_0, \tag{5b}$$

$$B_j x_j \leq b_j \quad \text{for } j = 1, \ldots, n, \tag{5c}$$

RESOURCE ALLOCATION IN NONLINEAR & DYNAMIC MODELS 123

and $x_j \geqq 0$   for $j = 1, \ldots, n$, (5d)

where

$x = (x_1, \ldots, x_n); c = (c_1, \ldots, c_n);$

$$C = \begin{bmatrix} C_{11} & \cdots & C_{1n} \\ \vdots & & \\ C_{n1} & \cdots & C_{nn} \end{bmatrix};$$

$c = \Sigma n_j$ element vector; $c_j$ is an $n_j$ element vector;

$x = \Sigma n_j$ element vector; $x_j$ is an $n_j$ element vector;

$C = \Sigma n_j \times \Sigma n_j$ matrix;

$C_{ij}, c'_{ji}$ are $n_i \times n_j$ matrices;

$A_j = m \times n_j$ matrix; $b_0$ is an $m$ element vector;

$B_j = m_j \times n_j$ matrix; $b_j$ is an $m_j$ element vector;

$C$ is a symmetric partitioned matrix.

Suppose that the sector $j$ has $K_j$ feasible extreme points that satisfy (5c) and (5d), and that they are denoted by $x_{jk}$ ($k$ ranging from 1 to $K_j$). Then each feasible $x_j$ can be written as:

$$x_j = \sum_{k=1}^{K_j} s_{jk} x_{jk} \tag{6a}$$

$$\sum_k s_{jk} = 1 \text{ and } s_{jk} \geq 0. \tag{6b}$$

We assume that (5c) and (5d) determine bounded polyhedral sets. If these sets are not bounded the method presented can be easily extended in the same way as Dantzig and Wolfe suggest.

Substituting (6) in (5) we have the following equivalent extremal problem in the decision variables $s_{jk}$:

$$\text{maximize} \sum_{j=1}^{n} \sum_{k=1}^{K_j} (c'_j x_{jk}) s_{jk} - \frac{1}{2} \sum_{j=1}^{n} \left( \sum_{k=1}^{K_j} x_{jk} s_{jk} \right)' C_{jj} \left( \sum_{k=1}^{K_j} x_{jk} s_{jk} \right)$$

$$- \sum_{j=1}^{n} \sum_{i \neq j=1}^{n} \left( \sum_{k=1}^{K_j} x_{jk} s_{jk} \right)' C_{jl} \left( \sum_{k=1}^{K_l} x_{lk} s_{lk} \right) \tag{7a}$$

subject to $\sum_{j=1}^{n} A_j \left( \sum_{k=1}^{K_j} x_{jk} s_{jk} \right) = b_0,$ (7b)

$$\sum_{k=1}^{K_j} s_{jk} = 1 \quad \text{for } j = 1, \ldots, n, \tag{7c}$$

$$s_{jk} \geq 0 \quad \text{for } k = 1, \ldots, K_j \tag{7d}$$
$$\text{and } j = 1, \ldots, n,$$

or equivalently:

$$\text{maximize } \sum_{j=1}^{n} \sum_{k=1}^{K_j} C_{jk} s_{jk} - \tfrac{1}{2} \sum_{j=1}^{n} \sum_{k=1}^{K_j} \sum_{k'=1}^{K_j} Q'_{kk} s_{jk} s_{jk'}$$

$$- \sum_{j=1}^{n} \sum_{l \neq j=1}^{n} \sum_{k=1}^{K_j} \sum_{k'=1}^{K_l} Q_{jk,lk'} s_{jk} s_{lk'} \tag{8a}$$

$$\text{subject to } \sum_{j=1}^{n} \sum_{k=1}^{K_j} P_{jk} s_{jk} = b_0, \tag{8b}$$

$$\sum_{k=1}^{K_j} s_{jk} = 1 \quad \text{for } j = 1, \ldots, n, \tag{8c}$$

$$s_{jk} \geq 0 \quad \text{for } j = 1, \ldots, n \tag{8d}$$
$$\text{and } k = 1, \ldots, K_j,$$

where $c_{jk} = c'_j x_{jk}$; $P_{jk} = A_j x_{jk}$;

$Q'_{kk} = x_{jk} C_{jj} x_{jk'}$;

and

$Q_{jk,lk'} = x_{jk} C_{jl} x_{lk'}.$

It can be easily shown that this equivalent transformed problem is a concave programming problem in $s_{jk}$. We can therefore apply the Kuhn–Tucker theory. Let $y$ denote the Lagrange multiplier vector associated with the extremal problem constraints (8b) and $y_j$ the Lagrange multiplier associated with the $j$th constraint under (8c). Note that $y$ is an $m$-element vector which is unrestricted in sign and $y_j$ is a real number unrestricted in sign.

The Lagrangean can be written as:

$$L = (a) + y' \left( (b) + \sum_{j=1}^{n} y_j(c)_j \right), \tag{9}$$

where $(a)$ denotes the quadratic form under (8a) that is maximized; $(b)$ denotes the expression $(b_0 - \Sigma\Sigma P_{jk} s_{jk})$; $(c)_j$ denotes the $j$th constraint under (8c), viz.,

$$\left(1 - \sum_{k} s_{jk}\right).$$

The Kuhn–Tucker conditions are:

$$\frac{\partial L}{\partial s_{jk}} \geq 0;\ s_{jk} \geq 0;\ j = 1, \ldots, n;\ k = 1, \ldots, k_j; \tag{10a}$$

$$s_{jk}\frac{\partial L}{\partial s_{jk}} = 0;\ j = 1, \ldots, n;\ k = 1, \ldots, k_j; \tag{10b}$$

$$\frac{\partial L}{\partial y_i} = 0;\ \frac{\partial L}{\partial y_j} = 0;\ j = 1, \ldots, n;\ i = 1, \ldots, m. \tag{10c}$$

Conditions (10a) and (10b) can equivalently be written as:

$$\frac{\partial L}{\partial s_{jk}} + U_{jk} = 0;\ s_{jk} \geq 0;\ U_{jk} \geq 0, \tag{10a'}$$

and

$$U_{jk}s_{jk} = 0. \tag{10b'}$$

To initiate the algorithm one starts with any set of $m + n$ positive variables $s_{jk}$ corresponding to a basis determined by linear equations (8b and 8c) which are $m + n$ in number. Other variables that may be at nonzero levels are the set of $m$ shadow prices $y$ and the $n$ shadow prices $y_j(j = 1, \ldots, n)$. Further in accordance with (10b') we set

$$\sum_{j=1}^{n} K_j - m - n$$

variables $U_{jk}$ at nonzero level, one corresponding to each $s_{jk}$ variable not in the basis. Thus in the initial solution with which we start the $U_{jk}$ variables are made to satisfy the condition (10b'), but they may not satisfy the non-negativity constraint required by (10a').

Any solution that satisfies (8b), (8c), (8d), and (10b') is called a feasible solution in the standard form. The algorithm moves from one feasible standard form solution that is not necessarily optimal to another, until an optimal solution is obtained.

Let $\{z_i\}$ be the values taken by the basic variables (i.e., $s_{jk}$ and $U_{jk}$ variables which are at nonzero levels) which are "considered" for leaving the basis at a particular iteration and $\{l_{ji}\}$ be the elements in the $j$th column of the tableau (in which basic variables are expressed as linear functions of all variables) which is the column of the variable to come into the basis. Then the variable to leave the basis is the one whose value $z_i$ is such that:

$$\min_i \left\{ \frac{z_i}{l_{ij}} \middle| \frac{z_i}{l_{ij}} \geq 0,\ l_{ij} \neq 0 \right\}. \tag{11}$$

The algorithm proceeds according to the following steps:

1. Determine the most negative $U_{jk}$ variable. If there is no $U_{jk}$ which is negative then the initial basic feasible solution is optimal.

2. Introduce into the basis the variable complementary to $U_{jk}$ chosen in step 1, viz., $s_{jk}$. The variable to be removed from the basis is chosen from among $s_{jk}$ variables in the basis and the $U_{jk}$ variable chosen in step 1. If the variable $U_{ju}$ of step 1 is removed using criterion (11) return to step 1; if not, go to step 3.

3. Introduce the $U_{jk}$ variable corresponding to the $s_{jk}$ variable which was just taken out in step 2. The variable to be taken out of the basis is chosen from the $s_{jk}$ variables in the basis and the $U_{jk}$ variables chosen in step 1. If an $s_{jk}$ variable is removed repeat step 3; if not, go back to step 1.

It is easy to note that corresponding to any basic feasible solution there is a set of provisional dual prices $y$ and $y_j$ from the linear equations (8b, 8c, and 8d).

Now let us consider the procedure under step 1. From (10a′) we have:

$$U_{jk} = -\frac{\partial L}{\partial s_{jk}} = -C_{jk} + x'_{jk}C_{jj}(\Sigma_{k'}x_{jk'}s_{jk'})$$

$$+ \sum_{\substack{l=1 \\ l \neq j}}^{n} x'_{jk}C_{jl}(\Sigma_{k'}x_{lk'}s_{lk'}) + y'P_{jk} + y_j. \qquad (12)$$

According to step 1, for each $j$ we have to determine that extreme point $x_{jk}$ for which $U_{jk}$ given by (12) is a minimum. This desired value of $U_{jk}$ and the corresponding $x_{jk}$ can be obtained for each $j$ by setting up the following LP problem for sector $j$:

maximize $c'_j x_j - x'_j C_{jj}(\Sigma_{k'} x_{jk'} s_{jk'})$

$$- \sum_{\substack{l=1 \\ l \neq j}}^{n} x'_j C_{jl}(\Sigma_{k'} x_{lk'} s_{lk'}) - y' A_j x_j - y_j, \qquad (13a)$$

subject to $B_j x_j \leq b_j$, $\qquad (13b)$

$x_j \geq 0.$ $\qquad (13c)$

When we start with any basic feasible solution to the extremal problem, the center that solves the extremal problem does not have full information on all the $n$ sectors. Hence the center computes

$$\left( \sum_{k'} x_{jk'} s_{jk'} \right)$$

and

$$\left( \sum_{\substack{l \neq j \\ l=1}}^{n} \sum_{k'=1} x_{lk'} s_{lk'} \right)$$

on the basis of the $s_{jk}$ values of the current basic feasible solution. The center then transmits the following directive to sector $j$:

$$\text{"maximize"}: \left[ c_j - C_{jj}\left(\sum_{k'} x_{jk'}s_{jk'}\right) - \sum_{\substack{l=1 \\ l=j}}^{n} C_{jl}(\Sigma x_{lk'}s_{lk'}) - A'_j y \right]' x_j$$

(subject to its own constraints). Note that this turns out to be identical with the Dantzig–Wolfe rule if the quadratic terms are absent. The center then gets both elements of the new information, i.e., $x_{jk}$ and the corresponding $U_{jk}$. The center introduces that particular $s_{jk}$ into the basis which has the minimum $U_{ju}$ value. It can be easily seen that this criterion of minimum $U_{ju}$ value is equivalent to choosing that particular $s_{jk}$ for which the *net benefit* is a maximum.* This algorithm sets at each iteration a constant reward per unit, a reward per unit that is independent of the level of operation. It is equivalent to saying that the center would buy the product (in any amount) at the price quoted by it. Interestingly enough, this is precisely the suggestion which Lerner (1944) gave for planning in an economy with monopolistic firms. He advocated setting up a central board of counter speculation that guarantees a price and agrees to buy any amount of the product at that price, the price being determined so as to clear the market.

In the subproblem (13) for sector $j$ we have a term in the objective function

$$\left(\sum_k x_{jk}s_{jk}\right).$$

We mentioned earlier that this value is computed by the center and given to the sector at each iteration based on the current levels of the $s_{jk}$ variables. This might seem to be a task that can be delegated to the sector itself at the risk of converting the sector problems into quadratic programming problems, thereby losing the finite termination property possessed by the above procedure of van de Panne and Whinston. This modification is suggested by Hass (1968).

*Application of decomposition techniques to educational systems*†

In some of our previous work (Fox et al. 1967; Sengupta and Fox 1969; Fox and Sengupta 1968) we have discussed the various techniques of decomposition applied to educational resource allocation LP (linear programming) models, particularly the algorithms of Dantzig–Wolfe and of Kornai–Lipták. In these applications it is assumed that the cen-

---

\* Refer to the interpretation given to the Dantzig–Wolfe algorithm on pp. 96–99.
† This section is based on a joint paper by Fox, Sengupta, and Sanyal (1969).

tral model optimizes the objective function of the dean, whereas the sectoral models refer to the optimizing decisions of several departmental heads. We have also discussed cases (Sengupta and Fox 1969) where the over-all LP model has infeasibility in the solution space, but tolerance measures are introduced to indicate the limits up to which constraint violations are permitted by the two groups of policymakers. These tolerance measures, in effect, may impart feasibility to an otherwise infeasible structure.

Two different interpretations of these tolerance measures are conceivable. One is the case in which the parameters of the LP model (i.e., the input coefficients, resource vector or net prices in the objective function) have margins of uncertainty so that the LP model in effect is only an approximation of possibly a more general nonlinear model. A second interpretation is that the linearity and separability assumptions of the LP model abstract from more general types of complementarity, substitution, and interdependence between activities and their prices. These tolerance measures allow the LP model to be embedded in a general nonlinear programming model.

For the case of a quadratic objective function and linear inequality constraints a decomposition algorithm has been developed recently by Jerome Hass (1968), which seeks to determine efficient demand-supply functions rather than prices. Successive iterations continue to shift the imputed demand and supply functions until the efficient functions are attained.

For applying the Hass algorithm we have considered as an illustration a very simple notional model from a university department system. The illustrative model is:

maximize $\pi = (5.0 - .01x_1)x_1 + (3.75 - .02x_2)x_2 + (2.75 - .03x_3)x_3$
$- .002(x_1 + x_2 + x_3 - R^*)(x_4 + x_5 + x_6 + x_7 + x_8 + x_9 + x_{10} - T^*)$
$+ 1.50(x_4 + x_5 + x_6 + x_7 + x_8 + x_9 + x_{10})$,

subject to

(R1) $\quad 3x_1 + x_2 - 2x_5 \leq 0$,

(R2) $\quad 3x_1 + 1.5x_2 + .75x_3 + 5.5x_5 \leq 18.646$,

(R3) $\quad x_1 + x_2 + x_3 \leq 1.973$,

(R4) $\quad x_7 + .5x_8 \leq 30.82$,

(R5) $\quad -10x_6 + .5x_8 \leq 0$,

(R6) $\quad -10x_4 - 10x_5 - 10x_6 + 24x_9 \geq 124$,

(R7) $\quad 3x_4 + 3x_5 + 3x_6 \leq 22$,

(R8)    $5.6x_6 \leq 17.2811,$
(R9)    $x_4 \leq 2.0,$
(R10)   $x_9 + x_{10} \leq 11.5,$
(R11)   $3x_4 + 3x_5 + 3x_6 - 6.5x_{10} \leq 0,$

all $x_j \geq 0, j = 1, \ldots, 10.$

Here $R^*$ and $T^*$ indicate desired levels of research and teaching respectively ($R^* = 5$, $T^* = 75$ preassigned, $x_1$, $x_2$, and $x_3$ are the variables corresponding to different research activities; $x_4$, $x_5$, and $x_6$ denote the numbers of M.S. degrees per year awarded to students supported by themselves, by research assistantships, or by teaching assistantships; $x_7$ and $x_8$ refer to the undergraduate class sections per year taught by faculty members separately or with the assistance of teaching assistants; $x_9$ denotes the number of graduate class sections taught per year; and $x_{10}$ refers to faculty time allocated to thesis supervision (in class section equivalent units). Assuming two divisions, research (division 1 with activities $x_1$, $x_2$, $x_3$) and teaching (division 2 with activities $x_4$ through $x_{10}$), there would be two common resources in restrictions R1 and R2. The quadratic facet of the objective function could be partitioned as:

$$\phi_1 = \begin{pmatrix} -.01 & 0 & 0 \\ 0 & -.02 & 0 \\ 0 & 0 & -.03 \end{pmatrix}, \quad \phi_2 = \begin{pmatrix} 0 & \cdots & 0 \\ \vdots & & \vdots \\ 0 & \cdots & 0 \end{pmatrix},$$

$$\phi_3 = \begin{bmatrix} -.001 & -.001 & -.001 & -.001 & -.001 & -.001 & -.001 \\ -.001 & -.001 & -.001 & -.001 & -.001 & -.001 & -.001 \\ -.001 & -.001 & -.001 & -.001 & -.001 & -.001 & -.001 \end{bmatrix}$$

in terms of divisional outputs $X$ and $Y$ of the two divisions separately and joint outputs ($\phi_3$) incorporating the interdependence between the two divisions. Note that the objective function is assumed positive definite.

In the first iteration the center (i.e., department head) neglects the interdependence between the two divisions, so that each division solves its own problem. The division 1 problem is:

$$\pi_1(X) = \max\ (5.15 - .01x_1)x_1 + (3.90 - .02x_2)x_2 + (2.90 - .03x_3)x_3$$

subject to $x_1 + x_2 + x_3 \leq 1.973$; $x_j \geq 0, j = 1, 2, 3$;

optimal solution $X_{(1)}$: $\begin{cases} x_1 = 1.973 \\ x_2 = 0 \\ x_3 = 0 \end{cases}$ and $\pi_1(X_{(1)}) = 10.124.$

The division 2 problem is:

$$\pi_2(Y) = \max 1.51(x_4 + x_5 + x_6 + x_7 + x_8 + x_9 + x_{10})$$

subject to restrictions R4 through R11 and $x_j \geq 0$;

optimal solution $Y_{(1)}$: $\begin{cases} x_4 = 0 \\ x_5 = 4.13 \\ x_6 = 3.08 \\ x_7 = 0 \\ x_8 = 61.64 \\ x_9 = 8.17 \\ x_{10} = 3.33 \end{cases}$ and $\pi_2(Y_{(1)}) = 121.331$.

Upon receipt of the first iteration plans for $\pi_1$ and $\pi_2$ from the two divisions, the department head has first to make accept/reject type decisions on the basis of adjusted demand curves $D_x$ and $D_y$:

If $\pi_1(X_{(1)}) \geq D_x$, then accept $X_{(1)}$ plan, reject otherwise.
If $\pi_2(Y_{(1)}) \geq D_y$, then accept $Y_{(1)}$ plan, reject otherwise.

The adjusted functions $D_x$, $D_y$ determine whether the over-all profitability will be improved by including the plans. Since this criterion is satisfied for the first iteration values of the two divisions, the department head now solves for the weights $(U, V)$ from another quadratic program, e.g.:

$$\max \pi(U, V) = 0.u_0 + 10.16265 \, u_1 - .03894 \, u_1^2 + 121.331 \, v_1 \\ - .317116 \, u_1 v_1$$

subject to
$$0.u_0 + 5.920 \, u_1 + 0.v_0 - 8.25936 \, v_1 \leq 0,$$
$$0.u_0 + 5.920 \, u_1 + 0.v_0 + 22.71324 \leq 18.646,$$
$$u_0 + u_1 = 1,$$
$$v_0 + v_1 = 1,$$

all $u_j, v_j \geq 0$;

optimal solution $\begin{cases} U = \begin{pmatrix} 1 \\ 0 \end{pmatrix}, \quad V = \begin{pmatrix} .179 \\ .821 \end{pmatrix}; \quad \pi(U, V) = 99.60, \\ \lambda_1 = 0, \lambda_2 = .0053 \ (\lambda_j = \text{shadow prices}). \end{cases}$

Thus at the end of the first iteration the current optimal values of $X_{(1)}$ and $Y_{(1)}$ are:

$\hat{X}_{(1)} = (0 \ 0 \ 0)'$,
$\hat{Y}_{(1)} = (0, 3.390, 2.530, 0, 50.602, 6.708, 2.732)'$.

Using these quantities $\hat{X}_{(1)}$, $\hat{Y}_{(1)}$ and the shadow prices $\lambda_1 = 0$, $\lambda_2 = .0053$ supplied by the department head, each division computes at the second iteration its respective demands and formulates its optimal plans. Thus the iterations continue until the over-all optimum is reached along with divisional optima. The solution at the fourth stage of iteration is:

$$x_1 = 1.635,\ x_2 = 0,\ x_3 = 0.338,\ x_4 = 2.0,\ x_5 = 2.126$$

$$x_6 = 3.086,\ x_7 = 0,\ x_8 = 61.64,\ x_9 = 8.172,\ x_{10} = 3.328;$$

$$\pi(\hat{X},\hat{Y}) = \pi(U,V) = 129.08.$$

This solution differs from the final optimal solution by less than 1.24 units in the value of the optimal objective function. Hence truncation at the fourth iteration may be quite acceptable.

However, when the dimension of the model is quite large, two types of additional problems may arise. The incidence of truncation may be difficult to evaluate, particularly with respect to the stability of the strategies of the divisions (Radstrom 1964). Also, the aspect of informational economy usually claimed for the decomposition algorithms is not obviously established; this is particularly important if only approximate results are sought after, since in the latter case even aggregation procedures (rather than decomposition) may be set up with suitable norms for the divisions which would have great informational economy. We feel it is still an open question how to evaluate the informational efficiency of alternative shadow-price-based algorithms. Further, in cases where the quadratic objective function is semidefinite rather than strictly positive-definite the computational algorithm may have additional difficulties such as the failure of monotonicity and some degree of instability.

*Generalizations of Dantzig-Wolfe and Kornai-Lipták methods*

The decomposition methods of Dantzig-Wolfe, Kornai-Lipták, van de Panne-Whinston, and Hass that we have described so far are particular cases of a general iterative method of communication needed to implement an optimal plan. Malinvaud (1967) has given an excellent conceptual outline of these methods. We shall describe the conceptual framework which he developed.

The central planning agency communicates certain information through a set of messages to each of the sectors. These messages are referred to as the "prospective indices." On the basis of these messages each sector provides a "proposal" to the center. Based on these proposals, the central agency modifies its draft plan. Then it communicates a new set of prospective indices to each of the sectors based on the new draft plan. After a certain amount of communication between the center and the sectors the central planning agency chooses a program which constitutes the plan.

The actual design of the plan depends on the answers to the following questions:

i) What variables or functions of the variables constitute the prospective indices? What constitutes a sector's proposal? How does the procedure start?
ii) What are the mechanisms by which the sectors generate their proposals?
iii) How does the central planning agency generate, at each stage, the prospective indices?
iv) How does the central planning agency determine when to stop receiving additional information and how does it determine the final plan?

A procedure is termed "well defined" if there exist solutions to the problems of determining the "prospective indices," the "proposals," and "the optimal plan."

A procedure is called "monotonic" if the utility or pay-off to the center at *any* iteration $k$ is at least as great as the utility at the previous iteration. It is termed strictly monotonic if there is a definite improvement or increase in the utility from iteration $k-1$ to iteration $k$ until the optimal plan is reached.

A procedure is convergent if when the number of iterations increases indefinitely the utility tends to its least upper bound over the set of feasible programs.

A procedure is finite if after only a finite number of iterations the utility assumes the value of its least upper bound.

Viewing the decomposition methods we discussed earlier in the light of these terms we find the following situation:

1) The Dantzig-Wolfe method is well defined if we include the appropriate modifications of the procedure in case of degeneracy in the restricted master problem and in the case of unbounded sectoral feasible sets. It is monotonic. It is convergent and finite.
2) The Kornai-Lipták method is well defined since it restricts itself to regular polyhedral games with evaluable "prospective indices" and "proposals." It is not monotonic. It is convergent, but not finite.

3) The van de Panne–Whinston method is well defined, monotonic, convergent, and finite.
4) The method of Hass is well defined, monotonic, and convergent but not finite.

Geoffrion (1968) classifies the decomposition methods into (i) resource-directive and (ii) price-directive types. He identifies (i) with primal methods and (ii) with dual methods of solving the over-all problem.

Consider the following over-all decomposable problem:

$$\text{maximize} \sum_{i=1}^{k} f_i(x_i) \tag{14a}$$

$$\text{subject to } x_i \in X_i \quad i = 1, 2, \ldots, k \tag{14b}$$

$$\text{and} \quad \sum_{i=1}^{k} G_i(x_i) \geq b, \tag{14c}$$

where $x_i$ is a $n_i.1$ vector, $X_i$ is a feasible region that is convex, $G_i$ is a vector function $(g_{i1}, \ldots, g_{im})$ and $b$ is an $m.1$ vector of constraints. The functions $f_i$ and $g_i$ are assumed to be concave on the convex sets $X_i$ and (14) is assumed to admit at least one feasible solution.

A resource-directive method similar to the Kornai–Lipták method can be formulated by determining iteratively $k$ vectors $(y_1, \ldots, y_k)$ ($m$-dimensional vectors) such that the optimal solutions of the $k$ sub-problems:

$$\text{maximize } f_i(x_i) \tag{15a}$$
$$\text{subject to } x_i \in X_i, \text{ and} \tag{15b}$$
$$G_i(x_i) \geq y_i, \tag{15c}$$

also solve problem (14).

At any iteration the $k$ vectors are chosen in such a way that the $k$ subproblem solutions yield a feasible solution to (14). This is achieved if the $y_i$ are chosen such that

$$\sum_{i=1}^{k} y_i \geq b.$$

This is the reason why this method is called a primal method.

The over-all problem (14) can now be written as:

$$\text{maximize} \sum_{i=1}^{k} f_i(x_i) \tag{16a}$$

$$\text{subject to } x_i \in X_i, \quad i = 1, \ldots, k; \tag{16b}$$

$$G_i(x_i) \geq y_i, \quad i = 1, \ldots, k; \text{ and} \tag{16c}$$

$$\sum_{i=1}^{k} y_i \geq b. \tag{16d}$$

Since the center does not know completely the feasible regions of the sectoral outputs we have to determine a problem involving the variables $y_i$ alone, which will be equivalent to (16). This is achieved by replacing the sectoral objective function and the sectoral constraints, viz. (16a, 16b, and 16c), by the response or reaction function of the allocation $y_1, \ldots, y_k$. By varying $y_i$ parametrically one obtains the response function $v_i(y_i)$ as a maximal value of the sectoral parametric programming problem:

$$\text{maximize } f_i(x) \tag{17a}$$

$$\text{subject to } x_i \in X_i \tag{17b}$$

$$\text{and} \quad G_i(x) \geq y_i \quad (y_i \text{ varied parametrically}). \tag{17c}$$

The central problem can then be written as:

$$\text{maximize } \sum_{i=1}^{k} v_i(y_i) \tag{18a}$$

$$\text{subject to } \sum_{i=1}^{k} y_i \geq b. \tag{18b}$$

It can be shown that $v_i(y_i)$ is a concave function. A gradient method to solve the concave programming problem (17) has been described by Sanders (1965). This may be termed a groping process because the center does not know the response functions $v_i(y_i)$ for the entire domain of $y_i$, but it learns or "gropes" more and more about them by means of the sectoral proposals.

The shadow price vector or Lagrangean multiplier vector $\lambda_i$ associated with the constraint (17c) satisfies the conditions:

$$\frac{\partial v_i}{\partial y_i} = \lambda_i \quad \text{if these partial derivatives exist; or} \tag{19a}$$

$$\left(\frac{\partial v_i}{\partial y_i}\right)_+ \leq \lambda_i \leq \left(\frac{\partial v_i}{\partial y_i}\right)_- \tag{19b}$$

when the partial derivatives do not exist;

$$\left(\frac{\partial v_i}{\partial y_i}\right)_+ \quad \text{and} \quad \left(\frac{\partial v_i}{\partial y_i}\right)_-$$

are the right- and left-hand partial derivatives which exist and are finite if the sectoral problem (17) satisfies the Kuhn–Tucker constraint qualification (Balinski and Baumol 1968).

Consider the linear decomposition model of Dantzig and Wolfe:

$$\text{maximize} \sum_{j=1}^{n} c_j x_j \tag{20a}$$

$$\text{subject to} \sum_{j=1}^{n} A_j x_j = b, \tag{20b}$$

$$B_j x_j = b_j, \tag{20c}$$

$$x_j \geq 0. \tag{20d}$$

This is a problem with coupling constraints (20b and 20c). Consider its dual:

$$\text{minimize} \ b'y + \sum_{j=1}^{n} b'_j y_j \tag{21a}$$

$$\text{subject to} \ A'_j y + B'_j y_j \geq c_j, \tag{21b}$$

$$y \text{ and } y_j \text{ unrestricted in sign.} \tag{21c}$$

This is a problem with coupling variables, $y$ for example. Notice that revising the objective functions of the sectoral problems implied in the Dantzig-Wolfe algorithm is equivalent to changing parametrically the right-hand side of the corresponding dual:

minimize $b'_j y_j$

subject to $B'_j y_j \geq (c_j - A'_j y)$.

Thus the primal resource-directive approach of Geoffrion is analogous to the dual methods of solving the Dantzig-Wolfe type of coupling constraint problem. In this respect Geoffrion's approach is closely related to the dual decomposition methods of Beale (1963), Abadie and Williams (1963), and Rosen (1963).

Geoffrion develops three approaches, namely (i) tangential approximation, (ii) large step subgradient, and (iii) piecewise. These three approaches share the property that they evaluate or approximate $v_i(y_i)$ only as needed.

*Decomposition in dynamic models: Control theory approach*

A certain class of dynamic models in which time is discrete can usually be reformulated* as a larger dimensional linear or nonlinear programming system by merely redefining the same variable at different time points as different variables. However, there are additionally two important reasons why the dynamic models must be given separate attention.

_____
* See for instance Sengupta and Fox (1969, pp. 115–18).

First, decisions taken at one point of time (e.g., investment expansion decisions) usually have intertemporal effects distributed over a future horizon. The system performance in this case is a function of both the state and decision variables over the entire future horizon. The dynamic analysis in this case is greatly facilitated by the application of control theory techniques. Second, an important characteristic of the activities of an educational system (e.g., an academic department within a university) is that activities are sequentially related over time (e.g., the products of activities such as teaching, research, and extension in one period largely go to feed the system in the next period as freshmen become sophomores, sophomores become juniors, and so on). Hence, in planning the expansion of such a system a relevant approach may be to examine how the activities within the system or department should be organized in order to keep pace with the growing demands placed on faculty resources by the inflow of students and other diversified needs.

It would be necessary in this case to know the requirements of the system or department if it is to grow over time while maintaining the same technological coefficients, describing the input-output relationships for different activities, as at present. In particular, the policymaker (e.g., the dean or the departmental chairman) may be interested in knowing the potential capacity for growth of the system or the department under the given circumstances. Von Neumann had questions basically of the same kind in mind when he formulated his model of balanced growth for an economy. His model has been extended and opened in several directions (Kemeny et al. 1956; Morishima 1969) in recent times. The policy question is whether his approach of balanced and optimal growth can be usefully applied in the partial equilibrium framework of planning an educational system. If the answer to this question is affirmative, then one can suggest a decentralization interpretation of the von Neumann model using the von Neumann prices as signals for optimal resource allocation over time. However, there remain in our opinion a great many operational problems to be solved before the concept of a von Neumann type intertemporal path can be meaningfully applied to problems of educational planning.

Hence, we shall restrict ourselves here to only that class of problems which can be described by the following optimal control problem:

$$\text{maximize} \int_{t_0}^{t_1} f(x,u,t)dt \tag{22a}$$

subject to $x(t_0) = x_0; x(t_1) = x_1,$ (22b)

$$\frac{dx}{dt} = G(x,u,t), \tag{22c}$$

and $\quad R(x,u,t) \leq 0 \quad$ (22d)

$(x = n \cdot 1; u = m \cdot 1; G = n \cdot 1; R = r \cdot 1.)$.

It is known (Kumar 1969) that under certain regularity conditions there exists an optimal solution to this problem. Associated with this problem (22) one can define a dual control problem:

$$\text{minimize} \int_{t_0}^{t_1} \left\{ f(x,u,t) - \lambda'(t) \left[ G(x,u,t) - \frac{dx}{dt} \right] - \mu'(t) R(x,u,t) \right\} dt \quad (23a)$$

subject to $x(t_0) = x_0; x(t_1) = x_1,$ (23b)

$$-f_x(x,u,t) + \lambda'(t) G_x(x,u,t) + \mu'(t) R_x(x,u,t) = d\lambda/dt, \quad (23c)$$

$$f_u(x,u,t) - \lambda(t) G_u(x,u,t) - \mu(t) R_u(x,u,t) = 0, \quad (23d)$$

$$\mu(t) \geq 0, \quad (23e)$$

where a function suffixed by a variable denotes the gradient (if it is a scalar function) or the Hessian (if it is a vector function); $\lambda(t) = n \cdot 1$; and $\mu(t) = r \cdot 1$.

Noting that $\mu(t)$ and $\lambda(t)$ are the marginal value imputations associated with the constraints (22c) and (22d) and the form of the dual objective function (23a), it is not difficult to see that the dual problem can be interpreted as the problem of minimizing the time stream of economic rents.

Under the further assumptions that $f(x,u,t)$ is concave in $x$ and $u$, $G(x,u,t)$ is concave in $x$ and $u$; $R(x,u,t)$ is convex in $x$ and $u$, and that their components $R_i(x,u,t)$ satisfy a certain constraint qualification, Mond and Hanson (1968) proved the following duality theorem on control:

If $(x^*,u^*)$ is an optimal solution of (22), then there exist functions $\lambda(t)$ and $\mu(t)$, such that $x^*(t), u^*(t), \lambda(t), \mu(t)$ is an optimal solution of (23) and the extreme values (i.e., pay-offs) of (22) and (23) are equal.

There are several problems that can be solved by means of condition (23d) and the differential equations (22c) and (23c) (i.e., using Pontryagin's maximum principle). For solving other more difficult problems one can use some of the computational techniques developed to solve optimal control problems.

As an illustration, consider the following generalization (similar to El-Hodiri's model [1966]) of the macroeducational planning problem. Suppose that the objective of the program is to maximize the discounted stream of total income benefits that accrue to the various occupational groups whose occupations require specific educational training. Suppose that we consider the stream of benefits during a particular horizon $[t_0, t_1]$. The salary structure for each occupation may be assumed to be a downward sloping function of the total number available for work under that occupational category.

Let $x_i^k(t)$ denote the number available for work in period $t$ in the occupational category $i$ who had their training from region $k$ or in an educational institution labeled $k$. Let $y_i^k(t)$ be the number of people trained for occupational category $i$ during the period $t$ by the production unit $k$. We can then write the change in stock for unit $k$ and category $i$ as:

$$\frac{dx_i^k}{dt} = (1 - \alpha_i^k)y_i^k - \beta_i^k x_i^k(t),$$

where $0 < \alpha_i^k < 1$ and $\alpha_i^k$ denotes the fraction of trained persons of period $t$ who do not enter the labor force (for example, this fraction includes those who seek more advanced training to move to a higher occupational category) and $\beta_i^k x_i^k$ denotes the number of people in occupational category $i$, trained at unit $k$ (from period 0 to $t$) who leave the labor force (for example, this number includes those who either die or retire from service).

Let $u_{ji}^k(t)$ denote the amount of resource $j$ used in period $t$ for producing $y_i^k(t)$ in production unit $k$. The production functions relating $y_i^k(t)$ to $u_{ji}^k(t)$ can be written as:

$$y_i^k(t) = f_i^k(u_{0i}^k(t), t), \tag{24}$$

where $u_{0i}^k(t) = (u_{1i}^k(t), \ldots, u_{ji}^k(t), \ldots, u_{m+m_k,i}^k(t))$.

Each educational institution labeled $k$ employs $m$ joint resources (resources commonly shared by more than one educational institution of the economy), and $m_k$ resources that are specific to that particular unit. We assume that the functions $f_i^k$ are continuous and have continuous second-order partial derivatives, monotone increasing, and concave.

Let $\bar{b}_j(t)$ denote the amount of joint resources available in period $t$ for $j = 1, 2, \ldots, m$; and let $b_j^k(t)$ denote the amount of the $j$th resource available for the educational institution labeled $k$. We assume the following demand functions describing the salary structures:

$$s_i(t) = a_i + b_i X_i(t) \qquad (b_i < 0), \tag{25}$$

where $X_i = \sum_{k=1}^{K} x_i^k$ (we are assuming that no [regional] salary differentials exist for the same occupational category).

The over-all educational planning problem can now be written as:

$$\text{maximize} \int_{t_0}^{t_i} e^{-rt} \sum_{i=1}^{n} (a_i + b_i X_i(t)) X_i(t) dt \tag{26a}$$

$$\text{subject to } x_i^k(t_0) = x_{i0}^k;\ x_i^k(t_1) = x_{i1}^k \tag{26b}$$

$$\text{for } i = 1, \ldots, n,$$

$$\frac{dx_i^k(t)}{dt} = (1 - \alpha_i^k) f_i^k(u_{0i}(t), t) - \beta_i^k x_i^k(t) \tag{26c}$$

$$\text{for } i = 1, \ldots, n,$$

$$\sum_{k=1}^{K} \sum_{i=1}^{n} u_{ji}^k(t) \leq \bar{b}_j(t) \qquad \text{for } j = 1, \ldots, m, \tag{26d}$$

$$\sum_{i=1}^{n} u_{ji}^k(t) \leq b_j^k(t) \qquad \text{for } j = m+1, \ldots, m+m_k \tag{26e}$$

$$\text{and for } k = 1, \ldots, K,$$

$$u_{ji}^k(t) \geq 0. \tag{26f}$$

This problem is in precisely the form in which we formulated the optimal control problem in (22). Even if the end points are not fixed (refer to the second condition in [22b] or [26b]) the above approach is applicable with a few modifications. Instead of the end condition we will have a set of relations to be satisfied by the end point $x(t_1)$ in (22). These end-point relations in the primal introduce a set of transversality conditions to be added to the dual problem formulation.*

Dynamic formulations, such as the above, can be solved by a double decomposition method. As the "maximum principle" of Pontryagin (1962) or the "optimality principle" of Bellman (1957) show, the dynamic problem can be replaced by a set of static problems, one optimization problem for each time period $t$. Within each time period we can use the decomposition methods we described in the previous sections. The iterative methods of computing an optimal control suggest one level of decomposition (over time). The iterative methods for solving each static problem constitute the second level of decomposition (Pearson 1966).

It should be mentioned, however, that the control theory approach has several other interesting aspects which have been applied to various problems of planning educational systems (Fox and Sengupta 1968,

---

* Refer to the standard literature such as Pontryagin et al. (1962) or Berkovitz (1961) for more details on these transversality conditions.

Sengupta and Fox 1970), although these are not discussed here. We may briefly refer in this connection to some interesting empirical applications (Plessner et al. 1968; Fox et al. 1969) of a linear activity analysis model of optimal allocation of resources in a university department. Although the model is static and linear, there are two essential dynamic ingredients in the model which could be utilized to formulate a dynamic control problem. First, the coefficients $c_j$ associated with output-like activities $x_j$ are derived from net discounted lifetime earnings of the recipients of degrees, i.e.:

$$c_j = R_j \frac{(1+r)^{n_j-k_j} - 1}{r(1+r)^{n_j-1}} - F_j \frac{(1+r)^{m_j-k_j} - 1}{r(1+r)^{m_j-1}},$$

where

$R_j$ = starting annual salary
$F_j$ = annual income foregone
$r$ = interest rate assumed exogenous
$k_j$ = years elapsed from the start of the program to the year of admission
$n_j$ = expected worklife plus $k_j$ and
$m_j$ = $n_j$ + years of study.

Note that from the viewpoint of the policymaker, who in this case is the departmental chairman, the growth of the vector $(dx/dt)$ of output-like activities $x_j(t)$ may be viewed as a function of the initial inputs or activities and the instruments or the policy vector $u(t)$ available to him in terms of budgetary support for teaching and research, reallocation of teaching load, and faculty man-hours between courses, etc., hence, a dynamic relationship may be postulated as a function:*

$$dx/dt = f(x(t), u(t)),$$

where naturally there will be constraints on $u(t)$ and even $x(t)$. One natural way the static objective function $c'x$ may be modified now is as follows:

$$\text{maximize } J = \lambda(x(\tau)) + \int_0^\tau \left[ e^{-st} \sum_{j=1}^n c_j(t) x_j(t) \right] dt,$$

where the scalar function $\lambda(x(\tau))$ may represent the implicit worth of attaining the desired terminal activity levels and the integral the capital-

---

* A view that such a formulation would be highly nonlinear and complicated for an entire university comprising many academic departments and that for that reason the concept of optimization would be very difficult to apply has been held by some authors, e.g., Keeney et al. (1967).

ized value of net benefits of all the services produced by the academic department under various static and dynamic restrictions. For such a control model, not only the optimum control is of great interest but also the feedback and other feasible controls (e.g., a feedback control selects $u(t)$ as a function of the current $x(t)$ state and it need not optimize a performance criterion).

A second aspect of the above resource allocation model is the treatment of problems posed by fixed and semifixed resources in a linear activity analysis model. This aspect will be referred to later in Chapter 6.

## Economic implications of applying decomposition techniques to educational and other systems*

Our analyses of several decomposition techniques of resource allocation have so far assumed the existence of a mathematical model and its solutions for the system being considered; also the dynamic considerations introduced into the model formulation are highly abstract and in particular they neglect the uncertainty and unforeseen changes which occur in real-life situations. In this section we indicate very briefly some of the basic difficulties of modeling, implementing, and evaluating the decomposition methods of decentralized decisionmaking, particularly under the realistic environment of educational or other systems which incorporate the characteristics of a quasi market and internal market described before in Chapter 4.

From an economic viewpoint there are three basic points common to the various methods of linear and nonlinear decomposition discussed before. First, there is a classification in levels of decisionmaking (i.e., hierarchy of decision stages) between the center (e.g., the firm as a whole) and the sectors (e.g., the divisions of a firm) for example, mainly through resources, part of which are specific to sectors only, while the remainder allocated by the center are resources common to all sectors. The concept of decentralization here implies that the sectors should be allowed complete freedom of choice in their optimization problems, except that the center provides co-ordination through guiding rules of price imputation based on the marginal productivities of common central resources. This stage of decentralization may be unworkable for several institutional reasons, e.g., (a) the anonymity of the prices declared by the center may fail, due to lack of a proper transmission of information flows; (b) those externalities not internalized in the institutional model may provide

---

\* This section is based on some notes prepared by J. K. Sengupta and partly summarized in Sengupta (1971a).

potential threats which may stifle the competitive spirit between sectors; and (c) indivisibility of some resources may prevent computation of marginal productivities.

Second, the formulation of guiding rules of adjustment by the center (e.g., price adjustment) should be such that in successive applications or iterations they specify a feasible and sequentially improving optimizing direction converging to the over-all optimum. Since these guiding rules are generally based on marginal productivities of some sort, they may be unworkable due to (a) the presence of significant indivisibilities and externalities of demand and supply; (b) the existence of significant scale economies or diseconomies in some sectors; and (c) the fact that the sectoral constraints may not be mutually consistent along the computational path. Of these, the role of indivisible components in the resource, the constraints, and the objective function is of utmost importance (although some types of indivisibility can be characterized by integer programming, there is some need here for specifying the implications of decomposition* in this context).

Third, the decomposition techniques reflect sectoral (or divisional) interdependence in the competition by each sector for higher allocations of the central resources whenever feasible; however, the desire of each sector to get higher allocations is unlikely to be realized after some iterations for at least some sectors, since the guiding rule of the center is to allocate to the highest bidder, when each sectoral bid is in terms of its marginal contribution to the over-all objective function. The competitive mechanism assumed here must be defined in terms of a hypothetical *tâtonnement* process, without any real transactions taking place, since otherwise this bidding mechanism disregards the various institutional rigidities in a system which prevents these experimental trial and error adjustments. For realism there is some need at this stage to analyze non*tâtonnement* adjustment processes which emphasize both prices (equilibrium and nonequilibrium) and the resource distributions between sectors. In a partial equilibrium set-up, when the number of sectors or divisions is few and the center is on the whole dominant, another basic question is whether there is any economic rationale for imputing a *tâtonnement*-type competitive mechanism, which disregards "fewness" and the fact that sectoral sovereignty is replaced by the central sovereignty. For an educational system (e.g., an institution of higher education) this question, which affects the whole question of freedom and

* Some recent attempts in this direction, which supplement the price-adjustment process by quota-allocation methods under the presence of increasing returns are available (Aoki 1971).

flexibility in the academic environment, is of fundamental concern for the entire community and society.

*Problems of modeling*

The modern proponents of decentralized resource allocation mechanisms (Hurwicz 1960) using decomposition-type techniques are quite aware of the type of environment required for the method to work, and they generally restrict the *tâtonnement*-type adjustment process to the system which is informationally decentralized, a term due to Hurwicz. The two requirements of informational decentralization are that there exists a rule for adjustment processes (through price or output changes) which is operational and that there is anonymity in the application of the rule so far as information flows are concerned.

Even excluding the role of sizable indivisibilities, externalities and scale economies (or diseconomies), the requirements of operationalism may not be fully satisfied for a system such as an academic institution, unless its resources, both physical and human, which are used to produce outputs and services can be quantified in terms of dollars and/or related economic quantities. If this quantification is done through imputation, then the question remains: Whose imputation is the most appropriate? If in a group of multiple policymakers a method for deriving an appropriate imputation method is evolved, as was suggested for example by van Eijk and Sandee's (1959) "imaginary interviewing," then the basis for the center's objective function has to be quantified and made compatible with those of other policymakers. Alternatively, the quantification may be done through analyzing the impact of national markets on the prices of some of the inputs and outputs of the educational system, but the most serious shortcoming of this approach is that it lacks a clear-cut objective relationship between the educational system and the market, at least in a partial equilibrium framework. University systems do not usually follow a full cost-pricing principle for their services, the market returns to degree outputs (e.g., market values of B.S., M.S., or Ph.D. degrees) are only very partially, if at all, returned to the universities, and state support and budget grants by legislatures are not always guided by the quality and quantity of the universities' performance.

Two types of economic reasoning may be advanced for supplementing the various decentralization methods and thereby building the basic ingredients of a theory of resource allocation for university systems. First, one may recognize that most of the outputs produced by a university system are in the nature of public goods, where potential demand may be as important as observed demand at any given point of time. In this view the market can reflect only a part of the value of the output generated by the university system. The quality of performance of a university may far exceed (or fall short of) the total market value of all its outputs, depending on the quality and performance of the students (and others) trained. A profit-oriented market system tends always to discourage the supply of public goods relative to private goods; also it fails to charge the producers for their external diseconomies (e.g., pollution and wastes). As a supplier of public goods, a university system need not be guided by profit motives, and in its job of knowledge creation, distribution, and utilization it should be concerned with broad economic and social goals of the present and future generations. One could still, we believe, develop a theory of efficient allocation of resources for the supply of public goods and apply the decomposition methods of decentralization; however, this requires the assumption or imputation of a social welfare function, as is frequently done in recent times in the Ramsay-type models of optimum growth (Cass and Yaari 1967). A second approach, different from the theory of public goods, would concentrate on the rationale of budget grants and state subsidies to the university system and point out its role as distributional equalizer. A democratic system of education provides a mechanism for allocation of economic power, since knowledge is power and its effective uses can be learned and disseminated among the community at large. The idea of a negative income tax related to basic educational needs may be as strong as that related to basic subsistence needs. This calls for a very different type of decentralization than has so far been discussed.

*Framework of implementation*

There are several basic problems which arise when one has to implement the framework of adjustment processes through decentralized methods of decomposition. First, the Lagrange multipliers interpreted as shadow prices at appropriate stages of a *tâtonnement* process are generally nonanalytic, in the sense that in static programming problems they can be computed only for given numerical problems; methods of parametric programming which exist are not yet very general, in the sense that comparison theorems for arbitrary programming problems are yet unavailable. When the marginal productivity of a resource is known not uniquely but within a range, what kinds of pricing rules are needed to sustain a method of decentralization? What are the criteria for the robustness of an optimal solution or an optimal set? Some of these questions can be partially answered in the control theory framework of a dynamic model, but when applied to an educational system in a partial equilibrium set-up, the most difficult problem is to characterize the resources which are semifixed or inflexible in the short run and to distinguish between capital goods and noncapital goods. To treat capital goods as bundles of service flows may provide a workable mechanism in a model of general equilibrium, but in the partial equilibrium set-up of a university system this is not very operational. Also, a fixed factor which is surplus in the short run (having, therefore, a zero shadow price in a static programming model) may not be so in the long run; hence the short-run and long-run needs of resource adjustment and expansion may be conflicting for an educational system. Since the long run is based on expectations and at times the past experiences of not all expectations being fulfilled, there is more need to allow slack resources in the system with potentials for somewhat uncertain changes in demand and for incompatibilities and conflicts between the short- and long-run goals.

Second, the information flows required by the decomposition algorithms are not only very specific and anonymous, but their costs are completely disregarded. The role of costs (both static and dynamic) associated with transmission of information flows has been emphasized by Tinbergen (1967) and others very strongly, particularly in relation to the institutional decisionmaking processes. Sometimes these costs can be avoided in practice by aggregative methods of planning and sometimes there are definite scale economies in these costs which could be utilized under a central co-ordinating mechanism. A decision on the most useful type and quality of information and its decentralization should precede any decomposition-type accounting procedure. This again requires institutional and organizational changes of a certain type which should not be taken for granted.

Third, if the model specification is not completely quantitative, since it may have imputed values and quality factors for its resources, it may be more realistic in some situations to analyze the costs of adjustment due to disequilibrium conditions of various sorts (i.e., supply-demand gap) and if possible to incorporate some of these costs in the decomposition algorithms. Mathematically speaking, the effects of some of these costs may be merely to truncate the convergence of the decomposition algorithms. An explicit allowance in the framework of model specification would be much more appealing from the viewpoint of institutional decisionmaking.

*Problems of evaluation*

The evaluation of alternative methods of decomposition and decentralization under a given institutional setting (e.g., an educational system) becomes a much more difficult problem due to the presence of elements such as indivisibility, externalities, and returns to scale which generally are not quite compatible with marginal cost pricing theory, unless special assumptions (e.g., a two-part pricing system) are introduced.

In the framework of our discussion in earlier sections, it remains however to mention the following basic problems which yet remain unsolved, in our opinion. These problems can be classified into three groups: (a) computational; (b) practical (from the viewpoint of firm management decisions); and (c) theoretical (from the viewpoint of the economic theory of resource allocation).

First, there are two basic computational problems in applying the decomposition or aggregation algorithms: (i) the relative costs of computation of alternative methods of decomposition and aggregation in LP models have never been actually compared (or its theory developed) although certain principles of comparison are available (Zoutendijk 1960) and (ii) the game theory methods of solving for coalitions of all orders, from one division coalition to higher order coalitions, which may be applied to resource and activity aggregation in LP models and some nonlinear models also, need to be explored and evaluated from an economic standpoint.

Second, from the practical viewpoint of a divisionalized firm there remain at least three basic types of problems to be solved, before the rules of co-ordination laid down by different decomposition and aggregation algorithms are accepted and implemented by the different divisions:

i) The rules of transfer pricing in decomposition algorithms are essentially designed to reallocate resources more productively and profitably from the viewpoint of the firm as a whole, particularly when there is interdependence in cost and demand between different divisions. The presence of joint costs, quasi-fixed resources and mild indivisibility of various sorts (e.g., qualitative structure of resources and of flexibility in cost structure in the multiproduct, multiprocess, and multidivision firm [Morris 1968]) has a tendency to make the specification of resource restrictions in terms of linear inequalities much less precise and quantitative than desired. Hence the rules of transfer pricing are always subject to challenge, since the competitive framework is only hypothetical, invented in the account book of the center.

ii) The risks of executive failure in a division or the feeling of this risk on the part of the divisional management when a division has to sell (i.e., transfer) a resource to another division internally at a marginal cost price below its average costs may induce biased and exaggerated reporting of marginal productivities to the center by different divisions.

This may even destroy the neutral competitive behavior of the divisions and the center altogether (Hirshleifer 1964); some historical cases are also available in the framework of economic planning in the socialist countries, which tend to confirm this tendency.

iii) The economic dictum that division of labor is limited by the size of the market does not easily carry over to the divisionalized firm model, since the internal market with internal prices (i.e., transfer prices) which the central management of the firm creates does not have (a) the conditions of free entry and free exit; (b) perfect information and knowledge of the consequences of deviating from the so-called internal prices; and (c) the conditions of quantity and price adjustment as in a perfectly competitive market, and hence the question of how much divisionalization remains (Dean 1955; Williamson 1964). A practical compromise between integration and divisionalization depends of course on the possibility of determining what may be called the optimum degree of divisions into which the firm has to be decomposed.

Third, from an economic viewpoint the question of resource or activity aggregation or decomposition raises at least two basic questions:

i) By what criteria can one compare an external market with actual prices faced by a firm and an internal market (comprising the same firm's different divisions) with its hypothetical internal prices? In particular, how real and identifiable are the *tâtonnement* processes from the non*tâtonnement* processes? The economic implications of the latter need much closer investigation in the framework of the theory of decomposition, divisionalization, and aggregation.

ii) The standard decomposition methods start from a given output or activity system and then develop a sequential (shadow) price system which in effect sustains an optimal output system. It seems, one may as well start from a given price (i.e., standard costs) system and then develop a sequential (shadow) output system which could in effect realize an optimal price system. A third method would be to start from a primal-dual system (i.e., a mixed output-price subsystem) and then develop sequential algorithms in terms of both (shadow) prices and (shadow) outputs. The economic implications of these alternatives remain yet to be explored, compared, and evaluated, particularly in partial equilibrium frameworks.

CHAPTER 6

# Economic Problems of Resource Allocation in Nonmarket Systems

Jati K. Sengupta

**General remarks**

The economy of a nonmarket system appears to be characterized in our view by the modification or partial replacement of those three essential ingredients which describe a market system, e.g., use of price signals, the rules of exchange, and the concept of an equilibrium or disequilibrium in a market or system of markets. In the framework of a competitive market model for homogeneous goods, discussed in earlier chapters, we referred to the implications of the rule of anonymity of market prices, their deviations from the equilibrium, and the fact that under suitable assumptions about consumer and producer behavior patterns the market equilibrium may also represent an optimum system of allocation of resources. However, in the real world the competitive model does not hold throughout any economy; even in a partial equilibrium set-up in which the price-guided methods of decomposition are conceivable and a Walrasian type *tâtonnement* process is considered useful, competitive models require a behavioristic interpretation of prices, the various adjustments, and the implicit notion of optimization behind an equilibrium.

Two kinds of goods which are highly important in our economic lives may not be amenable to such interpretations by a competitive model. One of them is public goods, for which markets as conceived in the competitive model do not exist in most cases. The services of the government sector in large part and the goods and services produced within and by the educational system are important examples. A second kind of good may be called the *prospects* of future goods and services, which are by their nature uncertain as viewed at present. For some private goods, futures markets exist and decisionmakers have the option of hedging against the uncertainty of their availability; in some other cases in which risks are insurable, insurance markets exist and in both of these types of markets competitive elements may be traced. However, for a large number of goods and services such markets for contingent goods do not exist in the present institutional framework, and hence the identification of potential buyers and sellers of such contingent goods and a Walrasian *tâtonnement* process of exchange between present and contingent goods appears impossible.

This point about the nonexistence of markets for contingent goods has raised two very basic questions about the meaningful interpretation of the Arrow–Debreu-type competitive model (Debreu 1959; Morishima 1964) which under certain interpretations of competitive consumer and entrepreneurial choice patterns led to stability and optimality of competitive equilibrium. First, the category of contingent goods for which institutional markets do not exist may not only thwart the rule of anonymity of prices for such goods but it may also lead under certain situations to non-*tâtonnement* types of adjustment, not all of which may be stabilizing. This destabilizing tendency (Stigum 1969; Hahn and Negishi 1962; Hahn 1966) may also be due in part to the relative dominance of risk-taking behavior over that of risk-aversion among the participants of the competitive system. Second, imperfections in the transmission of information flows and limitations in the computing capacities of participants in the competitive system raise serious doubts (Radner 1968) about the meaningfulness and practical generality of the notion of general equilibrium. One implication of this result is that truncations in the Walrasian-type adjustment processes are more likely than not and hence the world of partial equilibrium and the theories of second best should really provide the central focus of our attention.

The history and practice of national planning for investment and growth (Feinstein 1967; Grossman 1960) particularly in socialist economies (Zielinski 1968) have brought to the fore some of the basic problems of both centralized and decentralized planning. Two such problems relevant for our later discussion are due to the presence of indivisibilities in resource structure represented by fixed and semifixed resources such as capital, and the existence of inconsistencies and hence infeasibility in sectoral constraints and policies. It has been recently pointed out by a number of authors (Ellman 1969) that aggregative planning (i.e., resource allocation procedures based on aggregative variables rather than their disaggregative counterparts) has been practiced in most cases as a compromise measure, since it is practically impossible in disaggregative planning to ensure feasibility and mutual consistency. The use of various prices, shadow-price or otherwise, has also been replaced by other directives in the form of output quotas and lump sum transfers, which usually are not of the Walrasian *tâtonnement* variety (Portes 1969).

The role of indivisibility in the form of fixed and semifixed resources is not satisfactorily treated either in the theory of the firm or in that of over-all economic growth. The usual treatment of an indivisible resource, which is of course the least satisfactory, is to assume that an indivisible resource (e.g., a certain type of capital) is representable by an appropriate and equivalent bundle of service flows over time, such that the flows at any given time maintain the usual diminishing marginal productivity requirements; a similar attempt is to assume that the short-run decision problem can be separated from the long-run one in such a way that the latter, which involves fixed resources as decision variables, specifies the problem of optimal expansion of capacity; given an optimal capacity, the short-run resource-allocation problem merely concerns itself with variable resources to which marginal cost pricing principles can be easily applied.

In this view, however, there are two basic problems. First, even in the short run the rate of utilization of fixed resources can be varied, and to that extent marginal costs could include the costs of utilization (e.g. user costs [Keynes 1936]) and their variations. Second, the marginal cost pricing rule would imply a zero shadow price for any resource which is surplus relative to its optimal requirement. This is sometimes referred to as a competitive pricing mechanism. However, since a surplus resource could be imputed a fixed (and positive) shadow price by the decision-maker (e.g., by forcing it into the solution), the element (Nikaido 1964) in the shadow price can be built into the solution by the decision process (or through a budgeting procedure [Morris 1968]). These and other broad questions will be raised in the following sections in the framework of resource allocation in educational systems in particular and in non-market systems in general.

### Problems of imputation in benefit-cost analysis for public goods

The object of this section is to discuss some analytical problems related to the specification of optimality of resource allocation in educational systems, where part of the outputs produced are in the form of public goods, such that the potential value of "option demand" for some research and teaching activities may generate various nonmarket external economies through diffusion of knowledge beyond the confines of the educational system.

Consider a specific case, e.g., the degree output produced by a university. The returns to a specific degree such as the Ph.D. can be estimated as an average of discounted career incomes for that specialty (Plessner et al. 1968) although this may sometimes be a very crude estimate; similarly, the average gestation period for an average Ph.D. degree in a certain specialty and the average costs of tuition and living expenses would provide crude estimates of the costs of generating an average Ph.D.-type output. In both these cases there may arise two types of externalities which are neglected in the above cost-return estimates. These two externalities are basically similar to the two generic types discussed by Meade (1952) as the cases of "unpaid factors of production" and "the creation of atmosphere."

The first case arises when the various services of research and teaching by faculty that go into the making of a unit of degree output (e.g., one Ph.D.) are not charged at full cost, since tuition and other direct costs would cover only a fraction of the total; it follows, therefore, that if through state and private subsidies to the university the quality of its teaching and research services improves, with no corresponding effect on tuition and other direct costs charged to the students, there will exist an external economy in the system which could be internalized by institutional innovations, since for the system as a whole all economies external to the students are internal to the system. The same reasoning would apply to an external diseconomy. The second case arises when the creation of research and degree outputs helps in the process of spreading and generating new technology throughout the various segments of the over-all economy; only a fraction of the social pay-offs may return to the university system in the form of increased state and private subsidies from a community of improved quality.

In a very aggregative framework in which the education sector is viewed as one sector producing all forms of skilled manpower demanded by the second sector which comprises the whole economy in its industrial subsectors, we have a simple two-sector interdependence which may or may not be internalized by the two sectors independently. For instance, if the quality and efficiency of the first sector improved with no change in the market price, the second sector would obtain an extra benefit due to unpaid factors of production in the first sector. Again, some of the research done in the education sector may ultimately help improve the functioning rules and efficiency of the second sector insofar as the over-all economic goals of the society are concerned. This would then amount to an interdependence through creation and improvement of over-all atmosphere, which of course cannot ordinarily be internalized, and it may be far less meaningful to think of a pricing strategy to internalize it.

For a specific empirical illustration we consider a typical academic department in a moderate-sized university and ask how its resource allocation pattern can be evaluated when the objective function is only partially known or estimable. Imperfect knowledge of the coefficients of the objective function may be due to several factors, e.g., absence of explicit market prices, multiple policymakers, and differences in their relative weights. Attempts at imputation of prices for the objective function may be approached from two alternative standpoints, i.e., from the viewpoint of a policymaker (Plessner et al. 1968) and that of an imaginary interviewer (van Eijk and Sandee 1959).

The first approach views the problem of resource allocation in education from the standpoint of a department chairman (or the dean). The need for a departmental policy model, of course, varies with variations in the superstructure of the university and the various constraints. The program of any university, for instance, should be responsive to the state of the world, the state of science, the state of the labor market for graduates, and possibly to the economic condition of the state, if it is state-supported. These four sets of data, external to the university, are not ordinarily specified in quantitative form. Nevertheless, we believe they are researchable and should be explored, first with reasonable and imputed values of the policymaker's objective function and then with improved information through market trends and constraints. Logically, then, these data provide constraints on the set of alternatives over which the university's objective may be optimized. An empirical application and the economic implications of this approach are discussed in some detail in Plessner et al. (1968). This approach is easily extendable to a set of departments within a university, although in the latter case the problems of decomposition of multiple decision processes would provide more interesting challenges.

The second approach assumes that the basic ingredients of a resource allocation model, e.g., input-output relations and the various technical and policy constraints and boundary conditions, are already available in a consistent quantitative form and then it explores the implications of cost-based prices in a linear objective function and other subjective estimates of the objective function, as if these estimates were potentially available through imaginary interviewing. Like the hypothetical schemes of compensation in the various welfare criteria of welfare economics, these provide hypothetical sets of optimal solutions, which are then compared under alternative conditions of payments for the fixed and the semifixed resources that may be indivisible in some sense. The transition from a consistency model to an optimization model is greatly facilitated by the fact that the former is considered to be linear and in some sense parametric. It is presumed that such a consistency model of the activity analysis type can be built up from the input-output relations and other observed feasible decisions characterizing a given academic department (or a set of such departments). An example of such a model for Y-department is shown in Table 6.1, page 158.

The very construction of a consistency model may of course require alternative, and often approximate, calculation of several intended outputs and the required input costs, e.g., the faculty time required for committee work and various professional activities other than teaching and research. The policy problem is how to develop a tangible framework for evaluating alternative resource allocation patterns. Such evaluation would include, for example, estimating the relative costs of transfer of resources, such as faculty time between activities, particularly when externalities and complementarities prevail.

Several lines of attack on this policy problem may be suggested. First, in the absence of significant indivisibilities one may start by imputing prices for those inputs and outputs which do not have a clear-cut market framework. These imputed prices (e.g., a specified percentage mark-up over variable cost) may be used, along with the market prices of other inputs and outputs, in order to construct a pseudo-objective function. The sensitivity of this pseudo-objective function to variations in imputed prices in the framework of the activity analysis model provides two kinds of useful signals: first, it leads to an ordering of the solutions and a divisionalized view of the dual pricing process (Hirshleifer 1957; Shubik 1962), which though tentative may be analyzed by the decomposition algorithms (Sengupta and Fox 1969); and second, it permits the discussion of alternative incentive schemes (or compensation mechanisms) to attain particular and therefore desired allocation patterns. For linear activity analysis models this type of pseudo-optimization is computable, and in this framework the presence of an otherwise indivisible resource may have to be evaluated as a real-life complexity. The problem of incorporating indivisibility of resources in a linear activity analysis model has not been satisfactorily solved in general, although some theoretical work is available for special situations (Hirshleifer 1957; Shubik 1962).

Second, the scheme of imputed prices may be used only as a benchmark for initiating other kinds of resource evaluating procedures. The various decomposition algorithms and decentralization techniques (Baumol and Fabian 1964) developed in recent times have made us aware of the importance of two-stage planning procedures; it is now known that a linear activity analysis model may sometimes be interpreted as a competitive market model (Arrow and Hurwicz 1960), and in that case a specific objective function may indeed be unnecessary. We may require instead a method of estimating penalty costs for not satisfying some demand-supply constraints. In cases in which the concepts of tolerance measures or safety levels are applicable, the imposition of penalty costs could be studied usefully through methods of chance-constrained and two-stage programming, but even in deterministic cases it is useful to consider the ranking of different facets of the objective function according to their importance for the departmental goals. These ranking indices would then have to be incorporated in some sense in the resource allocation mechanism.

A simple computable method of incorporating this idea in the framework of an activity analysis model would be to identify the two categories of activities $x_A$ and $x_B$, where $x_A$ denotes current activities and $x_B$ those activities which are related to capacity measures or constraints of the environment, so to speak. If the analogy of the theory of the firm holds, then $x_B$ would involve costs associated with the plant, i.e., the mix of fixed and semifixed resources which are assumed given for the $x_A$ activities.

The accounting allocation of the so-called overhead costs needs a more careful analysis in educational resource allocation procedures, particularly with regard to its impact on the shadow prices of other current activities $x_A$ and resources. Sometimes the activities in $x_B$ could be related to decisions undertaken at a higher level of the administrative hierarchy (e.g., the dean's decisions may be based on $x_B$ activities, whereas a particular department chairman may be concerned with $x_A$ activities). If it is a fact that costs related to $x_A$ may be partially separable from those related to $x_B$, a two-stage decomposition process may show the implications of input-output interdependence among several departments.

Third, one may mention the method of setting desired output values as targets and then computing in some sense the implicit costs of deviations (van den Bogaard and Theil 1959) from these targets. If the targets are parametrically varied and satisfy the feasibility conditions derived from a consistency model, then the way the target variation and substitution affects the solution structure would provide important information on the optimizing direction. In practical cases, when the rates of trade-off between different targets (and/or instruments) are not constant, this would involve at least a quadratic programming problem. Again, the decomposition algorithms based on shadow price-guided resource allocation should be useful; in particular, they permit us to set up an optimizing direction.

Our objective is to illustrate some of the above approaches toward specification of an objective function and to build an activity analysis model capable of ordering alternative feasible policies derived from what is otherwise a consistency model. We are not trying to identify an objective function which is perceived, though perhaps vaguely, by the policymakers; instead we are concerned with analyzing the implications of alternative *specifications* of the objective function (Simon 1959).

Our approach emphasizes the following operational aspects of departmental resource allocation. First, it is argued that accounting costs based on the departmental budget data would provide the starting point for estimating average activity-specific unit costs. Special attention is needed here for the treatment of fixed and semifixed resources, as in the theory of the multiproduct firm (Pfouts 1962). Second, it is assumed that the over-all performance of an academic department could be analyzed through two interrelated facets, the first based on the detailed set of activities in the department and the second on an aggregate measure. For instance, denote by $x_j (j = 1, \ldots, n)$ the $j$th activity in the first group (e.g., graduate teaching activity for a given class size), then an aggregate measure based on some or all of the outputs of different activities could be specified as:

$$x_T = \sum_j \alpha_j x_j / \sum_j \alpha_j. \tag{1}$$

Here the $\alpha_j$ are suitable normalization factors (weights). The normalization factors may be based partly on the accounting costs of relevant activities, based possibly on long-run objectives and trends, and partly on the imputations by the departmental chairman to reflect the desired targets. It is now assumed that the resource allocation cost $C(x_1, \ldots, x_n; x_T)$ can be decomposed into two parts, one related to the activity-specific individual costs

$$\left( \sum_j v_j x_j \right)$$

and the other dependent on the aggregate measure* $(G(x_T))$, i.e.:

$$C(x_1, \ldots, x_n; x_T) = \sum_j v_j x_j + G(x_T). \tag{2}$$

* Note that this aggregate measure could be the yardstick in terms of which the higher-level decisionmaking authority evaluates the performance of different activities of different academic departments.

Here the $v_j$'s ($j = 1, \ldots, n$) are the unit variable costs assumed constant, and the aggregate (scalar) cost function $G(x_T)$ may have to satisfy several conditions (e.g., increasing in the positive domain of $x_T$ and convex) for the existence of meaningful solutions.

This type of two-part cost function has been analyzed by Kornai and Lipták (1962) in their production model for a multiproduct firm. They showed that a set of indifferent prices $p_j$ can be developed by following the rule:

$$p_j = v_j + \beta; p_j > 0; j = 1, \ldots, n \ (\beta \text{ arbitrary constant}) \tag{3}$$

for a given aggregate output $x_T$ within a feasible program. The condition that the objective function be independent of the composition of activities in a given program (i.e., with a given $x_T$) leads to an indifferent system of prices, which however may not be unique (i.e., other sets of such prices can be constructed). This pricing rule may be more generally interpreted as a two-part pricing process, i.e.:

$$p_j = v_j + \beta_j; (j = 1, \ldots, n), \tag{4}$$

where the departmental policy is to fix the price of its output by adding a price margin $\beta_j$. The price margin must be so determined that it covers the over-all costs $G(x_T)$ and any other costs of resource adjustment that may be planned with a view to meeting increased student enrollment.

We hasten to add two cautions about this type of pricing process. First, we do not imply that it should necessarily be related to the profit-maximizing type of objective function. Second, the collective-good aspect (Frisch 1959; Buchanan 1966; Davis and Whinston 1967) of teaching and research activities must be explicitly introduced as an external economy from production of such services. In other words, these activities may be thought of as producing two types of outputs: services of an individual consumption sort to actual users and potential or option services of a collective-consumption sort to nonusers and potential users. The latter raises difficult problems for evolving a pricing scheme dependent on full cost principles. However, its explicit recognition makes us aware of the existence of externalities which are not very adequately treated in linear activity analysis-type programming models.

A third aspect of our analysis refers to the multiproduct model of a firm as a possible construct that may be relevant to the resource allocation problem within an academic department. Since the transfer prices used in decomposition algorithms refer to *tâtonnement* processes of a market framework, we have to examine the characteristics by which an internal price-based market differs from the common notion of a market framework.

*Structure of alternative illustrative models*

Our empirical analysis is based on the input-output data* of an academic department $X$ which assume enrollment projections for 1972–73, a projected salary structure for teaching and research personnel, and an estimate of other department plans and needs (Fox 1968). The input-output matrix assumes that if part of a faculty member's time is used up on nondepartmental assignments, some reduction in output is sustained in department $X$. The matrix can help us to estimate the nature and magnitude of the reduction in $X$-department outputs (a) without internal readjustments and (b) with the best internal readjustments that can be made with our remaining resources. The prices of outputs and inputs are used in a notional sense; some of the input costs are, however, directly related to the salary structure and average budget allocations for specific research or extension activities. Since the time inputs of students, extension audiences, and readers of faculty research publications are explicitly included in the matrix, we need not limit ourselves to optimizing department $X$'s outputs with respect only to inputs included in the university budget. Alternatively, we could consider the implications of trying to optimize gross benefits received by undergraduate and graduate students, subject only to the limits of their own time and learning capacity. An interesting feature of the matrix is its inclusion of several intermediate goods; for example, one intermediate good is the value of training gained by experience as a research assistant, the pay-off coming in terms of increased research output per man-year when the former research assistant becomes a dissertation-stage research associate.

In the illustrations which follow, we did not use the complete model of department $X$; instead we used a subdepartment $Y$ of department $X$, primarily for simplicity and lower computational costs. The input-output structure of subdepartment $Y$ (Table 6.1) is, however, directly derived from that of department $X$ and hence incorporates the basic assumptions of the latter.

The following four groups of linear programming (LP) models are considered: (a) problems P1 to P5, in which the implications of developing a set of net prices on the basis of individual activity-specific costs $v_j$ are analyzed; (b) problems P6 to P29, in which the implications of over-

---

* These data, including the complete input-output matrix, are not reproduced here because of space limitations (Fox et al. 1969).

Table 6.1. Basic data of the $Y$-subdepartment model[a]

| $p_j$: | 39.2 | 22.4 | 67.2 | 61.6 | 112.0 | 100.8 | 39.2 | 22.4 | 67.2 | 61.6 |
|---|---|---|---|---|---|---|---|---|---|---|
| $v_j$: | 16.416 | 14.68 | 31.224 | 31.096 | 60.8 | 59.74 | 16.416 | 14.68 | 31.224 | 31.096 |
| $c_j$: | 2.388 | 1.526 | 2.152 | 1.981 | 1.842 | 1.687 | 2.388 | 1.526 | 2.152 | 1.981 |
| ACTIVITY: | $x_1$ | $x_4$ | $x_5$ | $x_8$ | $x_{11}$ | $x_{13}$ | $x_{15}$ | $x_{18}$ | $x_{19}$ | $x_{22}$ |
| IDENTIFICATION | | | | | | | | | | |
| 1. Cr. 306 | 35 | 35 | 70 | 70 | 140 | 140 | | | | |
| 2. Cr. 405 | | | | | | | 35 | 35 | 70 | 70 |
| 3. Cr. 544 | | | | | | | | | | |
| 4. Cr. 545 | | | | | | | | | | |
| 5. Cr. 564 | | | | | | | | | | |
| 6. Et | | | | | | | | | | |
| 7. Edi | | | | | | | | | | |
| 8. MST | | | | | | | | | | |
| 9. DIS | | | | | | | | | | |
| 10. Pub-2 | | | | | | | | | | |
| 11. Pub-1 | | | | | | | | | | |
| 13. RCO | | | | | | | | | | |
| 14. P-2 | .083 | | .111 | .083 | .167 | .083 | .083 | | .111 | .083 |
| 17. I-1 | | .083 | | .083 | | .167 | | .083 | | .083 |
| 19. CPS-P-2 | .010 | | .013 | .010 | .020 | .010 | .010 | | .013 | .010 |
| 21. FDO-P-2 | .007 | | .009 | .007 | .013 | .007 | .007 | | .009 | .007 |
| 24. C-2 | | | | | | | | | | |
| 25. Su | 2.19 | 2.19 | 4.38 | 4.38 | 8.75 | 8.75 | 2.19 | 2.19 | 4.38 | 4.38 |
| 26. Sg | | | | | | | | | | |
| 27. St | | | | | | | | | | |
| 28. Sdi | | | | | | | | | | |
| 29. Rpub-2 | | | | | | | | | | |
| 30. Rpub-1 | | | | | | | | | | |
| 32. P-2 | | | | | | | | | | |

[a] Special assumptions about resource availabilities enabled us to delete 17 of the 38 activities and 9 of the 32 restrictions.

head and fixed resource allocation problems are investigated; (c) problems P30 to P35, in which the implications of transfer activities are discussed; and lastly (d) problems Q1 to Q8, in which the implications of a two-part division of costs into individual and aggregate costs are analyzed:

P1: max $\Sigma p_j x_j$ under $Ax \leq b; x \geq 0$
where $p_j$ = gross benefit (imputed) for activity $x_j$.

P2: max $\Sigma r_j x_j$ under $Ax \leq b; x \geq 0$
where $r_j = p_j/v_j$ = benefit/cost ratio for activity $x_j$.

P3: min $\Sigma v_j x_j$ under $Ax \leq b; x \geq 0$
where $v_j$ = gross estimated cost per unit of activity $x_j$.

P4: max $\Sigma \hat{a}_j v_j x_j$ under $Ax \leq b; x \geq 0$
where $p_j = (1 + \hat{a}_j)v_j$, $\hat{a}_j$ preassigned.

P5: max $\Sigma v_j x_j$ under $Ax \leq b; x \geq 0$
where $v_j$ = gross estimated cost per unit of $x_j$.

P6–P13: max $\Sigma p_j x_j/(F_0 + \Sigma v_j x_j)$ under $Ax \leq b, x \geq 0$
with $F_0$ = overhead cost = 0, 5, 10, 15, 20, 25, 50, 100 (in some units).

# RESOURCE ALLOCATION IN NONMARKET SYSTEMS 159

| 112.0 | 110.8 | 66.53 | 66.53 | 44.36 | 8.9 | 16.75 | 35.6 | 5.0 | 5.0 | — | |
|---|---|---|---|---|---|---|---|---|---|---|---|
| 60.8 | 59.736 | 38.4 | 38.4 | 26.41 | 6.216 | 10.678 | 17.232 | 3.992 | 3.033 | — | |
| 1.842 | 1.687 | 1.733 | 1.733 | 1.811 | 1.432 | 1.569 | 2.066 | 1.253 | 1.649 | — | |
| $x_{25}$ | $x_{27}$ | $x_{29}$ | $x_{30}$ | $x_{31}$ | $x_{32}$ | $x_{33}$ | $x_{34}$ | $x_{36}$ | $x_{37}$ | $x_{38}$ | b |
| | | | | | | | | | | | = 210 |
| 140 | 140 | | | | | | | | | | = 280 |
| | | 30 | | | | | | | | | = 30 |
| | | | 30 | | | | | | | | = 30 |
| | | | | 20 | | | | | | | = 20 |
| | | | | | 4 | 4 | | | | | ≤ 8 |
| | | | | | | | 8 | | | | ≤ 32 |
| | | | | | 1 | 1 | | | | | ≥ 0 |
| | | | | | | | 1 | | | | ≥ 0 |
| | | | | | | | | 1 | 1 | | ≥ 0 |
| | | | | | | 1.57 | | | | | ≥ 0 |
| | | | | | | | | | .077 | | ≥ 0 |
| .167 | .083 | .083 | .083 | .083 | .049 | .150 | .098 | .111 | .077 | −.833 | = 0 |
| | .167 | | | | | | | | | | = 0.583 |
| .020 | .010 | .010 | .010 | .010 | .006 | .018 | .012 | .013 | .008 | −.100 | = 0 |
| .013 | .007 | .007 | .007 | .007 | .004 | .012 | .008 | .009 | .006 | −.067 | = 0 |
| | | | | | | .500 | | | .007 | | ≤ 1 |
| 8.75 | 8.75 | | | | | | | | | | ≥ 0 |
| | | 2.50 | 2.50 | 1.67 | | | | | | | ≥ 0 |
| | | | | | .500 | .167 | | | | | ≥ 0 |
| | | | | | | | 1.00 | | | | ≥ 0 |
| | | | | | | | | .125 | .125 | | ≥ 0 |
| | | | | | | .196 | | | | | ≥ 0 |
| | | | | | | | | | | 1 | ≤ 2 |

P14–P21: min $\Sigma v_j x_j$ under $Ax \leq b$; $w_j x_j \leq \lambda_j F_0 \sum_j w_j$

$\Sigma p_j x_j \geq z_0$; $z_0$ preassigned from P6–P13; $0 \leq \lambda_j \leq 1$; $x_j \geq 0$; $F_0$ varied as in P6–P13; $w_j$ = positive weights (preassigned).

P22–P29: min $\Sigma v_j x_j$ under $Ax \leq b$; $w_j x_j \leq \lambda_j F_0 \Sigma w_j$; $\Sigma p_j x_j \geq z_0$ ($z_0$ as above); $\lambda_j \leq 1$, $\Sigma \lambda_j = 1$; $\lambda_j$, $x_j \geq 0$; $F_0$ varied as above.

P30–P32: max $\Sigma p_j x_j$ under $Ax \leq b$; $h'\hat{x} \leq u_0 x_{38}$; $u_0 = .450$, $.583$, $.667$; $x$, $\hat{x}$, $x_{38} \geq 0$, where $\hat{x}$ denotes teaching and advising activities only and $u_0$ is the fraction of faculty time of type $x_{38}$ available. (Note that $u_0$ is parametrically varied); $h$ = vector of constants.

P33–P35: max $\Sigma p_j x_j$ under $Ax \leq b$; $e'\tilde{x} \geq v_0 x_{38}$; $v_0 = .100$, $.200$, $.300$; $x$, $\tilde{x}$, $x_{38} \geq 0$, where $\tilde{x}$ denotes the activities of undergraduate teaching alone and $v_0$ = fraction of faculty time of type $x_{38}$ available (this is parametrically varied); $e$ = vector of constants.

Q1: max $\Sigma \hat{\alpha}_j v_j x_j - G(x_T)$ under $v_{jl} x_{jl} \leq M_L$, $M_L$ preassigned; $Ax \leq b$, $x_T = \Sigma \hat{\alpha}_j x_j / \Sigma \hat{\alpha}_j$, $\hat{\alpha}_j$ preassigned, $x$, $x_T \geq 0$; where

$x_{jl}$ is the activity in the $l$th group (e.g., graduate teaching) where the total number of activities is divided into $l$ groups, $M_L$ is the average of costs for each activity $(v_j x_j)$ averaged over $l$th group of activities and the preassigned value of $\hat{\alpha}_j$ is estimated from the mark-up rule $p_j = (1 + \hat{\alpha}_j)v_j$; also $G(x_T)$ is the type of cost function mentioned before in (1.2). Here we consider it as a linear form, i.e., $G(x_T) = k^0 x_T$ where $k^0$ is estimated by max $v_j/\Sigma v_j$.

Q2–Q3: max $\Sigma \hat{\alpha}_j v_j x_j - k x_T$ under the same conditions as Q1 but with $k = .5, 1.0$.

Q4: max $\Sigma p_j x_j / (\Sigma v_j x_j + k^0 x_T + F_0)$ under the same conditions as Q1 except that $k^0$ is estimated by max $v_j/\Sigma v_j$ and $F_0$ preassigned, as $F_0 = 20$ (in some units).

Q5–Q6: same problem as Q4 except that $k^0$ is replaced by $k = .5, 1.0$.

Q7–Q8: same problem as Q2 except that its coefficient $k$ is replaced by $k^0$ estimated by max $v_j/\Sigma v_j$ and the restriction on $x_T$ replaced by $\Sigma \hat{\alpha}_j x_j / \Sigma \hat{\alpha}_j = \beta x_T$; $\beta = 5.0, .50$ preassigned.

The results of numerical computations of these LP models are presented in Tables 6.2A through 6.2E. Since our results are only illustrative, we will emphasize the implications of the structures of different models rather than their specific solution values.

a) For the first group of models (P1 to P5), we note that models P1 and P3 are only partial specifications of the complete model P4 if $\hat{\alpha}_j$'s are so preassigned that we get $c_j = p_j - v_j$ as the net price coefficients of the objective function in P4. In other words, given a measure of aggregate costs, the objective function in P1 maximizes total returns, whereas given a measure of aggregate output the objective function in P3 minimizes total costs. The duality between costs and output is the crucial characteristic which links the objective functions of the three models P1, P3, and P4. However, if a measure of aggregate output can be introduced in the decision space, then the model of type P3 becomes interesting. This is the motivation for introducing $x_T$ and its associated cost function $G(x_T)$ in the fourth group of models Q1 through Q8.

b) Note also that if the weight coefficients $\hat{\alpha}_j$ are restricted to be nonnegative by following a mark-up rule, then we cannot avoid sometimes getting a situation like P5, where we end up maximizing rather than minimizing aggregate costs; e.g., if all $\hat{\alpha}_j$'s are equal and positive we obtain P5 from P4. Denoting the objective function optimum values by $z$, it is seen in our calculations that $z(P4) < z(P3) < z(P5)$, which is not difficult to explain. So long as the measure of aggregate output is not given, even the rule of indifferent prices mentioned in (6.3) will not lead to any determinate result.

c) An interesting case arises when we consider preassigning $\hat{\alpha}_j$ as a problem of decisionmaking under uncertainty in problem P4. The policymaker is now assumed to have a set of subjective estimates for the net price vector $c = (c_j)$, $c_j = \alpha_j v_j = p_j - v_j$ out of which a decision set $D$ of price vectors has to be selected. Now any choice of a specific vector $c^0$ in the decision set $D$ (assumed to be convex, closed, and bounded) would lead to an optimal solution in the activity space, provided the feasible region is nonempty. However, since there is price uncertainty around $c$ in $D$, the imputed objective function of the policymaker

$$\phi(c,x) = c'x, \ c \in D, \ x \in X = \{Ax \leq b, x \geq 0\}$$

is no longer exact and deterministic. The source of this uncertainty may be partly subjective (Arrow 1964), partly objective in terms of past experiences and reactions (Cyert and March 1959), or partly both. The fact that the probability distribution of $c$ is either unknown or irrelevant (since it may be a once-for-all decision [Shackle 1955]) makes the case more interesting and more difficult analytically.

Two types of operational procedures may now be suggested. One is to consider the most pessimistic and the most optimistic estimates of the price vector $c$ in terms of the corresponding basic estimates of input costs and output values for different activities and then build up a sequence of bounds on the optimum values of the objective function. A second method is to consider the application of various decision criteria under uncertainty, e.g.:

minimax criterion (Wald): $\max_{x \in X} \min_{c \in D} \phi(c,x)$;

mixed minimax (Hurwicz):

$$\max_{x \in X} \left\{ w \min_{c \in D} \phi(c,x) + (1-w) \max_{c \in D} \phi(c,x) \right\},$$

$0 \leq w \leq 1$: weight constant;

expectation criterion (Bayes): $\max_{x} E \, \phi(c,x)$. (The expectation operator $E$ may refer to prior or posterior distributions in $c \in D$.)

Similarly, other criteria (Luce and Raiffa 1957) can be introduced to specify a consistent procedure of decisionmaking, although these do not

Table 6.2A. Optimal solutions of $Y$-subdepartment activity models

| Variables or Activities | P1 | P2 | P3 | P6 | P7 | P8 |
|---|---|---|---|---|---|---|
| $x_1$ | | | | | | |
| $x_2$ | | | | | | |
| $x_3$ | | | | | | |
| $x_4$ | | 6.0 | | 6.004 | 6.000 | 5.992 |
| $x_5$ | | | | | | |
| $x_6$ | | | | | | |
| $x_7$ | | | | | | |
| $x_8$ | .194 | | | | | |
| $x_9$ | | | | | | |
| $x_{10}$ | | | | | | |
| $x_{11}$ | 1.403 | | 1.5 | | | |
| $x_{12}$ | | | | | | |
| $x_{13}$ | | | | | | |
| $x_{14}$ | | | | | | |
| $x_{15}$ | | | | | | |
| $x_{16}$ | | | | | | |
| $x_{17}$ | | | | | | |
| $x_{18}$ | 6.830 | 1.024 | 6.884 | 1.023 | 1.024 | 1.024 |
| $x_{19}$ | | | | | | |
| $x_{20}$ | | | | | | |
| $x_{21}$ | | | | | | |
| $x_{22}$ | | | | | | |
| $x_{23}$ | | | | | | |
| $x_{24}$ | | | | | | |
| $x_{25}$ | .292 | 3.488 | .419 | 1.747 | 1.744 | 1.741 |
| $x_{26}$ | | | | | | |
| $x_{27}$ | | | .069 | | | |
| $x_{28}$ | | | | | | |
| $x_{29}$ | 1.000 | 1.000 | 1.000 | 1.000 | 1.000 | 1.000 |
| $x_{30}$ | 1.000 | 1.000 | 1.000 | 1.000 | 1.000 | 1.000 |
| $x_{31}$ | 1.000 | 1.000 | 1.000 | 1.000 | 1.000 | 1.000 |
| $x_{32}$ | | 1.342 | | | | |
| $x_{33}$ | 2.000 | .658 | 2.000 | .708 | .705 | .705 |
| $x_{34}$ | 4.000 | 4.000 | .831 | 4.004 | 4.000 | 3.996 |
| $x_{35}$ | | | | | | |
| $x_{36}$ | | 2.488 | | | | |
| $x_{37}$ | | | | | | |
| $x_{38}$ | | | | | | |
| Obj. Func. $z$ | 711.60 | 360.76 | 360.76 | 688.34 | 687.74 | 687.08 |
| Dual Variables | | | | | | |
| $y_1$ | +.88 | +.0388 | −.3958 | +.1336 | +.1320 | +.1303 |
| $y_2$ | +.88 | +.0388 | .7916 | +.1336 | +.1320 | +.1303 |
| $y_3$ | +1.938 | +.0171 | −2.1092 | −.4028 | −.3341 | −.2671 |
| $y_4$ | +1.938 | +.0171 | −2.1092 | −.4028 | −.3341 | −.2671 |
| $y_5$ | +1.971 | +.0296 | −2.5641 | −.4792 | −.3896 | −.3022 |
| $y_6$ | +4.608 | +.3409 | −3.7925 | 0 | 0 | 0 |
| $y_7$ | +4.590 | +.2411 | 0 | +.8181 | +.8465 | +.8741 |
| $y_{14}$ | 0 | 0 | 0 | 0 | 0 | 0 |
| $y_{17}$ | +101.205 | +2.011 | +156.9 | −99.31 | −94.64 | −90.079 |
| $y_{19}$ | +18,760 | −2,198 | −38,366 | −23,869 | −21,192 | −18,581 |
| $y_{21}$ | +28,000 | +3,314 | +55,395 | −35,626 | −31,629 | −27,733 |
| $y_{33(F_o)}$ | | | | +1.7688 | +1.7464 | +1.7245 |
| $z_{LFF}$ | | | | 1.7688 | 1.7464 | 1.7245 |
| $t$ | | | | .00257 | .00254 | .00251 |
| $\sum v_j x_j$ | 402.872 | | | | | |
| $\sum p_j x_j$ | | | 620.034 | | | |

*Notes:* 1. Objective function optimal values denoted by $z$ above refer to the value of the numerator only for linear functional fractional problems, e.g., P6–P13, etc.
2. The notation $z_{LFF}$ denotes optimal objective function values for the linear fractional functional problems.
3. $t$-values denote the fractions relating the $x$ vectors and the $q$ vectors say when $q = t \cdot x$, when the linear functional program is solved in terms of $q$ vectors.
4. The signs of the dual variables for equality restrictions may have to be properly adjusted.

# RESOURCE ALLOCATION IN NONMARKET SYSTEMS 163

| | | | Problems | | | |
|---|---|---|---|---|---|---|
| P9 | P10 | P11 | P12 | P13 | P5 | P4 |
| | | | .195 | | | |
| 5.991 | 6.013 | 5.991 | 5.801 | 5.995 | 6.0 | |
| | | | | | | |
| 1.024 | .831 | .829 | 1.217 | .829 | 1.02 | |
| | .195 | .192 | | .196 | | |
| 1.742 | 1.699 | 1.693 | 1.692 | 1.693 | 3.49 | |
| 1.000 | 1.000 | 1.000 | 1.000 | 1.000 | 1.000 | |
| 1.000 | 1.000 | 1.000 | 1.000 | 1.000 | 1.000 | |
| 1.000 | 1.000 | 1.000 | 1.000 | 1.000 | 1.000 | |
| | | | | | .908 | |
| .706 | 2.004 | 2.000 | 2.000 | 2.000 | 1.092 | |
| 3.996 | 4.008 | 4.000 | 4.000 | 4.000 | 4.000 | |
| | | | | | 1.910 | |
| | | | | | .289 | |
| | | | | | 2.000 | |
| 687.19 | 712.74 | 710.87 | 711.12 | 711.31 | 514.46 | 308.79 |
| +.1287 | +.1346 | +.1433 | +.1840 | +.2532 | .760 | .437 |
| +.1287 | +.1346 | +.1433 | +.1840 | +.2532 | .760 | .437 |
| −.2017 | −.1652 | −.1406 | −.0259 | +.1693 | 1.166 | .689 |
| −.2017 | −.1652 | −.1406 | −.0259 | +.1693 | 1.166 | .689 |
| −.2171 | −.1745 | −.1494 | −.0324 | +.1668 | 1.149 | .696 |
| 0 | +.0386 | +.0920 | +.3412 | +.7654 | 1.016 | 1.893 |
| +.9011 | +.9397 | +.9824 | +1.1815 | +1.5204 | 1.616 | 2.421 |
| 0 | 0 | 0 | 0 | 0 | 52.615 | |
| −85.63 | −84.50 | −84.69 | −85.60 | −87.16 | −143.66 | −91.24 |
| −16,035 | −15,333 | −15,373 | −15,560 | −15,878 | 379.27 | −16,727 |
| −23,933 | −22,884 | −22,944 | −23,223 | −23,698 | −675.42 | −24,966 |
| +1.7031 | +1.6828 | +1.6631 | 1.5713 | +1.4151 | | |
| 1.7131 | 1.6828 | 1.6631 | 1.5713 | 1.4151 | | |
| .00248 | .00236 | .00234 | .00221 | .00199 | | |

Table 6.2B.  Optimal solutions of $Y$-subdepartment activity models

| Variables | P14 | P15 | P16 | P17 | P18 | P19 | P20 | P21 |
|---|---|---|---|---|---|---|---|---|
| $x_1$ | | | | | .202 | .187 | .189 | |
| $x_2$ | | | | | | | | |
| $x_3$ | | | | | | | | |
| $x_4$ | | | | | .258 | .197 | .205 | |
| $x_5$ | | | | | | | | |
| $x_6$ | | | | | | | | |
| $x_7$ | | | | | | | | |
| $x_8$ | | | | | | | | |
| $x_9$ | | | | | | | | |
| $x_{10}$ | | | | | | | | |
| $x_{11}$ | 1.5 | 1.5 | 1.5 | 1.5 | 1.385 | 1.404 | 1.401 | 1. |
| $x_{12}$ | | | | | | | | |
| $x_{13}$ | | | | | | | | |
| $x_{14}$ | | | | | | | | |
| $x_{15}$ | | | | | | | | |
| $x_{16}$ | | | | | | | | |
| $x_{17}$ | | | | | | | | |
| $x_{18}$ | 7.02 | 7.02 | 7.02 | 7.02 | 6.766 | 6.827 | 6.819 | 6. |
| $x_{19}$ | .07 | .07 | .07 | .07 | | | | |
| $x_{20}$ | | | | | | | | |
| $x_{21}$ | | | | | | | | |
| $x_{22}$ | | | | | | | | |
| $x_{23}$ | | | | | | | | |
| $x_{24}$ | | | | | | | | |
| $x_{25}$ | .417 | .417 | .417 | .417 | .617 | .586 | .591 | . |
| $x_{26}$ | | | | | | | | |
| $x_{27}$ | | | | | | | | |
| $x_{28}$ | | | | | | | | |
| $x_{29}$ | 1.0 | 1.0 | 1.0 | 1.0 | 1.0 | 1.0 | 1.0 | 1. |
| $x_{30}$ | 1.0 | 1.0 | 1.0 | 1.0 | 1.0 | 1.0 | 1.0 | 1. |
| $x_{31}$ | 1.0 | 1.0 | 1.0 | 1.0 | 1.0 | 1.0 | 1.0 | 1. |
| $x_{32}$ | | | | | | | | |
| $x_{33}$ | .170 | .186 | .204 | .201 | | | | |
| $x_{34}$ | 3.59 | 3.57 | 3.54 | 3.54 | 4.0 | 4.0 | 4.0 | 4. |
| $x_{35}$ | | | | | | | | |
| $x_{36}$ | | | | | | | | |
| $x_{37}$ | | | | | | | | |
| $x_{38}$ | | | | 1.15 | 1.20 | 1.197 | 1.197 | |
| $z$ | 388.77 | +388.52 | +388.25 | 388.29 | 400.28 | 399.33 | 399.46 | 399. |
| $y_1$ | −.0694 | −.0694 | −.0694 | −.0694 | | | | 0 |
| $y_2$ | −.1387 | −.1387 | −.1387 | −.1387 | | | | 0 |
| $y_3$ | −.5646 | −.5646 | −.5646 | −.5646 | −.2743 | −.2743 | −.2743 | −. |
| $y_4$ | −.5646 | −.5646 | −.5646 | −.5646 | −.2743 | −.2743 | −.2743 | −. |
| $y_5$ | −.6345 | −.6345 | −.6345 | −.6345 | −.2828 | −.2828 | −.2828 | −. |
| $y_6$ | | | | | | | | |
| $y_7$ | | | | | +.1413 | +.1413 | +.1413 | +. |
| $y_{14}$ | | | | | | | | |
| $y_{17}$ | −6.673 | −6.673 | −6.673 | −6.673 | −41.02 | −41.02 | −41.02 | −41. |
| $y_{19}$ | −11,483 | −11,483 | −11,483 | −11,483 | −7,407 | −7,407 | −7,407 | −7,407 |
| $y_{21}$ | +16,913 | +16,913 | +16,913 | +16,913 | +11,054 | +11,054 | +11,054 | +11,054 |

imply that such consistent decision processes are necessarily rational and unequivocal.

Note, however, that the decision set $D$ where $c \in D$ can be interpreted to include the case where the resulting problem becomes one of vector optimization. For instance, assume that there are $K$ policymakers, each with his subjective estimate $c^{(k)}$ ($k = 1, \ldots, K$) of vector $c$ in the objective function. Define vector

RESOURCE ALLOCATION IN NONMARKET SYSTEMS 165

| Variables | P14 | P15 | P16 | P17 | P18 | P19 | P20 | P21 |
|---|---|---|---|---|---|---|---|---|
| $\lambda_1$ | | | | 1.0 | .0003 | .0003 | .0003 | .0003 |
| $\lambda_2$ | | | | | | | | |
| $\lambda_3$ | | | | | | | | |
| $\lambda_4$ | | | | 1.0 | .0003 | .0002 | .0002 | .0002 |
| $\lambda_5$ | | | | | | | | |
| $\lambda_6$ | | | | | | | | |
| $\lambda_7$ | | | | | | | | |
| $\lambda_8$ | | | | | | | | |
| $\lambda_9$ | | | | | | | | |
| $\lambda_{10}$ | | | | | | | | |
| $\lambda_{11}$ | .0026 | .0026 | .0026 | .0026 | .0024 | .0024 | .0024 | .0024 |
| $\lambda_{12}$ | | | | | | | | |
| $\lambda_{13}$ | | | | | | | | |
| $\lambda_{14}$ | | | | | | | | |
| $\lambda_{15}$ | | | | | | | | |
| $\lambda_{16}$ | | | | | | | | |
| $\lambda_{17}$ | | | | | | | | |
| $\lambda_{18}$ | .0092 | .0092 | .0092 | .0092 | .0089 | .0090 | .0090 | .0090 |
| $\lambda_{19}$ | .0001 | .0001 | .0001 | .0001 | | | | |
| $\lambda_{20}$ | | | | | | | | |
| $\lambda_{21}$ | | | | | | | | |
| $\lambda_{22}$ | | | | | | | | |
| $\lambda_{23}$ | | | | | | | | |
| $\lambda_{24}$ | | | | | | | | |
| $\lambda_{25}$ | .0007 | .0007 | .0007 | .0007 | .0011 | .0010 | .0010 | .0010 |
| $\lambda_{26}$ | | | | | | | | |
| $\lambda_{27}$ | | | | | | | | |
| $\lambda_{28}$ | | | | | | | | |
| $\lambda_{29}$ | .0015 | .0015 | .0015 | .0015 | .0015 | .0015 | .0015 | .0015 |
| $\lambda_{30}$ | .0012 | .0012 | .0012 | .0012 | .0012 | .0012 | .0012 | .0012 |
| $\lambda_{31}$ | .0016 | .0016 | .0016 | .0016 | .0016 | .0016 | .0016 | .0016 |
| $\lambda_{32}$ | | | | | | | | |
| $\lambda_{33}$ | .0002 | .0002 | .0002 | .0002 | | | | |
| $\lambda_{34}$ | .0052 | .0052 | .0051 | .0051 | .0058 | .0058 | .0058 | .0058 |
| $\lambda_{35}$ | | | | | | | | |
| $\lambda_{36}$ | | | | | | | | |
| $\lambda_{37}$ | | | | | | | | |
| $\lambda_{38}$ | | | | —negligible— | | | | |

$$u(x) = \begin{pmatrix} c^{(1)\prime}x \\ \vdots \\ c^{(K)\prime}x \end{pmatrix} \text{ and } x \in X.$$

Also define a vector $\bar{x}$ to be the vector optimum (i.e., efficient point) if there exists no other feasible $x \in X$ satisfying the vector inequality:

$$u(x) \geq u(\bar{x}), \; x \neq \bar{x}.$$

Table 6.2C. Optimal solutions of $Y$-subdepartment activity models

| Variables | P22 | P23 | P24 | P25 | P26 | P27 | P28 | P29 |
|---|---|---|---|---|---|---|---|---|
| $x_1$ | | | | | | | | .191 |
| $x_2$ | | | | | | | | |
| $x_3$ | | | | | | | | |
| $x_4$ | | | | | .055 | .010 | .016 | .211 |
| $x_5$ | | | | | | | | |
| $x_6$ | | | | | | | | |
| $x_7$ | | | | | | | | |
| $x_8$ | | | | | .202 | .187 | .189 | |
| $x_9$ | | | | | | | | |
| $x_{10}$ | | | | | | | | |
| $x_{11}$ | 1.5 | 1.5 | 1.5 | 1.5 | 1.385 | 1.404 | 1.401 | 1.399 |
| $x_{12}$ | | | | | | | | |
| $x_{13}$ | | | | | | | | |
| $x_{14}$ | | | | | | | | |
| $x_{15}$ | | | | | | | | |
| $x_{16}$ | | | | | | | | |
| $x_{17}$ | | | | | | | | |
| $x_{18}$ | 7.02 | 7.02 | 7.02 | 7.02 | 6.766 | 6.827 | 6.819 | 6.813 |
| $x_{19}$ | .071 | .071 | .071 | .071 | | | | |
| $x_{20}$ | | | | | | | | |
| $x_{21}$ | | | | | | | | |
| $x_{22}$ | | | | | | | | |
| $x_{23}$ | | | | | | | | |
| $x_{24}$ | | | | | | | | |
| $x_{25}$ | .417 | .417 | .417 | .417 | 0.6168 | .586 | .591 | .594 |
| $x_{26}$ | | | | | | | | |
| $x_{27}$ | | | | | | | | |
| $x_{28}$ | | | | | | | | |
| $x_{29}$ | 1.0 | 1.0 | 1.0 | 1.0 | 1.0 | 1.0 | 1.0 | 1.0 |
| $x_{30}$ | 1.0 | 1.0 | 1.0 | 1.0 | 1.0 | 1.0 | 1.0 | 1.0 |
| $x_{31}$ | 1.0 | 1.0 | 1.0 | 1.0 | 1.0 | 1.0 | 1.0 | 1.0 |
| $x_{32}$ | | | | | | | | |
| $x_{33}$ | .167 | .186 | .204 | .201 | | | | |
| $x_{34}$ | 3.59 | 3.566 | 3.539 | 3.543 | 4.0 | 4.0 | 4.0 | 4.0 |
| $x_{35}$ | | | | | | | | |
| $x_{36}$ | | | | | | | | |
| $x_{37}$ | | | | | | | | |
| $x_{38}$ | 1.154 | 1.154 | 1.154 | 1.154 | 1.201 | 1.197 | 1.197 | 1.198 |
| Obj. func. $z$ | 388.77 | 388.52 | 388.25 | 388.29 | 400.28 | 399.33 | 399.46 | 399.56 |
| Dual variables | | | | | | | | |
| $v_1$ | −.0694 | −.0694 | −.0694 | −.0694 | | | | |
| $v_2$ | −.1387 | −.1387 | −.1387 | −.1387 | | | | |
| $v_3$ | −.5646 | −.5646 | −.5646 | −.5646 | −.2743 | −.2743 | −.2743 | −.274 |
| $v_4$ | −.5646 | −.5646 | −.5646 | −.5646 | −.2743 | −.2743 | −.2743 | −.274 |
| $v_5$ | −.6345 | −.6345 | −.6345 | −.6345 | −.2828 | −.2828 | −.2828 | −.282 |
| $v_6$ | | | | | | | | |
| $v_7$ | | | | | −.1413 | −.1413 | −.1413 | −.141 |
| $v_{14}$ | | | | | | | | |
| $v_{17}$ | −6.673 | −6.673 | −6.673 | −6.673 | −41.02 | −41.02 | −41.02 | −41.02 |
| $v_{19}$ | −11,483 | −11,483 | −11,483 | −11,483 | −7,407 | −7,407 | −7,407 | −7,407 |
| $v_{21}$ | +16,913 | +16,913 | +16,913 | +16,913 | +11,054 | +11,054 | +11,054 | +11,054 |

*Note:* See the notes at the end of Table 6.2A.

It is known (Sengupta and Fox 1969) that if such a vector optimum or efficient point $\bar{x}$ exists, then there must exist a set of non-negative Lagrange multipliers $\bar{v} = (\bar{v}^{(1)}, \ldots, \bar{v}^{(K)})$ such that the equivalent scalar optimization problem, i.e.:

$$\max_{x} \bar{v}' u(x), \ x \in X,$$

| Variables | P22 | P23 | P24 | P25 | P26 | P27 | P28 | P29 |
|---|---|---|---|---|---|---|---|---|
| $\lambda_1$ | .978 | .978 | .978 |  | .9770 | .9770 | .9770 | .9770 |
| $\lambda_2$ |  |  |  |  |  |  |  |  |
| $\lambda_3$ |  |  |  |  |  |  |  |  |
| $\lambda_4$ |  |  |  |  | .0001 | .0000 | .0000 | .0002 |
| $\lambda_5$ |  |  |  |  |  |  |  |  |
| $\lambda_6$ |  |  |  |  |  |  |  |  |
| $\lambda_7$ |  |  |  |  |  |  |  |  |
| $\lambda_8$ |  |  |  | .978 | .0002 | .0002 | .0002 |  |
| $\lambda_9$ |  |  |  |  |  |  |  |  |
| $\lambda_{10}$ |  |  |  |  |  |  |  |  |
| $\lambda_{11}$ | .0026 | .0026 | .0026 | .0026 | .0024 | .0024 | .0024 | .0024 |
| $\lambda_{12}$ |  |  |  |  |  |  |  |  |
| $\lambda_{13}$ |  |  |  |  |  |  |  |  |
| $\lambda_{14}$ |  |  |  |  |  |  |  |  |
| $\lambda_{15}$ |  |  |  |  |  |  |  |  |
| $\lambda_{16}$ |  |  |  |  |  |  |  |  |
| $\lambda_{17}$ |  |  |  |  |  |  |  |  |
| $\lambda_{18}$ | .0092 | .0092 | .0092 | .0092 | .0089 | .0090 | .0090 | .0090 |
| $\lambda_{19}$ | .0001 | .0001 | .0001 | .0001 |  |  |  |  |
| $\lambda_{20}$ |  |  |  |  |  |  |  |  |
| $\lambda_{21}$ |  |  |  |  |  |  |  |  |
| $\lambda_{22}$ |  |  |  |  |  |  |  |  |
| $\lambda_{23}$ |  |  |  |  |  |  |  |  |
| $\lambda_{24}$ |  |  |  |  |  |  |  |  |
| $\lambda_{25}$ | .0007 | .0007 | .0007 | .0007 | .0011 | .0010 | .0010 | .0010 |
| $\lambda_{26}$ |  |  |  |  |  |  |  |  |
| $\lambda_{27}$ |  |  |  |  |  |  |  |  |
| $\lambda_{28}$ |  |  |  |  |  |  |  |  |
| $\lambda_{29}$ | .0015 | .0015 | .0015 | .0015 | .0015 | .0015 | .0015 | .0015 |
| $\lambda_{30}$ | .0012 | .0012 | .0012 | .0012 | .0012 | .0012 | .0012 | .0012 |
| $\lambda_{31}$ | .0016 | .0016 | .0016 | .0016 | .0016 | .0016 | .0016 | .0016 |
| $\lambda_{32}$ |  |  |  |  |  |  |  |  |
| $\lambda_{33}$ | .0002 | .0002 | .0002 | .0002 |  |  |  |  |
| $\lambda_{34}$ | .0052 | .0052 | .0051 | .0052 | .0058 | .0058 | .0058 | .0058 |
| $\lambda_{35}$ |  |  |  |  |  |  |  |  |
| $\lambda_{36}$ |  |  |  |  |  |  |  |  |
| $\lambda_{37}$ |  |  |  |  |  |  |  |  |
| $\lambda_{38}$ |  |  |  |  |  |  |  |  |

—negligible—

will also lead to the same optimal vector $\bar{x}$. In a sense, this new objective function $\bar{v}'u(x)$ is a weighted average of the individual utility functions $c^{(k)}{}'x$, $(k = 1, \ldots, K)$. If the $K$ policymakers belong to a hierarchy in the organizational structure, then this average may be more meaningfully interpreted by the chairman or the dean (who is co-ordinating the individual decisionmakers) in terms of the relative contributions of individ-

Table 6.2D. Optimal solutions of $Y$-subdepartment activity models

| Variables | P30 | P31 | P32 | P33 | P34 | P35 |
|---|---|---|---|---|---|---|
| $x_1$ | | | .194 | | | |
| $x_2$ | | | | | | |
| $x_3$ | | | | | | |
| $x_4$ | | | | | | |
| $x_5$ | | | | | | |
| $x_6$ | | | | | | |
| $x_7$ | | | | | | |
| $x_8$ | | | | | | |
| $x_9$ | | | | | | |
| $x_{10}$ | | | | | | |
| $x_{11}$ | 1.5 | 1.5 | 1.451 | 1.5 | 1.5 | |
| $x_{12}$ | | | | | | |
| $x_{13}$ | | | | | | |
| $x_{14}$ | | | | | | |
| $x_{15}$ | .194 | | | .194 | .192 | |
| $x_{16}$ | | | | | | |
| $x_{17}$ | | | | | | |
| $x_{18}$ | 7.02 | 6.830 | 7.02 | 7.02 | 7.02 | |
| $x_{19}$ | | | | | | |
| $x_{20}$ | | | | | | |
| $x_{21}$ | | | | | | |
| $x_{22}$ | | .194 | | | | |
| $x_{23}$ | | | | | | |
| $x_{24}$ | | | | | | |
| $x_{25}$ | .195 | .195 | .244 | .195 | .196 | |
| $x_{26}$ | | | | | | |
| $x_{27}$ | | | | | | |
| $x_{28}$ | | | | | | |
| $x_{29}$ | 1.0 | 1.0 | 1.0 | 1.0 | 1.0 | |
| $x_{30}$ | 1.0 | 1.0 | 1.0 | 1.0 | 1.0 | |
| $x_{31}$ | 1.0 | 1.0 | 1.0 | 1.0 | 1.0 | |
| $x_{32}$ | | | | | .022 | |
| $x_{33}$ | 2.0 | 2.0 | 2.0 | 2.0 | 1.978 | |
| $x_{34}$ | 4.0 | 4.0 | 4.0 | 4.0 | 4.0 | |
| $x_{35}$ | | | | | | |
| $x_{36}$ | | | | | | |
| $x_{37}$ | | | | | | |
| $x_{38}$ | 1.498 | 1.498 | 1.498 | 1.498 | 1.496 | |
| Obj. func. | | | | | | |
| $z$ | 711.60 | 711.60 | 711.60 | 711.60 | 711.41 | |
| $y_1$ | +.880 | +.880 | +.880 | +.880 | +1.366 | |
| $y_2$ | +.880 | +.880 | +.880 | +.880 | +1.366 | |
| $y_3$ | +1.938 | +1.938 | +1.938 | +1.938 | +1.315 | |
| $y_4$ | +1.938 | +1.938 | +1.938 | +1.938 | −1.315 | |
| $y_5$ | +1.971 | +1.971 | +1.971 | +1.971 | +1.037 | —Infeasible— |
| $y_6$ | +4.608 | +4.608 | +4.608 | +4.608 | +1.244 | |
| $y_7$ | +4.590 | +4.590 | +4.590 | +4.590 | +3.469 | |
| $y_{14}$ | 0.0 | 0 | 0 | 0 | 0 | |
| $y_{17}$ | −101.20 | −101.20 | −101.20 | −101.20 | −306.02 | |
| $y_{19}$ | −18,760 | −18,760 | −18,760 | −18,760 | −40,393 | |
| $y_{21}$ | +28,000 | +28,000 | +28,000 | +28,000 | +61,570 | |
| $y_{32}$ | 0 | 0 | 0 | 0 | 0 | |
| $y_{33}$ | 0 | 0 | 0 | 0 | 429.70 | |

*Note:* See the notes at the end of Table 6.2A.

Table 6.2E. Optimal solutions of $Y$-subdepartment activity models

| Variables | Q1 | Q2 | Q3 | Q4 | Q5 | Q6 | Q7 | Q8 |
|---|---|---|---|---|---|---|---|---|
| $x_1$ | | | | | | | .152 | |
| $x_2$ | | | | | | | | |
| $x_3$ | | | | | | | | |
| $x_4$ | 6.0 | 6.0 | | 5.736 | 5.732 | 5.728 | 5.848 | 5.696 |
| $x_5$ | | | | | | | | |
| $x_6$ | | | | | | | | |
| $x_7$ | | | | | | | | |
| $x_8$ | | | | .130 | .130 | .130 | | .1522 |
| $x_9$ | | | | | | | | |
| $x_{10}$ | | | | | | | | |
| $x_{11}$ | | | | | | | | |
| $x_{12}$ | | | | | | | | |
| $x_{13}$ | | | | | | | | |
| $x_{14}$ | | | | | | | | |
| $x_{15}$ | | | | | | | | |
| $x_{16}$ | | | | | | | | |
| $x_{17}$ | | | | | | | | |
| $x_{18}$ | .87 | .87 | | 1.155 | 1.155 | 1.155 | 1.176 | 1.176 |
| $x_{19}$ | | | | | | | | |
| $x_{20}$ | | | | | | | | |
| $x_{21}$ | | | | | | | | |
| $x_{22}$ | .15 | .15 | | | | | | |
| $x_{23}$ | | | | | | | | |
| $x_{24}$ | | | | | | | | |
| $x_{25}$ | 1.71 | 1.71 | | 1.711 | 1.711 | 1.707 | 1.706 | 1.706 |
| $x_{26}$ | | | | | | | | |
| $x_{27}$ | | | | | | | | |
| $x_{28}$ | | | | | | | | |
| $x_{29}$ | 1.0 | 1.0 | | 1.0 | 1.0 | 1.0 | 1.0 | 1.0 |
| $x_{30}$ | 1.0 | 1.0 | | 1.0 | 1.0 | 1.0 | 1.0 | 1.0 |
| $x_{31}$ | 1.0 | 1.0 | | 1.0 | 1.0 | 1.0 | 1.0 | 1.0 |
| $x_{32}$ | .418 | .418 | | | | | .418 | .418 |
| $x_{33}$ | 1.582 | 1.582 | | 1.582 | 1.582 | 1.582 | 1.582 | 1.582 |
| $x_{34}$ | 4.0 | 4.0 | | 4.0 | 4.0 | 3.992 | 4.0 | 4.0 |
| $x_{35}$ | | | | | | | | |
| $x_{36}$ | | | | | | | | |
| $x_{37}$ | | | | | | | | |
| $x_{38}$ | 1.446 | 1.446 | | 1.418 | 1.418 | 1.418 | 1.446 | 1.446 |
| $x_{39}=x_r$ | .779 | .779 | | .770 | .766 | .766 | .1576 | 1.559 |
| Dual variables | | | | | | | | |
| $y_1$ | +.437 | +.437 | | +.135 | +.135 | +.135 | +.437 | +.437 |
| $y_2$ | +.437 | +.437 | | +.135 | +.135 | +.135 | +.437 | +.437 |
| $y_3$ | | | | −.165 | −.164 | −.163 | | |
| $y_4$ | +.689 | +.688 | | −.165 | −.164 | −.163 | +.689 | +.689 |
| $y_5$ | +.696 | +.695 | | −.174 | −.174 | −.173 | +.696 | +.696 |
| $y_6$ | +.796 | +.793 | | | | | +.796 | +.795 |
| $y_7$ | +2.420 | +2.417 | | | | | +2.421 | +2.420 |
| $y_{10}$ | −6.229 | −6.231 | | | | | −6.230 | −6.229 |
| $y_{15}$ | +33.668 | +33.375 | | −2,438 | −2,426 | −2,412.6 | +33.69 | +33.63 |
| $y_{16}$ | −27.850 | −28.040 | | | | | −27.835 | −27.87 |
| $y_{17}$ | −91.246 | −91.329 | | −84.52 | −84.67 | −84.84 | −91.243 | −91.26 |
| $y_{19}$ | −16,723 | −16,711 | | −15,330 | −15,315 | −15,296 | −16,726 | −16,721 |
| $y_{20}$ | | | | −20,514 | −20,410 | −20,293 | | |
| $y_{21}$ | +24,959 | +24,942 | | +22,882 | −22,857 | −22,830 | +24,964 | +24,957 |
| $y_{61}$ | +.538 | +.538 | | | | | +.538 | +.538 |
| $y_{68}$ | +.411 | +.411 | | +.014 | +.013 | +.012 | +.411 | +.411 |
| $y_{69}$ | | | | +.436 | +.435 | +.433 | | |
| $y_{201}$ | +.054 | +.5000 | | +.091 | +.841 | +1.680 | +.011 | +.108[a] |
| $y_{301}$ | | | | +1.682[b] | +1.681 | +1.680 | | |
| Obj. func. $z$ | 306.92 | 306.57 | | 703.763 | 703.763 | | | |
| Obj. func. $z_{LFF}$ | | | | 1.682 | 1.681 | 1.680 | | |
| TVC: | 569.84 | 569.84 | | 398.25 | | | 400.96 | 400.96 |

*Note:* 1. See notes at the end of Table 6.2A.
2. The optimal basis for Q2 is maintained in Q3, hence the separate results for Q3 are not mentioned.
[a] (imputed cost for $x_r = x_{39}$)
[b] (Shadow price for $F_0$)

ual objective functions to the over-all objective perceived by the chairman or the dean. The point that the different basic feasible solutions of the set $X$ can be candidates for optimal solutions under a particular $c^{(k)\prime}x$ is of some importance in exploring the implications of $c^{(k)}$ varying in the decision set $D$.

d) Note also the implications of imputing prices on the basis of variable costs alone in the problems P3 to P5. The optimal solution vectors for P3 and P5 are not the same, and the sensitivity of the optimum objective functions to variations in the input-output coefficients is also different in the two cases; this implies that the difference in the two optimal solution vectors may not be insignificant. It is useful in a policy framework to introduce a distance function $d(x,\bar{x})$ for distinguishing the significantly different solution vectors from those which are not. For instance, $d(x,\bar{x})$ may be the Euclidean distance between the two vector points $x$ and $\bar{x}$ and the policymaker may preassign the scalar $r$, such that if $d(x,\bar{x}) > r$ then the two solution vectors $x,\bar{x}$ may be considered significantly different. (In case $d(x,\bar{x}) \leq r$, the solutions $x,\bar{x}$ are not significantly different.) In this interpretation, if one of the vectors, say $\bar{x}$, represents a state desired by the policymaker on subjective grounds, then the distance function $d(x - \bar{x}) = [(x - \bar{x})'(x - \bar{x})]^{\frac{1}{2}}$ may represent penalty costs for deviating from the desired state.

However, one limitation of the first group of models (P1–P5) is that it neglects the role of indivisible fixed resources such as overheads. In the LP models, divisible fixed resources are imputed their shadow prices, and if at the optimal feasible solution a particular such fixed resource has a positive slack, its shadow price is equated to zero. There are several reasons why such imputation of zero shadow prices may be very inappropriate for semi-indivisible or indivisible fixed resources. First, the organization theorists have laid great emphasis on the importance of "organizational slack" in any system (Naslund 1967), and presumably some of these slacks (e.g., computing, library, and other research facilities) are very important in educational systems. (For example, the accounting practice at Iowa State University requires computing university overhead costs at about 60 percent of total salary and wage costs on research grants, and this ratio is applied to all departments equally.) Second, a theory of imputing positive prices to the slacks and excess fixed or semifixed resources has been developed by some authors (Dhrymes 1964) for the case in which there is some uncertainty in constraint specification and its feasibility. Third, the theory of the multiproduct firm introduces for its semidivisible fixed resources a positive and convex cost function (called relocation cost [Nikaido 1964]) representing the cost of shifting these resources from one set of activities to another.

The second group of models (P6–P29) discusses the problem of overhead cost allocation in a limited way. Again the point comes up that an aggregate (possibly scalar) output measure of the activity mix, if it could be meaningfully defined in our context, would be of great help in the overhead cost allocation problem, since it could then be related to capacity costs. A somewhat different method is followed in the second group of models (P6–P29). Here the cost equivalent $F_0$ of fixed resources is incorporated either in a modified objective function (P6–P13) or in terms of additional decision variables $\lambda_j$ (P14–P29). A third method that has been suggested in the context of linear programming is to allow a monopolistic price imputation (Nikaido 1964) for the fixed and semifixed factors which are not allocated in the LP structure.

a) For the second group of models (P6–P29) we note that the models P6–P13 are linear fractional functional (LFF) programs which could of course be solved by LP routines (Sengupta and Fox 1969). The motivation for considering the maximization of a ratio of gross revenue to total costs is twofold. The ratio of output to input costs has been considered in several situations as an efficiency measure (Simon 1960), and it is of course different from the usual linear objective function. Nevertheless, this ratio index may be helpful, as Kornai and Lipták have shown (1962), in developing a set of imputed prices $\hat{p}_j$ on the basis of individual costs $v_j$ and the optimal relation between fixed costs $F_0$ and a measure of aggregate output $x_T$, say, where $F_0 = G(x_T)$. The parametric variations in $F_0$ are supposed to reflect the cost variations due to variations in $x_T$, although the aggregate activity $x_T$ is not explicitly introduced in P6–P13. A second reason for maximization of the ratio is that the shadow price associated with $F_0$ can be directly computed. Note that for problems P6–P13 the shadow price of $F_0$ becomes identical with the optimal value of the objective function of the LFF programs; but as $F_0$ increases from zero to 20, a new activity ($x_{22}$) enters into the optimal basis. Although the optimal value of the objective function of the LFF programs decreases as $F_0$ increases, the effect on total gross receipts ($\Sigma p_j x_j$) is not that definite. The explicit introduction of $F_0$ and its parametric variation shows that all other shadow prices are conditional on the level preassigned for $F_0$.

b) The $\lambda_j$ coefficients in models P14–P21 have two specific implications. As decision variables they specify optimal allocation of the fixed resource $F_0$, provided a measure of comparability of different activities is introduced in the activity space. The normalized value weights

$w_j/\Sigma w_j$ associated with each $x_j$ fulfill this role; it is apparent that developing the concept of an aggregate output measure like the concept of GNP (gross national product) becomes very important and fundamental. The allocation coefficients are such that they have to enter into the optimal solution at a positive level, if the corresponding activity is positive at the optimal solution; note, however, that the reverse need not be true. Hence, only the activities which are used at a positive level share the use of fixed overheads $F_0$. The numerical results for models P14–P21 show that the optimal overhead cost allocation ratios tend to increase (decrease) when the corresponding optimal activity levels increase (decrease). In problems P22–P29 the sum of the allocation coefficients ($\Sigma\lambda_j$) is forced to equal unity.

The problems P30–P35 are intended to analyze the implications of incorporating an aspect of allocable fixed resources which is commonly called "transfer activities." These transfer activities (e.g., faculty time transferred from graduate to undergraduate teaching) have played very crucial roles in our previous optimization models for educational institutions (Fox et al. 1967; Plessner et al. 1968). The basic counterpart of these transfer activities is found in the theory of the multiproduct firm when units of fixed factors are transferred from the production of one type of output to another (Pfouts 1962). For instance, if the machines of a plant represent fixed resources, then these have to be adapted to process a different product, storage spaces may have to be readjusted, and so on. These costs do not change continuously with the output of a particular product, but they do change as the product mix of the firm is changed.

To represent such costs, which do not belong either in the category of variable costs or in that of fixed costs, one needs to introduce a relocation cost function $c(F_{11}, F_{12}, \ldots, F_{1p}, F_{21}, \ldots, F_{np})$ in terms of the $j$th fixed factor used in the production of the $i$th output ($F_{it}$). If this function could be assumed (or approximated) to be linear, then one simple way to estimate the marginal transfer cost would be to compute the relative cost of transferring the $j$th fixed factor to the $i$th type of output for several feasible solutions and then consider either the most pessimistic (relevant for an austerity situation) or the most optimistic (relevant for an expansion phase) relative cost. However, since in the basic input-output data of Table 6.1 no allowances were made for variations in quality, estimation of transfer cost is attempted here only indirectly through adjoining additional constraints to model P1. These constraints stipulate, for example, that some minimum amount of faculty time has to be transferred to either undergraduate teaching or to departmental work other than teaching or research. The minimum faculty time allocation is then varied parametrically. Problem P35 shows that in some cases we would encounter infeasibility if the minimum faculty time allocation were set too high. Some means of evaluation of the cost of infeasibility seems to be required in this connection. Again, if subjective probability estimates can be reasonably introduced in the field of relocation costs, then the methods of two-stage (Sengupta and Fox 1969) and chance-constrained programming can be applied. The scheme of developing imputed prices should now include, besides the individual activity-specific costs $v_j$ and shadow prices of divisible fixed resources, an estimate of penalty costs associated with fixed resource transfers and the fact that a slack resource may have a positive implicit price as Naslund has argued (1967). The latter aspect is more important when the student enrollment data (forecast) have to be used in calculation, since the latter may have margins of uncertainty in details.

The fourth group of models (Q1–Q8) is structured so that the educational resource allocation problem may be viewed as a multiproduct firm model, except that an academic department's objective function may have several facets. The theoretical constructs here follow very closely the work of Kornai and Lipták (1962), who later developed (1965) decomposition techniques for two-level planning. Here a measure (i.e., index) of aggregate output $x_T$ is explicitly introduced and its associated cost function $G(x_T)$ is linearly approximated. Our calculations, however, differ in three important respects from the line followed by Kornai and Lipták. First, our measure $X_T$ is not a technical measure independent of monetary and valuation units, since the weights $\alpha_j$ used to define it are derived from the profitability ratio (i.e., $\alpha_j = (p_j - v_j)/v_j$) for activity $x_j$. Second, the role of indivisible fixed resources $F_0$ is explicitly introduced in a ratio-maximization problem, and the method of solution is obtained through the convenient technique of linear fractional functional programming. Third, our activities are grouped into broad groups such as graduate teaching, research, etc. for setting up additional constraints so that the single measure $x_T$ of aggregate activities does not force extreme rigidities into the solution structure.

Some remarks are in order here about our numerical calculations for Q1–Q8. First, the two-part division of costs permits the application of decomposition-type algorithms* even in nonlinear cases (i.e., nonlinear $G(x_T)$ function) and hence the dual prices of $x_T$, which differ for different

* Refer to Chapter 5 for an empirical application of the quadratic decomposition algorithm developed by Hass (1968) which seeks to determine efficient demand-supply functions rather than prices (Whinston 1964).

models in this group, play some interesting roles. Since alternative aggregate measures for $x_T$ would have to be tried for arriving at a final output measure, these shadow prices compared to other (resource) shadow prices may suggest some stability or otherwise of the optimal basis. Second, an optimal mix of total variable and fixed costs may now be defined; hence, a scheme of price imputation on this basis may be developed, although it may not be necessarily unique. In more general cases, the two-facet cost function may be extended to include more than two facets and also some nonlinearities in the $G(x_T)$ function.

However, the aggregate measure $x_T$ and its associated cost function $G(x_T)$ can be given a very interesting interpretation on the lines of neoclassical models of economic growth, which stipulate that aggregate GNP (gross national product), aggregate capital, and aggregate labor are well-defined quantities subject to diminishing marginal returns and constant returns to scale. If $x_T$ can be considered an output variable just like the GNP, the next step is to presume a policymaker (i.e., a higher-level central authority, e.g., the dean or the president in some cases) who considers a desired value of $x_T$ by evaluating the costs $G(x_T)$ and benefits $R(x_T)$ of alternative levels of $x_T$, subject to the policy restrictions $h_i(x_T)$ on the variability of $x_T$. Assuming these functions to be measurable, we may pose the aggregate policy problem as follows:

$$\max f(x_T) = R(x_T) - G(x_T), \tag{5a}$$

$$\text{subject to } h_i(x_T) \geq 0,\ x_T \geq 0;\ i = 1, \ldots, N. \tag{5b}$$

Note that the set of restrictions $h_i(x_T)$ must include the demand constraint (e.g., $x_T - d_T \geq 0$, where $d_T$ is the forecast value of aggregate demand for the output and the policymaker plans to meet at least the forecast demand). Also, if the functions $R(x_T)$, $G(x_T)$, $h_i(x_T)$ are linear, this will be a linear programming problem.

Let the optimal solution vectors for this aggregate problem be denoted by $\bar{x}_T$ and $\bar{y}_T$, where $\bar{y}_T$ is the vector of shadow prices. Given these solutions, each of the sectors (or departments) seeks to solve for the optimal solution vector $\bar{x}^{(k)}$ ($k = 1, \ldots, K$, when $K = $ total number of sectors or departments), subject to its own constraints and the given aggregate measures $\bar{x}_T$ and $\bar{y}_T$. For instance let $\bar{x}_T$ be such that the central policymaker views it as an average over $K$ sectors, i.e.:

$$\bar{x}_T = \sum_{k=1}^{K} w_k x^{(k)}, \text{ where } w_k \geq 0,\ \sum_k w_k = 1, \tag{6}$$

with $w_k$ preassigned. Then for the $k$th sector the decision problem is to

$$\max c^{(k)\prime} x^{(k)},$$

subject to $A^{(k)}x^{(k)} \leq b^{(k)}$, (7a)

$x^{(k)} \leq \lambda_k \bar{x}_T; \ x^{(k)} \geq 0; \ \lambda_k \geq 0.$ (7b)

Here the subscript $k$ denotes the particular sector (or department), and $\lambda_k$ is a non-negative scalar which may be parametrically varied by the center so as to satisfy the condition (6). The set of problems (7) and the problem (5) have a basic structure of decomposition and decentralization of decisionmaking. First, the center alone computes the aggregate demand forecast $d_T$ and concerns itself with over-all budgetary and fiscal policies. Given this decision, each individual sector behaves as a price-taker and optimizes its individual objective function, subject to its own constraints and an additional constraint imposed by the center. The latter generally comes in the form of a budget allocation by the center. For a university system, the central model (5) may represent the decisions of the president or similar top administrator, whereas the sectoral model (7) is an attempt to model the decisions by one department or division of the university. If the total budget or state support is cut, it is first felt in (5), then it is transmitted to the sectors in (7) through central allocations $\lambda_k$. Second, the long-run planning problem of the university may only concern the intertemporal extension of the central model (5), since it must be in relation to trends and requirements of aggregate demand. This leads, naturally, to the various techniques of decomposition we discussed in Chapters 4 and 5.

*Implications of optimal control theory*

This section suggests some lines of application of recent ideas from optimal control theory to the problems of growth of educational systems at two different levels, e.g., at the sectoral (national) and the university level.

The policy framework of recent theories of optimal growth under neoclassical conditions of aggregate production functions usually conceives the role of the public sector as somewhat different from that of the private sector. In two sector models with public and private sectors, two different, though related, approaches are identifiable: (a) In Uzawa's approach (1966) the public sector having a separate production function is subject to the competitive market assumptions, very similar to the private sector except that the entire output of the public sector is consumed and the short-run policies in the public sector are geared to maintain a long-run optimal savings program for the economy; (b) in the Arrow–Kurz approach (1970) the public sector does not have a separate production function, but the aggregate production function of the economy has two types of capital, public and private, and the aggregate utility function has two arguments, consumption and public sector's capital, the latter representing the services of public goods generated by the use of public capital.

These two approaches can be utilized to formulate a general model in which the public sector may be assumed to produce outputs, partly for current consumption and partly for investment, by utilizing three kinds of inputs, physical capital $K_1$, human capital in the form of skill-formation $H_1$, and labor $L_1$. Denoting the private sector (subscript 2) production function by $F_2(K_2,H_2,L_2)$ and the aggregate utility function in per-capita terms by:

$$U = U\left[\frac{C_1(t)}{L(t)}, \frac{C_2(t)}{L(t)}, \frac{\mathbf{Z}_1(t)}{L(t)}, \frac{\mathbf{Z}_2(t)}{L(t)}\right],$$

the optimal policy problem may be posed as follows: Find the time path of the control variables $(K_1(t), K_2(t), H_2(t), L_1(t), L_2(t), C_1(t), C_2(t), \mathbf{Z}_1(t), Z_1(t), \mathbf{Z}_2(t), Z_2(t))$ for which the utility functional

$$\int_0^T \exp(-\delta t) \cdot U dt$$

is maximized, subject to the production, allocation, and capital accumulation constraints:

$$C_1(t) + Z_1(t) + \mathbf{Z}_1(t) \leq F_1(K_1,H_1,L_1),$$

$$C_2(t) + Z_2(t) + \mathbf{Z}_2(t) \leq F_2(K_2,H_2,L_2),$$

$$K_1(t) + K_2(t) \leq K(t),$$

$$H_1(t) + H_2(t) \leq H(t),$$

$$L_1(t) + L_2(t) \leq L(t),$$

$$\dot{K}_i = dK_i/dt = Z_i - m_i K_i; \ (i = 1,2),$$

$$\dot{H}_i = dH_i/dt = \mathbf{Z}_i - h_i H_i; \ (i = 1,2),$$

$$L(t) = L(0) \exp(nt): \text{exogenous},$$

$$K(0), L(0) \text{ given at initial time } t = 0.$$

Here $Z_i$, $\mathbf{Z}_i$ denote respectively the investments in physical and human capital, where $m_i$ and $h_i$ are the corresponding depreciation rates assumed constant; capital is assumed freely transferable between sectors, and the production functions are assumed to be homogeneous of degree one, following the neo-classical tradition. Note that this model allows for the role of the education sector in two ways: first in the use of skills generated through knowledge creation and dissemination, and second in the utility function where the level of felicity is assumed to be dependent on the education level of the community. By applying the usual methods of optimization (e.g., Pontryagin's maximum principle) one could derive from the above model an optimal path of growth of the education sector.

From the viewpoint of economic policy, two important types of questions can be related to the above approach. First, one may compute a long-run stationary solution of the above system (assuming that $T \to \infty$ and that such a solution exists) and determine equilibrium ratios of consumption and two types of investment to national income. Denote these by $\alpha$, $\beta_1$, $\beta_2$. How could one use a detailed short-run model to choose instrument variables such as tax rate variation $\tau$, rate of deficit financing $\theta$ and transfer payments* $\phi$, such that the short-run values of $\alpha$, $\beta_1$, $\beta_2$ denoted by $\hat{\alpha}$, $\hat{\beta}_1$, $\hat{\beta}_2$ are as close as possible to the long-run optimal values? If in the above, a choice is made of a point on the long-run optimal trajectory (denoted by asterisks) other than the stationary solution, then the short-run policy problem is to choose the control variables $\tau$, $\theta$, $\phi$ such that:

$$\hat{\alpha}(\tau,\theta,\phi) = \alpha^*,$$

$$\hat{\beta}_1(\tau,\theta,\phi) = \beta_1^*,$$

and

$$\hat{\beta}_2(\tau,\theta,\phi) = \beta_2^*,$$

where $(\alpha^*,\beta_1^*,\beta_2^*)$ specifies the chosen equilibrium point. Note that this approach allows the flexibility of using detailed econometric models in the short run in order to determine the controls which should be applied to converge to the desired values $(\alpha^*,\beta_1^*,\beta_2^*)$. Second, we may consider the short-run optimization problem (i.e., the maximization of the current value Hamiltonian function as it is called) implicit in the above long-run problem, along with some predicted values for $\dot{K}_i$, $\dot{H}_i$ (for example, $\dot{K}_i = r_i K_i$ and $\dot{H}_i = q_i H_i$ with $r_i$, $q_i$ being fixed positive constants would be predictions of a balanced view of growth of capital). Taking this as a short-run equilibrium model we may compare the shadow prices generated with the set of market prices, thus providing us with an implicit trade-off between resources used in the two sectors having a specific education sector. The relative costs of nontransferability of capital between the two sectors can also be appraised in this framework.

* This instrument is closely related to Lindahl's theory of public expenditure (Johansen 1965).

At the university or the department level, applying the above ideas of optimal growth theory is difficult for two reasons: (i) outputs such as research and teaching services cannot be invested within the system, since there is no feedback; and (ii) the demand for output in the form of enrollment of new students is largely exogenous to the system. However, it is possible to identify a set of production functions for any department of a university relating its outputs $(y_i, \ldots, y_n)$ to the various inputs $(x_1, \ldots, x_m)$, i.e.:

$$y_i = f_i(x_1, \ldots, x_m); i = 1, \ldots, n.$$

The various inputs may be, for example, the administrative personnel, capital (in the form of net expenditures on plant and equipment), and the teaching-cum-research personnel, and the typical outputs are various degree outputs and research. Assume that the enrollment projection for a specific department is $\Delta d_i = r_i d_i$, where $r_i$ is constant, and assume that initially there is equilibrium between supply and demand (i.e., $d_i(t) = y_i(t)$ in appropriate units). A consistency model would then ask: What is the appropriate growth in inputs which would maintain the scheme of equilibrium? Using the production function the answer would be:

$$\Delta d_i = \Delta y_i = \sum_{j=1}^{m} (\partial f_i/\partial x_j) \cdot \Delta x_j.$$

If the matrix $F: [\partial f_i/\partial x_j]$ can be assumed constant, then we have the required input vector $\Delta x = (\Delta x_j)$, assuming $F$ to be square and nonsingular,

$$\Delta x = F^{-1}\Delta d, \text{ where } \Delta d = (\Delta d_i).$$

If this rate of input provision is not allowed in the system, imbalances will result in various implicit costs reflected in relative declines of various services (library facilities, instruction quality, etc.) per student unit.

A meaningful control problem can be set up in this framework if one can assume that there are some inputs in the production function above, which are long-run in the sense that they affect the capacity of the system, and that the decision problem differentiates between the long-run capacity expansion problem and the short-run adjustment problems. Let us then consider those inputs (e.g., the inputs in the form of overheads, capital expenditures, library facilities, stock of teaching faculty) in the production function which are elements determining capacity, i.e., $x_i, i = 1, \ldots, \bar{m}$, say, $\bar{m} < m$. Then define $D_i, Y_i$ as the cumulative demand and output of type $i$ starting from some base period, so that $\Delta D_i = \dot{D}_i = d_i$ and $\Delta Y_i = \dot{Y}_i = y_i$. Any long-run divergence between the cumulative demand (i.e., cumulative enrollment) and cumulative output is assumed to entail costs $C_i = C_i(D_i - Y_i)$ as a function of the divergence. It may be assumed that this cost function has the property of positively increasing marginal costs, such that it is zero if and only if $D_i = Y_i$ at every point of time. Now the long-run control problem is one of determining the time paths of the capacity-inputs $x_i(t), \ldots, x_{\bar{m}}(t)$ so as to minimize the discounted cost function over the long-run planning horizon $[O,T]$:

$$\text{minimize} \int_0^T \exp(-\delta t) \left[ \sum_{i=1}^n C_i(D_i - Y_i) \right] dt,$$

subject to

$$\dot{Y}_i = y_i = f_i(x_1, \ldots, x_{\bar{m}}), i = 1, \ldots, n$$

$Y_i(0), D_i(0)$ given at initial time $t = 0$;

here it is assumed that the discount rate $\delta_i$ is the same ($\delta_i = \delta$) for all the cost components.

Note that this control problem specifies only the long-run optimal capacity expansion path for an education unit. Given a point (e.g., a stationary point if it exists) on this optimal trajectory when it exists, one could specify various short-run policies defined through a detailed activity analysis approach in order to allow short-run adjustments and flexibility so that the policymaker could converge to the desired point on the long-run optimal trajectory. Note that in the short-run, activity analysis models or decomposition-type analyses help to provide a means of adjustment, staying as close as possible to the optimal long-run point. The analogy with the optimal neo-classical growth models can be easily extended now (provided the respective production functions can be interpreted to be homogeneous of degree one).

*Goal programming and efficiency in decision models for educational institutions**

Since the outputs of educational institutions are such that obtaining a set of relative prices for them is at best a difficult task, it may prove useful to consider decision models which do not rely heavily upon such a price vector. Models which employ goal programming or which compute efficient output vectors (see Charnes and Cooper [1961], Ijiri [1965], and Lee and Clayton [1969]) allow the policymaker to choose directly the

* This section has been contributed by Gene Gruver, Department of Economics, University of Pittsburgh.

vector of outputs he prefers, and the explicit vector of prices or relative weights for the outputs is only marginally important for such models. There is a very close relationship between the approach of goal programming and the concepts of fixed and variable targets formulated by Tinbergen for quantitative economic planning. In institutions in which decisions are to be made in a decentralized but hierarchical manner a set of subgoals and priority weightings may be effectively employed (see Charnes, Clower, and Kortanek [1967]).

A model which computes efficient output vectors is valuable since a policymaker is assured that to increase the level of any particular output in an efficient vector he will be forced to accept decreases in the level of other outputs. This fact follows directly from the definition of efficiency, since a vector is said to be efficient if and only if it can be produced from available resources and there exists no other feasible vector which has at least as much of each output and strictly more of some outputs.

To give concreteness to the above statements, we will indicate how a linear decision model could be specified, different ways in which goals and subgoals could be formulated, and how linear programming could be used to optimize the resulting goal programming problem. We will also indicate how the same model could be employed to compute an efficient output vector and ensure that the output vector chosen will be efficient.

Let us specify, for example, a linear activity analysis model with the following structure to aid in making short-run decisions at the departmental level in a large university:

$$A_F x - I y_F = 0$$
$$A_I x = 0$$
$$-A_p x \leq -N$$
$$x, y_F \geq 0$$

The constraints $-A_p x \leq -N$ require that the amount of primary commodities used be not more than the amount available per-time unit. The minus signs result from the convention of treating inputs as negative values. Likely commodities to be included in the vector $N$ would be: time of various classifications of faculty and students available, budget, and physical space. The constraints $A_I x = 0$ force the production and consumption of intermediate commodities to balance, and the constraints $A_F x - I y_F = 0$ essentially require that the vector of final output, $y_F$, be equal to $A_F x$. The designation of intermediate commodities is largely a matter of definition; however, it may be useful to consider combining primary commodities, such as graduate student time and dollars, from the budget to form an intermediate commodity, such as the services of a teaching or research assistant. The model then uses the intermediate commodity so formed in producing final commodities. Final commodities in a university department would probably include different instructional and research activities at least. The objective then is to choose in some optimal fashion a vector of final commodities $y_F$ and a corresponding vector of production activity levels $x$.

Suppose that a linear activity analysis model has been specified which accurately expresses the resource availabilities and production capabilities of a university department. A high level policymaker, such as the dean, may choose a vector of output levels $\hat{y}_F$, which he instructs the department to consider as minimum goals to be met if feasible. If they are not feasible then they are to be met as closely as possible in the sense that a weighted sum of the difference between the goals $\hat{y}_F$ and the output vector $y_F$ is to be minimized. A vector of weights $c_\epsilon$, indicating the relative importance of not meeting each of the minimum goal levels, must be specified by the high-level policymaker.

A vector $y_F$ which meets minimum goal levels as nearly as possible will not, in general, be an efficient vector of outputs. Suppose the departmental policymaker views his role as, first of all, meeting the goals of the higher-level policymaker as closely as possible. Next, given that the high-level goals are met as closely as possible he wishes to ensure that an efficient vector of outputs is produced. Finally, given that the vector will be efficient and that high-level goals are met as nearly as possible he may wish to maximize certain subgoals. If the amounts of final output over and above the minimum goal levels $\hat{y}_F$ are designated as $\bar{y}_F$, and if $c_y > 0$ is a vector of relative prices for the commodities of $\bar{y}_F$, then the following model may be employed to implement the above decision-making process:

$$c_y' \bar{y}_F \geqq g_y$$
$$c_\epsilon' \epsilon \leqq g_\epsilon$$
$$A_F x - I \bar{y}_F + I \epsilon_F \geqq \hat{y}_F$$
$$A_I x \qquad\qquad = 0$$
$$-A_p x \qquad\qquad \leqq -N$$
$$x, \bar{y}_F, \epsilon_F \qquad\quad \geqq 0$$

The above constraints are for a series of three linear programming problems which must be computed in sequence to obtain the desired vector. First we set $g_y = 0$ and $g_\epsilon$ equal to a very large number, so that neither of these first two constraints will be binding for the first solution.

Then the first linear program to be solved is to minimize $c'_\epsilon \epsilon$, subject to the constraints. The optimal vector $\epsilon^0$ will equal the positive difference between the high-level goals and the vector of final outputs, i.e., $\epsilon^0 = y_F - y_F^0$, when those goals have been met as nearly as possible. The optimal value of the objective function will represent the minimum sum of weighted positive deviations between $y_F$ and $y_F^0$. Thus, if $c'_\epsilon \epsilon \leq c'_\epsilon \epsilon^0$ then the high-level goals are met as nearly as possible. Therefore, set $g_\epsilon = c'_\epsilon \epsilon^0$ in the above set of constraints. Then, subject to the constraints, the policymaker may proceed to his next objective, which is to insure that the vector of final outputs will be efficient. To accomplish this the second linear program in the sequence must be computed, in which the new objective function is to maximize $c'_y \bar{y}_F$. Let an asterisk denote the optimal solution of this program. The resulting optimal solution will produce an $x^*$, such that the corresponding vector of final output, $y_F^*$, which equals $A_F x^*$ will be an efficient vector of final output. For theoretical verification of this point see Charnes and Cooper ([1961], pp. 312–17). If the constraint set is again changed so that $g_y = c'_y \bar{y}_F^*$, then the resulting constraint $c'_y \bar{y}_F \geq g_y$ will ensure that any feasible solution will be such that $y_F$ is efficient.

At this point the policymaker may maximize certain subgoals by solving the third linear program in the sequence. By choosing a vector $c_x$ of relative weights or prices for the vector of activities $x$ and maximizing $c'_x x$, subject to the constraint set, the policymaker can maximize subgoals while ensuring that he will meet high-level goals as nearly as possible and that the vector of final output will be efficient. The optimal $x$ vector and corresponding $y_F$ vector are the desired solution to the whole decision problem.

Note that the above procedure does require that policymakers specify three different vectors $c_\epsilon$, $c_y$, and $c_x$, each of which indicates the relative importance of different outputs and can be considered to be relative price vectors. However, these relative prices are only marginally important since $c_\epsilon$ and $c_y$ apply only to commodity additions or subtractions around a particular vector of outputs, $\hat{y}_F$. The vector $c_x$ is also only marginally important since it applies only to changes in activity levels which do not violate higher-level objectives. Thus, the ability of the policymaker to specify his preferences in the form of output goals $\hat{y}_F$ is much more important in the above procedure than is his ability to specify his preferences in the form of relative prices.

The possibility of implementing a decentralized hierarchical decision process is also evident. The high-level policymaker can set his goals with top priority in terms of a few highly aggregated outputs and leave to lower-level policymakers the decisions concerning which specific activities can best be used to meet the aggregated outputs. That is, he can leave for lower-level policymakers the responsibility for setting and optimizing subgoals.

An illustrative numerical model is specified in Table 6.3. The numerical values are based on specific assumptions about acceptable class sizes, course loads, teaching loads, and the like, which will not be discussed here. To keep the example of manageable size it is cast as a short-run decision model, so that more long-term decisions, such as classroom space and the budget for faculty salaries, can be taken as given and need not enter this model.

The upper left-hand (6 × 26) submatrix corresponds to $A_F$, the middle left-hand (8 × 26) submatrix corresponds to $A_I$, and the lower left-hand (10 × 26) one to $A_p$. The final commodity activities and the level of available primary commodities $N$ are given by the last seven columns of the table.

Table 6.4 shows the solutions to the three linear programs outlined above, where the model of Table 6.3 is used. The vector of high-level goals is given in the column labeled $\hat{y}_F$. The $c$ vectors used for each program are given in the columns labeled $c_\epsilon$, $c_y$, and $c_x$. The remaining three columns give optimal values of the vector of final outputs $y_F$ and the $x$ vector for each of the three different linear programs. The last column on the right is the vector of final outputs and activities which would be finally chosen using the procedure discussed.

Note that all minimum goals can be satisfied in this example, that the $y_F$ values for the second program make it obvious that the first $y_F$ was not efficient and that, even though $y_F$ is not changed by the third program, two of the three subgoals were increased. The $c_x$ vector in this case is specified, such that the subgoals would be to have as many large principles lectures taught by undergraduate faculty as possible, to have as many junior- and senior-level courses taught by graduate faculty as possible, and to have as many teaching assistants at the M.S. course level as possible (i.e., to have the $x$ variables XLPU, XI2G, and XTAC be as large as possible, given that the minimum goals $\hat{y}_F$ are met and that $y_F$ is efficient).

The column of Table 6.5 labeled "minimum goals" shows comparable results when $y_F$ is changed by increasing the number of standard research years, YSRY, from 55 to 100. The solutions to the first two linear programs were identical in this example, implying that the $y_F$ vector which met the goals as closely as possible was also efficient. Those values for $y_F$ are given. No subgoal problem was computed for this example.

Table 6.3. Goal programming: Basic model

|  |  |  | Instruction |  |
|---|---|---|---|---|
|  |  | Small principles section using instructor | Large principles section using undergrad. faculty | Large principles section using graduate faculty |
| Commodity | Code | XSPI | XLPU | XLPG |
| Undergrad. instruction | UI | 105.00000 | 840.00000 | 840.00000 |
| M.S. level instruction | MI |  |  |  |
| Ph.D. level instruction | DI |  |  |  |
| M.S. thesis | MT |  |  |  |
| Ph.D. dissertation | DD |  |  |  |
| Standard research year | SRY |  |  |  |
| Teaching assistants | TA |  | −1.00000 | −1.00000 |
| Instructors | INST | −.08333 |  |  |
| Research assistants (M.S. course level) | RAMC |  |  |  |
| Research assistants (M.S. thesis level) | RAMT |  |  |  |
| Research assistants (Ph.D. course level) | RADC |  |  |  |
| Research assistants (Ph.D. dissertation level) | RADD |  |  |  |
| Secretarial services | SEC | −.02000 | −.03000 | −.03000 |
| Computing | COMP |  |  |  |
| Undergrad. faculty | UF |  | −.08333 |  |
| Graduate faculty | GF |  |  | −.08333 |
| M.S. students (course stage) | GSMC |  |  |  |
| Ph.D. students (course stage) | GSDC |  |  |  |
| M.S. students (thesis stage) | GSMT |  |  |  |
| Ph.D. students (dissertation stage) | GSDD |  |  |  |
| Undergrad. students (Fresh. & Soph.) | US12 | −2.18750 | −17.50000 | −17.50000 |
| Undergrad. students (Jr. and Sr.) | US34 |  |  |  |
| Budget | BUDG |  |  |  |
| Grad. student and secretarial offices | GSSO |  |  |  |

*Note:* All blank positions in the matrix indicate zero elements.

The above examples are not rich enough to present the full versatility of goal programming. There exists the possibility of setting fixed goals in which both positive and negative deviations from the values are considered undesirable. Different criteria for minimization of deviations from goals can be chosen. One obvious possibility would be to minimize a weighted sum of squared deviations. This, however, would require a different computational technique. Either quadratic programming or a generalized inverse method might be used (see Ijiri [1965] and Contini [1968] for examples).

On the other hand, minimizing the weighted sum of absolute deviations from goals, or minimizing the maximum weighted absolute deviation, may be set as the criterion for "closeness" to goals. Each of these may be computed by linear programming (see Ijiri [1965] and Zukhovitskiy and Avdeyeva [1966] for further information).

The original numerical model can be used to give a numerical example for each of the two criteria just mentioned. The following program will find the vector $y_F = A_F x$, which minimizes the weighted sum of absolute deviations from goals $\hat{y}_F$:

# RESOURCE ALLOCATION IN NONMARKET SYSTEMS 185

activities

| Fr.-Soph class undergrad. faculty | Fr.-Soph. class grad. faculty | Jr.-Sr. class undergrad. faculty | Jr.-Sr. class grad. faculty | M.S. course instruction | Ph.D. course instruction |
|---|---|---|---|---|---|
| XIIU | XIIG | XI2U | XI2G | XIM | XID |
| 105.00000 | 105.00000 | 90.00000 | 90.00000 |  |  |
|  |  |  |  | 90.00000 |  |
|  |  |  |  |  | 90.00000 |
|  |  |  |  |  |  |
| −.0200 | −.02000 | −.02000 | −.02000 | −.02000 | −.02000 |
| −.08333 |  | −.08333 |  |  |  |
|  | −.08333 |  | −.08333 | −.08333 | −.08333 |
|  |  |  |  | −2.50000 |  |
|  |  |  |  |  | −2.50000 |
| −2.18750 | −2.18750 |  |  |  |  |
|  |  | −1.87500 | −1.87500 |  |  |

$$\min c'_\epsilon \epsilon_F$$

subject to

$$c'_\epsilon \epsilon_F \leq g_\epsilon,$$
$$A_F x - I \epsilon_F \leq \hat{y}_F,$$
$$A_F^+ x - I \epsilon_{F+} \geq \hat{y}_F^+,$$
$$A_I x = 0,$$
$$-A_p x \leq -N, \quad x, \epsilon_F \geq 0.$$

If all goals are to be fixed goals (i.e., quotas of final outputs which should not be over- or underfulfilled) then $A_F = A_F^+$, $\epsilon_F = \epsilon_F^+$, and $\hat{y}_F = \hat{y}_F^+$. However, for any commodity which is to have only a minimum goal (i.e., where only underfulfillment of the goal is to be minimized) then the corresponding row of $A_F$, $\epsilon_F$, and $\hat{y}_F$ must be dropped from $A_F^+$, $\epsilon_F^+$, and $\hat{y}_F^+$. For the example solution the rows corresponding to YMI and YDI were dropped from $A_F^+$, $\epsilon_F^+$, and $\hat{y}_F^+$. In other words, the $\hat{y}_F$ values shown in Table 6.5 represent quotas of fixed goals for all com-

Table 6.3. (continued)

|  | Research, dissertation, and thesis activities ||||||| 
| | Research activity no. 1 | Research activity no. 2 | Research activity no. 3 | Research activity no. 4 | Research activity no. 5 | M.S. thesis supervision | Ph.D. dissertation supervision |
|---|---|---|---|---|---|---|---|
| Code | XRES1 | XRES2 | XRES3 | XRES4 | XRES5 | XSM | XSD |
| UI | | | | | | | |
| MI | | | | | | | |
| DI | | | | | | | |
| MT | | 4.00000 | 4.00000 | | 2.00000 | 1.00000 | |
| DD | | | 2.00000 | | 1.00000 | | 1.00000 |
| SRY | 1.00000 | 2.33333 | 3.66667 | 1.66667 | 3.66667 | | |
| TA | | | | | | | |
| INST | | | | | | | |
| RAMC | | | | −1.00000 | −1.00000 | | |
| RAMT | | −2.00000 | −2.00000 | | −1.00000 | | |
| RADC | | | | | −1.00000 | | |
| RADD | | | −2.00000 | | −1.00000 | | |
| SEC | −.30000 | −.60000 | −1.00000 | −.40000 | −1.00000 | | |
| COMP | −.30000 | −1.00000 | −1.50000 | −.60000 | −1.20000 | −.15000 | −.30000 |
| UF | | | | | | | |
| GF | −1.00000 | −1.00000 | −1.00000 | −1.00000 | −1.00000 | −.04900 | −.09800 |
| GSMC | | | | | | | |
| GSDC | | | | | | | |
| GSMT | | | | | | −.45000 | |
| GSDD | | | | | | | −.90000 |
| US12 | | | | | | | |
| US34 | | | | | | | |
| BUDG | | | | | | | |
| GSSO | | | | | | | |

*Note:* All blank positions in the matrix indicate zero elements.

modities except graduate student instruction at both the M.S. and Ph.D. The $\hat{y}_F$ values for graduate student instruction represent only minimum goals.

The optimal solution to the above program produces the $y_F$ vector given under the column labeled "Minimum sum of absolute deviations." For the initial minimization $g_\epsilon$ is set equal to a very large number so as not to be constraining; then once the optimal solution has been obtained $g_\epsilon$ can be set equal to $c'_\epsilon \epsilon_F^0$ and subgoals can then be maximized if desired.

To find the vector which minimizes the maximum weighted absolute deviation from goals the following linear program must be solved:

min $\epsilon_1$,

subject to

$$\epsilon_1 \leq g_\epsilon,$$
$$A_F x - c_\epsilon \epsilon_1 \leq \hat{y}_F,$$
$$A_F^+ x + c_\epsilon \epsilon_1 \geq \hat{y}_F^+,$$

# RESOURCE ALLOCATION IN NONMARKET SYSTEMS

| | | | Intermediate commodity activities | | | | | |
|---|---|---|---|---|---|---|---|---|
| Teaching assistant course stage | Teaching assistant thesis stage | Instructor course stage | Instructor dissertation stage | Research assistants M.S. course stage | Research assistants M.S. thesis stage | Research assistants Ph.D. course stage | Research assistants Ph.D. dissertation stage | Secretarial services |
| XTAC | XTAT | XINC | XIND | XRAMC | XRAMT | XRADC | XRADD | XSEC |
| .50000 | .50000 | .50000 | .50000 | .50000 | .50000 | .50000 | 1.00000 | 1.00000 |
| −.50000 | −.50000 | −.50000 | −.50000 | −.50000 | −.50000 | −.50000 | −1.00000 | |
| −2.70000 | −2.70000 | −3.60000 | −3.60000 | −2.70000 | −2.70000 | −3.60000 | −7.20000 | −7.20000 |
| −1.00000 | −1.00000 | −1.00000 | −1.00000 | −1.00000 | −1.00000 | −1.00000 | −1.00000 | −1.00000 |

$$A_I x = 0,$$
$$-A_p x \leq -N, \; x, \; \epsilon_1 \geq 0.$$

Note that $\epsilon_1$ is a scalar and $c_\epsilon$ and $c_\epsilon^+$ are column vectors.

The plus superscript has the same interpretation as in the last problem. As before, $g_\epsilon$ is initially a very large number and if subgoals are to be maximized, $g_\epsilon$ is set equal to $\epsilon_1^0$. For the example calculation $\epsilon_1^0$ was 14.336 and the resulting $y_F$ is given in Table 6.5 under the column labeled "Minimum maximum absolute deviation."

### Aggregation, disaggregation, and consistency problems of policymaking

Various methods (Dantzig and Wolfe 1960; Arrow 1959; Sengupta and Fox 1969) have been proposed in recent years for decomposing a large programming model, suitable for national planning, into subprograms linked through a set of prices which can be sequentially co-ordinated

Table 6.3. (*continued*)

|  | \multicolumn{7}{c}{Intermediate commodity activities} | | | | | | |
| --- | --- | --- | --- | --- | --- | --- | --- | --- | --- |
|  | Computational services | Undergrad. instruction | M.S. level instruction | Ph.D. level instruction | M.S. theses | Ph.D. dissertations | Standard research years | | | |
| Code | XCOMP | YUI | YMI | YDI | YMT | YDD | YSRY | | | |
| UI | | −1.00000 | | | | | | = | 0 |
| MI | | | −1.00000 | | | | | = | 0 |
| DI | | | | −1.00000 | | | | = | 0 |
| MT | | | | | −1.00000 | | | = | 0 |
| DD | | | | | | −1.00000 | | = | 0 |
| SRY | | | | | | | −1.00000 | = | 0 |
| TA | | | | | | | | = | 0 |
| INST | | | | | | | | = | 0 |
| RAMC | | | | | | | | = | 0 |
| RAMT | | | | | | | | = | 0 |
| RADC | | | | | | | | = | 0 |
| RADD | | | | | | | | = | 0 |
| SEC | | | | | | | | = | 0 |
| COMP | 1.00000 | | | | | | | = | 0 |
| UF | | | | | | | | ≥ | −20.0 |
| GF | | | | | | | | ≥ | −40.0 |
| GSMC | | | | | | | | ≥ | −120.0 |
| GSDC | | | | | | | | ≥ | −60.0 |
| GSMT | | | | | | | | ≥ | −40.0 |
| GSDD | | | | | | | | ≥ | −30.0 |
| US12 | | | | | | | | ≥ | −600.0 |
| US34 | | | | | | | | ≥ | −375.0 |
| BUDG | −1.00000 | | | | | | | ≥ | −1,000.0 |
| GSSO | | | | | | | | ≥ | −260.0 |

*Note:* All blank positions in the matrix indicate zero elements.

and revised by the central agency until the optima of the subprograms lead also to the over-all optimum of the original program. These prices, discussed in Chapters 4 and 5, have been variously termed in the economic literature, e.g., interim shadow prices, provisional dual variables, transfer prices, internal prices, or prices with specific rules of imputation. The term "transfer price" (Hirshleifer 1957) brings out clearly the economic implications of its role in bringing about the convergence of subprogram optima to the over-all optimum through successive transfer of resources between the subprograms.

The methods of decomposition through transfer pricing have raised the most fundamental questions about the general economic theory of resource allocation and optimization at different levels; national planning for economic systems comprising several sectors has provided one natural framework for discussion, whereas a divisionalized firm (Hirshleifer 1957) (i.e., a firm with several divisions with some resources specific to a division and others common to all divisions) with its problem of optimal decisionmaking has provided another basic framework for discussing decomposition methods. In the context of firm behavior the

RESOURCE ALLOCATION IN NONMARKET SYSTEMS 189

Table 6.4. Goal programming: Solutions to the three linear programs

|  |  |  | min $c'_\epsilon \epsilon$ |  | max $c'_y \bar{y}_F$ |  | max $c'_x x$ |
|---|---|---|---|---|---|---|---|
| Code | $y_F$ | $c_\epsilon$ | $g_\epsilon = 100{,}000$<br>$g_y = 0$ | $c_y$ | $g = 0$<br>$g^\epsilon_y = 0$ | $c_x$ | $g_\epsilon = 0$<br>$g^\epsilon_y = 1117.103$ |
| YUI | 46,800.000 | 1.000 | 46,800.000 | 1.000 | 46,800.000 |  | 46,800.000 |
| YMI | 3,600.000 | 1.000 | 3,600.000 | 1.000 | 4,320.000 |  | 4,320.000 |
| YDI | 1,800.000 | 1.000 | 1,800.000 | 1.000 | 2,160.000 |  | 2,160.000 |
| YMT | 40.000 | 1.000 | 40.000 | 1.000 | 77.102 |  | 77.102 |
| YDD | 30.000 | 1.000 | 30.000 | 1.000 | 30.000 |  | 30.000 |
| YSRY | 55.000 | 1.000 | 55.000 | 1.000 | 55.001 |  | 55.001 |
| XSPI |  |  | 5.833 |  | 0.000 | 0.000 | 0.000 |
| XLPU |  |  | 0.000 |  | 0.000 | 1.000 | 2.304 |
| XLPG |  |  | 0.000 |  | 2.304 | 0.000 | 0.000 |
| XI1U |  |  | 40.096 |  | 40.096 | 0.000 | 237.792 |
| XI1G |  |  | 228.357 |  | 215.756 | 0.000 | 18.060 |
| XI2U |  |  | 200.000 |  | 200.000 | 0.000 | 0.000 |
| XI2G |  |  | 0.000 |  | 0.000 | 1.000 | 200.000 |
| XIM |  |  | 40.000 |  | 48.000 | 0.000 | 48.000 |
| XID |  |  | 20.000 |  | 24.000 | 0.000 | 24.000 |
| XRES1 |  |  | 0.000 |  | 0.000 | 0.000 | 0.000 |
| XRES2 |  |  | 0.000 |  | 0.000 | 0.000 | 0.000 |
| XRES3 |  |  | 5.000 |  | 15.000 | 0.000 | 15.000 |
| XRES4 |  |  | 0.000 |  | 0.000 | 0.000 | 0.000 |
| XRES5 |  |  | 10.000 |  | 0.000 | 0.000 | 0.000 |
| XSM |  |  | 0.000 |  | 17.101 | 0.000 | 17.101 |
| XSD |  |  | 10.000 |  | 0.000 | 0.000 | 0.000 |
| XTAC |  |  | 0.000 |  | 0.000 | 1.000 | 0.000 |
| XTAT |  |  | 0.000 |  | 4.608 | 0.000 | 4.608 |
| XINC |  |  | 0.000 |  | 0.000 | 0.000 | 0.000 |
| XIND |  |  | 0.972 |  | 0.000 | 0.000 | 0.000 |
| XRAMC |  |  | 19.999 |  | 0.000 | 0.000 | 0.000 |
| XRAMT |  |  | 40.000 |  | 60.000 | 0.000 | 60.000 |
| XRADC |  |  | 19.999 |  | 0.000 | 0.000 | 0.000 |
| XRADD |  |  | 20.000 |  | 30.000 | 0.000 | 30.000 |
| XSEC |  |  | 25.686 |  | 25.626 | 0.000 | 25.626 |
| XCOMP |  |  | 22.500 |  | 25.065 | 0.000 | 25.065 |

Note: All values rounded to three decimal places.

Table 6.5. Goal programming: Solutions in the parametric case

|  |  | Minimum goals |  | Fixed and minimum goals |  |  |  |
|---|---|---|---|---|---|---|---|
|  |  | max $c_y \bar{y}_F$ |  | Minimum |  | Minimum |  |
| Code | $\hat{y}_r$ | $c_\epsilon, c_y$ | $g_\epsilon = 15.271$<br>$g_y = 0$ | $c_\epsilon$ | Sum of absolute deviations | $c_\epsilon$ | Maximum absolute deviations |
| YUI | 46,800.000 | 1.000 | 46,800.000 | 1.000 | 46,800.000 | 1.000 | 46,785.666 |
| YMI | 3,600.000 | 1.000 | 3,600.000 | 1.000 | 3,600.000 | 1.000 | 3,585.664 |
| YDI | 1,800.000 | 1.000 | 1,800.000 | 1.000 | 1,800.000 | 1.000 | 1,785.664 |
| YMT | 40.000 | 1.000 | 80.000 | 1.000 | 40.000 | 1.000 | 54.334 |
| YDD | 30.000 | 1.000 | 30.000 | 1.000 | 30.000 | 1.000 | 27.168 |
| YSRY | 100.000 | 1.000 | 84.729 | 1.000 | 76.126 | 1.000 | 85.664 |

Note: All values rounded to three decimal places.

transfer prices are all internal prices (Shubik 1962) to the firm, in the sense that these are nonmarket prices and hence may contain all sorts of imputations and arbitrary elements, unless other suitable interpretations are considered.

In recent years several important theoretical and practical questions have been raised concerning the various decomposition methods of planning, which are essentially based on the use of prices to guide decentralized resource transfers and allocation. First, in a general nonlinear programming framework (or even in the Kornai–Lipták scheme applied to linear programming) it is difficult to guarantee that any of the existing decomposition techniques would preserve the two properties called feasibility and monotonicity by Malinvaud (1967), i.e., there may be lack of feasibility at any stage other than the optimum, and successive applications of the decomposition procedure do not ensure monotonic increases in the objective function. Lack of feasibility may also arise when the aggregate model constraints are built out of the sectoral constraints, where the latter may be mutually conflicting intersectorally. As a matter of fact, it is sometimes argued with reference to actual planning experiences in socialist countries that aggregation in planning is the cause (Ellman 1969) of inconsistency in detailed plan formulations. The danger of infeasibility is, of course, a serious limitation of the practicality of application of price-guided allocations. Also, the assumption of convex production possibility sets is basic to all of the decomposition techniques, so that even limited economies of scale and its associated nonconvexities are not admissible. This has led to alternative methods of planning without prices (Heal 1969; Aoki 1971), based on outputs and marginal productivities of inputs given the demand constraints.

Second, the two roles of prices, for expressing planner's commands and also for securing efficient allocation according to relative scarcities, may at times be seriously conflicting. If shadow prices are really used to guide resource allocation and decentralization, this fact should minimize and tend to eliminate the use of central command and quota allocations (Levine 1966). In the linear programming models of decomposition discussed in Chapter 4, it is tacitly assumed that the resource vector is in terms of quantities and that for each effective inequality there exists a positive shadow price. However, if the resource vector is not in quantities but in value terms (due to aggregation or planner's commands), it already incorporates a price. Conflicts may arise when these two prices are varied with differing objectives, the shadow price for efficient resource allocation and the imputed resource price for planner's priorities.

Third, the relative fixity of a resource (i.e. inelasticity of supply) is the basic reason for imputing a shadow price in a linear programming (or nonlinear programming) framework, which is nothing but a quasi rent to a fixed factor inelastic in supply in the short run. In a competitive private market system, the relative fixity of some inputs and their associated costs can be estimated by reference to their market value (or salvage value), whereas in a centrally directed system, the planner has some degree of freedom in determining the degree of relative fixity. To this extent, the planner's decisions regarding the user costs of fixed resources are likely to have variable effects on resource transfer unlike that of lump-sum tax schemes discussed in the theory of welfare economics.

*Decomposition and aggregation*

Technically speaking decomposition techniques refer to the various methods of subdividing one master programming problem into subproblems (each of which is a programming problem), such that the subproblems are linked in some fashion (e.g., through successive revision of net prices in the subproblem objective function in the Dantzig–Wolfe algorithm) to allow the sequence of subproblem optima to converge to the over-all optimum of the objective function of the original program. For LP (linear programming) models it is possible in principle to classify at least five types of decomposition methods:

1. the decomposition algorithms for the block-triangular-type LP models which distinguish between central and sectoral (i.e., divisional) resources, developed by Dantzig and Wolfe (DW) (1960);

2. the methods of two-level planning developed by Kornai and Lipták (KL) (1965), in which the resource vector is reshuffled sequentially to attain conformability and optimality of sector programs with the over-all program;

3. the active approach developed by Tintner and Sengupta (TS) (Sengupta et al. 1963; Sengupta and Fox 1969) in connection with stochastic linear programming, in which the resource vector is partitioned into a linear combination of allocation vectors, as in the KL approach, but the partitioning of the over-all problem into subproblems is done in a manner different from the KL approach. Also it has been shown elsewhere (Sengupta and Tintner 1971) that the TS approach combines in a sense the partitioning method of the KL approach with the simplex-type computation procedure of the DW approach. The fact that the TS approach was developed much earlier than the KL and DW approaches is also worth mentioning;

4. the methods of decentralization developed by Arrow and Hurwicz (AH), in which alternative rules of adjustment through implicit prices (i.e., dual variables) using the gradient methods of different versions (1960) are adopted for showing the convergence of subproblem optima to the over-all optimand; and

5. the delegation models of activity analysis type developed by Koopmans (1951) and others based, for example, on methods of analyzing an LP model with a vector objective function into a sequence of properly constructed and linked LP subprograms. The optimality characterized by an optimal activity vector in this framework has been termed K-efficiency by Charnes and Cooper (1960) and shown to be more general than the ordinary concept of optimality associated with a standard LP model.

From an economic viewpoint there are three basic points of similarity common to the above five types of decomposition. Since most of the above types of decomposition have been discussed in Chapters 4 and 5, we mention here only the basic points of similarity between these methods. First, there is a classification (i.e., a decentralization) in levels of decisionmaking between the center (i.e., firm as a whole) and the sectors (i.e., divisions of a firm), for example, mainly through resources some of which are specific to individual sectors while the remainder, allocated by the center, are common to all sectors.* The concept of decentralization here implies that the sectors should be allowed complete freedom of choice in their optimization problems, except that the center provides co-ordination through guiding rules of price imputation based on the marginal productivities of common, central resources allocated to different sectors.

Second, the formulation of guiding rules of price adjustment should be such that in successive applications or iterations they specify a feasible and sequentially improving optimizing direction converging to the over-all optimum. These guiding rules are generally based on the marginal productivities (or some functions thereof as in the AH approach) of the common central resources allocated to the sectors in terms of their marginal contributions to the over-all objective function of the original master LP model. This implies that sectors (or divisions of a firm) having higher marginal productivities of a specific set of central resources at any stage or iteration tend to receive higher allocations (more precisely, not lower than before) of those central resources, until at the over-all optimum point no further reallocation of central resources between sectors could improve the value of the over-all objective function of the master program.

Third, the sectoral (or divisional) interdependence is here reflected in

* Note that the university as a whole may be like the "center," while the different academic departments are the "sectors." Also, a single department chairman could be the central planner, whereas various subdepartment heads could be sectoral planners.

the competition by each sector to get a higher allocation of the central resources; however, the desire of each sector to get higher allocations is unlikely to be realized (after some iterations) for at least some sectors, since the guiding rule followed by the center is to allocate to the highest bidder, when each sectoral bid is in terms of its marginal contribution to the over-all objective function.

For any decomposition method for a given LP problem there are three distinct identifiable stages: the central LP model, the set of divisional (or sectoral) LP submodels, and a rule of aggregation linking the central and the divisional LP models. Three different types of analysis are now conceivable:

1. Given the central and the divisional LP models, how to determine the linking rule, such that it allows the sequential convergence of the set of divisional optima to the over-all optimand? The usual algorithms (DW, KL, AH) of decomposition raise this basic question and develop computational methods for its solution.

2. Given the divisional LP's and a rule of aggregation (or allocation), how to determine an appropriate central LP model which is optimal in a class of central LP models? This question was raised earlier by several authors (Klein 1946; May 1946; Theil 1954) in the context of estimation of micro and macro relations, but the LP version of this problem brings new additional complications due to the presence of inequalities and optimizing objective functions.

3. Given any central model and a rule of disaggregation of central resources or activities, how to determine a set of divisional LP models linked in some fashion and having the optimality property in a class of divisional LP models? This question leads to methods of decomposing (or subdividing) the over-all central LP model conditional on the specific rule of disaggregation. This method has been found very useful in the active approach of TS in stochastic linear programming (Sengupta 1970), particularly in analyzing the statistical distribution (e.g., mean, variance, etc.) of optimal profits in the over-all LP model conditional on the specific rule of disaggregation.

Note that the class of problems (2) and (3) which are basically problems of aggregation or disaggregation is outside the realm of decomposition techniques developed so far. We consider some basic aspects of these problems and their characterizations in an economic framework.

Consider a typical example* of problem (2) mentioned above. Assume

* For resources which are transferable between academic departments, this example would be applicable to a set of academic departments in a university system.

there are $K$ subdepartments of a large academic department, with the activity vector of subdepartment (or unit) $k = 1, 2, \ldots, K$ denoted by $x_k$ and its LP problem as:

$$\max z_k = c'_k x_k \text{ subject to } A_k x_k \leq b_k; x_k \geq 0, \tag{8}$$

where $(c_k, b_k, A_k)$ is the set of coefficients assumed given.

The problem is how to aggregate the $K$ models (8) to arrive at a central LP model with an activity vector $X$ and the parameter set $c, b, A$, such that $X$ satisfies a given rule:

$$X = R(x_1, x_2, \ldots, x_K) \tag{9}$$

of aggregation and there are certain restrictions on the relationship between the parameter sets $(c, b, A)$ and $(c_k, b_k, A_k; k = 1, 2, \ldots, K)$. A particular case of the latter restrictions is:

$$c_k = L_k \cdot c; \; b_k = M_k \cdot b; \; A_k = A_0; \; k = 1, 2, \ldots, K, \tag{10}$$

where $L_k$ and $M_k$ are fixed scalar numbers $0 \leq L_k, M_k \leq 1$ and $A_0$ is the *optimal* basis matrix contained in the matrix $A$ of the central LP model. Likewise, a particular example of the rule (9) of aggregation is:

$$X = \sum_{k=1}^{K} x_k, \tag{11}$$

where the activity vectors $x_k$ are to be suitably redefined if necessary by including dummy activities, so that the dimension of the activity vector of $K$ different subdepartments is identically equal to that of the subdepartment having the largest number of activities to choose from. In this framework defined by (10) and (11), the class of central models is specified by the following central LP model:

$$\max Z = c'X \text{ subject to } A_0 X \leq b, \; x \geq 0. \tag{12}$$

Since $b$ and $b_k$, $c$ and $c_k$ are linearly dependent vectors and $A_k = A_0$, it is easy to prove (Day 1963) that the optimal solution of this central problem denoted by $X_0$ and its optimal basis $A_0$ is related to the optimal solution vectors (denoted by $\bar{x}_k$) of sectoral LP models (8). As a matter of fact if the non-negative weights $L_k$, $M_k$ in (10) are such that:

$$\sum_{k=1}^{K} L_k = 1 = \sum_{k=1}^{K} M_k, \tag{13}$$

then it follows that:

$$X_0 = \sum_{k=1}^{K} \bar{x}_k, \tag{14}$$

$\bar{x}_k$ is the optimal vector of the $k$th subdepartment model, and

$$Z_0 = c'X_0 = \sum_{k=1}^{K} c'_k \bar{x}_k = \sum_{k=1}^{K} \bar{z}_k. \tag{15}$$

Two points about this aggregation may be noted. First, the optimal basis $A_0$ is invariant under either the aggregation of LP submodels (8) into the central model (12) or the decomposition of the central LP model (12) into divisional LP submodels (8). Second, this scheme specifies the condition of *perfect* aggregation, which has been defined by Theil (1954) for equational systems as follows: "The rule of perfection for a macroequation obtains when there is no contradiction between the macroequation and the microequations corresponding to it, whatever values and changes assumed by the microvariables." In this case the central LP model (12) is the macrosystem corresponding to the microsystems (8) and the macroparameters $(c,b,A)$ are related to the microparameters $(c_k,b_k,A_k)$ as follows:

$$\sum_k c_k = \sum_k L_k \cdot c = c; \sum_k b_k = \sum_k M_k \cdot b = b; A_k = A_0 \subseteq A.$$

The changes in values of microvariables are, of course, restricted to the domain of feasibility of each subproblem (8); note that the presence of errors in the microparameters (e.g., in the form $c_k = L_k \cdot c + u_k$, $b_k = M_k \cdot b + v_k$, where $u_k$, $v_k$ are mutually independent errors with zero means and variances unity) would not disturb this scheme of perfect aggregation or perfect disaggregation (i.e., decomposition), if it does not violate the linear independence of the columns of $A_k = A_0$ (i.e., if it preserves the same optimal basis as before); the only change required would be to replace the previous objective functions and other random parameters by their expected values (Sengupta et al. 1963).

Note, however, that the above example of perfect aggregation is a very special case, which could be generalized in several directions. Three types of generalization will be mentioned here: (a) resource aggregation without activity aggregation; (b) resource aggregation with activity aggregation; and (c) resource aggregation with a decision rule but without any activity aggregation.

In the first case of resource aggregation without activity aggregation, the central model could be formulated as:

$$\max Z = \sum_k c'_k x_k \text{ subject to } A_k x_k \leq U_k \cdot \sum_k b_k; x_k \geq 0, \tag{16}$$

where $k = 1, 2, \ldots, K$ and $U_k$ denotes the $k$th row of an allocation matrix $U$ of order $K \cdot m$ (assuming there are $m$ resources for each of $K$

subdepartments), a typical element $u_{ki}$ of which denotes the proportion of resource $i = 1, \ldots, m$ allocated to the $k$th unit ($k = 1, \ldots, K$) such that:

$$u_{ki} \geq 0, \sum_{k=1}^{K} u_{ki} \leq 1. \tag{17}$$

Denote the aggregate resource vector by $\beta$:

$$\beta = \sum_{k} b_k;\ \beta,\ b_k:\ m.1;\ k = 1, \ldots, K. \tag{18}$$

Then the aggregate model (12), compared to the divisional models (8) has the following economic interpretation: If the $K$ individual subdepartments, each having an LP model of the form (8), agree to pool their resources into an aggregate vector $\beta$ and then solve for its optimal reallocation $u_{ki}(k = 1, \ldots, K; i = 1, \ldots, m)$ along with a new optimal activity vector $\bar{x}_k$, then they can always guarantee a level of aggregate profits at least as great as (or greater than) the sum of optimal individual profits. Generally speaking the aggregate optimal profits will be greater, i.e.:

$$\bar{Z} = \sum_{k} c'_k \bar{x}_k \text{ of } (12) > \sum_{k} \bar{z}_k = \sum_{k} c'_k \bar{x}_k \text{ of } (8), \tag{19}$$

since the matrix $U$ with rows $U_k^k$ of allocation ratios, which is a decision variable just like $x_k$ in the central model (12), allows better utilization of resources available to each subdepartment.

In the language of game theory (Radstrom 1964), the inequality (19) says that by entering into coalition in terms of pooled resources the subdepartments can improve their aggregate profits. Note, however, that whenever the inequality (19) holds, there is a problem of distribution of the excess profits $E$:

$$E = \bar{Z} - \sum_{k} \bar{z}_k > 0. \tag{20}$$

The game theory approach (Shapley 1959) introduces a set of imputations expressing possible schemes of distribution of this excess profit $E$ among the $K$ individual units. An imputation is a vector $w$ of $K$ elements $(w_1, w_2, \ldots, w_k)$ with the following two properties (for $k = 1, 2, \ldots, K$):

$$w_k \geq \bar{z}_k = c'_k \bar{x}_k,\ \bar{x}_k \text{ is the optimal vector for (8), and} \tag{21a}$$

$$\sum_{k=1}^{K} w_k = \bar{Z},\ \bar{Z} \text{ is the optimal profit for (12).} \tag{21b}$$

Note that in the above framework of aggregation of subdepartment models, several choices are open for selecting an imputation vector satisfying the two properties of (21). For instance, one obvious choice of the imputation vector is

$$w_k = \bar{Z} \cdot \left(\bar{z}_k / \sum_{k=1}^{K} \bar{z}_k\right); k = 1, 2, \ldots, K, \tag{22}$$

which updates optimal profits for each subdepartment by a proportion given by

$$\bar{Z} / \sum_k \bar{z}_k$$

(i.e., this is the proportion by which the optimal dual vector $\bar{y}_k$ of each LP problem [8] is multiplied). Several other choices are conceivable (Harsanyi 1956), and different sharing principles (Rosenfeld 1964) have been proposed in the context of $n$-person game theory. Two points are worth mentioning here. First, the imputation vector, if it is not empty, provides one important difference between the aggregation and disaggregation procedures for a set of LP models. Second, although the imputation vector is not unique, unless other conditions are suitably imposed, yet the range of variation of its elements can be laid down precisely, e.g., the share of each subdepartment in the increased level of aggregate profits $\bar{Z}$ must lie between the ratios $\bar{z}_k / \bar{Z}$ and one, depending on the bargaining strengths of different units.

Now consider the case of activity aggregation along with the resource aggregation defined above. Assume that the input coefficient vector for each activity (e.g., undergraduate teaching) is identical for all $K$ subdepartments (technological homogeneity of production), and denote by $x_{jk}$ the activity $j$ produced by the $k$th subdepartment with its input-coefficient vector $\alpha_j (j = 1, 2, \ldots, n)$. Denote the aggregate activity $j$ by:

$$X_j = \sum_k x_{jk}; k = 1, 2, \ldots, K; j = 1, \ldots, n, \tag{23}$$

and let the element of the net returns (i.e., its estimates are assumed available) vector $c_k$ be denoted by $c_{jk}$ for the $j$th activity and the $k$th subdepartment. Then, one version of the central model under aggregation of both resources and activities turns out to be:

$$\max Z = \sum_k \sum_j c_{jk} x_{jk} \text{ subject to } \sum_j \left(\alpha_j \sum_k x_{jk}\right) \leq \sum_k b_k; x_{jk} \geq 0. \tag{24}$$

Note that the restriction set of problem (24) is the union of the restriction sets of problem (8) with the additional condition of technological homogeneity. Hence the optimal profits solved from (24) can never be less than the sum of optimal profits of individual unit LP models (8).

Again we have to introduce imputation functions for distributing the excess profits, if any. Note that the aggregate problem formulation in (24) assumes that all $K$ subdepartments pool their resources and activities. If we assume instead that the first $K_1$ units agree to pool their resources and activities in a coalition, separately from other groups $K_2$, $K_3, \ldots, K_N$ of $N$ coalitions, under the assumption $1 \leq K_n \leq K$, $n = 1, 2, \ldots, N$, where $K$ denotes the total number of units, then we get several other versions of the aggregate model (24).

Now consider the case of resource aggregation with a decision rule but without any activity aggregation. This method adjoins in effect a separate decision rule constraint to the aggregate formulation (16). One type of decision rule constraint is:

$$\lambda_k \sum_{m=1}^{K} x_m \leq x_k \leq \mu_k \sum_{m=1}^{K} x_k; \lambda_k, \mu_k \geq 0; \sum_k \lambda_k \leq 1, \sum \mu_k \leq 1, \qquad (25)$$

where $\lambda_k, \mu_k$ are preassigned non-negative (scalar) numbers which express, in a sense, the lower and upper flexibility coefficients of the $k$th unit's adjustment behavior (Day 1963a, b). In other words, these preassigned coefficients allow the $K$ individual units to stay close, in some sense, to their individual optimal solutions of individual LP models (8). For example, $\lambda_k$ in (25) may be preassigned by the $k$th unit from the optimal solution vectors $\bar{x}_k$ of the individual LP models (25) as:

$$\lambda_k \cdot \sum_{m=1}^{K} \bar{x}_m = \bar{x}_k; k = 1, 2, \ldots, K. \qquad (26)$$

Several remarks on this type of formulation may be made. First, choices of decision rules other than that mentioned in (25) and (26) are available, particularly in dynamic (Fox et al. 1966) and stochastic models (Howard 1960). Further, the set $(\lambda_k, \mu_k; k = 1, 2, \ldots, K)$ need not be preassigned in a general formulation, in which it could provide additional decision variables to allocate the increased level $\bar{Z}$ of optimal profits, thus eliminating the need for introducing separate imputation functions. However, this general formulation would be basically nonlinear. Second, note that the aggregate optimal profits in this type of aggregation can never be higher than those given by the resource aggregation model (24), although this type of aggregation may have more acceptability with subdepartment-level decisionmakers, since the identities of individual units and their relative positions in the group are maintained. This consideration may be important in terms of implementation of over-all policy toward aggregation or disaggregation of subdepartments.

The models of aggregation, as opposed to disaggregation or decomposition presented in the earlier section, have mainly considered the primal maximization problems, to each of which an appropriate dual minimization problem can be associated. Each dual LP problem has a set of shadow prices for each resource in its optimal solution, which is usually interpreted as the marginal productivity or profitability of that resource at the optimum. Now consider any specific resource present in the individual LP models (8) and the aggregate LP model (16), for example, assuming that the excess profit condition (19) or (20) is satisfied. For this specific resource, three types of shadow prices are in principle conceivable:

a) shadow prices ($K$ in number) for each of $K$ models (8);
b) a shadow price (one in number) for the aggregate model (16); and
c) updated shadow prices ($K$ in number) for each of the $K$ subdepartments obtained by multiplying the individual shadow prices of model (8) by the ratio

$$\left(\bar{Z}/\sum_{k} \bar{z}_k\right)$$

of optimal aggregate profits in (16) to the sum of individual optimal profits in (8).

Regarding the shadow prices in (b), note, however, that different types of aggregation would define different shadow prices; similarly, there could be different types of updating rules in (c).

Consider now the aggregate model (16) and denote the optimal decision vectors by $\bar{x}_k$ and $\bar{U}_k$ (i.e., $\bar{U}$) and optimal aggregate profits by:

$$\bar{Z} = Z(\bar{x}_k, \bar{U}_k; k = 1, 2, \ldots, K). \tag{27}$$

Any decision vector feasible but not necessarily optimal is denoted by $(x_k, U_k; k = 1, 2, \ldots, K)$. Now it is obvious from the specification of the aggregate model (16) that:

$$Z(\bar{x}_k, \bar{U}_k; \text{all } k) \geq Z(\bar{x}_k, U_k; \text{all } k) \geq Z(x_k, U_k; \text{all } k); \tag{28}$$

that is, if the resource aggregates are not optimally allocated among the $K$ participants (e.g., subdepartments or firms as it may be), then the aggregate optimal profits may be increased (or maintained at the same level) by reallocation of resource aggregates which implies reallocation of resource-specific shadow prices.

Note that if the allocation ratio $U_k^0$ is so preassigned that:

$$b_k = U_k^0 \cdot \sum_{k} b_k; \; k = 1, 2, \ldots, K, \tag{29}$$

where $U_k^0$ denotes a specific selection of $U_k \subseteq U$, satisfying the feasibility conditions (17), then the aggregate LP problem (16) can be uniquely decomposed into $K$ submodels, each being of the type (8). In other words, if the central model is given in the form (16) and the rule of disaggregation of the central resource $\beta = \Sigma b_k$ is given by $U_k^0 \subseteq U^0$ satisfying (29) and (17), then there is a unique set of $K$-divisional LP models in the form (8) into which the central model can be decomposed. (Note that this provides one example of the third type of decomposition method mentioned before.) This emphasizes the important property of invariance of the central model (16) and the individual (divisional) LP models (8) relative to the resource allocation rule $U_k^0$ given in (29). This may be termed $U_k^0$-relative invariance.

It is obvious now that under the condition of $U_k^0$-relative invariance, the three sets of shadow prices mentioned at the beginning of this section are equal for any given resource. A system of central and divisional LP models ([16] and [8]) may fail to maintain $U_k^0$-relative invariance in at least two ways: either the decomposition of the central model (16) or the aggregation of divisional LP models (8) does not follow the rule $U_k^0$ of allocation. However, if the rule $U_k^0$ is such that it is equal to the optimal vector $\bar{U}$, then the $\bar{U}$-relative invariance of the decomposition and/or aggregation would be stable, in the sense that once reached it would tend to be maintained in the class of resource coalitions of order $K$ (i.e., all $K$ subdepartments and no less are to pool their resources).

Now denote the vector of shadow prices of resources for the divisional models (8) by $\bar{p}_k = p_k(\bar{U}_k)$ and $p_k^0 = p_k(U_k^0)$ and for the central model (16) by $\bar{P}^k = P^k(\bar{U})$ and $P^0 = P(U^0)$. If we interpret $\bar{P}$ as *the price vector* of a competitive market, then the precise manner in which $p_k^0$ converges to $\bar{P}$ as $U^0$ converges to $\bar{U}$ becomes crucially important. For the decomposition-aggregation discussion three aspects of this convergence are important from an economic viewpoint. First, the competitive market framework may be real or hypothetical, and this determines whether the sequence of compensations implied in the successive revisions of shadow prices and allocation ratios is actual or hypothetical. If it is actual, then the cost and time to convergence must be economically evaluated (Marschak 1964). In some cases this cost and time could be reduced considerably by a scheme of forecasts for the so-called "correct" price vector $\bar{P}$ (Wolfe 1967). Different types of forecasting rules (Sengupta 1964) become important then.

Second, the degree of competitiveness of the otherwise competitive market framework (i.e., the degree of imperfection in the competitive system associated with unequal bargaining powers of different participants in the $K$-order coalition) would not only determine the speed of convergence of successive reallocations ($U^0 \to \bar{U}$) and shadow prices ($p_k^0 \to \bar{P}$) but also the need for having imputations to share the excess profits. For example, a specific resource (such as a particular type of research) may have a high and positive shadow price $p_{0k}$ for the $k$th subdepartment in the individual model (8), although the same resource has a far lower shadow price $p_0 \ll p_{0k}$ in the central model (16) at the optimal allocation rule $\bar{U}_k \subseteq \bar{U}$. In particular, $p_0$ may be zero. However, if this $k$th subdepartment is dominant in the group in the sense that it can maintain (i.e., impute or impose) its own shadow price $p_{0k}$ in the aggregate central model (16), then the earlier sequence ($p_k^0 \to \bar{P}$) of convergence may be terminated by imputations.

Third, the resource aggregation in (16) implies transferability of resources between subdepartments, which may only be partially realized for those fixed and semifixed resources which are specific to each unit. In dynamic models over time the existence of quasi-fixed or fixed resources in the short run (e.g., durable capital goods) may block the convergence (or its continuity) of the pricing process. Hence in dynamic models of multisectoral balanced growth (e.g., in the von Neumann model [Kemeny et al. 1956]) we require special assumptions to maintain the continuity of the convergence process.

Note also that in each of the decomposition methods the successive revisions of shadow prices and resource reallocations prior to the optimal stage are only hypothetical subject to a Walrasian *tâtonnement* process. The *tâtonnement* process is based on the assumption that price-setting proceeds by comparing supplies and demands at various hypothetical shadow prices without any actual transactions taking place at these interim hypothetical prices. A non-*tâtonnement* process of competitive adjustment involves instead transactions actually taking place at both equilibrium (i.e., optimal) and nonequilibrium shadow prices.

A competitive adjustment process based on non-*tâtonnement* rules of exchange would have stability characteristics much different from a *tâtonnement* process as Hahn and Negishi (1962) have observed, since it may allow transactions (i.e., resource transfers between sectors by the center) at any price, imputed or forecast and not necessarily the price calculated by the center. To see the implication of this remark, consider the price vectors $\bar{p}_k = p_k(\bar{U})$, $p_k^0 = p_k(U_k^0)$ defined before, and assume that each of the $K$ subdepartments has a set of price imputations (i.e., a vector $y_k^0$ of dimension equal to that of $p_k^0$), such that

$$\bar{p}_k = p_k^0 \pm y_k^0; y_k^0 \geq 0, \text{ for all } k = 1, 2, \ldots, K; \qquad (30)$$

then the set of imputations $\{y_k^0, k = 1, 2, \ldots, K\}$, if not empty, defines a nonequilibrium price set for the central model (16). Nikaido (1964) has interpreted $y_k^0$ as the price vector monopolistically determined by each subdepartment, whereas the price vectors $\bar{p}_k$ and $p_k^0$ are competitively determined. This interpretation is based on an additive decomposition of the shadow-price vector $\bar{p}_k$ for the aggregate system (16). A multiplicative decomposition method, already discussed before in (22), would be:

$$\bar{p}_k = \lambda p_k^0; k = 1, 2, \ldots, K \text{ and } \lambda = \bar{Z}/\sum_k \bar{z}_k, \tag{31}$$

where the ratio $\lambda$ of optimal aggregate profits to the sum of individual optimal profits is defined in (22) before; in other words $\lambda p_k^0$ defines the set of updated shadow prices. In principle, one could also formulate a general linear transformation, i.e.:

$$\bar{p}_k = \lambda_0 p_k^0 \pm \lambda_1 y_k^0; k = 1, 2, \ldots, K, \tag{32}$$

where $\lambda_0, \lambda_1$ are scalar non-negative constants to be determined and $y_k^0$ is a set of prices monopolistically imposed, i.e., imputed or preassigned. This sort of imposition or imputation (i.e., premium or penalty prices) may be defended in terms of either the bargaining theory of games (Harsanyi 1963) or the need for certain types of stability in non-*tâtonnement* exchange processes illustrated by an example by Hahn and Negishi (1962).

*Problems in decomposition*

The methods of decomposition and aggregation have one common assumption, i.e., that the central and the divisional LP models are feasible. This implies that the conflict (i.e., infeasibility) of constraints either between divisions (or sectors) or between the center and the divisions may defeat the entire sequential process. However, the degree or intensity of infeasibility may be unequal for different division (or sectors or subdepartments), and hence we need some principle for optimal allocation of infeasibility in some sense.

Several partial solutions may be offered for specifying decomposition algorithms under conditions of infeasibility. First, the conflict between the divisional resource constraints and the central resource constraints may be minimized or eliminated by allowing sufficient reserve resources as "organizational slack" in the system. This requires a chance-constrained interpretation of the central and the divisional constraints so that infeasibility of constraints is allowed up to specific tolerance levels (Sengupta 1969). Second, a penalty cost function approach, as in the theory of two-stage programming under uncertainty (Dantzig and

Madansky 1961), may be adopted. In this approach specific penalty functions for violation (or infeasibility) of constraints are imputed (e.g., penalty cost may be proportional to the resource deficit $Ax - b \geq 0$), and the expected value of this imputed penalty cost function is adjoined to the objective function of the original LP model (Beale 1961). However, in any given situation the penalty costs may be difficult to determine. Third, the bargaining solution in terms of game theory is available (Nyblen 1951) and the possibility of coalition of different groups (of divisions or subdepartments) and of different orders (Luce and Raiffa 1957) has to be considered. Fourth, we may seek a least-squares type solution as in the Gauss approach (Kuhn 1963) by considering a solution vector $(x^*, y^*)$, where $x^*$ is the primal vector and $y^*$ is the dual, which minimizes the Euclidean distance between this point and other points defined by $(x_N, y_N)$, $N = 1, 2, \ldots$, where $x_N$ and $y_N$ are primal and dual variables for the $N$th subproblem (i.e., it could be either a central or a divisional problem) considered separately. The distance between the point $P$ with co-ordinates $(x^*, y^*)$ and the points $Q_N$ with co-ordinates $(x_N, y_N)$ may be weighted, if suitable weights reflecting the intensity of infeasibility could be preassigned. Note that if this least square solution vector $(x^*, y^*)$ exists, it would *not* satisfy all constraints; however, it would be least infeasible in the sense of least squared distance described above. This type of approach is most appropriate in situations where some or all parameters (i.e., the resources, input-coefficients, and net prices in the objective functions) of the mutually conflicting LP models can be interpreted to contain random errors which are normally and independently distributed, so that the Gaussian theory of errors can apply. Note that the distance function above may be defined in terms of profits rather than primal-dual variables, since the presence of infeasibility by definition implies less profits than otherwise.

Fifth, there is the Tchebycheff method of approximation* for the solution of a system of linear equations (i.e., inequalities converted to equalities through addition of slack or artificial variables as in LP models) on the divisional activity vectors $x_k$ and the central activity vector $x$, such that the greatest of the absolute values of the residuals is as small as possible. For example, rewrite the divisional models (8) and the central model (16) as (33) and (34), respectively:

$$A_k x_k - b_k = \xi_k \text{ and } c'_k x_k - z^0_k = s_k, \tag{33}$$

$$A_k x_k - U^0_k \cdot \Sigma b_k = \bar{\xi}_k \text{ and } \sum_k c'_k x_k - Z^0 = \bar{s}, \tag{34}$$

*Note that this is basically the method followed in goal-programming discussed on pages 179-87.

where $s_k$, $\bar{s}$ are scalar slack variables, superscript zero denotes prescribed values, $\xi_k$, $\bar{\xi}_k$ are residual vectors, and the systems of inequalities in (8) and (16) are written here as equalities by incorporating appropriate slack variables in the redefinition of $x_k$ in (33) and (34). It is assumed that $U_k^0$ is such that $Z^0$ is not equal to

$$\sum_k z_k^0;$$

the vectors $\xi_k$ and $\bar{\xi}_k$ are interpreted as residuals. If the profits $z_k^0$, $Z^0$ are so preassigned that $s_k$ and $\bar{s}$ are not equal to zero, then these are also residual variables like $\xi_k$ and $\bar{\xi}_k$. Now it is assumed that the two linear systems (33) and (34) are mutually conflicting for preassigned $U_k^0$, $z_k^0$, $Z^0$, in the sense that there exists no solution $X = \{\bar{x}_k\}$ for $\xi_k = 0 = \bar{\xi}_k$ and $s_k = 0 = \bar{s}$, i.e., the linear systems (33) and (34) cannot be solved exactly with all residual variables zero. By Tchebycheff's method of approximation we seek in this case a solution vector $X = \{\bar{x}_k\}$ for the system comprising (33) and (34), such that the greatest of the absolute values of the above residual variables is as small as possible. While the Gauss approach of least squares is appropriate when the inconsistency of a linear system of equations is due to statistical errors, the Tchebycheff method of approximation is appropriate when the linear system may be viewed as approximations to nonlinear functions. Nef (1967) has shown in great detail that the Tchebycheff method of approximate solution for a linear system leads to a linear programming scheme and the usual simplex routine can be applied. Hence, this method has much to recommend it for computational purposes.

Note that in our discussion of the aggregate model (16) and the individual models (8) there is always a degree of conflict in distribution or allocation of aggregate resources so long as it holds for some $U_k$ that:

$$b_k \neq U_k \cdot \sum_k b_k$$

in the notation of the section beginning on page 187. In other words, the presence of conflict is in terms of the deviation of any arbitrary allocation ($U_k$) from the optimal allocation scheme $\bar{U} = \{\bar{U}_k\}$ defined on page 199.

In the framework of our discussion on LP models of decomposition, several basic problems yet remain unsolved in our opinion. These problems can be classified into three groups: (a) computational; (b) practical (from the viewpoint of management decisions); and (c) theoretical (from the viewpoint of the economic theory of resource allocation).

First, there are two basic computational problems in applying the decomposition or aggregation algorithms: (i) the relative costs of computation (due to information processing) of alternative methods of decomposition and aggregation in LP models have never been actually compared (or the theory developed) although certain principles of comparison are available (Zoutendijk 1960) and (ii) the game theory method of solving for coalitions of all orders, from a one-firm coalition to a $K$-firm coalition, as applied to resource and activity aggregation in LP models needs to be explored and evaluated from an economic standpoint.

Second, from the practical viewpoint of a divisionalized firm there remain at least three basic types of problems to be solved, before the rules of co-ordination laid down by different decomposition and aggregation algorithms are accepted and implemented by the different divisions.

i) The rules of transfer pricing in decomposition algorithms are essentially designed to reallocate resources more productively and profitably from the viewpoint of the firm as a whole, particularly when there is interdependence in cost and demand between different divisions. The presence of joint costs, quasi-fixed resources, and indivisibility of various sorts, qualitative resources and of flexibility in cost structure in the multiproduct, multiprocess, and multi-division firm (Morris 1968) has a tendency to make the specification of resource restrictions in terms of linear inequalities much less precise and quantitative than desired. Hence, the rules of transfer pricing are always subject to challenge, since the competitive framework is only hypothetical, invented in the account book of the center.

ii) The risks of executive failure in a division or the feeling of this risk on the part of the divisional management when a division has to sell (i.e., transfer) a resource to another division internally at a marginal cost price below its average costs may induce biased and exaggerated reporting of marginal productivities to the center by different divisions. This may even destroy the neutral competitive behavior of the divisions and the center altogether (Hirshleifer 1964); some historical cases (Jasny 1951) are also available in the framework of economic planning in the socialist countries, which tend to confirm the existence of this tendency.

iii) The economic dictum that division of labor is limited by the size of the market does not easily carry over to the divisionalized firm model, since the internal market with internal prices (i.e., transfer prices) which the central management of the firm "creates" does not have (a) the conditions of free entry and free exit; (b) perfect information and knowledge of the consequences of deviating from the so-called internal prices; and (c) the conditions of quantity and price adjustment, as in a perfectly competitive market, and hence the question of how much divisionalization remains (Dean 1955; Cook 1955; Williamson 1964). A practical compromise between integration and divisionalization depends of course on the possibility of determining what may be called the optimum number of divisions into which the firm should be decomposed.

Third, from an economic viewpoint the question of resource or activity aggregation or decomposition raises at least two basic questions:

i) By what criteria can one compare an external market with actual prices faced by a firm with an internal market (comprising the same firm's different divisions) with its hypothetical internal prices? In particular, how real and identifiable are the *tâtonnement* processes from the non-*tâtonnement* processes? The economic implications of the latter need much closer investigation in the framework of the theory of decomposition, divisionalization, and aggregation.

ii) The standard decomposition methods start from a given output or activity system and then develop a sequential (shadow) price system which in effect sustains an optimal output system. It seems that one may as well start from a given price (i.e., standard costs) system and then develop a sequential (shadow) output system which could in effect realize an optimal price system. A third method would be to start from a primal-dual system (i.e., a mixed output-price subsystem) and then develop sequential algorithms in terms of both (shadow) prices and (shadow) outputs. The economic implications of these alternatives remain yet to be explored, compared, and evaluated.

A few words may be added about the relevance of the above discussion for planning educational systems, where allocations of divisible and transferable economic resources are considered. First, the university as a whole, or for that matter a large academic department, may in some sense be considered very similar to a multiproduct firm, except that its objective function may be in terms of an imputed value of performance rather than private profits. The decisionmaker for the university as a whole is much like a central planner who has to plan ahead against his best forecast of aggregate demand and the state of the future support by government. The sectoral planners are the component divisions. The transferable resources are budget allocations, and therefore additions to faculty and other services, between departments. Second, the presence of multiple decisionmakers at the sectoral level and the lack of any real *tâtonnement*-type exchange process render infeasibility unavoidable, so to speak, although in most organizations these infeasibilities are resolved through mutual exchange of information, consolidation of activities, and allowing some slacks to permit some flexibility. The important policy question is to what extent such informal procedures of resolving conflicts and infeasibilities can be quantified, at least for those decisions which are mostly quantitative. Whenever a consistent set of relations or inequalities can be developed to specify a consistency model for an educational system, it would presume that implicit optimization procedures have already been considered to remove infeasibilities.

*Econometric versus optimizing models for educational systems*

Econometric models based on estimates of the production and cost structure obtained through cross-section or time-series data (Cartter 1966; Lindsay 1964; Lind 1959–65) seem to offer an interesting alternative to the optimizing models for educational systems, e.g., a set of academic departments or colleges. The advantage of an econometric model is that it does not require an explicit objective function for its specification, although the estimation method it uses or the form of the function it specifies may assume implicit optimization, as does least squares, or some particular behavior pattern. An interesting attempt by Southwick (1969) may be mentioned in this connection; this is an econometric study estimating the production and cost relationships in the U.S. land grant colleges and universities for the period 1956–57 to 1962–63, using the financial, enrollment, and employment data as published by the U.S. Office of Education. Three outputs are distinguished: undergraduate education (measured by the full-time equivalent undergraduate students, $V$), graduate education (measured by graduate enrollment, $G$), and knowledge via research (measured by sales of research or research contracts, $R^*$). Also, three categories of inputs are distinguished, e.g. (a) common inputs in the form of administrative staff (measured by the total number of professional persons acting as university administrators, $SA$), capital (measured by the net value of plant and equipment excluding land, $K$) and library staff; (b) teaching inputs in the form of senior teaching staff (measured by the full time equivalent number of teaching faculty with rank of instructor and above), junior teaching staff and research staff; and (c) other inputs in the form of extension and other staff.

For illustrative purposes consider two of the aggregate production function results:

$$SA = a_{11} V + a_{12} G + a_{13} R^*, \qquad (35)$$

$$K^* = a_{21} V + a_{22} G + a_{23} R^*, \qquad (36)$$

where $K^*$ and $R^*$ are measured in millions of dollars. The cross-section estimates (based on sixty-eight institutions) for the seven-year period are as follows:

| Year | $a_{11}$ | $a_{12}$ | $a_{13}$ | $r^2$ | $a_{21}$ | $a_{22}$ | $a_{23}$ | $r^2$ |
|---|---|---|---|---|---|---|---|---|
| 1963 | 0.0070* | .0100 | 2.66* | 0.894 | 0.0050 | .0124 | 0.602 | 0.926 |
| 1962 | .0054 | .0124 | 0.92 | .895 | .0054 | .0093 | .609 | .920 |
| 1961 | .0039 | .0219 | 0.34 | .690 | .0058 | .0071 | .669 | .916 |
| 1960 | .0029 | .0264 | −0.03 | .556 | .0059 | .0071 | .659 | .920 |
| 1959 | .0030 | .0157 | −1.05 | .329 | .0052 | .0091 | .466 | .916 |
| 1958 | .0009 | .0294 | −1.58 | .288 | .0043 | .0014 | .251 | .917 |
| 1957 | .0003 | .0177 | −1.13 | .292 | .0036 | .0010 | .390 | .907 |

*Note:* 1. In this table an asterisk above the coefficient indicates a change significant at the 0.05 level over the seven-year time span.
2. The coefficient of multiple correlation is denoted here by $r^2$ to avoid confusion with $R^*$.

These estimates, admittedly very aggregative (and referring to an "average" land grant school representing the sixty-eight institutions in some sense) should reflect certain national trends, provided the coefficients can be meaningfully interpreted.

For example, (35) in 1963 implies that each of the following changes would be associated on the average with an addition of one full-time person to the administrative staff: (a) an increase of 143 undergraduate students enrolled; (b) an increase of 100 graduate students enrolled; or (c) an increase of 0.376 million dollars in the volume of research contracts. None of these figures is inherently implausible. However, the movements of $a_{11}$, $a_{12}$, $a_{13}$ and $r^2$ from 1957 to 1963 suggest a high and increasing degree of intercorrelation among $V$, $G$, and $R^*$. The shift of $a_{13}$ from negative to positive supports this inference. Also, the value of $a_{11}$ in 1957 implies one additional administrator for each increase of 3,333 undergraduates, suggesting that the marginal productivity of an administrator in the undergraduate program was (3,333/143) or 23 times as large in 1957 as in 1963! Hence, we must not read too much into the coefficients of (35).

In 1963, (36) implies that an increase in enrollment of one underduate student would be associated on the average with an increase of $5,000 in the value of plant and equipment, while an additional graduate student would be associated with an increase of $12,400; an increase of one million dollars in the annual volume of research contracts would be associated with an increase of $602,000 in the value of plant and equipment. Again, these figures are plausible enough, and the coefficients $a_{21}$ and $a_{23}$ are much more stable from 1957 to 1963 than are $a_{11}$ and $a_{13}$ in (35). Methods used to estimate the value of university plant and equipment probably changed very little between 1957 and 1963; in contrast, methods of using, classifying, and reporting numbers of administrative personnel may have changed a great deal. The lines between full-time administrators, part-time co-ordinators, and faculty committees as means for accomplishing the same task are not sharply drawn; they may change over time in a given university and may vary widely as between universities.

How useful are econometric estimates such as (35) and (36) in the context of a specific land grant university so far as policy decisions are concerned? First, divergences from these national (or over-all industry-wide) relationships would be more likely than not and the sources of these divergences would need to be spelled out among various departments (as a matter of fact, computation of similar coefficients using cross-section data for different academic departments within a university may be required at this stage). Second, we would have to use the first-stage calculations to arrive at a set of corrected coefficients for a specific university, relating this to different levels of decisionmaking, e.g., depending on whether the dean, the departmental chairman, or the subdepartment co-ordinator make the effective decisions. This means that for each of the aggregate output indicators $V$, $G$, $R^*$ there would have to be derived a consistent set of vectors representing various activities as discussed before (see p. 157). Note that the models of decomposition would be relevant in this connection. Third, given the validity of the first two stages, the econometric relationships (35) and (36) may be useful for the following policy questions: (a) suppose the student enrollment is forecast to follow an upward trend, resulting in an uptrend for $V$ and $G$ for the next three years, what would be the requirements in terms of administrative personnel and capital which would maintain the present balance?; (b) what would be the cost of divergence if the growth of the common and other inputs cannot follow a balanced path? Whenever a scheme of balanced growth cannot be maintained for one reason or another, one has to go beyond the aggregate production relations such as (35) and (36) to the detailed resource and output constraints of different departments in considering different input mixes and output mixes as an adjusting scheme. This means we have to pass from the aggregate production function to the detailed activity analysis-type models; the consistency of the aggregate planning procedure is maintained, as it were, by considering alternative feasible solutions of activity models.

It seems that some methods of linking the two types of models, the econometric and the optimizing, may prove very useful. For instance, the aggregate relationships, such as (35) or (36) estimated for a specific university (or a suitable cluster of departments) may provide a long-run calculation of requirements, assuming a certain projected pattern of student enrollment (this would be very similar to the capacity expansion policies [Sengupta and Fox 1969] of a firm). The short-run decision models would then be of detailed activity analysis type, showing the interdependence of different departments in costs and output (the policy constraints would play very important roles here). Alternatively, one might start with detailed activity analysis-type models with possibly imputed objective functions and then derive, in a sense, the aggregate indicators of outputs and inputs, as in the production function (35) and (36). In our opinion, this type of consistency analysis offers a very fruitful field for research in educational planning.

## The indivisibility problem and suboptimization

The economic theory of competitive pricing characterizes the concept of efficiency in resource allocation under two basic assumptions (Arrow 1969):

($C$) convexity of household indifference maps and the firm production possibility sets; and

($M$) the universality of markets implying anonymity of market prices to all households and all producers.

For some types of resources, which are given in this section the generic name of "indivisible resources," both these assumptions may fail either partially or completely, thus undermining the very basis of efficiency and therefore optimality of the competitive price mechanism. For instance, if there were increasing returns to scale due to the presence of an indivisible input, then the assumption ($C$) would not hold for the production set, and hence a competitive (shadow or efficiency) price which would sustain a Pareto-optimal resource allocation could not easily be defined. In this case the discussion of the various techniques of decomposition in Chapters 4 and 5 would be inapplicable. Again, if there were significant economies of scale due to the internal or external effects of an indivisible resource (Meade 1952) and the firm continued to follow the marginal cost pricing rule, then its losses would cumulate until it went out of the market, unless there were a subsidy or compensation.

It is apparent that the resources considered in the competitive model must have certain characteristics, such that the indivisibility elements or aspects can be reduced and, if possible, eliminated. Otherwise there would be problems in defining efficiency prices which would sustain a Pareto-optimal resource allocation and also in maintaining the stability of such efficiency prices. Ideally this objective could be achieved if all the relevant economic (scarce) resources satisfy the properties of $(D)$ divisibility in any amounts and proportions, of $(S)$ separability between households, producers, and markets as regards their decisions, and of $(Q)$ quantifiability of resources (inputs, outputs), prices, and information flows. Any economic resource satisfying these properties $(D)$, $(S)$, and $(Q)$ may be called divisible, so that the generic name of "an indivisible resource" would apply in our view to any resource which fails to satisfy any or all of the three properties $(D)$, $(S)$, and $(Q)$.

The most common situation in which the property $(D)$ fails to hold arises when the activities or solutions are required to be integral, e.g., in some situations a faculty member has to be hired on an all or none basis, a project may or may not be selected for funding. An economic situation where $(S)$ may fail to hold arises in the case called "unpaid factor of production" by Meade (1952), when one firm's production activity generates through interfirm production-interdependence cost economies to other firms, although there is no market for pricing these external economies. In the educational system, the benefits of research in universities which are not project-guided *per se* are not all internalized, since the industry and the society at large may reap the external economies or diseconomies. The case in which $(Q)$ may fail to hold has been least discussed in economic literature, except in methodological terms in the form of measurability of economic quantities through index numbers and other aggregate variables. In the theory of the firm and also of the over-all growth of an economy, the measurement of capacity poses a situation in which $(Q)$ may fail to hold. As a matter of fact, the Cambridge theory of economic growth (Kaldor and Mirrlees 1962) has consistently criticized the concepts of aggregate capital, aggregate labor, and aggregate production function used in the neo-classical models of growth (Solow 1956; Cass 1965) as meaningless, since they are not quantifiable in the same sense as sectoral quantities and markets for aggregate capital, labor, and output do not exist. Also, the practice of "two-part tariff" rules of pricing for services of public enterprises (Turvey 1968), one part covering parts of overhead indivisible costs, also reflects in a sense a failure of the competitive pricing rule, to the extent that this allows two prices for the same product or service. The existence of two or more prices for the same good or service is sometimes associated with discriminatory pricing practiced by a discriminating monopolist selling in two markets having unequal elasticities of demand (e.g., dumping).

For models of educational planning at the university level, indivisibility due to failure of (D) enters into the decision problem when the university or some of its departments have to plan for optimal expansion due to rising enrollment, when there may be significant economies (or diseconomies) of scale. Determining the optimal sizes of the university, the central library, the central computing facility, and their optimal expansion paths are the important decision problems in this area of long-range planning. The existing models (Sengupta and Fox 1969) of optimal capacity expansion for the firm which are available in the current economic literature are very useful in this regard. At the national level, similar problems arise in planning the scale of higher education (Blaug 1968; Sengupta and Fox 1970), in investment programming for the education sector (Fox and Sengupta 1968) relative to other sectors, and in exploring the interdependence of investment decisions for skill formation and for future research needs (O.E.C.D. 1967).

Indivisibility due to failure of (S) enters into the decision problem, mainly as a result of incomplete characterization of various interdependencies existing in the university or the education sector as a whole, e.g., the interdependence of several academic departments in the M.S. and Ph.D. programs in U.S. universities, when students are required to take courses in more than one department, the joint appointment of faculty members in two or more departments, or research and consulting by faculty members outside the department or the university for at least part of the calendar year. For undergraduate teaching in a specialty, some faculty members may be transferable from one course to another, although for graduate teaching such transfer possibilities are far more limited.

Indivisibility due to failure of (Q) is the most important but the least characterized in modeling for educational systems. We have seen some implications of imputing prices and values to quantities for which ordinary market signals may not exist (p. 156). There are other cases, of course, in which markets may not exist, e.g., markets for many forms of risk-bearing and many future goods and services which have elements of uncertainty. In the absence of a market, the allocative efficiency of prices is difficult to characterize, and there is always the possibility of conflict of the two roles of prices as allocative signals and as administrative directives, to which we have referred (p. 202). There are two other very important cases, discussed in some detail by Arrow (1969), in which the presence of indivisibility due to failure of (Q) may generate failure of the competitive market mechanism and its pricing system through (1) high costs of exclusion of nonbuyers from buyers and (2) through high transaction costs associated with information flows (about indivisible resources and externalities), which may also include costs of disequilibrium and/or wrong decisions.

The point that some indivisible resources exist in the educational system, in which quality and other nonquantitative factors are important and in which markets do not ordinarily exist, does not mean that interuniversity or interdepartment comparisons are not feasible (or not done), but the costs of transaction and communication in getting a unique "correct" price for each indivisible resource may be so large that it may not be worthwhile to conceive of a market system. The possibility of two or more prices (subjective estimates) for a given indivisible resource may only be avoided by transmitting appropriate information flows to the relevant decisionmakers, but this may be very expensive; also, the information itself may be indivisible, to a large extent, with economies of scale. As Arrow (1969) has mentioned: "The welfare implications of transaction costs would exist even if they were proportional to the size of the transaction, but in fact they typically exhibit increasing returns. The cost of acquiring a piece of information, for example, a price, is independent of the scale of use to which it will be put" ([Arrow 1969], p. 60).

In the economic literature two types of attempts have been made to incorporate the effects of indivisibilities, if they are not significantly large. By the latter we mean that by suitable modifications of $(C)$ and $(M)$ these not-too-large indivisibilities may be incorporated. More appropriately, these indivisibilities should be called "limited divisibility," e.g., integer requirements for some activities. First, there is a group of methods which assume initially that the firm production possibility sets are not convex, but that there exists a transformation which causes the reduced production set to be convex. For instance, a very important criterion of integer convexity has been formulated by Frank (1969), according to which one postulates a smallest convex set called the "convex hull," $\bar{Y}$, say, of the set $Y$ of production possibilities, where the set $Y$ contains some integral outputs (or inputs) and it need not be convex. The generalized notion of integer convexity then allows one to associate a concept of "efficiency" price. Second, there are a number of methods for combining the pricing mechanism with directives, so that the assumption $(M)$ may be modified to include central directives. For instance, the methods of two-part prices, of prices with lump-sum tax or subsidy, or of prices combined with some central norms or standards are instances in which the effects of indivisibilities are incorporated (political processes or negotiation may be considered alternative methods of solution not using prices).

*Integer convexity criterion*

Two important uses of the integer convexity criterion emphasized by Frank (1969) are of great relevance for models of resource planning in which some resources (inputs or outputs) are integers. First, if the integer convexity postulate is satisfied, then although the set of indivisible commodities (e.g., outputs as integral numbers) may not be convex, one may be able to define an efficiency point in the Pareto-optimal sense. This efficiency point may not always be on the boundary of $\bar{Y}$, the convex hull of the production possibility set $Y$, but it lies at least relatively close and, what is more important, there exists a boundary point of $\bar{Y}$ which lies just above and to the right of an efficient point which is not on the boundary point of $\bar{Y}$. This is called the near-profit maximization theorem (Frank 1969, p. 77). The policy implication of this result is that in the presence of such integral indivisibility, the profit goal should be replaced by a near-to-maximum level of profits. Second, a special kind of two-part pricing procedure may be developed as an alternative to perfectly competitive pricing, i.e., "Another way of stating it is that in order for a firm to be induced to produce at a point of increasing returns, a higher price must be charged for the first units of output than the price charged for later units of output and a lower price must be charged for the first units of input than for later units. Otherwise, if the prices for all units were the same, either it would pay the firm to expand (if the prices of outputs were high enough and the prices of inputs low enough) or it would pay to shut down (if prices were such that a loss was being made)" (Frank 1969, p. 89).

However, one should note that the concept of nearness in the near-profit maximization theorem is dependent on a particular form of distance function; in effect, it allows a condition of ordering between several points near to the efficient point which is not on the boundary of the convex hull $\bar{Y}$. Second, the construction of a suitable convex set containing the nonconvex production set presumes a particular transformation; other transformations (e.g., in a somewhat different context a logarithmic convexity criterion for positive functions is used in geometric programming for nondiscrete cases [Klinger 1968; Duffin et al. 1967]) are possible. Also, the computing question is not yet well settled in the area of integer programming; in particular the convergence may be very, very slow, and hence, practically useless for application in decomposition routines. Third, the policy implications of multiple pricing (or discriminatory pricing) may be much different from its theoretical advantages. Methods of combining fixed prices with other directives, including lump-sum transfers, may be more useful in practice. Fourth, the efficiency point defined in the Pareto-optimal sense by Frank (1969) has associated with it a nonnegative price, the implication presumably being that a negative price is meaningless. Apparently he is implying the existence of a private competitive market. Whenever the market does not exist, due to high transaction costs as in university systems, the concept of a nonnegative price may have to be revised. For instance, if a particular output is desired by the decisionmaker and forced into the constraints as an equality, its associated Lagrange multiplier is, in general, arbitrary in sign (i.e., it could be either positive or negative). The implications of taxes and subsidies, not necessarily of the lump-sum variety, can then be easily incorporated.

*Logarithmic convexity criterion*

In order to illustrate that there are other methods of incorporating a nonconvex production possibility set, we should mention the case of logarithmic convexity. A scalar positive function $g(x)$ of a vector $x$ is defined to be logarithmically convex (or, in short, $L$-convex), if $\log g(x)$ is convex. If a function $g(x)$ is $L$-convex on a convex set $X$, then it is necessarily convex on $X$, although the converse is not true.

Suppose we consider a case in which there are increasing returns to scale, so that competitive equilibrium is not compatible with it. Let $x_{ij}$ denote the amount of fixed resource $i$ ($i = 1, \ldots, m$) allocated to produce $j$ ($j = 1, \ldots, n$), where

$$x_j = \prod_{i=1}^{m_j} c_j x_{ij}^{\alpha_{ij}}; \; m_j = \text{integers } 1, 2, \ldots \tag{37}$$
$$j = 1, \ldots, n$$
$$i = 1, \ldots, m$$

and $c_j > 0$ is assumed strictly positive. If

$$\sum_i \alpha_{ij} > 1$$

we have increasing returns to scale. However, even in this case the following model would define equilibrium solutions at their optimum and hence their dual prices:

$$\min C(x) = \sum_{j=1}^{n} \sum_{i=1}^{m} p_i x_{ij} \tag{38a}$$

subject to

$$\prod_{i=1}^{m_j} c_j x_{ij}^{\alpha_{ij}} \geq \bar{x}_j, \; \bar{x}_j > 0 \text{ preassigned}; \; \sum_j m_j = m, \tag{38b}$$

$$x_{ij} > 0, \text{ continuous.} \tag{38c}$$

Here the $p_i$ are the actual or imputed prices of fixed inputs $x_{ij}$ which, of course, are assumed here to be divisible in limited amounts. The form of the programming model (38a) through (38c) is a typical geometric program and explicit computational algorithms exist for computing its solutions (Wilde and Beightler 1967). The important point is that even under the conditions of nonconstant returns to scale this model would define an optimal solution with a dual vector of shadow prices which could be given a Pareto-efficiency interpretation. Also, extensions of computing algorithms to situations in which $c_j$ is not necessarily positive in (37) are available through generalized polynomial programming (Passy and Wilde 1967).

Two remarks may be added at this stage. First, the dual variables or shadow prices may be defined even in cases where the production set is not fully convex, thus implying that the concept of a market *tâtonnement* to sustain a dual variable may be artificial. Second, one should explore several methods of incorporating the scale effects, due to indivisibilities of various sorts, into the framework of a meaningful solution, so that alternative meaningful solutions may then be compared by a policy-maker either directly or through imaginary interviewing. Each meaningful solution may at best be a suboptimum. However, through a separate ordering criterion these different suboptima may be compared and the optimum optimorum located. In a framework where markets do not exist, one should explore the conditions and requirements of a system of replacement.

### Implications of second-best policies and partial optimization

When the constraints and objectives are exactly known and there are no specification errors in modeling a system in terms of a programming model with a scalar objective function, there should be no interest in computing a second-best solution, since the first-best would be computable and preferable by definition. However, for most economic models, especially for nonmarket or quasi-market models, prices, constraints, and objectives are rarely known with complete exactitude, and even when they are known, the post-optimal situation may be slightly different from that obtaining in the pre-optimal, and this necessitates the investigation of second-best optimal solutions. In the activity analysis-type models of educational systems just considered (pp. 157–75), we have seen that the objective function coefficients may contain imputed subjective elements and other components because the good produced by the system has special characteristics and the market framework is not fully operative in public financing policies for educational systems. However, there are various reasons why second-best optimum policies are sometimes pursued, which by definition are policies which aim at partial optimization, since complete information is not available or not likely to be available.

From an operational viewpoint it is useful to classify the following sources of second-best policies when a quantitative programming model, linear or nonlinear, is assumed to characterize an optimal policy either first-best or second-best, viz.:

1) externalities in production and consumption (Meade 1952; Buchanan and Stubblebine 1962; Buchanan 1966);
2) presence of an indivisible good with a high fixed cost but negligible marginal cost (Samuelson 1954; Davis and Whinston 1967);
3) failure of Pareto-optimality conditions due to at least one additional constraint which violates Pareto-type marginal conditions (Lipsey and Lancaster 1956–57; Davis and Whinston 1965; Bohm 1967; McManus 1967);
4) objective functions may be altered due to at least one decision-maker changing his relative weights for different activities or goods (Phelps and Pollack 1968; Pollack 1968; Davis and Whinston 1962); and
5) uncertainty in the parameters of the objective function, the constraints, or the resources (Sengupta 1966, 1969; Radstrom 1964; Tisdell 1968).

In each of the five cases, a first-best optimum solution (vector) is assumed to exist if none of the five sources is present or effective at the first-best optimum solution, i.e., if there are no externalities, no indivisible goods, no conditions to violate Pareto optimality, no change in the parameters and the specific form of the objective function, and no uncertainty in the parameters of the programming problem, then under certain assumptions (e.g., convexity of the production possibility sets, etc.) the first-best solution is defined. A second-best solution may then be due to any of the five reasons mentioned above.

We have already discussed the case (1) of externalities in production, in which competitive pricing would ordinarily fail to allocate economies in cost which are external to the firm (e.g., Meade's case of unpaid factors of production), unless the externalities can be internalized and a modified system of pricing can be developed. Another interesting case, more relevant in a dynamic model of intertemporal growth, has been discussed by Sheshinski (1967), in which externality is due to technological interdependence of labor and capital due to a learning-by-doing type of production technology; in this case it is impossible for both capital and labor to be paid the values of their marginal products, as would be the case in a competitive framework, thus necessitating corrective fiscal or other policies of tax subsidies. In educational systems, so far as the research output is concerned there are external economies in consumption, since the benefits of research lead in general to diffusion of related knowledge. This sort of good (e.g., research) has some characteristics of a public good, since once the results are published in a professional journal, its use by one consumer would not limit its availability and use by another consumer. Also, it may be difficult to exclude potential users from actual users at any given time. The existence of such externalities, which are not internal to the university system, suggests that the internal resource allocation problems of a university can at best attempt to seek second-best solutions.

Case (2), which has been termed "Non-Samuelsonian public goods" by Davis and Whinston (1967), since it does not have all the characteristics of Samuelsonian public goods, such as cost of private provision and exclusion, would include most of governmental activity and also a class of goods, such as roads and bridges, which have high fixed costs but negligible (or declining) marginal costs. The latter class of goods may be particularly relevant in some situations of educational planning, e.g., decisions on the size of computer facilities or other overhead goods which cater to the needs of the whole university. Computer models are such that there are significant economies in scale associated with larger sizes (e.g., IBM 360/75 compared to 360/45); also computer services may be hired from outside. It may be of some relevance here to discuss the two-good model considered by Davis–Whinston (1967), in which there are at times $t = 1, \ldots, T$ two goods, one private $x_1(t)$, $y_1(t)$, and the other governmental $x_2(t)$, $y_2(t)$, where $x_j^i$ denotes the consumption of good $j$ by individual $i = 1, \ldots, m$, and $y_j(t)$ denotes the production of good $j$. Representing by $\alpha_i$ the unspecified but assumed positive reciprocal of the $i$th consumer's marginal utility of income, the decision problem in a Pareto-optimality framework may be presented as follows (Davis and Whinston 1967):

$$\text{maximize} \sum_{i=1}^{m} \sum_{t=1}^{T} [\alpha_i u_{1t}^i(x_1^i(t)) + \alpha_i u_{2t}^i(x_2^i(t))] \tag{39a}$$

subject to

$$\sum_{i=1}^{m} x_1^i(t) \leqq y_1(t), \ t = 1, \ldots, T; \tag{39b}$$

RESOURCE ALLOCATION IN NONMARKET SYSTEMS 219

$$\sum_{i=1}^{m} x_2^i(t) \leq y_2(1), t = 1, \ldots, T; \tag{39c}$$

$$h_1(y_1(1)) + h_2(y_2(1)) \leq 0; \tag{39d}$$

$$g(y_1(t)) \leq 0, t = 2, \ldots, T; \tag{39e}$$

$$x_j^i(t) \geq 0, j = 1, 2; y_j(t) \geq 0, j = 1, 2; \tag{39f}$$

$$t = 1, \ldots, T,$$

$$i = 1, \ldots, m.$$

Here the utility function of the $i$th consumer $U_t^i(x_1^i(t), x_2^i(t))$ is assumed separable as:

$$U_t^i(x_1^i(t), x_2^i(t)) = u_{1t}^i(x_1^i(t)) + u_{2t}^i(x_2^i(t)).$$

The constraint (39d) sets up an implicit production function relating available resources to the quantities of the two goods produced in the initial period (also [39e] specifies the production possibility function for later periods $t = 2, \ldots, T$). Constraint (39c) indicates that no more of the governmental good can be consumed in any period than is made available in the first period. Now if an optimum (feasible) solution exists for this problem, assuming that the functions $u_{jt}^i$, $-h_1$, $-h_2$, $-g$ are concave and satisfy the Kuhn–Tucker constraint qualifications, then at the optimum the following conditions must hold on the demand and supply side for public goods:

$$\alpha_i(\partial u_{2t}^i/\partial x_2^i(t)) - \lambda(t) \left\{ \begin{matrix} \leq \\ = \end{matrix} \right\} 0 \text{ if } x_2^i(t) \left\{ \begin{matrix} = \\ > \end{matrix} \right\} 0. \tag{40a}$$

$$i = 1, \ldots, m$$

$$t = 1, \ldots, T$$

$$\sum_t \lambda(t) - \beta(\partial h_2/\partial y_2(1)) \left\{ \begin{matrix} \leq \\ = \end{matrix} \right\} 0, \text{ if } y_2(1) \left\{ \begin{matrix} = \\ > \end{matrix} \right\} 0, \tag{40b}$$

where $\lambda(t)$ and $\beta$ are the respective Lagrange multipliers associated with constraints (39c) and (39d). Note that one obtains for the governmental good in the optimal solution a vector of consumption quantities $(x_2^i(1), \ldots, x_2^i(T))$ for each individual consumer $i$ and a number $y_2(1)$ which is the quantity (i.e., capacity) available in each period and a vector of shadow prices or charges $(\lambda(1), \ldots, \lambda(T))$. This solution is obviously Pareto-optimal but it cannot be decentralized period by period.

Now consider this model for the resource allocation problem of a university, which is assumed to produce two goods, the first of which is just like a private good (e.g., consulting work or undergraduate instruction in a private school in which each student is charged the full cost of his instruction), and the second is a public good, in the sense that it is supplied for nonmarket considerations. Under this interpretation the above two-good model has two very striking implications that have been emphasized by Davis and Whinston. First, the optimality condition (40b) for the public good can be interpreted as (with $\lambda(t)$, $\beta$ given):

$$\max_{y_2(1) \geq 0} \left\{ \sum_t \lambda(t) y_2(1) - \beta h_2(1) \right\}, \tag{41}$$

which means that "if the governmental good is to be supplied, then that quantity (capacity) should be chosen in the initial period which will equate the sum of the prices to the marginal cost of supplying the selected quantity" (Davis and Whinston, 1967, p. 371). Second, the capacity (i.e., quantity supplied) of the public good should not be selected so large that the constraint (39c) never becomes binding. In other words, for some period $\lambda(t)$ must be positive. If the demand for the public good is such that the charge $\lambda(t)$ can never become positive, then that public good or facility is not justified. (Note that much of the academic research which is not directly related to the profit motives of private industries may be supported on the ground that its potential implicit worth may be positive for some time in terms of its likely contribution to human knowledge and social goals.)

However, two basic difficulties in the above formulation remain. First, the implicit price or worth $\lambda(t)$ cannot be forecast or extrapolated, since it is dependent on the parameters $\alpha_i$ of the objective function and other parameters, and, hence, predetermining $\lambda(t)$ in advance would not be meaningful. Second, the notion of demand for a public good may be very difficult to ascertain in an *ex ante* sense, and to some extent such demand may be influenced through information about supply (e.g., a new course in the curriculum may be offered on a trial basis in order to estimate potential demand). Also, the above formulation does not make clear the dichotomy of a firm's pricing rule under competition regarding the fixed and variable resources. An individual firm in a competitive market would operate in the short run if at the current price of its output none of its fixed costs were covered. However, the long-run prospect of price improving over time must exist for the firm to continue if only variable costs are covered. This argument is of great relevance for the potential outputs produced by an educational system, which may only charge the equivalent of its variable costs, the fixed costs being recouped from lump-sum or other transfers through state and local support.

Case (3) has led to considerable debate and discussion in the current literature (Lipsey and Lancaster 1956–57; Davis and Whinston 1965; Bohm 1967; McManus 1967), because of the specific implications and interpretations due to the addition of a new constraint into a general equilibrium Pareto-optimal system, which prevents the attainment of one of the Paretian marginal conditions. In one view, held by Lipsey and Lancaster, the other Paretian conditions, although attainable (except for the one violated by one additional constraint), are in general no longer desirable. However, in this view the violation of one Paretian condition is assumed to be of a very special form; also the dual prices (i.e., Lagrange multipliers) in the first-best and second-best situations may not be comparable, since they are nonanalytic, marginal, and dependent on the assumption of separability of resources from the input coefficients and from the objective function. A second view, advanced by Davis and Whinston (1965) claimed that when the additional constraints contained only variables subject to the choice of the deviant, then except for the deviant the Pareto and second-best conditions and behavioral rules are the same. In other words, in the absence of external effects the perfect competition framework, coupled with utility maximization by consumers and profit-maximization by producers, leads under certain regularity assumptions to the Pareto-optimal demand-and-supply functions (which are best behavior or decision rules in the Pareto sense). If, however, the actual behavior rules for one or more decision units are different from the above best behavior rules, and these actual behavior rules cannot be altered by any policy, the decision units are then termed deviants, and we have a second-best problem according to Davis and Whinston, who solve the original maximization problem under the additional constraints due to the deviants' behavior and derive the second-best optimum conditions for nondeviants.

From a policymaking viewpoint several objections have been raised against the argument of Davis and Whinston. First, the restrictions due to additional constraints must be more clearly related to the set of policy measures available in the system, since a certain state of the economy (i.e., a Pareto-optimal state) can be achieved by several combinations of policy measures. Tax subsidy and other nonprice measures are conceivable which can, in effect, obtain optimality in resource allocation in suitable situations. Second, as McManus (1967) has emphasized, the approach fails to distinguish between the shadow prices and the market prices, when the latter are measured in arbitrary financial units of account. The shadow prices (i.e., Lagrange multipliers) may in some situations be interpreted like market prices, but to impute to them the real significance of a market price would be meaningless (since the shadow price may be negative for an equality constraint and it may have arbitrary units). Third, the question of comparison between first-best and second-best situations in general cannot be completely settled from an economic viewpoint unless the welfare implications of various corrective measures from ad valorem taxes or subsidies to price variations are introduced, compared, and evaluated through a social welfare function.

The case (4) arises typically in a Ramsay-type growth model (Phelps and Pollack 1968; Davis and Whinston 1962; Pollack 1968) in which the present generation cannot commit the future generations to save the optimal amount which the present generation wishes them to save. If the present generation (or the central planner) could commit the future generation, then the optimal savings and growth determined in such a framework would be the first best, since future generations' restrictions are already committed by the present. Otherwise, the optimal saving decision problem of the present generation becomes a second-best problem, since the saving objectives of the future generation (which may not be completely known) become additional constraints for the present generation. This second-best type situation may also arise in the optimal capacity expansion problem of a single enterprise, when it plans on the basis of expected prices of output and availability of fixed resources; however, conditions in the future may be different from those anticipated by the enterprise. If the risks due to changed market conditions are great, the enterprise may prefer more flexible policies or one-period optimization to committing itself entirely over a period. In resource allocation models for educational systems this type of flexibility, although it may lead to partial optimization, may be desirable in some situations in which some of the educational inputs and outputs contain elements imputed on the basis of national market trends. The basic problems of this second-best type characterization are as follows: First, it may sometimes lead to very conservative policies, in the sense of lack of innovation, for fear of restricting future decisions, and this may be economically most expensive in situations having significant economies of scale. Second, the expected changes or shifts in the objective function likely to prevail in the future must be evaluated now by the present policymaker or policymakers and some means of adaptive forecasting may have to be built into the system. Since different degrees of risk associated with policies of different degrees of cautiousness may be explicitly introduced, it may be useful to compare and evaluate the various suboptimal policies before second-best policies are considered preferable.

The case (5) typically arises in situations in which there is some uncertainty, say, in the net price vector $c$ of a linear programming model:

$$\max z = c'x, \ Ax \leqq b, \ x \geqq 0$$

and various deterministic equivalents are sought. For instance, if the expected value $Ec$ of $c$ is considered to compute an optimal deterministic solution $\bar{x}(Ec)$, then since the optimal objective function

$$\bar{z} = z(\bar{x}(Ec)) = Ec'x(Ec)$$

is convex in $C$ it follows by Jensen's inequality that:

$$Ez(x(c)) = Ec'x(c) \geqq z(\bar{x}(Ec)) = Ec'\bar{x}(Ec)$$

when $x(c), \bar{x}(Ec) \, \epsilon \, X = \{x \, | \, x \geq 0, \, Ax \leq b\}$.

However, the above inequality suggests that different basic solution vectors of a linear program may have unequal degrees of stability, when stability is measured by the standard deviation of profits at that basic feasible solution relative to the expected profits. In particular, the second-best feasible solution may have far lower variance of total profits than the first best. This is the basic reason why in stochastic linear programming the active approach (also called the "here and now" approach) is sometimes preferred to the passive approach (also called the "wait and see" approach) as a means of obtaining a level of profits which is very stable in terms of low coefficient of variation.

This type of situation may arise in problems of allocation of resources to research activities in university systems. Evaluations of research performance as in the R & D (research and development) budgeting systems, where future returns are sometimes uncertain, are most difficult to quantify. This sometimes leads to underemphasis of research capacity as a second priority item, where the first priority of academic departments goes to teaching, especially undergraduate teaching. However, as the size of the academic departments and of the university increases more emphasis on research may be the outcome. The decision problem is one of determining appropriate budgetary and other allocations for different types of research in some optimal fashion. Methods of quantifying price uncertainty and other sources of uncertainty are yet to be developed in this field.

Finally, our discussion of the five different, although sometimes related, types of second-best situations and policies has been based on the premise that the competitive market model requires various sorts of modifications in real world situations. However, given proper safeguards and corrective measures the market failures of a competitive system may be remedied, partially at least, by various fiscal policies, external quota allocations, and nonprice strategies. For quasi-market or nonmarket economies, the various planning procedures have sometimes adopted these corrective measures through fiscal and other means without using prices. This point is of great relevance for problems of educational resource allocation.

CHAPTER 7

# The Systems Approach to Resource Allocation in Educational Planning

*Bikas C. Sanyal*

**Objectives of a systems approach**

The approach of systems planning developed by management scientists and operations researchers is a generic name for a collection of methods which analyze the informational network for decisions and actions taken at different levels in the hierarchy of an organization or a system. The feedback from information flows to decisions, the need for analyzing the decisionmaking processes for a large and complex organization into simpler structures, and the specification of changes in functional requirements and information processing technology due to changes in or modifications of goals and subgoals of the organization are some of the essential ingredients of a systems planning approach. Note that this approach is not limited in its application to industrial systems such as firms and corporate businesses in which outputs, inputs, and profits can be definitely quantified in their physical and institutional connotations. For systems such as a government organization or an academic institution a quantitative specification of input-output and other characteristics may not be completely adequate, but since decisions are continually made in these systems and policies result in action, the systems planning approach takes the most operational attitude in identifying and classifying these decisions (e.g., sequential, nonsequential, routine or nonroutine), their informational bases, the potential alternatives forgone, and in developing a reasonable method of comparison of alternative decision rules or policies. This operational attitude is basically similar to the approach of Tinbergen and Theil in their theory of economic policy (Fox et al. 1966) although the systems analysts focus more intensively on the information systems underlying important decisions and the functional hierarchy within which information flows are processed, may be quantified, economized and made consistent. Forrester (1961) has made this point quite succinctly: "the economist . . . looks upon the entrepreneur as a man who maximizes his profit without asking whether or not he has the available information sources and the mental computing capacity to find the maximum (p. 71)."

Methods most frequently used in systems planning can be broadly classified into three groups:

i) methods for modeling a complex interconnected system by analyzing the details of its working, from the building of information to decision and in some sequential cases from decisions to model revisions (e.g., characterization of a system by a feedback type consistency model);

ii) techniques for implementing the models formulated for an interconnected system in terms of their feasibility relative to computational algorithms (e.g., the decomposition techniques of linear and nonlinear programming); and

iii) methods of simulation for generating alternative feasible policies or decisions which may be worth while considering under conditions of change to which the system may be subject in a dynamic framework (e.g., imputing a lag between inputs and outputs and observing its impact on stability in a production model).

In a logical sense the first group of methods is intended to describe a system in its interconnected parts by making a choice among alternative models (usually optimization goals or subgoals are not required in such descriptions, unless they are explicit or quantified in the information flows available). The second group of methods specifies the operational and computational implications of those languages which are selected to describe (or model) a system. (Usually at this stage some optimization criteria are introduced, either explicitly through an objective function or implicitly through an imputed cost function representing costs of information processing and computing the optimum.) The third group of methods is intended to relax the rigidities of the language structure implicit in the computer algorithms which have to be numerical and nonextrapolative (i.e., nonanalytic).

## A systems analysis framework for educational systems

A number of attempts have recently been made to specify econometric models for planning educational systems (Fox and Sengupta 1968; Sengupta and Fox 1970; O.E.C.D. 1965, 1967, 1969) at various levels, at the national level, at the level of a particular university or public school system, and at more detailed levels (e.g., problems of resource allocation in a particular department or discipline in a specific university). Our discussion will be limited, for reasons of space, to those models which are potentially or currently capable of being applied to institutions of higher learning (e.g., components of a university system). Even in this framework the range of problems and techniques (O.E.C.D. 1969) is too large to be analyzed in a section; hence we will focus primarily on the problems of resource allocation and select a few typical models in systems analysis for illustrating the various decision problems arising in an educational system. From a dynamic viewpoint of growth, change, and diversification of resource allocation patterns, the quantitative models of educational systems have adopted three interrelated approaches. First, the growth of the education sector, as supplier of skilled manpower of various types, has been related (Correa and Tinbergen 1962; Moser and Redfern 1965b; O.E.C.D. 1961–62) to the more important structural variables characterizing over-all growth of real national income (e.g., population growth, trend of investment, and growth of the industrial sector, etc.) and the various policy variables (Adelman 1966; Smith and Armitage 1967) affecting the relative levels of demand and supply (e.g., public policies for financing the expansion of university systems, guidelines for allocation of research funds through state subsidies, etc.).

Second, a systems analysis approach has been developed at a more dynamic level (Stone 1965; Ryans 1965; Rath 1968) for the input and output components of an educational system which is defined to be a system of interconnected processes including different forms of education, training, and retraining, their inputs and outputs. Needs for consistent decisionmaking in a large-scale system with considerable information flows through the component subsystems have frequently led to the wide usage of electronic computers in this field and those techniques (e.g., activity analysis, program planning and budgeting (PPB), scheduling, simulation, etc.) which have proved their usefulness in other applied fields of management science have been most frequently redesigned and suitably modified for application to educational systems.

Third, a decomposition approach based on implicit or explicit optimization criteria (e.g., cost-benefit criterion), mostly on the lines of control theory and the techniques of price *tâtonnement* processes, has been developed, which seeks to specify various characteristics of an optimal or quasi-optimal resource allocation over time for an educational system (Alper 1966; Bowles 1965; Reisman 1966; Stoikov 1964; Intriligator and Smith 1966; Fox et al. 1967). Resource allocation between teaching and research, requirements of capacity expansion in line with prospective demand over time for different skills, and the characterization of investment in human capital in an economic growth model are some of the important areas of educational planning where optimality, efficiency, and the concepts of shadow prices have been most frequently explored.

In the generic sense the systems analysis approach could include all the three groups of methods mentioned above. However, we will consider here mostly the second group of methods for our selective illustration of the techniques of systems analysis as developed by the management scientists and operations researchers, since the remaining two groups of methods have been discussed in earlier chapters in great detail. In particular we will discuss very briefly the methodology of applications of systems analysis to a university framework in relation to (a) the general set-up of instructional development and media innovation; (b) the various levels of decisionmaking about the direction and use of resources in a university; and (c) a simplified view of interdependence of resource flows through activities and their costs and returns, some of which may be partly imputed.

*A general systems approach to education*

The development of instructional systems at a proper level is one of the most important functions of a university. A quantitative analysis of this development is complicated by changes in enrollment patterns, difficulties of co-ordination of learning and teaching resources, technological changes in media of communication, and also the lack of sound methods for measuring observed and opportunity costs associated with alternative schemes of instructional systems development. A general systems approach to analyze these complexities and understand their implications is due to Barson and his team (Barson 1965), who reported a series of interviews with faculty members and media specialists to obtain informational data which were used in part for appraising instructional media, their design, and innovational aspects for courses at Michigan State University over the past several years. The data were also analyzed to identify the rationale used by course developers in reaching their decisions on course development and to determine if, from the viewpoint of faculty time and costs, a given sequence could be determined as the most appropriate or optimal. The flow diagram (Fig. 7.1) summarizes the post interview data analysis and the information-decision network. The appraisal of alternative media innovation procedures for instructional development and their implications for administrative

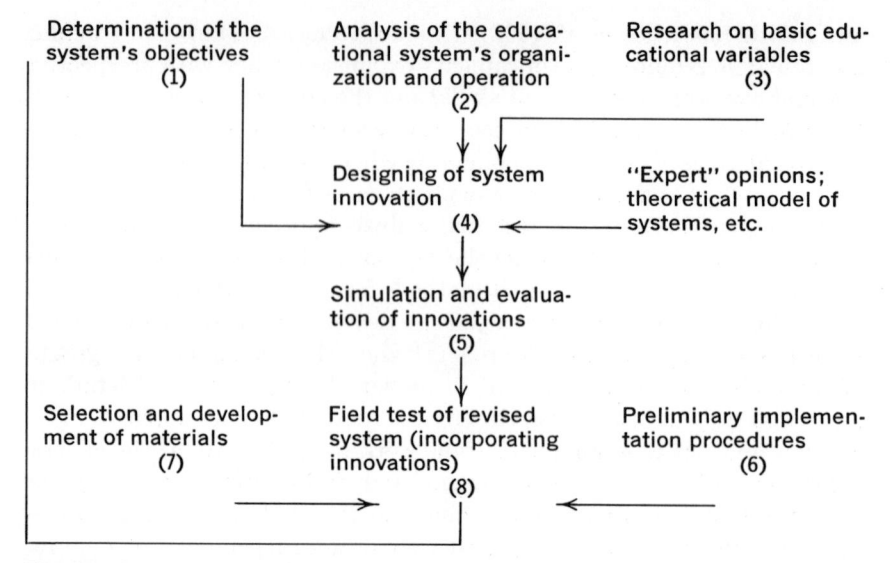

```
Determination of the       Analysis of the educa-      Research on basic edu-
system's objectives        tional system's organi-     cational variables
       (1)                 zation and operation               (3)
                                   (2)
                                    ↓    ↓
                           Designing of system          "Expert" opinions;
                           innovation                   theoretical model of
                                  (4)      ←─────────── systems, etc.
                                    ↓
                           Simulation and evalua-
                           tion of innovations
                                  (5)
                                    ↓
Selection and develop-     Field test of revised        Preliminary implemen-
ment of materials          system (incorporating        tation procedures
       (7)                 innovations)                        (6)
                                  (8)
                    ─────────→              ←─────────
```

Fig. 7.1. General systems approach to education. Source: A modification from Ryans (1963).

organizational set-up and the budgetary procedures of planning were facilitated greatly by the interview data and other statistical facts related to specifically selected courses of study, such as accounting, chemistry, physical education, etc. at Michigan State University at East Lansing. One aspect of this appraisal is described by Barson and his associates:

> A significant problem encountered in the analysis was determining the relevance of accumulated information to instructional development and media innovation. This difficulty was somewhat eased by the use of conceptual techniques derived from the province of systems analysts.
> 
> Two systems were considered of chief concern to the investigators: (1) activities which comprise classroom teaching—the instructional system (IS) and (2) the planning and preparation of classroom teaching activities—the instructional development system (DS), essentially a system for producing systems. It was the DS or series of DS's which were designed and simulated in the search for a viable model.
> 
> In developing a series of hypothetical models of the DS, the investigators were in essence synthetically determining relatively standardized sets of procedures which should most efficiently meet specific instructional objectives. The synthesis of these models followed a thorough analysis of: (1) the successes and failures within the past and present Michigan State University media innovation activities; (2) related situations within the literature; and (3) a consensus of "expert" opinion (p. 9).

Although the system analysis design here is very specific to a particular issue (i.e., instructional development), one should note its several features of generality in the specification of the sequence: information → data evaluation → models and decisions → decision evaluation → action. First, such a scheme is potentially applicable for appraising some other forms of resource development in an academic system (e.g., the development of research and extension services, appraisal of the development of a co-ordinated information system in an academic department, etc.). Second, the empirical contacts through interviews and the reactions of a group of experts involved in the system and its performance suggest very clearly the focal points where more information is required at both quantitative and qualitative levels. Much of the indivisibility of the system relationship may be due to lack of information about alternative situations or modes of development. Third, the procedure of revisions and modifications built into the system analysis design suggests very vaguely its resemblance to the *tâtonnement* processes of decentralization discussed in Chapters 4 and 5, except for two points. The system decision model may not be as numerical as a programming model (unless we agree on a common set of index numbers to represent various qualitative aspects of resources used in the system); also it may be more feasible and economic from the viewpoint of information costs that the system decision model retains flexibility in the organizational decision structure in the various stages of discussion and interaction leading to the final and hopefully optimal action under the circumstances.

One should note in this connection that in situations where the interview method of obtaining statistical data about system operation is not feasible, due either to cost factors or to the dimension of the problem, more reliance has to be placed on simulation techniques and the experiences of similar universities. Some important work on this line has been carried on by R. Judy and his associates (Judy et al. 1968; Judy 1969) on the experiences at the University of Toronto. Note that these simulation techniques do not assume an explicit objective function in dollar terms which could be maximized or minimized; however, in considering the various alternative hypothetical frames of reference and decision situations, they, in effect, provide a choice to the potential decisionmaker. Making a choice between alternatives is very similar to the analogy of "imaginary interviewing" of policymakers suggested by van Eijk and Sandee (1959) in relation to the theory of economic policy.

*A decisionmaking model in a university system*

The decisionmaking model of system analysis in a university framework considered in this section is due to Brink (1966); similar approaches to other aspects of decisionmaking in a university system are available in the growing literature (Keeney et al. 1967; Kershaw and McKean 1959; Williams 1966; O.E.C.D. 1969) on educational planning.

The systems model developed by Brink (1966, p. 235) is outlined as a flow diagram in Figure 2.1 (page 34), which should be referred to at this time. The information network underlying the flow diagram is based on quite substantial statistical data about the different educational parts of the University of Pennsylvania for five or six years, and the flow diagram is designed to reflect not only the difficulty of decisionmaking in the complex and interrelated subsystems of a university system, its logistics, and financing problems but also the economic problems of allocating available intellectual resources among major competing activities, such as teaching, research, and other services. The following quotation emphasizes the potential usefulness of such a flow diagram-type analysis for modeling a university system in general:

> This figure shows the completed system plus what we believe to be the logical decision points. These are designated as those which can and usually are made within the university and conversely those outside. There are in this concept of a university decision-making system 25 decision points. Seven are outside and eighteen are inside.
>
> There is every realization that many of the individual "boxes" in this system must eventually be "blown up" to recognize the system within it. For example, INSTRUCTION. At the University of Pennsylvania there are 19 faculties, 19 deans, 4 Vice-Provosts, 2 academic Vice-Presidents, 1 Provost and the President, not to mention such advisory bodies as the university council.
>
> Once the systems and decision points have been established, we can examine their utility for analysis. Consider the hypothetical case in which a new course of instruction is being contemplated by one of the faculties of the university. Assume that some new faculty will be needed and some present faculty diverted. Horizontally there are some questions to be answered first. First, there is availability, regardless of cost, then willingness to make appointments by the university as a whole. That is to say that the individual faculty may be convinced of the merits of the potential staff, but the University Appointing Committee may not. Looking ahead, as most good planners do, a dean might question the overall balance of his faculty with respect to retirement, etc. Vertically, of course, we start at operating funds and ask what drain can be expected at research facilities, teaching facilities and, of course, faculty salaries. At this point it is logical to examine the possibility of outside aid to supplement operating funds. Finally, looking at the existing amount of operating funds as a fixed amount, we can see the other decision points that will be affected by this decision. Some may be

quite evident, such as student housing. Others, such as the way research from this programme will enhance reputation and increase the body of knowledge, are difficult. Here is where value theory and objectives which I have mentioned must come into play (Brink 1966, pp. 235–36).

The above-mentioned design of systems analysis for decisionmaking in a university complex comprising interrelated subsystems must have a number of interesting implications for planning efficient allocation of various instructional and other resources in a university. First, the various methods of decentralization using decomposition techniques discussed in Chapters 4 and 5 implicitly assumed that the levels of decisionmaking are clear-cut, distinct, and identified; in the actual experiences of a university system subject to dynamic change these are sometimes the unknowns to be determined very carefully. Decisions which are not completely internal to the university system may have to be treated differently from those which are internal. A two-part pricing system may be considered feasible for those cases of resource allocation decisions which refer to divisible and quantified resources, such as finance; here one part would depend on the internal decisions, the other on the external. However, the characteristics of the two decision systems and markets may be much different from those usually associated with the economists' theory of competitive markets.

Second, a question important for organizational efficiency arising in this connection is to what extent the external decisions and the externalities resulting from internal decisions could be profitably internalized in the organizational hierarchy. In some state-supported universities, the government financing and support of the university system is handled through an autonomous body, such as the board of regents or the university grants commission, which may sometimes allow the university considerable autonomy and power in deciding or changing the cost of tuition and other services offered by the university system. Again, since a large part of the benefits of research outputs of the university system are not directly returned *quid pro quo* to the university, since the external benefits are uncompensated by the private market structure, although the community and society as a whole gain through the increased body of knowledge, there is a great scope for measuring the potential contribution of the university vis-à-vis the observed costs.

Third, this systems network emphasizes very clearly the need for combining the pure economic and technical analysis of educational resource allocation with the experience of successes and failures of alternative organizational frameworks possessed by the educational administrators involved in conscious decisionmaking at various stages. For this reason any quantitative formulation in mathematical terms of the various loops and casual relationships in the flow-diagram in Figure 2.1 must be sufficiently flexible to allow for the possibilities of successive modification and revision of the specification of the model and its specified goals, if any. Finally, at some levels of internal decisionmaking (e.g., allocation of budget funds) the economic problems of resource allocation may have to be tackled in a partial equilibrium set-up, much in the spirit of the theory of the second best, in which a number of optimum conditions of the Pareto-efficiency criteria may not be realized.

*Activity analysis model of a university department*

Activity analysis has long offered economists and management scientists a versatile tool which can be applied to various decision situations. It can be designed for checking the mutual consistency of decisions of different subsystems of a university system, when the latter can be expressed in quantitative activity levels. Given an explicit or implicit objective function, it can also be used to show the optimal solution and other feasible solutions, whenever they exist, and their implications.

For the economists, activity analysis offers two important generalizations. First, it generalizes the old concepts of production and cost functions and their technology by relating inputs and outputs through a set of "activities" properly defined. Second, it provides a method, which is sometimes operational and useful, by which a variable, such as a unit of capital stock, can be broken down into a bundle of flows in terms of its services during its lifetime. This latter aspect provides a way of incorporating in a short-run model some of the implications of relatively fixed resources, which may have short-run user costs (i.e., costs of using rather than keeping idle). For the management scientists, activity analysis provides a more flexible tool for analyzing partial indivisibilities and interdependence in production scheduling and project evaluation. The facts that some activities can take only integer values, that some depend contingently on other activities, and that there are some the choice of which in a solution automatically excludes some others provide a very wide degree of flexibility in system designs for production sequences and interdependent projects.

This section describes a specific optimization application of activity analysis in a university department (Plessner et al. 1967; Sengupta and Fox 1969). It grew out of a need felt at Iowa State University by the editor for an information system and a model for analyzing alternative programs that would hopefully carry conviction to the relevant college and university-level administrators when their support was required to implement departmental proposals.

The need for a departmental policy model varies with variations in the superstructure. Thus, a department in a four-year college of limited size requires little major decisionmaking compared with a department combining undergraduate and graduate studies, as well as research and extension activities, in a rapidly expanding university. The need is perhaps greatest when such a complex department belongs to a university which has special obligations to serve the people of a state. In such an institution the administrative environment confronting a department chairman is frequently benign but always imperfectly co-ordinated.

The program of any university should be responsive to the state of the world, the state of science, and the state of the labor market for graduates. The program of a state-supported university should also be responsive to the state of the state. These four sets of data, external to the university, are not ordinarily specified in quantitative form. Nevertheless, they are researchable and should not be left wholly to verbal debate. Logically, these data provide constraints on the set of alternatives over which the university's objective is being optimized. They imply "barter terms of trade" between various outputs or policy targets.

The university president is thus a multiple-goal decisionmaker.* Between the president and the department chairman there may be a number of administrators, such as the vice-president for research, the dean of the graduate college, and the director of the extension service, each of whom contributes to only one of the president's goals.† Their actions impose constraints on the department chairman, whose decisions must take cognizance of several of the presidential goals. The valuation of these constraints as reflected in resource allocation is subject to estimation, once certain pricing mechanisms are accepted.

The attempt at valuation is not limited to superimposed constraints. Every university department operates under self-imposed constraints which manifest themselves in standards of excellence, tradition, academic freedom, etc. An economics faculty should be particularly sensitive to such an attempt and capable of carrying through an analysis of its programs and the impact of various constraints upon its productivity.

* As is, actually, the president of any firm. Regarding the latter, however, we can often assume that the profit goal is dominant without being led to serious mistakes. Such a dominant objective is not usually present in a university.

† We assume that the university president has separate goals for major categories of activities, such as research, graduate education, undergraduate education, extension, and others.

Naturally, the appraisal of the impact of constraints on both inputs and outputs will be made in terms of the department's currency. But this currency should be convertible into that of the aforementioned administrators and ultimately into that of the university president, who must translate his currency into dollar requests from the state legislature and other sources.

It is our belief that a departmental policy model can be helpful in clarifying the objectives of the faculty and increasing the consistency of its recommendations. Such a model can also serve as a precursor of improved decisionmaking in the superstructure by providing viewpoints and information which are not often available at present.

As observed above, the problem confronting us is much like the one confronting a government or any other nonprofit, multiple-goal institution. The term "welfare function" is frequently used to describe the objective of the decisionmaker in such a setting. We shall limit our use of this term to national targets; in speaking of the objective of a university, a department, or other entity of less than national size we will refer to its "policy function."

The activity analysis model is summarized in Table 7.1 in the form of a simplex tableau, assuming a linear structure and an imputed set of net prices for the objective function. This model is potentially applicable to other university departments, with very minor modifications, and is capable of being generalized in several directions, e.g., nonlinear interaction between activities and quadratic objective functions. Similar models for other departments could be combined with this one, using a decomposition technique for allocating college or university-level resources among the departments.

The assumptions of this specific model are: (a) the graduates with each academic degree of a university department have the same starting earning power as the average U.S. economist with that degree; (b) the extension services of the department are predetermined; (c) tuition policy and admission standards are prescribed; (d) the department's own output of graduates has no appreciable effect on the national salary structure for economists; and (e) student dropouts equal the number of student transfers from other curricula and addition of students with a so far undecided major subject. (This last assumption was made only because the effects of drop-outs were not examined.) The actual model constitutes a four-year plan, with interdependence between the years, for an academic department which produces B.S., M.S., and Ph.D. graduates. The Ph.D. candidates are subdivided into (1) those who do not have any income from university sources; (2) those who are half-time instruc-

Table 7.1. Activity analysis model of a university department: The simplified simplex tableau

| No. | Activity no.: Objective coefficient | 1 Undergraduates (B.S.) $c_1$ | 2 Master's students $c_2$ | 3 Ph.D. candidates UP $c_3$ | 4 Ph.D. candidates IP $c_4$ | 5 Ph.D. candidates RP $c_5$ | 6 Hiring new faculty $c_6$ | 7 Research by existing faculty $c_7$ | 8 Research by new faculty $c_8$ | 9 Office space addition $c_9$ | 10 Transfer of existing faculty time to under-graduate teaching | 11 Transfer of existing faculty time to graduate teaching | 12 Transfer of new faculty time to undergraduate teaching | 13 Transfer of new faculty time to graduate teaching | 14 Transfer of new faculty time to graduate administration | 15 Transfer of new faculty time to undergraduate administration | Right-hand side |
|---|---|---|---|---|---|---|---|---|---|---|---|---|---|---|---|---|---|
|  |  |  |  |  |  |  |  |  |  |  | 0 | 0 | 0 | 0 | 0 | 0 |  |
| *Restrictions:* |
| 1 | Manpower for undergraduate teaching | $a_{11}$ |  |  | $-a_{14}$ |  |  |  |  |  | $-1$ |  | $-a_{1,12}$ |  |  |  | $b_1$ |
| 2 | Manpower for graduate teaching |  | $a_{22}$ | $a_{23}$ | $a_{24}$ | $a_{25}$ |  |  |  |  |  | $-1$ |  | $-a_{2,13}$ |  |  | $b_2$ |
| 3 | Pool of existing manpower |  |  |  |  |  | $-1676$ | 1 |  |  | 1 | 1 |  |  |  |  | $b_3$ |
| 4 | Pool of new manpower |  |  |  |  |  |  |  | 1 |  |  |  | 1 | 1 | 1 | 1 | 0 |
| 5 | Manpower for undergraduate administration | $a_{51}$ |  |  |  |  |  |  |  |  |  |  |  |  |  |  | $b_5$ |
| 6 | Manpower for graduate administration |  | $a_{62}$ | $a_{63}$ | $a_{64}$ | $a_{65}$ |  |  |  |  |  |  |  |  | $-1$ |  | $b_6$ |
| 7 | Office space |  |  |  | $a_{74}$ | $a_{75}$ | $a_{76}$ |  |  | $-1$ |  |  |  |  |  | $-1$ | $b_7$ |
| 8 | Admission of undergraduates | 1 |  |  |  |  |  |  |  |  |  |  |  |  |  |  | $b_8$ |
| 9 | Admission of graduates |  | 1 | 1 | 1 | 1 |  |  |  |  |  |  |  |  |  |  | $b_9$ |
| 10 | Ratio of IP to undergraduates | $-1$ |  |  | $a_{10,4}$ |  |  |  |  |  |  |  |  |  |  |  | 0 |
| 11 | Ratio of M.S. to graduates |  | $-.75$ | $.25$ | $.25$ | $.25$ |  |  |  |  |  |  |  |  |  |  | 0 |
| 12 | Manpower of RP |  |  |  |  | $-a_{12,5}$ |  | $a_{12,7}$ | $a_{12,8}$ |  |  |  |  |  |  |  | 0 |
| 13 | Dissertation supervision |  | $a_{13,2}$ | $a_{13,3}$ | $a_{13,4}$ | $a_{13,5}$ |  | $-a_{13,7}$ |  |  |  |  |  |  |  |  | 0 |
| 14 | Existing manpower transferable to undergraduate teaching |  |  |  |  |  |  |  |  |  | 1 |  |  |  |  |  | $b_{14}$ |
| 15 | New manpower transferable to administration |  |  |  |  |  | $-a_{15,6}$ |  |  |  |  |  |  |  | 1 | 1 | $b_{15}$ |
| 16 | Research |  |  |  |  |  | $-a_{16,6}$ | 1 |  |  |  |  |  |  |  |  | $b_{16}$ |

235

tors; and (3) those who are half-time research assistants. The norms for the duration of studies are: four years for B.S. and instructors; three years for research assistants and free students, and two years for M.S. students. A unit of research output is whatever emerges from one hour of faculty time devoted to research. The $c_j$ coefficients for each graduate are computed as follows:

$$c_j = R_j \frac{(1+r)^{n_j-k_j}-1}{r(1+r)^{n_j-1}} - F_j \frac{(1+r)^{m_j-k_j}-1}{r(1+r)^{m_j-1}},$$

where $R_j$ = starting annual salary; $F_j$ = annual income forgone; $r$ = interest rate; $k_j$ = years elapsed from the start of the program to the year of admission (i.e., if the program covers 1966–69, and a student enters the system in 1968, $k_j = 2$; $n_j$ = expected work-life + $k_j$ and $m_j = n_j$ + years of study. $F_j$ was taken to be the starting salary of the holder of the immediately preceding degree.

The activities include teaching degree candidates (namely, B.S., M.S., and three kinds of Ph.D. aspirants), hiring new faculty, research activity, office-space addition, and transfer activities, such as transfer of existing and newly hired faculty to undergraduate teaching and graduate teaching and transfer of new faculty to undergraduate and graduate administration. The department was assumed to have a planned expansion in enrollment. Distribution of workload of the existing staff was assumed to remain the same. The additional burdens were distributed among the newly hired faculty. In some applications of the model, it was assumed that new faculty members could supervise dissertations only after three years' experience. The objective function could thus be rewritten as:

$$Z = \sum_{j=1}^{n} \sum_{t=0}^{T} \frac{c_j}{(1+r)^t} x_{jt},$$

where $T$ is the planning period and $x_{jt}$, $j = 1, 2, \ldots, n$; $t = 0 \ldots T$ represents the activity level of a basic variable $x_j$ for period $t$. The $c_j$ coefficient for hired faculty was the starting salary, for research activity it was the total research expenditure (minus faculty and student salaries) per hour of faculty research, for office-space addition it was the cost of new building per square foot, and for the transfer activities it was zero. The actual model considered four years and had fifteen time-specific outputs in each year; i.e., in all sixty activities.

The resource vector $b$, represented by:

$$(b_{10}, b_{20}, \ldots, b_{m0}, b_{11}, b_{21}, \ldots, b_{1T}, b_{2T}, \ldots, b_{mT}),$$

where $b_{it}$ represents the resource of the $i$th category at the $t$th period, describes the resource limit for undergraduate teaching, graduate teaching, for undergraduate administration, graduate administration, office space, admission of undergraduates and graduates, and for research assistants available. Formulation of restrictions for undergraduate and graduate admissions was simplified by assumption (c). The number of courses taught by instructors was also restricted to maintain quality of instruction. Dissertation supervision was restricted up to a certain period of time to existing faculty with more than three years' experience. Experienced faculty members (in the model) were permitted to keep undergraduate teaching to a fixed proportion of their total effort. The newly hired faculty was to take charge of undergraduate administration for a fixed proportion of their total working hours. As regards manpower capacity, two "pools" were created of persons who could teach both undergraduate and graduate students, one for new faculty members and another for existing faculty members. These gave two more restrictions. There were sixteen restrictions considered in the actual model; i.e., $m = 16$. Since each of these was stipulated for each of four years ($t = 0, 1, 2, 3$), we had sixty-four restrictions.

The input-output coefficients of the matrix $A$ are estimated from existing departmental data from a survey conducted among faculty members and on the basis of some common practices regarding the curricula. For the initial year of the program no new resources were needed. Expansion of enrollment in the subsequent years resulted in additional resource requirements. Some teachers retired. These factors were taken into account. As in the case of input-output analysis in a dynamic situation, students are moved through the departmental system from level to level. As they move through the system, they engage in instructional activities as prescribed by the curricula. The form of the matrix* was:

$$A = \begin{bmatrix} A_0 & & & \\ A_1 & A_0 & & \\ A_2 & A_1 & A_0 & \\ A_3 & A_2 & A_1 & A_0 \end{bmatrix}, \text{ for } t = 3,$$

where $A_t$ is an $m.n$ matrix, for $t = 0, 1, 2, 3$; in this instance

$$A_t = (a_{ij}(t)), i = 1, 2, \ldots, 16, j = 1, 2, \ldots, 15.$$

* Note that the matrix $A_0$ represents the one given in Table 7.1, while matrices $A_1$, $A_2$, $A_3$ have different structures which characterize the movement of students and other flows through the system over time.

Thus the model is:

$$\text{maximize: } Z = \sum_{j=1}^{n} \sum_{t=0}^{T} c_j (1+r)^{-t} x_{jt}$$

subject to: $Ax \leq b; x \geq 0$,

where $x$ is a $4n.1$ vector, $A$ is a $4m.4n$ matrix, and $b$ is a $4m.1$ vector. This is a simple linear programming problem—the dynamic aspect being considered in the parameters. As such it has a lot of flexibility. Many modifications could be made in the parameters to analyze the effects of policy changes, technological changes, and changes in the salary structure for graduates, by introducing "revise" subroutines in the computer program. Some specific numerical applications are discussed in Fox et al. 1967; Plessner et al. 1968; Sengupta and Fox 1969; and Fox et al. 1969.

### Activity analysis, state space, and scheduling models

The three types of analysis discussed in the previous section are different facets of the more popular term called "systems analysis" applied in industry. "Systems design is such a modish, if not faddish, word at the moment that I don't want to exaggerate the amount of well-understood technique that stands behind it," commented Herbert A. Simon (1965) in 1965, while talking about the usefulness of systems analysis. "The good systems analyst is a 'chochem,' a Yiddish word meaning wise man with occasional overtones of wise guy. His forte is creativity," said Aaron Wildavsky (National Affairs, Inc., 1967).

While facing problems of choice, one always finds it convenient to think about the consequences of alternative policies instead of choosing one of them at random. While thinking, one uses some sort of model (or alternative models) of the real situation. When these problems of choice confront a university president, say, the models, taken in the form of mathematical relationships approximately representing the real situation, may help him judge the alternative ways of achieving efficiency in his administration, the nature of efficiency depending on the goals set up for the university.

Systems analysis does not replace the experienced judgment of the decisionmaker. It helps the manager to synthesize in his own way both the anticipated effectiveness and the projected resource requirements of all the competing program sets and to choose, in some cases, a course of action extending over several time periods interrelated in such a way that the actions in one time period materially affect the actions possible in the subsequent time period, recognizing the multiple decisionmakers within and without the university. University decisionmakers may benefit from systems analysis in various ways which have been experienced in other public service areas (McKean 1958; Buchanan and Tullock 1962; March 1965; Tullock 1966; McKean and Hitch 1967).

In some lower-order problems, such as inventory control and maintenance and replacement of equipment, it is easier to formulate objective functions and to undertake optimality analysis. As we move from operating problems to planning problems, the difficulties of specifying objective functions increase. But the potential pay-off from successful application of systems analysis also increases. Much can be done to improve the efficiency of educational administration and the allocation of scarce resources, and to save large amounts of money (and students' time) that may otherwise be misspent. Systems analysis provides a logical program to aid university administrators in the over-all allocation of resources to achieve their stated objectives and to establish a rational basis for evaluating alternative allocation policies under the assumption that the university has varied and perhaps conflicting goals defined by those entrusted with decisionmaking responsibilities. The model or "systems analysis" is never a substitute for the decisionmaker.

*Activity analysis models*

The activity analysis approach described earlier may sometimes involve assumptions relating to value judgments that are not always recognized and when recognized cannot always be handled in practice. There may be no single criterion or objective function in the near future which is agreed on by the relevant decisionmakers for judging among conflicting objectives. Sometimes to make the analyses applicable the original objectives have to be changed, which is *a priori* an undesirable situation. Under such circumstances, however, a creative amalgamation of means and unachievable ends is made. The analyst solves the problem very crudely at the first stage, then improves on the formulation, and, hopefully, the approximate solution iteratively, to get closer to the objective. New objectives are defined, new assumptions made, new models constructed, until a creative amalgam is arrived at which is better than others, even if it is not optimal in any sense. In this spirit the following application is presented.

An interesting activity analysis model* is designed and applied to a university department by McCamley (1967), based on the notional data of a department of economics. The model is static and it assumes that

---
* This section is based on (McCamley 1967).

decisions are made under conditions of certainty and are quantifiable in an operational sense. It is designed to find the desirable or the optimum levels of both inputs and outputs. Some of the available input levels are treated as fixed. The arguments of the departmental preference function are limited to output levels. The summer months are ignored in the model so far as its activities of teaching and research are concerned. The amount of resources which college deans and other higher-level decision-makers supply to the department depend on the quality of the output. Faculty members and students also influence the preference function of the department. The state's preference in terms of its emphasis on the undergraduate education of state residents is recognized. To maintain consistency with these goals, the department's preference function could involve both fixed and flexibile targets. Under the circumstances, undergraduate output levels appear to be the most relevant fixed targets.

The model assumes the preference function to be approximately linear in the flexible targets. Some of the resources are assumed to be specific to the department. The faculty positions allotted to the department are assumed to be distributed among three specializations within the economics discipline, each of which has some source of research funds. The department produces Master's and Ph.D. degrees in economics. Financial support to the students, although limited, is available as research or teaching assistantships.

The teaching budget is decided by the college dean. This model does not include truly fixed costs in the budget. One-half the salary of the department chairman and his secretarial assistance is the major cost considered fixed in the model. The proportion of faculty salaries included in the teaching budget is determined endogenously. Restrictions are imposed to insure that faculty members are paid. The college dean also allocates office space and classroom space to the department, and he allocates teaching resources furnished to the economics department by other supporting departments. The supply function confronting the department for faculty members of the $i$th type includes not only salary levels but other factors also.

Let $q_i = f_i(z_i)$ be the $i$th supply function, where $z_i$ is the vector of arguments which the department chairman can control. The following set can be defined:

$$Q_i = \{q_i | q_i \geq \bar{q}_i\},$$

where $\bar{q}_i$ is the number of positions authorized to the department for employment in the $i$th specialty. The department chairman is, therefore, limited to $z_i$ vectors which belong to the set:

$$z_i = f^{-1}(Q_i) = \{z_i | f_i(z_i) \geq \bar{q}_i\}.$$

In the model, $z_i$ has been assumed to have seven components: salary and benefits from the teaching budget, salary and benefits from a research budget, proportion of a faculty member's time allotted to research, amount of undergraduate teaching per year per faculty member, amount of graduate teaching per year per faculty member, and amount of time spent on committees and public service, which is assumed to be a given proportion of the amount of time spent in teaching functions. The time allotted to research by a faculty member also has to be proportional to the amount of his salary paid from that research budget.

Other restrictions may be imposed by the higher-order decisionmakers. Let $Q'_i$ be the set of vectors which belong to $Q_i$ and also satisfy these latter restrictions. If $Q'_i$ is convex, elements $z'_j$ of $Q'_i$ may be used to construct activity vectors for the model relating to faculty allocation. The model considers activities in which the total salary of a faculty member is independent of his activity mix. The total workload for each member adds up to the equivalent of twelve contact hours per week. The model assumes that secretarial and clerical personnel can be employed up to the desired number at the going wage rate. The same assumption is made concerning the students on various types of appointments. It was also assumed that a student who is on a research assistantship during his entire Ph.D. program is likely to finish sooner than if he had been a part-time instructor during some portion of the program.

McCamley's model consists of 57 "commodities" (outputs) and 82 activities. The activities have been grouped into seven interrelated classes: degree activities, research activities, faculty allocation activities, undergraduate teaching and advising activities, graduate teaching, advising and theses supervision, secretarial activities, and graduate student appointments. For reasons of space only one of them will be described, namely, the degree activities.

Table 7.2 shows the activity numbers, commodity numbers, and the different activities for this group. Activity number $e_{19}$ involves production of the target level of undergraduates (indicated by a minus sign) each of whom has to take 3 courses in economic principles, 2 courses in "specialty one" undergraduate instruction, 4 in specialty two undergraduate instruction, and 3 in specialty three undergraduate instruction, so that he will have $3(3 + 2 + 4 + 3) = 36$ credit hours in economics for his B.S. major in that subject. He will also have 13 "units" of advising from the economics department. Activity $e_{20}$ denotes that each "specialty two" Master's degree student in economics (denoted by commodity number $e_{49}$) has to have 5 courses in specialty one graduate instruction in economics, 3 courses in specialty two, one course in specialty three, 4 units of thesis work (each unit is 3 credit hours), 3 courses in another

Table 7.2. Activity analysis model of a university department: Degree activities

| Activity numbers<br>Commodity<br>numbers | $e_{19}$ | $e_{20}$ | $e_{21}$ | $e_{22}$ | $e_{23}$ |
|---|---|---|---|---|---|
| $e_1$ | −1 | | | | |
| $e_2$ | 3 | | | | |
| $e_3$ | 2 | | | | |
| $e_4$ | 4 | | | | |
| $e_5$ | 3 | | | | |
| $e_6$ | | 5 | 6 | 6 | 7 |
| $e_7$ | | 3 | 1 | 5 | 2 |
| $e_8$ | | 1 | 2 | 1 | 4 |
| $e_{34}$ | 13 | | | | |
| $e_{35}$ | | 6 | 6 | 10 | 10 |
| $e_{36}$ | | 4 | | 8 | |
| $e_{37}$ | | | 4 | | 8 |
| $e_{38}$ | | 3 | 3 | 5 | 4 |
| $e_{39}$ | | 1 | 1 | 2 | 2 |
| $e_{49}$ | | 1 | | | |
| $e_{50}$ | | | 1 | | |
| $e_{51}$ | | | | 1 | |
| $e_{52}$ | | | | | 1 |

*Source:* (McCamley 1967).

department (say, mathematics), and one course in a second department (say, statistics) which is the equivalent of $3(5 + 3 + 1 + 4 + 3 + 1) = 51$ credit hours, assuming each course to be equivalent to three credit hours. He will also have 6 units of counseling from the economics department. The activity $e_{21}$ can be explained exactly in the same way for specialty three Master's degree candidates. Commodity number $e_{37}$ is the thesis supervision of specialty three graduate students and $e_{50}$ stands for specialty three Master's candidates admitted. Activity $e_{22}$ has the same meaning for specialty two Ph.D. candidates as $e_{20}$ does for specialty two M.S. candidates. Commodity $e_{51}$ stands for specialty two Ph.D. candidates admitted. Activity $e_{23}$ has the same meaning for specialty three Ph.D. candidates as $e_{21}$ has for specialty three M.S. candidates. The total number of credit hours needed for a Ph.D. degree is

$$3(6 + 5 + 1 + 8 + 5 + 2) = 81 = 3(7 + 2 + 4 + 8 + 4 + 2).*$$

The Ph.D. candidate receives 10 units of counseling in the economics department. Commodity number $e_{52}$ stands for specialty three Ph.D. candidates. Some of the commodity constraints for the degree activities are as follows:

* Assuming that attrition rates are not zero and students sometime have more courses than necessary. The credit requirements for B.S., M.S., and Ph.D. have been assumed to be 36, 51, and 81 instead of 30, 45, and 63 respectively.

$y_{ed} \leq -100,$

$0 \leq y_{e_{49}} \leq 6.0,$

$0 \leq y_{e_{50}} \leq 8.0,$

$0 \leq y_{e_{51}} \leq 3.0,$

and

$0 \leq y_{e_{52}} \leq 4.0.$

The other relevant constraints also involve other groups of activities and are omitted to avoid confusion. The objective function weights for the activities $e_{20}$, $e_{21}$, $e_{22}$, and $e_{23}$ (the flexible targets) were $-2.4$, $-2.4$, $-4.8$, and $-4.8$, respectively.

This discussion of McCamley's model will not be complete if we do not bring out its special feature of identifying intermediate products as well as final ones. Faculty services for undergraduate teaching of different types, teaching services provided by graduate instructors and teaching assistants, secretarial and clerical assistance used by teaching and research activities, research assistance provided by M.S. and Ph.D. candidates, faculty research services of different types, counseling and advising of graduate and undergraduate students, and thesis supervision "commodites" have been incorporated into the model in such a way that they have the properties of intermediate products in Koopmans' sense (1957).

Although this type of activity analysis application to a university system has its limitations, due to the assumptions of divisibility in the definition of activities and the static features, some of these could be relaxed partially through simulation and other approaches.

*State-space approach*

The state-space approach considered in this section provides a dynamic view of interdependence of the subsystems of an educational system through the possible application of control theory techniques and also methods of dynamic decomposition.

Any quantitative method for analysis of a system is based on a set of equations which show the interdependence among the component variables which characterize the system. If the set of equations is all algebraic in form (linear or nonlinear), like those we have considered so far, the model is called a static model. If the set contains at least one differential or difference equation of any order it is called a dynamic model.

If all the differential or difference equations are of the first-order form, it is called a state-space model.

A state-space model is very easy to treat mathematically and computationally. This fact has caused it to be widely used in modern system science. The state-space model of an educational system which will be discussed in this section has been developed by Koenig, Keeney, and Zemach (Zemach 1967; Keeney et al. 1967). The structure of the model is represented diagramatically in Figure 7.2.

The model consists of a demand sector and various production sectors.

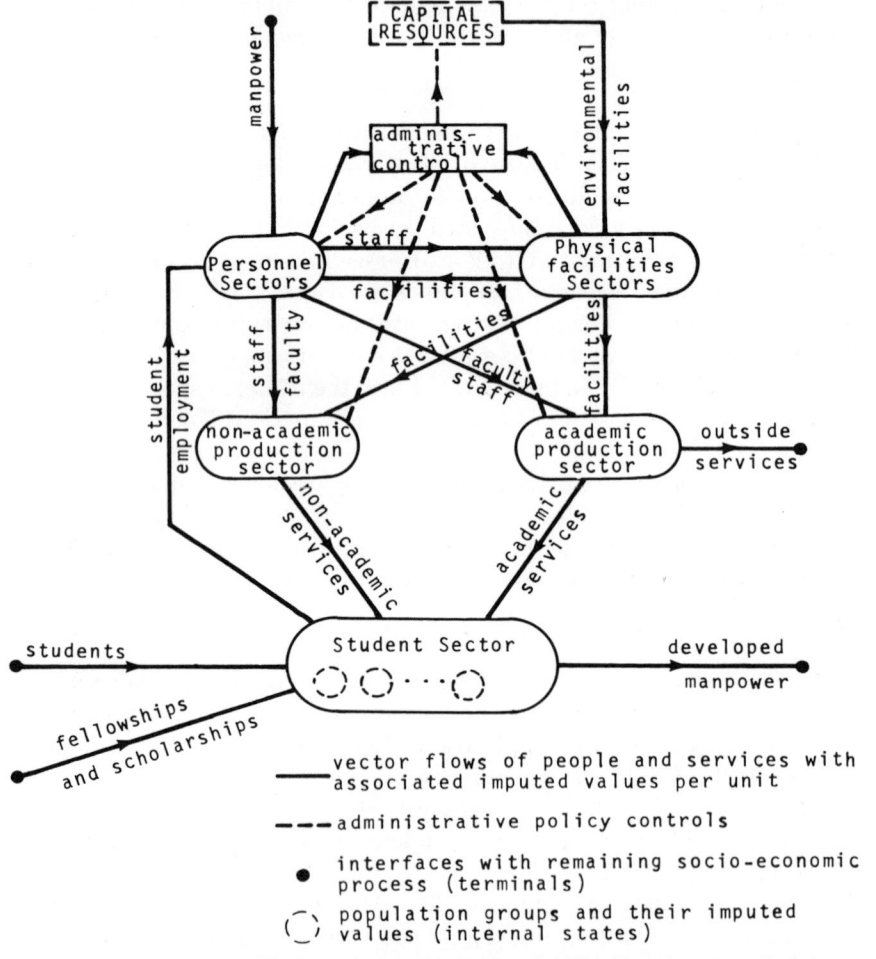

**Fig. 7.2. A systems model for a university. Source: Koenig and Keeney (1969).**

The demand sector reflects the demands placed on the system by the students in various academic programs. Patterns of behavior of large subgroups of students in selecting their programs have been considered. The graduate programs which involve thesis research have been especially considered in the model. The production sectors describe the allocation of resources in terms of man-hours of faculty and staff and of support facilities which include nonacademic programs and also classroom and laboratory space.

These two sectors are modeled separately and then coupled together by imposing constraints on flow rates and unit values, forming a state-space model of the system which represents the interrelationship between the sets of inputs, outputs, and internal states as a function of a set of control variables.

The model of the demand sector treats the number of fellowships and graduate assistantships as control variables which can be changed and the decisionmaker can study the effects of changes of financial assistance offered to students on the manpower output of the university. The students place demand for credit hours of courses and research on the institution. The model then works out an imputed value in terms of cost of faculty input and other support facilities. The state equation is defined as:

$$\bar{x}(t+1) = P(t)\bar{x}(t) + \bar{d}(t)s(t) + B_1\bar{g}(t) + B_2\bar{r}(t), \tag{1}$$

where $\bar{x}(t)$ is an $n.1$ vector, the $i$th element of which represents the number of students in category $i$ during the $t$th time interval $(t = 1, 2, \ldots, n)$; $P(t)$ is an $n.n$ matrix whose $i, j$th element represents the proportion of those students of category $j$ at time $t$ which goes to category $i$ in time $t + 1$ $(i = 1, 2, \ldots, n; j = 1, 2, \ldots, n)$; $\bar{d}(t)$ is an $n.1$ vector whose $i$th element represents the proportion of new students entering category $i$ at time $t$; $s(t)$ is the number of new students entering the university at time $t$; $B_1$ and $B_2$ are $n.n$ matrices which represent that part of the enrollment in each category which is attributable to the financial assistance; $\bar{g}(t)$ is an $n.1$ vector whose $i$th element gives the number of teaching assistantships offered; $\bar{r}(t)$ is an $n.1$ vector whose $i$th element gives the number of other financial aids, namely, research assistantships, fellowships, scholarships, and tuition concessions; $\bar{x}(t + 1)$ represents the $n.1$ vector of student population at time $(t + 1)$ for the $n$ categories.

The first term on the right-hand side of equation (1) gives the distribution of students of different categories who come from within the university independent of any financial inducements. The second term gives the new arrivals for different categories, independent of any financial inducement. The third and fourth terms give the number of students of different categories on financial assistance who would otherwise not continue their education in the particular university.

Corresponding to the state vector equation the output vector equation for the university is given as:

$$\tilde{v}(t) = \Delta(t)\tilde{x}(t) - C_1\tilde{g}(t) - C_2\tilde{r}(t), \qquad (2)$$

where $\tilde{v}(t)$ is the $n.1$ vector of manpower departing from the institution in $n$ categories; $\Delta(t)$ is the $n.n$ diagonal matrix whose $j$th diagonal element $S_j(t)$ represents the proportion of students of category $j$ who leave at the end of time $t$ (note that

$$S_j(t) = 1 - \sum_{i=1}^{n} P_{ij}(t))$$

and $C_1$ and $C_2$ are $n.n$ matrices reflecting the proportion of assistantships and other aids offered to students already *within the institution* who could not otherwise continue their education.

Student demand for credit hours for course and research work can be represented by the following equation, assuming that the unconstrained demands are directly proportional to the components of the state vector $x(t)$, as follows:

$$\begin{bmatrix} h_1(t) \\ h_2(t) \end{bmatrix}_{2n.1} = \begin{bmatrix} H_1 \\ H_2 \end{bmatrix}_{2n.n} x(t), \qquad (3)$$

where $h_1(t)$ and $h_2(t)$ are $n.1$ vectors representing numbers of student course and research credit hours for each category; and $H_1$ and $H_2$ are $n.n$ matrices representing credit requirements by course and by category of students.

The average imputed value of a student in category $i$ during the $(t+1)$th time interval is given by:

$$\hat{x}_i(t+1) = \sum_{j=1}^{n} q_{ij}(t+1)\hat{x}_j(t) + \frac{d_i(t)s(t)}{x_i(t+1)} \hat{x}_i(t) - k_i(t+1), \qquad (4)$$

where

$$q_{ij}(t+1) = \frac{p_{ij}(t)x_j(t)}{x_i(t+1)}$$

equals proportion of students in category $i$ in period $(t+1)$ who were from the $j$th category of period $t$;

$$\frac{d_i(t)s(t)}{x_i(t+1)}$$

is the proportion of new students in category $i$ in period $t+1$; and $\hat{x}_j(t)$, $\hat{x}_i(t)$ are the elements of the state vector representing the average value of investment at period $t$ in a student of the $j$th and the $i$th category, respectively. The imputed value of a student who enters at an advanced level is assumed to be the same as that of a corresponding student developed inside the institution. For accounting purposes, such values are negative, signifying the unit costs of output of the demand sector. Further, $k_i(t+1)$ represents the average value added to the student of category $i$ during the time interval $(t+1)$ by means of teaching and research (since the values of teaching, research, and support facilities are input to the demand sector, this will have a positive sign); and $\hat{x}_i(t+1)$, therefore, consists of the average imputed value of students coming from within the university, the average imputed value of new arrivals, and the value added during the period.

In vector notation for all categories of students we have:

$$\hat{x}(t+1) = Q(t+1)\hat{S}(t) + \hat{d}(t+1) - H_1'\hat{h}_1(t+1)$$
$$- H_2'\hat{h}_2(t+1), \quad (5)$$

where the $n.j$ vectors $\hat{h}_1(t+1)$ and $\hat{h}_2(t+1)$ denote the unit costs of course credit hours and research credit hours, respectively:

$$Q(t+1) = [q_{ij}(t+1)];$$

$$\hat{d}(t+1) = \frac{d_i(t)s(t)}{x_i(t+1)}\hat{x}_i(t) \quad (t = 1, 2, \ldots, n);$$

and $H_1'$ and $H_2'$ are the transposes of the matrices $H_1$ and $H_2$ in (3) above.

The model of the production sector is built in such a fashion as to take care of the demands of the students. The products are credit hours of education and research which are partly used in the educational process and partly sent outside. The resources are faculty, graduate assistants, and support facilities. The model assumes a feedback loop representing the fact that part of the graduate students are used as graduate assistants to meet faculty requirements. There are $m$ areas of study in the system. The input-output model of the production sector for the $i$th production unit (i.e., the $i$th area of study) is given by the following vector-matrix equations:

$$\begin{bmatrix} f(i,t) \\ g'(i,t) \\ e(i,t) \end{bmatrix} = \begin{bmatrix} F_1(i) & F_2(i) & F_3(i) \\ G_1(i) & G_2(i) & G_3(i) \\ E_1(i) & E_2(i) & E_3(i) \end{bmatrix} \begin{bmatrix} h'_1(i,t) \\ h'_2(i,t) \\ 0(i,t) \end{bmatrix}, \tag{6}$$

where

$f(i,t)$ is the $n_1.1$ vector of units of faculty manpower of $n_1$ types required in the $i$th area of study in period $t$;

$g'(i,t)$ is the $n_2.1$ vector of units of graduate assistant manpower of $n_2$ types in the $i$th study area at time $t$;

$e(i,t)$ is the $n_3.1$ vector representing items of various kinds of support facilities used in the $i$th study area;

$h'_1(i,t)$ represents the vector of the course credit hours associated with the $i$th study area at all levels;

$h'_2(i,t)$ represents the vector of research credit hours of the $i$th study area at all levels; and

$0(i,t)$ represents the vector of numbers of units of outside services, namely, contract research or special seminars for businessmen. These units are "sold" by the university in area $i$; and

$F_j(i)$, $G_j(i)$, $E_j(i)$, $j = 1, 2, 3$ are matrices whose elements are coefficients of proportionality used in measuring the input-output flows.

The costs of production of units of output (the imputed values) in the $i$th area of study are:

$$\begin{bmatrix} \hat{h}'_1(i,t) \\ \hat{h}'_2(i,t) \\ \hat{0}(i,t) \end{bmatrix} = -\begin{bmatrix} F_1(i) & F_2(i) & F_3(i) \\ G_1(i) & G_2(i) & G_3(i) \\ E_1(i) & E_2(i) & E_3(i) \end{bmatrix}' \begin{bmatrix} \hat{f}(i,t) \\ \hat{g}'(i,t) \\ \hat{e}(i,t) \end{bmatrix}. \tag{7}$$

The costs relate to the costs of course credits, research credits, and outside services and are assumed to be linear functions of faculty, graduate assistants, and support facilities. The negativity is due to the fact that these are output costs of the production sector. The ratios $F_j(i)/E_j(i)$ measure technical innovation and may be regarded as policy coefficients which need updating with time.

The system model is developed by combining these two unconstrained models using the feedback loop due to the use of graduate students (demand sector) in part as graduate assistants (production sector). The final reduced form equations of the system model contain a set of dynamic relations for (a) the growth of student population; (b) the imputed values of students; (c) changes in student output and resources; and (d) the cost of outside services.

The above model can be updated from time to time in two ways:

(1) the system model can be modified by addition, aggregation, or redefinition of its sectors and variables, and (2) the numbers in the equations may be re-evaluated from time to time on the basis of current data or according to changes in the operating policies. The model has been applied to the Michigan State University system and a computer program has been developed in a time-sharing computer system using numerical values for all policy parameters and variables. It starts with a projection of next year's enrollment, based on current policy and behavioral parameters and exogenous variables previously stored in the program. The outside service amount is entered into the program as a known quantity which is determined by the general policy of the university in promoting research, extension education, and other public services. A definite breakdown of these services is not given.

The program does *not* give an optimal solution; it gives only alternative amounts of inputs and outputs, dependent on the policymaker's choice. The model considers only those features of the educational process which can be expressed in terms of flow rates of numbers of people, goods, and services and the associated unit costs expressed in dollars. The model also does not consider the aspects of quality and effectiveness of an educational program.

The model is designed to incorporate through simulation experiments with alternative allocation and control policies (a) the stochastic and dynamic aspects of changes in parameters and variables and (b) the implications of alternative imputed costs (i.e., accumulated costs of education) for the "real flows" of the system. The most important feature of this system model is that its parameters are given as explicit functions of measurable behavioral and policy parameters of the demand and production sectors of the institutions belonging to the university system.

However, this system model does not emphasize the scope for partial optimization which exists in the different subsystems and component decision levels (e.g., decomposition techniques) nor does it emphasize the elements of externalities and social costs present in the calculation of imputed cost of education. Also, the model fails to bring out the importance of setting desirable goals or targets for the different subsystems and thereby focuses on the objectives of the university system as a whole, some of which are quantitative and some qualitative. Grambsch and Gross (1967) in their study on the goals and objectives of a university specify a set of forty-seven goals and subgoals which one or another university may try to achieve, depending upon several factors, such as size, source of support, nature of organization, and so on. They classify these goals into several major categories, as shown in Figure 7.3. It is our

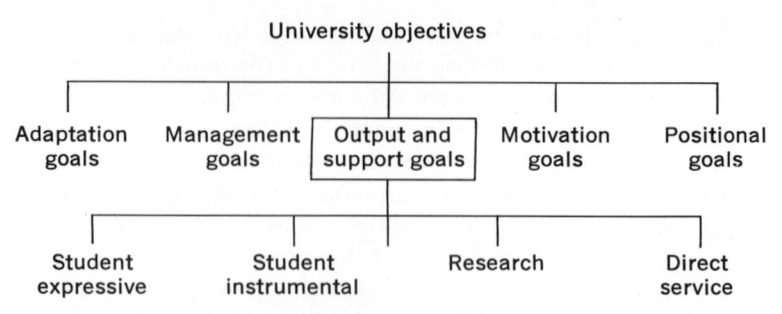

```
                           University objectives
        ┌──────────┬──────────────┬──────────────┬──────────┬──────────┐
   Adaptation   Management    Output and      Motivation   Positional
     goals         goals     support goals      goals        goals
                            ┌──────┬──────┬──────────┐
                         Student  Student  Research   Direct
                       expressive instrumental        service
```

**Fig. 7.3. Objectives of a university. Source: Adapted from Grambsch and Gross (1967).**

opinion that some of these objectives need to be analyzed and incorporated into quantitative models in order to facilitate better and more efficient policy formulation in university systems.

*Scheduling models*

Models of scheduling emphasize the aspects of sequencing involved at various stages of decisionmaking in the university. The courses, curricula, examinations, etc., all are required to follow some schedule for consistency purposes, but the schedules may be decided from the viewpoint of the objectives of the students (i.e., costs of education) or the faculty (i.e., convenience of the academic department), or the university system as a whole. The cost of time and the flexibility of the schedules in some sense provide one important aspect investigated in the scheduling models. The second most important factor is the evaluation of opportunity costs, due to the fact that using a resource in one area at a given time precludes its use elsewhere. In this aspect scheduling models emphasize the PERT (program evaluation and review techniques) and PPB (program planning and budgeting) techniques (O.E.C.D. 1968, 1969).

As an example of a scheduling model in an educational system, we may consider the problem of sequencing of curriculum subject to the constraints of faculty inputs and the fact that the students' utilization of class instruction for greater proficiency depends on its proper scheduling. It is assumed that better utilization of students' time can be achieved through better sequencing of the curriculum; indirectly the faculty input also can be better utilized. Due to unplanned distribution of subject matter contents in the schedule of a student, he may retain very little of some of the courses studied when he graduates. It has been observed that some distributions of subject matter produce higher levels of mastery at graduation than others. The object, therefore, is to work out that distribution of courses in a schedule which maximizes the student's mastery of the entire curriculum, not only on graduation but also after graduation (Taft and Reisman 1967).

The education potential $p$, representing the level of mastery achieved by a student at time $t$ relative to an initial base $p$, is dependent on the type of subject matter $S$, the type of student $L$, the type of teaching method $M$, the cumulative learning time $t_L$, the forgetting time $t_D$, the number of repetitions of the subject in other courses $(R)$, and an interaction factor $I$ between $S$, $L$, and $M$, and is given under certain conditions by:

$$p = IMH(1 - S^{-L(t_L)^2})S^{-At_D}, \tag{8}$$

where

$A = (H - Bt_L)/MLR$ and

$B$ is an empirically derived constant.

Here, $I$ is the ratio of the empirically determined $p$ and the $p$ which is calculated from the model without $I$, and $H$ is the total amount of time given for a subject matter $S$ (time to teach the subject under average conditions and the indirect time to be devoted to the repetition of the subject matter in other courses).

For $n$ courses in the $j$th schedule the relation (8) can be written as:

$$P_j = \sum_{i=1}^{n} p_i = \sum_{i=1}^{n} I_i M_i H_i (1 - S_i^{-L_i t_L}) S_i^{-A_i t_D}. \tag{9}$$

One has to maximize $P$ over all schedules $j$. Several algorithms are available to solve this problem (Taft and Reisman 1967; Buffa et al. 1964).

Scheduling programs have been developed to achieve higher rates of utilization of school facilities to save considerable construction expenses (Glasserman 1968). Programs for master schedules of classes and assignment of students to classes have also been developed to schedule students via computer programs (Oakford and Chatterton 1966–67). The program evaluation and review technique has been used extensively to plan and control research projects (Cook 1966). A modification of the above has been made in the convergence technique which has been applied to a research program aimed at understanding the reading process (Carresse and Barker 1967).

## Simulation techniques in educational planning

In the case of a university system for which not all the parameters of a decision system are known, for which no finite number of decision alternatives has been specified, and in which the objective functions of different members of the decision hierarchy are imcompatible the decision system cannot be uniquely defined. Such a situation calls for the use of a simulation model which may be defined as a collection of mathematical expressions that attempts to interrelate analytically all the parameters which define the major components of the university system. Such a model is intended to have the same predictive response to a chosen set of values of specified variables as the actual response of the real system to the same set of variables.

To formulate such a model, the first task is to identify and quantify all the parameters in a logical fashion. To compare the resource impact of changes in the parameters in a particular network, it is convenient to assess the final results in terms of a common denominator, say, dollars. The results provide a versatile and useful computer-based model for decisionmaking within the university, which will compute the resource consequences of academic planning and other decisions or of policy proposals.

The traditional methods of decisionmaking, namely, the historical view of costs and the formula models, are often misleading and allow the costing of only one alternative confined by the built-in assumptions; this is of very limited value (Nance et al. 1965; Rath 1966; Swanson et al. 1966). The rational objections to these methods concern the concepts of marginal costs and marginal benefits. In this discussion, marginal cost will be considered as the additions to the total systems costs required to accommodate an activity or, alternatively, the marginal cost of an activity consists of those resource costs which could be avoided if the activity were not undertaken. Similarly, the marginal benefit of an activity is defined as the additions to the total systems benefits that are attributable to that activity.

An important use of a simulation model is in dealing with uncertainty surrounding some system parameters and activities. This uncertainty may be the result of imperfect estimation and projection and the random nature of certain variables, such as enrollment in different courses, popularity of different major subjects, and so on. The simulation model is allowed to run repeatedly while probabilistic variables are assigned different values within a range on the assumption that the variables follow specific probability distributions. This will result in a frequency distribution of resource requirements, enlightening the decisionmaker about the range over which these requirements may vary and providing estimates of their probability distribution. This approach is called the Monte Carlo technique (Hoggatt and Balderston 1963). When this technique seems appropriate, the simulation model may be used to allow for variation in the values of uncertain parameters within a range to study their impact on resource requirements and to indicate the sensitivity of plans to such variations, helping the decisionmaker to avoid plans which are too sensitive to capricious variation in the system parameters and activity levels. Where it is impossible to avoid sensitive plans, the simulation model assists planners to prepare contingency plans for "insurance."

*A university cost simulation model*

G. Weathersby (1967) has developed a simulation model for the University of California which is useful both for input-output and efficiency analysis. The model consists of a set of mathematical expressions which describe the analytical relationships between the simulated parameters and the numerical values for the descriptive parameters of a campus. For the purpose of computer operation the analytical relationships are contained in the program, while the parameter values are supplied by the data deck. This enables investigation of both the independent and jointly distributed variables in the university system.

The costs involved in the resource requirements of the university are divided into five categories (Firmin et al. 1967):

1. Instruction: All of the relevant faculty salary costs generated by students taking courses.
2. Instructional support: The requisite support personnel, supplies, equipment, and facilities needed to serve the faculty in their teaching and departmental research efforts.
3. Organized research and activities: The costs of the university generated by separate research institutes, bureaus, studies, and centers.
4. Campuswide administration/service functions: The costs of general administration, libraries, student aid, housing, etc.
5. Physical space and maintenance of operation of the above.

These categories and the subsequent cost elements within each category are selected for their unique and significant characteristics. Each of these five general categories is dependent upon the other four in some global sense; however, the operation of each is taken to be autonomous within its own domain. This assumption reduces the problem of multistage joint determinacy to sequential single-stage determinacy, which is easier to handle analytically. The assumption and the categories are pictorially shown in Figure 7.4.

```
Instruction ─────────────────▶   Total university
Instructional support ───────▶   systems costs:
Organized research and activities ▶  Dollars
Campuswide activities ───────▶   Personnel
Physical facilities ─────────▶   Equipment
                                 Physical facilities
```

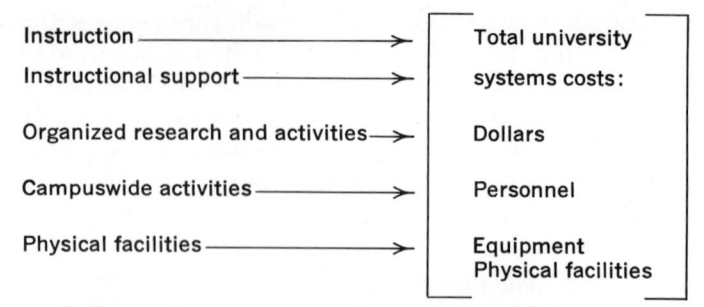

**Fig. 7.4. General flow chart of the university cost simulation model. Source: Weathersby (1967).**

We shall discuss the instruction and instructional support model first and then indicate how others could be developed. Consistent with the existing physical space standards, reporting classifications and the data base, aggregation may be made at a discipline level. For any year of interest, total annual resource requirements may be computed for the five categories shown in Figure 7.4 by applying regression analysis\* on the basis of normal sampling theory. Structural changes within the college may be simulated and compared with the existing mode of operation. Exogenously supplied enrollment figures help form an enrollment matrix $[e_{ij}]$ $i = 1, \ldots, m; j = 1, \ldots, n$, where $i$ stands for student major subject field and $j$ for the academic level of the student [freshman, sophomore, junior, senior, M.S. (and first-stage Ph.D.) students; Ph.D. (dissertation-stage) students; and nondegree students; $n = 7$]:

| Field ($i$) and Level ($k$) of instruction | Level of student in economics ($j$) | Freshman (1) | Sophomore (2) | Junior (3) | Senior (4) | Masters (5) | Ph.D. (6) | Special-nondegree (7) |
|---|---|---|---|---|---|---|---|---|
| 1. Mathematics | | | | | | | | |
| | 100 | $E_{1,1,1}$ | $E_{1,2,1}$ | $E_{1,3,1}$ | $E_{1,4,1}$ | | | $E_{1,7,1}$ |
| | 200 | $E_{1,1,2}$ | $E_{1,2,2}$ | | | | | $E_{1,7,2}$ |
| | 500 | | | | | | | |
| 2. Statistics | | | | | | | | |
| | 100 | | | | | | | |
| | 200 | | | | | | | |
| | 500 | $E_{2,1,5}$ | $E_{2,2,5}$ | | | | | $E_{2,7,5}$ |

\* The budget data are based upon annual departmental allocations and the past actual figures; personnel data upon payroll statistics; instructional data upon the schedule of class reports and past and forecasted enrollment figures; and physical space data upon accepted standards.

Assuming that the enrollment matrix $[e_{ij}]$ is known, the course load that these students would induce, both in their major subjects and minor subjects, may be displayed by a preference matrix as follows for a particular major subject—economics, say: where $E_{ijk}$ is the number of student credit hours a full-time equivalent student majoring in economics at an academic level $j$ ($j = 1, 2, \ldots, 7$) takes in subject field $i$ of level $k$. There will be as many such matrices as there are major subjects. They can be arranged one after another in columns. The total number of student credit hours taken by all students in any level of instruction in any of the subject fields is obtained by multiplying the appropriate preference matrix by the corresponding enrollment vector and summing up like quantities horizontally. From the figures on student credit hours, time spent by students and faculty in contact with each other and in using physical facilities may be evaluated for each level of instruction within each major subject field. From these figures, the weekly faculty contact hours per weekly student hour for each rank of faculty within each level of instruction of each major subject field can be obtained. This enables the academic planner to specify class size in a meaningful way. An average annual salary may be associated with each rank of faculty in each major subject field to obtain the associated salary costs. From the above information, the instructional support costs may be obtained in the second phase of the model as follows: (i) $y_1 = a_0 + a_1 f_a$; (ii) $y_2 = a_2 + a_3 f_a + a_4 f_r$; (iii) $y_3 = a_5 + a_6 f_a + a_7 g$, where $y_1 =$ nonacademic personnel, $y_2 =$ general assistance personnel, $y_3 =$ supplies, expenses, equipment, and facilities; $f_a$, $f_r$, and $g$ are academic personnel, research personnel, and graduate students, respectively; and $a_0, a_1, \ldots, a_7$ are constants. All personnel are expressed in full-time equivalents. The relationships are estimated by regression analysis as before. A salary cost is associated, as before, with each type of personnel. The model is pictorially represented in Figure 7.5.

The outputs of the above operations induce other responses in the system, namely, in organized research and organized activities. These activities may be assumed to be functionally related to the number of academic personnel and graduate students. While some may be nonlinear, nonlinear functions should be avoided if possible to retain the flexibility of the simulation model.* The cost of maintaining and operating the physical plant and the additional outlay of capital funds needed for new and remodeled facilities may be simulated in the model. The total amount of assignable square feet for each type of nonresidential facilities, such as classrooms, laboratories, research and office space, physical education, organized research and activities, and library, may be com-

* Nonlinear functions can be approximated by one or more linear segments.

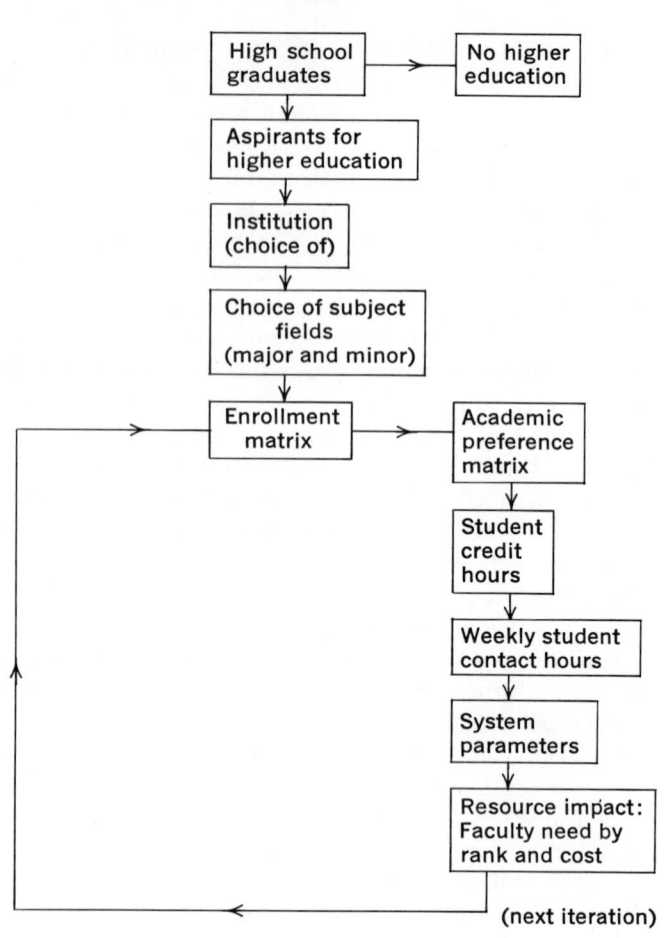

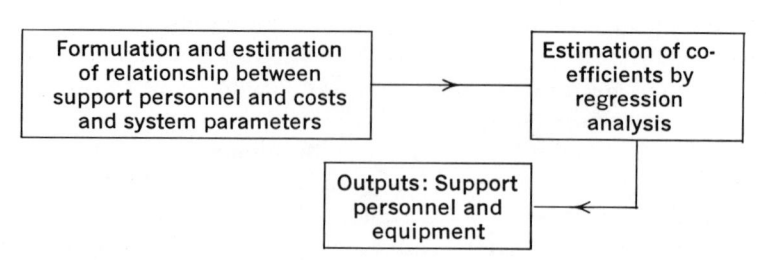

**Fig. 7.5. Instruction and instructional support model. Source: Adapted from text description in Weathersby (1967), p. 31.**

puted. A routine may be included which would recognize the requisite fund flow preceding the actual occupancy of the facilities; annual operating costs also may be computed. The model also enables the college administrator to associate with a discipline its accompanying capital outlay and operating expenditures in the college where the classrooms are allocated from a central pool. The college administrator may also determine an enrollment matrix which is consistent with the value systems of the controlling forces within the university. The distribution of faculty by rank may be considered as a policy variable with feasible rates of change limited to such factors as faculty recruitment, rigid and possibly noncompetitive salary schedules, inadequacy of physical space, etc., at a particular point of time. The sequential annual phasing inherent in the model enables the planner to asymptotically approach the desired distribution within the perceived physical and market constraints. The fact that the model enables the decisionmaker to associate with each discipline its accompanying capital outlay and operating expenditures in the college where the classrooms are allocated from a central pool makes the model very useful and operational.

*Remarks on simulation techniques*

Lack of facilities for experimentation with alternative policies and their implementations had led in recent years to a considerable growth in interest in the techniques of simulation for generating hypothetical data. Applications of these simulation techniques to planning problems of educational systems have been motivated by at least three broad groups of needs; (a) the need for forecasting the endogenous variables of a quantitative and dynamic systems model and appraising the consequences of alternative policies under a specific model; (b) the need for analyzing the sensitivity of the model equations and objective function to variations in coefficients and control variables around their equilibrium or desired values; and (c) the need for allowing some degree of flexibility due to uncertainty of information evolving in the future.

The first group of needs is emphasized in the simulation model developed by Weathersby (1967) for the University of California, while the second is pursued in the systems model developed by Keeney, Koenig, and Zemach (1967) for Michigan State University, and the third objective is emphasized in economywide models, particularly when structural changes and shifts may be expected in the system (Stone 1965; Scarborough and Daniel 1968; Judy 1969). However, as yet the simulation techniques are only exploratory; they provide only hypothetical alternatives, and the final decision is up to the decisionmaker or decisionmakers in the system.

CHAPTER 8

# Some Empirical Problems Involved in Specifying Quantitative Models for Educational Planning

*Karl A. Fox*

In this chapter we will look at the problems of defining and measuring inputs and outputs of institutions of higher education in terms of operating records actually kept and measurements which could in principle be made by the administrators of a particular institution. We will introduce these problems in terms of an illustrative model for a small college. We will then consider such problems as (1) comparing workloads and performance among departments and colleges within a given university; (2) comparing departments in the same discipline in different universities; (3) developing workload, cost, and quality measures for a given department; and (4) aggregating such measures at various levels from individual students, classes, and professors through departments, colleges, and universities to national totals.

### Illustrative model for a small college

The basic model used in this section and represented by equations (1) through (6) is taken directly from an article by Herbert A. Simon (1967). The arithmetical illustrations and extensions are by the editor.

*Basic relationships and identities*

Simon defines the following variables:

$S$ = number of students; $F$ = number of faculty; $r = S/F$ = student–faculty ratio; $W$ = average faculty salary; $\phi$ = the overhead cost percentage, expressed as a markup over the total cost of faculty salaries; $E$ = total expenditures; $h$ = average student course load; $c$ = average class size; $t$ = average teaching load; $i$ = direct (tuition) income per student; and $I$ = other income.

The basic constraints under which a small college operates are indicated in equations (1) through (6):

$$Ftc = Sh; \tag{1}$$

hence

$$\frac{S}{F} = r = \frac{tc}{h}. \text{ Also,} \tag{2}$$

$$I + iS = FW(1 + \phi) = E \tag{3}$$

so that

$$W = \frac{I + iS}{F(1 + \phi)}; \tag{4}$$

i.e.,

$$W = \frac{Ir}{S(1 + \phi)} + \frac{ir}{(1 + \phi)}; \tag{5}$$

therefore

$$W = \frac{r}{(1 + \phi)}\left(\frac{I}{S} + i\right). \tag{6}$$

For concreteness, let us assume that $S = 1{,}000$; $F = 66.67$; $r = 15$; $W = \$15{,}000$; $\phi = 0.6$; $E = \$1{,}600{,}000$; $h = 16$ credit hours per quarter, or 16 3-credit-hour courses per year; $c = 20$; $t = 12$ hours of classroom teaching per week, or 12 3-credit-hour courses per year; $i = \$1{,}000$; and $I = \$600{,}000$.

We have chosen these figures in such a way that the total bill for faculty salaries $FW$ is $1,000,000, precisely the same as the amount of income from student tuition fees. Other income $I$ is equal to $\phi FW$.

Equation (1) states that the total number of credit hours taken by students is identically equal to the total number of student credit hours taught by faculty members. If $S$ and $h$ are fixed, any reduction in average teaching load per faculty member must be offset by an increase in the number of faculty members and/or by an increase in average class size. Similarly, a reduction in average class size would have to be offset by an increase in the number of faculty members and/or an increase in average hours of teaching per faculty member. Further, if tuition per student does not change, these compensating adjustments of $F$, $t$, and $c$ must take place within a total faculty salary budget of $1,000,000. Under our particular assumptions that $I = \$600,000$ and $\phi = 0.6$, the average faculty salary $W$ is equal to $ri$. Hence, the average faculty salary can be increased only by increasing the student-faculty ratio or by raising tuition per student.

In practice, the college president will find that he must keep his tuition fees fairly close to those charged by similar institutions regionally and nationally. A sharp increase in tuition will offend the students currently enrolled (and their parents) and reduce the likelihood that younger brothers and sisters, friends and relatives will enroll in subsequent years. Similarly, both faculty members and president are constrained in salary negotiations by regional and national markets for college teachers. Finally, in striving to increase other (nontuition) income, the president finds himself in competition with other worthy causes. The chief executive of a nonmarket institution is in fact hemmed in by market and quasi-market forces.

*Measures of performance*

Most colleges use credit hours to define their requirements for graduation. Each course in the college catalog carries a certain number of credit hours; for example, graduation from a four-year college may require, say, 192 credit hours, if the college is on the quarter (rather than the semester) system. For simplicity, let us assume that every course carries three credit hours per quarter; then graduation in four years implies an average of sixteen three-credit-hour courses per year.

We assume that the basic unit of instructional activity is a class in which one faculty member meets three hours a week with a certain number of students for the duration of an academic quarter. The numbers we have chosen for our example imply that there will be 800 of these basic units (or "behavior settings") during the academic year, and the average class will consist of one faculty member and twenty students (Barker 1968).*

A. *Student grades and performance.* When a professor and twenty students enter a classroom to begin an hour of instruction, it is clearly intended that something of value will be produced. At the end of the quarter, each student is expected to be able to do certain measurable things that he could not have done at the beginning of the quarter. What he learns in the course is intended to modify his behavior when con-

\* For an elaboration of the concept of behavior settings.

fronted with specified situations. Typically, he receives a grade at the end of the course, which is an estimate of the extent to which his behavior has been modified in the intended respects.

Consider an array in which each of the 800 classes is represented by a column, each faculty member (numbered from 1 through 67, with the 67th faculty member having a two-thirds-time appointment) is represented by a row, and each of the 1,000 students is represented by another row. We assume that each faculty member is assigned during the academic year to 12 of the 800 classes, and that each student enrolls in 16 of the 800 classes. Within any given academic quarter, a "rational" student will allocate his classroom and homework or library time among his five or six courses in such a way that the expected rewards from the last hours invested in each course are equal.† Each student is also allocating his total time between class-related behavior settings and all of his other activities.

Similarly, a "rational" faculty member, teaching four courses during a quarter, will allocate his preparation time among them in such a way that the expected rewards resulting from the last hour applied to each will be equal. The faculty member also allocates his total time between class-related behavior settings and all of his other activities.

The complete matrix has 1,067 rows and 800 columns, giving a total of 853,600 elements, of which only 16,800 are nonzero (800 for faculty members and 16,000 for students). Each of the 16,000 nonzero elements for students results in an entry on a student's transcript, showing a course number and title, a number of credit hours, and a grade. The 800 nonzero elements for faculty members invite an attempt to evaluate their effectiveness in each class.

One of the most basic measurement problems in an educational institution is that of determining the effect of each course upon each student. One approach is to give the student an examination at the beginning of the course which is essentially a random drawing from the same population of questions (or tasks) that will be included in the final exam. The increase in score from the initial to the final exam is an estimate of what has been learned during the course—the extent to which specific behavior has been modified in the direction of the course objectives. If the expected behavior modification resulting from course $j$ is perceived by student $i$ to be among the 64 most desirable outcomes of available courses, he will presumably enroll in it.

† It should be stressed that expected rewards need not be perceived by students or faculty members in monetary terms. "Rewards" are used in Talcott Parsons's sense (1968) to include all outputs from a social system to a personality.

It may be readily granted that the final results of a college education are not identical with a simple aggregate of things learned in 64 courses. The student spends 16 hours a week in classes and 96 waking hours in other behavior settings. If 32 of these hours are spent on homework, there remain 64 hours for other activities. It is to be expected that these 64 hours will have at least as much influence on his life style and life chances as will the 48 hours spent in classes and on homework.

What can be learned from an array of 16,000 grades assigned by 67 faculty members to 1,000 students? We could perform an analysis in which the total variance of the 16,000 grades about their general mean was partitioned into the effects of (1) differences among students; (2) differences among faculty members; and (3) an interaction term. If the average grade given by each faculty member were almost identical with the general mean (i.e., if the $F$ ratio for variance attributed to differences among faculty members were nonsignificant), it would not be possible to identify particular faculty members as high graders or low graders.

However, to the extent that two professors teach different sections of the same course and use the same (objective) final exam, the more effective teacher should produce a higher average score and a different distribution around the average. (It is difficult to say *a priori* that one distribution is better than another, but lower variance in logarithmic terms would seem to be a logical outcome of more effective teaching, given that every student had met appropriate standards for admission to the course.)

The variance analysis covering all 16,000 grades given by faculty members to students is equivalent to the following multiple regression analysis in terms of zero-one variables:

| Grades given to students | Faculty member 1 2 3 ... 67 | Class 1 2 3 ... 800 | Student 1 2 3 ... 1,000 |
|---|---|---|---|
| $g_1$ | 1 0 0 0 | 1 0 0 0 | 1 0 0 0 |
| $g_2$ | 1 0 0 0 | 1 0 0 0 | 0 1 0 0 |
| $g_3$ | 1 0 0 0 | 1 0 0 0 | 0 0 1 0 |
| $g_{16,000}$ | 0 0 0 1 | 0 0 0 1 | 0 0 0 1 |

$$g_i = a + \sum_{j=1}^{67} b_j F_{ji} + \sum_{k=1}^{800} c_k C_{ki} + \sum_{r=1}^{1,000} d_r S_{ri} + u_i.$$

Suppose now that each student is required to assign a grade to each professor in each class he attends. The 16,000 effectiveness grades

$e_i (i = 1, 2, \ldots, 16{,}000)$ could be subjected to a multiple regression analysis in terms of the same variables as above, yielding:

$$e_i = \alpha + \sum_{j=1}^{67} \beta_j F_{ji} + \sum_{k=1}^{800} \gamma_k C_{ki} + \sum_{r=1}^{1{,}000} s_i S_{ri} + v_i.$$

The two regression equations take account of all the information contained in the two sets of grades for the given academic year. They do not take account of predetermined or exogenous factors. They assume that the identity of each student rating each faculty member (coded, perhaps) is part of the computer input.

The equations should permit standardized calculations of the following type:

1) Estimated average grades of all faculty members if rated by the same 240 students; and

2) Estimated average grades of all students if rated by the same 16 faculty members.

If various plausible standardizations have little effect on the relative grades of different students and different faculty members, the actual average grades may capture virtually all of the useful information contained in such a reporting system.

B. *Faculty grades, assignments, and salaries.* To what extent should grades given professors by students be used as a basis for administrative decisions?

If students rate a professor considerably higher in one course than another, this fact may call for a supply response by the professor to bring the second course up to par with the first—if the professor really wants to teach the second course. If he does not, a reassignment response by his chairman may be appropriate.

Salaries are cardinal numbers. If grades given to professors are to be used in salary determination, the grades themselves should be translatable into cardinal numbers. If Professor X's students average 60 correct answers on a standard final exam and Professor Y's students average 50, shall we say that Professor X's teaching performance was worth $(60/50) = 1.2$ times as much as Professor Y's in that course? If there were different numbers of students in the two classes, should we multiply the quality ratio 1.2 by the enrollment or quantity ratio $n_x/n_y$?

In practice, past performance and expected future performance in a variety of courses and roles are reflected in a faculty member's salary; it has the inertia of a weighted moving average. Higher grades in classroom teaching should be rewarded with higher salaries *ceteris paribus*; this requires an appraisal of each faculty member's total contribution to the objectives of the college through teaching, formal administration, student advising, committee work, research and publication (if these are specifically included in the college's mission), and perhaps work with alumni or other support groups.

C. *Other measures of student performance.* The principle of measuring what a student has learned in each course can be extended to an appraisal of what the student has learned cumulatively during his four years of college education. If the same batteries of nationally administered tests were taken by entering freshmen and graduating seniors in a large number of colleges, an average measure of learning could be computed for each college, and these measures could be compared between colleges. The effects of superior teaching in particular departments or clusters of departments might be detected in the scores made by graduating seniors on particular components of, say, a graduate record examination; it is less likely that the influences of individual professors could be thus observed.

It is perhaps too much to expect that the measurable outputs of a four-year liberal arts college education could be related to future earnings or future life satisfactions in convincing ways. Presumably, out of such an education a student develops a "model of the world" which helps him to cope with it as a participant in the economic, political, family, ecclesiastical, and other subsystems of his society. Also, the student's synthesis of what he has learned from his college courses is something more than a simple aggregate of those courses. This synthesis may owe as much to interaction and discussion with his fellow students as it does to his professors.

A student's self-image or *ego ideal*, shaped partly before and partly during his college years, indicates approximately how he intends to allocate his energies, assuming that he has appraised his talents realistically and can indeed secure given levels of rewards in specified activities with given degrees of effort. In all probability, a differential desire to make money (i.e., a difference in ego ideal) is a far better predictor of future income than are differences in amounts and kinds of things learned in academic subjects.

What professors and courses have caused what modifications in a student's ego ideal during his college years? National figures and fellow students may have been at least as important as professors in these modifications. The question should be researchable, on a qualitative level, by asking graduating seniors to write their own interpretations of how their ego ideals have changed and for what reasons.

Each student's ego ideal would have undergone some changes if he had gone to work directly out of high school or following some kind of vocational or technical training. The distinctive ways in which the ego ideals of basically similar seventeen-year-olds are modified by their differential educational and work experiences during the ensuing four years should also be researchable.

*Effects of increasing size and complexity: The transition from college to university*

Equation (1) might be taken quite literally as implying a small college of uniform structure, with each faculty member teaching the same number of classes of identical size for the same salary and with each student taking the same course load.

In practice, many types of differentiation are possible. Courses may be distinguished by levels of instruction, such as lower division (freshman and sophomore) and upper division (junior and senior). Courses with large enrollments may be handled in classes of larger size, the professor receiving some help from readers and graders. Teaching loads may be varied among faculty members, depending upon such things as the number of separate preparations required during the year and the greater effort required to keep up to date in the more advanced courses. Faculty salaries may be differentiated according to rank, years of experience, and field of specialization.

Consider the implications of successive doublings of enrollment as we pass from a four-year college with 1,000 students to a very large university with (say) 32,000 students. Opportunities and incentives for a number of changes in organizational structure and staffing patterns emerge as total enrollment increases.

1. If enrollment increases within a four-year college framework, every course may expand in the same proportion. With 1,000 students in total, the largest feasible lecture group might include about 100 students in a required lower division course. If enrollment reached 16,000 in a four-year college framework, lecture groups of as many as 1,600 students would become theoretically possible. More likely, lecture groups ranging from 200 to 500 students would be used and premium salaries paid to professors who were unusually effective in this pattern. Machine-graded examinations might be used, or seniors might be employed as readers and graders.

2. As enrollment increases within a four-year college framework, it appears that the student-faculty ratio may increase moderately without

serious diminution in quality of instruction. (Where readers and graders are used, they supplement the total man-years of instructional staff.) Also, greater specialization becomes possible as greater numbers of sections of specified courses are required during the academic year. Professors may specialize at the level of money and banking rather than at the level of economics. The increased degree of specialization and the larger number of graduating seniors both encourage the development of an M.S. (or M.A.) program.

An M.S. program provides support for teaching assistants and laboratory assistants. The greater specialization of those faculty members who teach upper division and beginning graduate courses is complementary with a limited amount of research and publication; in conjunction with these activities, there emerges a role for research assistants. Research assistantships are themselves complementary with writing M.S. theses.

At this stage, two categories of teaching personnel, professors and teaching assistants, would be involved in the lower division courses. Depending upon the relative numbers of professors and teaching assistants, the cost of instructional salaries per student quarter could be held constant or even diminished, while the average salaries of professors increased from, say, $15,000 up to $18,000. A significant proportion of the total student contact hours would be handled by teaching assistants.

3. Expanding enrollment increases the number of faculty members per department and therefore increases the amount of time and level of judgment required to co-ordinate their activities. The role of department chairman may rise to a half-time or even a full-time job in the largest departments. Full-time deans may be required to span groups of related departments.

4. Continued expansion of undergraduate enrollment requires still more professors per department and makes possible a still further deepening of specializations at such levels as monetary economics, international economics, industrial organization, and the like. Increased depth in particular specialities makes possible more frequent and active participation by faculty members in national scientific communities, involving research, conferences, and journal publication. These activities are complementary with the supervision of doctoral dissertations. As employees of the university, doctoral students with M.S. or equivalent training may lecture to their own small classes of lower division students and, in some cases, of upper division students in their special fields. Young (part-time) instructors who are also doctoral candidates may be more nearly up to date in the current tools and methods of their field

than are the majority of established faculty members in four-year colleges. On the other hand, they are less experienced as teachers.

In any event, the existence of Ph.D. programs makes possible the use of at least three categories of teaching personnel, namely, teaching assistants, predoctoral instructors, and professors. Temporary assistant professors or postdoctoral instructors and research associates provide still another category of personnel in the presence of nationally recognized Ph.D. programs and distinguished graduate faculties.

As undergraduate enrollment expands and successive layers of graduate programs are superimposed, class sizes and staffing patterns tend to become differentiated by levels of instruction. Some professors teach exclusively at the graduate level and others at both graduate and undergraduate levels; course loads and teaching loads are differentiated as between graduate and undergraduate levels; and such measures as the student-faculty ratio, the average teaching load, and the average class size become increasingly difficult to interpret. Instead of one category (professors) with average salary $W$, there may be three or four categories of instructional personnel, each with a distinctive salary level.

The workloads of professors teaching graduate courses expand to include a considerable amount of time spent in supervising doctoral dissertations and serving on graduate committees. To be an effective supervisor of doctoral candidates, a professor must be actively involved in research of a relatively advanced and original nature. Professional journal articles and advanced monographs become highly complementary with doctoral dissertations; research becomes highly complementary with teaching in the broad sense of graduate training. The doctoral candidate modifies his behavior not only on the basis of what he learns in his graduate courses but also on the basis of what he learns by doing his dissertation research.

Research conducted without the intention of modifying the behavior of those participating in it is not a teaching activity and must be justified on other grounds. Research done on contract is, in effect, priced in a market. The results are supposed to be embodied in a product desired by the contracting firm or agency, and not in modified behavior on the part of the research personnel.

### Comparing workloads and performance among departments within a university

A major university is made up of colleges, each of which includes a number of departments. Within a college, the departments may show considerable variation in size and in the structure of the teaching load by levels (lower division, upper division, and graduate).

Departments within a college compete for the college dean's resources. The dean is interested in seeing that the resources allocated to different departments are roughly in line with the amount of work to be done.

Consider a situation in which a college's budget contains separate funds for teaching and research, and in which many faculty members receive portions of their salaries from both funds. The percentage of faculty salaries allocated to research in the budgets of different departments may vary widely. We would like to determine whether the teaching budget is being used effectively and whether it is being allocated equitably among the teaching budgets of different departments within a college.

One measure which suggests itself is based on Simon's equation (1), namely:

$$Ftc = Sh. \tag{7}$$

Dividing both sides of the equation by $F$, we obtain

$$tc = \frac{Sh}{F}. \tag{8}$$

The left-hand side of the equation, $tc$, represents student credit hours per full-time instructor. We proceed to calculate this measure for each of a number of departments in a university. For convenience, we will denote this measure for the $i$th department by $m_i = (tc)_i$.

Within the largest and most diverse college of the university, $m_i$ in a particular quarter ranged from 94 to 529 around a college-wide average of 298. Some of the lower figures were for departments with large graduate programs and some of the higher ones were for departments with small graduate programs or none at all.

Additional information was available on the percentage distribution of total student credit hours taught in each department according to levels of instruction. We will characterize these levels as lower division, upper division, and graduate.

It is well known that average class sizes at the graduate level are considerably smaller than at the undergraduate level. The number of graduate students in a typical university department is much smaller than the number of undergraduates; furthermore, the graduate program is more specialized, so that the limited number of graduate students is distributed among a considerable number of courses.

On the surface, values of $m_i$ ranging from 94 to 529 can scarcely be regarded as equitable. The apparent inequities might be substantially

EMPIRICAL PROBLEMS IN QUANTITATIVE MODELS          269

reduced, however, if we took account of differences among departments in the composition of their total student credit hours by levels of instruction. We will approach this problem by means of linear multiple regression analysis.

*Comparisons among science departments with nationally recognized graduate programs*

In the first example, we consider eight departments, all within the sciences and all having nationally recognized graduate programs as evidenced by ratings of 2.5 or better in a recent report by Roose and Andersen (1970).

The rationale for choosing these eight departments for the initial example is essentially this: in the process of maintaining nationally recognized graduate programs for a number of decades, these departments have had to recruit and hold faculty members, and recruit and place graduate students, in national competition. Hence, it seems likely that their staffing and teaching patterns reflect national standards in their disciplines. Furthermore, competition for resources among departments within each major university has tended to bring standards of faculty quality and teaching loads in the different sciences into a fairly realistic equilibrium. Hence, science departments with nationally recognized graduate programs should be relatively free from local aberrations.

The relevant data for the eight scientific departments are as follows:

| Department | Student credit hours per full-time instructor $X_1$ | Lower division $X_2$ | Upper division $X_3$ | Graduate $X_4$ |
|---|---|---|---|---|
| 1 | 144 | .200 | .573 | .227 |
| 2 | 157 | .012 | .677 | .310 |
| 3 | 258 | .850 | .046 | .104 |
| 4 | 283 | .795 | .123 | .081 |
| 5 | 279 | .627 | .287 | .085 |
| 6 | 251 | .792 | .111 | .098 |
| 7 | 217 | .407 | .432 | .161 |
| 8 | 368 | .800 | .165 | .036 |
| Arithmetic mean: | 244.6 | .560 | .302 | .138 |

Proportion of student credit hours at each level of instruction shown in columns $X_2$, $X_3$, $X_4$.

The appropriate linear regression set-up is as follows:

$$\hat{X}_1 = a_{1.23} + b_{12.3}X_2 + b_{13.2}X_3. \tag{9}$$

We cannot add $X_4$ to this equation, because $X_2 + X_3 + X_4 = 1$ for each department, and once $X_2$ and $X_3$ are specified, $X_4$ is fully determined; i.e., the set $X_2$, $X_3$, and $X_4$ is collinear. Equation (9) avoids this difficulty and has the following logic:

If we set $X_2 = 1$, we imply that $X_3$ and $X_4$ must each be zero; then

$$\hat{X}_1 = a_{1.23} + b_{12.3}(X_2 = 1) \tag{10}$$

is the estimate of $X_1$ for a department which teaches only lower division courses.

If we set $X_3 = 1$, we imply that $X_2$ and $X_4$ must each be zero; then

$$\hat{X}_1 = a_{1.23} + b_{13.2}(X_3 = 1) \tag{11}$$

is the estimate of $X_1$ for a department which teaches only upper division courses.

If we set $X_2 = 0$ and $X_3 = 0$ at the same time, we imply that $X_4 = 1$; then in principle

$$\hat{X}_1 = a_{1.23} \tag{12}$$

is the estimate of $\hat{X}_1$ for a department which teaches only graduate courses.

It turns out that equation (12) requires us to extrapolate far beyond the observed values of $X_4$, which range from 0.036 to 0.310. Equations (10) and (11) also involve extrapolation beyond the range of the data, though not very far (the highest observed values of $X_2$ and $X_3$ are 0.850 and 0.677, respectively, and we must extrapolate to 1 in each case).

For the eight departments, equation (9) becomes

$$\hat{X}_1 = -531.2 + 877.6 X_2 + 941.3 X_3; \tag{13}$$
$$\phantom{\hat{X}_1 = -}(305.2)\ \ (315.0)\ \ \ \ \ (427.8)$$

$\bar{R}^2_{1.23} = 0.786;\ \bar{S}_{1.23} = 33.48;\ s_1 = 72.37;$

the figures in parentheses are standard errors of the respective regression coefficients. Some 78.6 percent of the variance of $X_1$ is associated with variations in the structure of the teaching load.

When $X_2 = 1$ we obtain

$$\hat{X}_1 = -531.2 + 877.6 = \underline{346.4};$$

when $X_3 = 1$ we obtain

$$\hat{X}_1 = -531.2 + 941.3 = \underline{410.1};$$

and when $X_2 = 0$ and $X_3 = 0$ we obtain

$$\hat{X}_1 = \underline{-531.2}.$$

A hypothetical department which best represented the common characteristics of these eight departments (in a least squares regression sense) would respond as follows to specified distributions of its teaching load by levels of instruction:

|  | Proportion of student credit hours at each level: | | | Student credit hours per full-time instructor: |
|---|---|---|---|---|
| Case no. | Lower division | Upper division | Graduate | (Estimated from equation [13]) |
| 1 | 1.000 | 0 | 0 | 346.4 |
| 2 | 0 | 1.000 | 0 | 410.1 |
| 3 | 0.500 | 0.500 | 0 | 378.2 |
| 4 | 0.500 | 0.400 | 0.100 | 248.1 |
| 5 | 0.500 | 0.300 | 0.200 | 190.0 |
| 6 | 0.500 | 0.200 | 0.300 | 95.9 |

Cases 1 and 2 imply that such a department would score from 346.4 to 410.1 on the student credit hours measure, if it confined itself to undergraduate courses; Case 3 illustrates the midpoint of the strictly undergraduate range.

Cases 3, 4, 5, and 6 illustrate the trade-off which equation (13) implies between graduate and upper division teaching while the proportion of lower division instruction is held constant at 0.500. The proportion of graduate level teaching is permitted to range from 0 to 0.300, which is approximately the range of the data for the eight departments. For each increase of 0.100 in the graduate proportion (and simultaneous decrease of 0.100 in the upper division proportion), the estimate of student credit hours drops by 94.1. Thus, the equation yields reasonable estimates within the range of the observed data, even though the implied estimate of $-531.2$ for a department teaching only graduate courses is, of course, absurd.

The actual and estimated values of $X_1$ for the eight departments compare as follows:

| | Student credit hours per full-time instructor: | | |
|---|---|---|---|
| Department | Actual $X_1$ | Estimated from eq. (13): $\hat{X}_1$ | Residual $X_1 - \hat{X}_1$ |
| 1 | 144 | 184 | $-40$ |
| 2 | 157 | 117 | 40 |
| 3 | 258 | 258 | 0 |
| 4 | 283 | 282 | 1 |
| 5 | 279 | 289 | $-10$ |
| 6 | 251 | 268 | $-17$ |
| 7 | 217 | 233 | $-16$ |
| 8 | 368 | 326 | 42 |
| Arithmetic means: | 244.6 | 244.6 | 0 |

While the results from this analysis seem very reasonable, the use of full-time equivalent instructors as a measure of input is potentially misleading; dollars should be a better one. All of these eight departments used teaching assistants and/or part-time instructors (who were also graduate students) for a large proportion of their student contact hours at the lower division level. There were many small laboratory and recitation sections at this level, but they were taught by low salaried personnel. At the upper division level, most of the courses were taught by professors; the classes averaged somewhat larger than in the lower division, but the dollar cost of instructional salaries per student credit hour must have averaged considerably higher.

*Comparisons among heterogeneous groups of departments*

The same approach was applied to two other groups of departments which were known to be quite heterogeneous.

A. *Sixteen departments in College 1.* The same three variables used in equation (13) yielded the following results:

$$\hat{X}_1 = -132.0 + 432.1 X_2 + 592.2 X_3; \qquad (14)$$
$$(247.4) \quad (254.0) \quad\quad (297.1)$$

$\bar{R}^2_{1.23} = 0.116;\ \bar{S}_{1.23} = 116.6;\ s_1 = 124.0.$

Only 11.6 percent of the variation in $X_1$ (which ranged from 94 to 529) was associated with variations in the proportions of student credit hours taught at the various levels. If all instruction were lower division level, $X_1$ would be estimated at 300.0; if all instruction were at the upper division level, $\hat{X}_1$ would be estimated at 460.2.

The data permitted a further subdivision of graduate courses between essentially M.S. and Ph.D. levels, so a variable $X_5$, the proportion of student credit hours at the M.S. level, was added to the above equation with the following results:

$$\hat{X}_1 = -1148.6 + 1398.5 X_2 + 1566.9 X_3 + 5374.8 X_5; \qquad (15)$$
$$(521.2) \quad\quad (502.7) \quad\quad (524.2) \quad\quad (2500.9)$$

$\bar{R}^2_{1.235} = 0.309;\ \bar{S}_{1.235} = 103.1;\ s_1 = 142.0.$

Some 30.9 percent of the variation in $X_1$ was associated with the three independent variables, implying that a separation of graduate clock-hours into M.S. versus Ph.D. levels had some explanatory value, raising $\bar{R}^2$ from 0.116 to 0.309. However, the regression coefficients suggest that an increase in the proportion of M.S level instruction would increase $\hat{X}_1$, while an increase in the proportion of Ph.D. level instruction would decrease $\hat{X}_1$. Only one department in this set had more than 2.6 percent of its credit hours at the Ph.D. level, and it had 39.4 percent; hence, the apparent effect of Ph.D. level instruction depends heavily upon a single observation. The other 15 departments may be distributed over a range within which an increase in M.S. level instruction is associated with a greater use of faculty members with Ph.D. degrees (assigned to large classes) and a reduced dependence on full-time instructors with B.A. or M.A. degrees (assigned to small classes).

In any event, equation (15) leaves 69.1 percent of the variation in $X_1$ untouched by the composition of teaching loads according to levels of instruction; other and better measures of performance, including dollar cost, are needed.

B. *Sixteen departments in College 2.* The same three variables used in equations (13) and (14) yielded the following results in this case:

$$\hat{X}_1 = 89.9 + 189.8X_2 + 135.0X_3; \qquad (16)$$
$$(76.7) \quad (104.8) \quad (110.2)$$

$$\bar{R}^2 = 0.102; \bar{S}_{1.23} = 81.7; s_1 = 86.2.$$

Adding $X_5$ to this set did not increase the value of $\bar{R}^2$.

The coefficients in equation (16) imply the following estimates for $X_1$:

If $X_2 = 1$ (i.e., all teaching at the lower division level),

$$\hat{X}_1 = \underline{280.7};$$

if $X_3 = 1$ (i.e., all teaching at the upper division level),

$$\hat{X}_1 = \underline{224.9}; \text{ and}$$

if $X_2 = 0$ and $X_3 = 0$, implying that $X_4 = 1$ (i.e., all teaching at the graduate level),

$$\hat{X}_1 = \underline{89.9}.$$

These estimates are not at all unreasonable. However, only 10.2 percent of the variation in $X_1$ (which ranges from 91 to 408) is associated with variations in $X_2$, $X_3$, and (implicitly) $X_4$. A much richer information base is evidently needed to appraise the significance of variations in student credit hours per full-time instructor as between departments.

C. *Some tentative conclusions.* The regression analysis for the eight science departments suggests that the $m_i = (tc)_i$ measure may be useful for comparing departments *which are known on other grounds to be similar* (e.g., in having nationally recognized graduate programs and in using graduate assistants, and/or part-time instructors who are also graduate students, for a large proportion of total student contact hours at the lower division level).

Even for such departments, the picture would be much clearer if the equivalent number of full-time instructors used at each level of instruction were subdivided into the categories of (1) graduate assistants; (2) instructors who are candidates for graduate degrees; (3) other instructors; and (4) assistant, associate, and full professors. The total salary cost should be specified for each level of instruction, along with the average salary cost per full-time instructor and the average salary cost per student credit hour.

This pattern would indicate how each department was allocating its resources by categories of personnel and by dollar cost per student credit hour as among the different levels of instruction.

This kind of display would also dramatize the differences between departments at different stages of development, so far as graduate work is concerned. The basic unit underlying this display would most logically be the individual section of the individual course, with its staffing pattern and its salary cost per equivalent full-time instructor and per student credit hour.

These basic units in turn should be elements of a more comprehensive system of workload estimates which would include supervision of theses and dissertations, other graduate committee roles, all administrative and co-ordinating roles, committee work, and research.

*Summary comments on workload comparisons*

Differences in the composition of total man-years used at the different instructional levels might be reflected by weighting each category of personnel in proportion to a typical or average salary level for that category. For example, if professorial salaries (assistant professor and above) averaged $18,000, part-time instructors' salaries $9,000, and teaching assistants' salaries $6,000 per academic man-year, a weight of 1.00 might be assigned to each man-year of professorial time, one of 0.50 to each man-year supplied by part-time instructors, and one of 0.33 to each man-year supplied by teaching assistants.

Thus, if average salaries for each category of personnel were similar (perhaps within 10 or 20 percent of one another) in all departments, and if the average salary for the professorial ranks were, say, $18,000, our measures of student credit hours taught per equivalent full-time professor would also approximate student credit hours taught per $18,000 of instructional salaries. (If our student credit hour figures related to a single academic quarter, the cost per equivalent full-time professor would be $6,000.)

Suppose a department taught 10,000 student credit hours in a given quarter, including 1,000 at the graduate level, 3,000 at the upper division level, and 6,000 at the lower division level. Suppose further that man-years in terms of equivalent full-time professors totaled 20.0, with 5.0 used at the graduate level, 7.5 at the upper division level, and 7.5 at the lower division level. Then student credit hours per equivalent full-time professor would average 500 for the department as a whole, 200 for graduate courses, 400 for upper division courses, and 800 for lower division courses.

As we have assumed an average professorial salary of $6,000 per quarter, the preceding figures imply an instructional cost of $7.50 per student credit hour at the lower division level, $15.00 at the upper division level, and $30.00 at the graduate level. Alternatively, in terms of student quarters of three credit hours each the instructional costs would be estimated at $22.50, $45.00, and $90.00 at the lower division, upper division, and graduate levels respectively. Total instructional salaries would be estimated at $120,000 per quarter or $360,000 per academic year, and the average salary cost per student quarter (all levels combined) would be $36.00. Such an approach might lead to more equitable comparisons among departments without publicizing differences in the actual salary levels of the same categories of personnel in different departments.

The low percentages of variation in teaching loads in our heterogeneous groups of departments explained by differences in the student credit hour distribution among instructional levels suggest that the teaching budget is supporting other activities in addition to classroom teaching and preparation. These other workload components may include the following (the list is not exhaustive):

1) Advising undergraduate students who are majoring in the department;
2) Recruiting, placing, assigning and advising graduate students pursuing M.S. or Ph.D. degrees in the department;
3) Supervising M.S. theses and Ph.D. dissertations, serving on dissertation and other graduate student committees, and administering preliminary examinations for Ph.D. candidates;
4) Administrative time put in by the department head or chairman and other faculty members with co-ordinating roles;

5) Serving on department, college, and university committees;
6) Participating in national professional association activities, refereeing manuscripts submitted to professional journals, and the like; and
7) Public service activities of a professional nature.

If faculty members are being assigned wisely and/or are using their own time wisely, the last hours of each faculty member's time spent in each of the above named activities and in classroom teaching should be of equal value to the university. Thus, an equitable comparison of the educational workload between departments should include in its numerator a measure of total workload (other than research), rather than simply a measure of student credit hours taught.

This assumes that it is possible to make a neat separation between time allocated to research and publication and time allocated to all instructional activities, or that the same guidelines for reporting the two categories of activities are followed in all departments. This was probably not the case in our heterogeneous groups. A comprehensive workload measure, including research as well as instruction, should reduce some of the evident disparities.

**Comparisons among universities**

To begin with, it is not clear how much detail identified with specific departments should be made generally available, even to members of the same discipline in other universities. We shall consider first the problem of comparisons among departments within the same discipline but in different universities.

*Comparisons of departments within a discipline*

Something can be inferred about the faculty of a four-year college on the basis of such factors as the percentage of regular faculty members holding Ph.D. degrees and the universities from which these Ph.D. degrees were received. Standards of faculty quality tend to be similar across the departments of a given college. High school seniors are not likely to discriminate among alternative four-year colleges on the basis of a single department.

In choosing among graduate schools, however, the reputations of individual departments are of crucial importance. A Ph.D. candidate will take most of his courses in a single department, and his dissertation will be supervised and his examinations administered by members of that department's faculty. The reputations of one or two related departments (in addition to his major department) may influence a student in his choice of graduate schools; however, this usually means that complementaries among these disciplines are recognized in most universities, and the quality standard at a given university tends to be fairly uniform within such related clusters.

In recent years the American Council on Education has sponsored two assessments of the quality of graduate education in the United States. The first of these was based on questionnaires circulated in April 1964 and the second on similar questionnaires circulated in April 1969. The results of the April 1964 survey were reported by Allan M. Cartter (1966). As Cartter was an economist, he made special analyses of the data for economics departments, some of which we will draw upon here.

A. *Quality of graduate faculty.* A total of 173 economists rated 71 economics departments that reported the award of one or more doctorates from July 1952 through June 1962. The respondents were selected (according to a prescribed sampling scheme) by the respective graduate deans. Each respondent was to rate the graduate faculty in each economics department as "distinguished," "strong," "good," "adequate," "marginal," or "not sufficient to provide acceptable doctoral training," or to indicate that he had insufficient information to make a rating. The adjective ratings were converted to numerical scores ranging from 5.00 down to less than 2.00. Departments with average point ratings of 4.00 or above were called "distinguished," those rated between 3.00 and 3.99 were called "strong," those rated between 2.50 and 2.99 were called "good," and those with ratings of 2.00 to 2.49 were called "adequate plus."

In economics as in other fields, the "distinguished" departments were generally found in such universities as Harvard, M.I.T., Chicago, Yale, California (Berkeley), Stanford, Princeton, and a few others. These departments were highly visible, as indicated by Figure 8.1; virtually all respondents felt qualified to rate them. Similarly, 90 to 95 percent of the respondents felt qualified to rate the "strong," and some of the "good" graduate faculties.

The "distinguished" departments also rated high in terms of research and publication, as indicated by Figure 8.2. The ten most productive departments in terms of Cartter's publications index accounted for 56

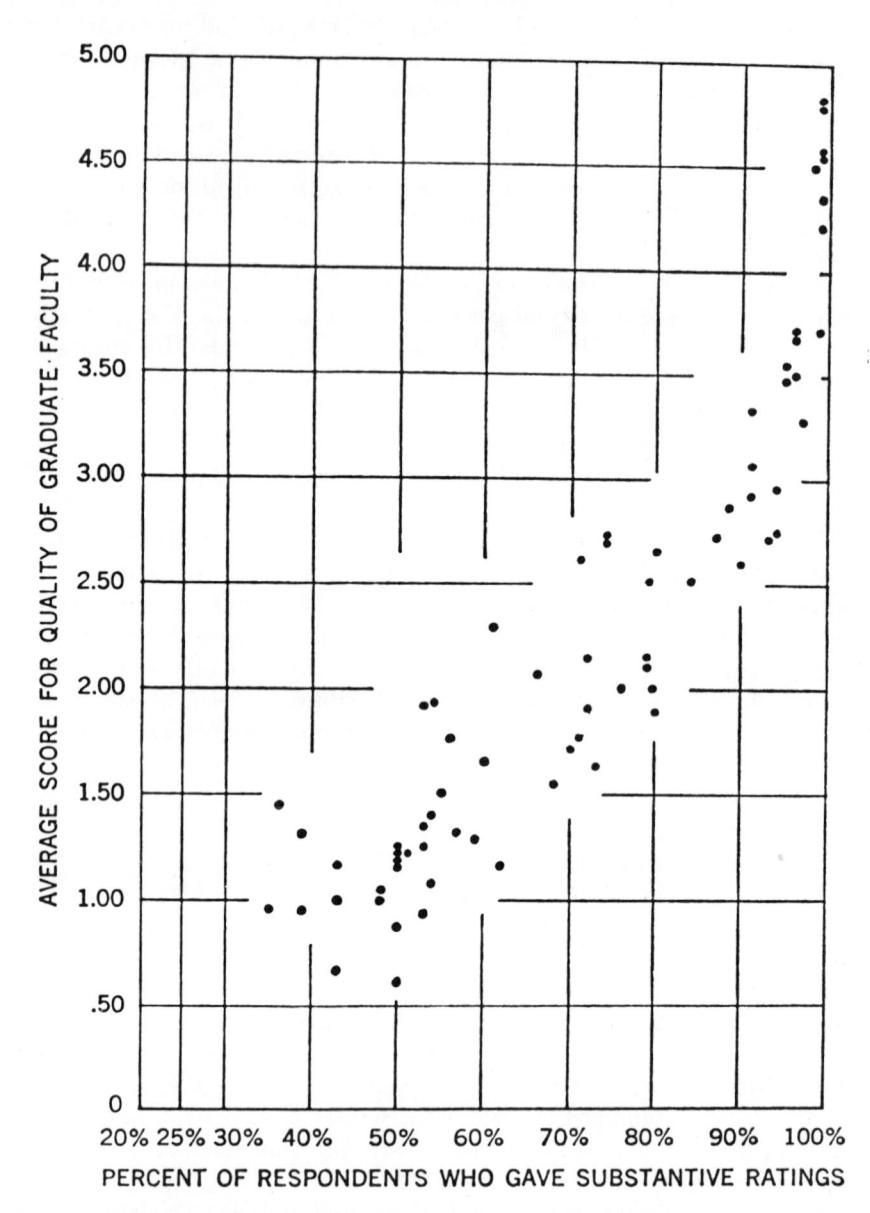

Fig. 8.1. Rated quality of economics faculty, by percent of respondents providing ratings. Source: Cartter (1966).

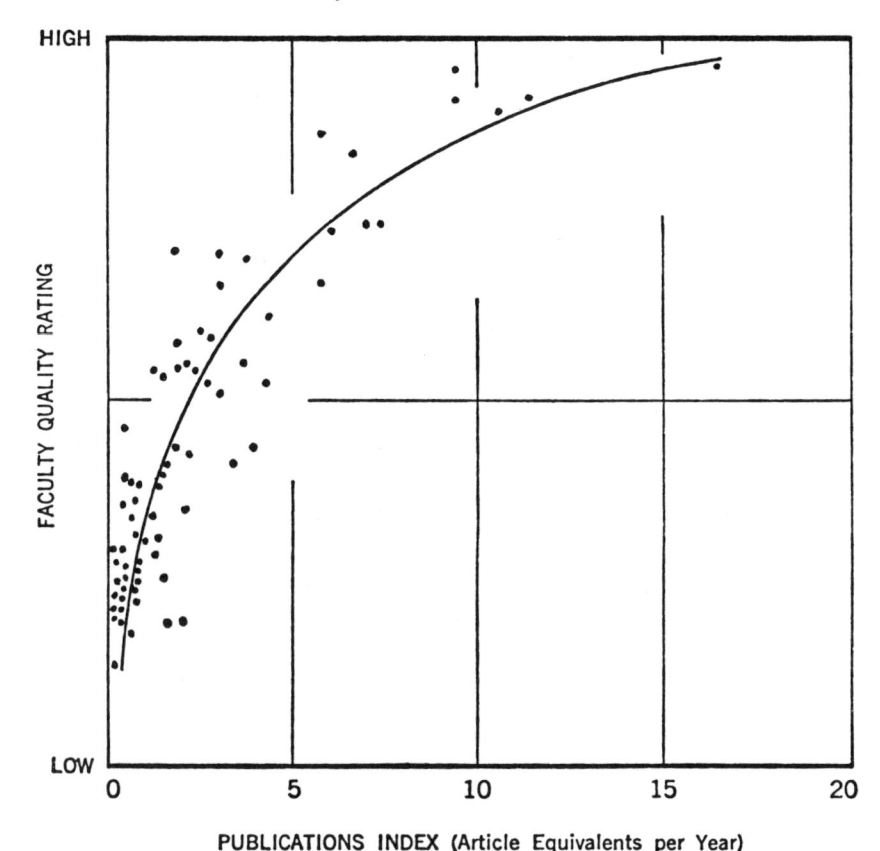

EMPIRICAL PROBLEMS IN QUANTITATIVE MODELS 279

**Fig. 8.2. Relationship of rated quality of graduate faculty to index of publications, 71 economics departments. Source: Cartter (1966).**

percent, and the 25 most productive departments for nearly 90 percent of all publications eligible for inclusion in this index.*

* Cartter describes the construction of his index as follows (1966, p. 80):
Six major journals in the field of economics—journals which publish most of the general theoretical and expository articles, not the highly specialized contributions in public finance, labor, economic history, or land economics—were selected, and all articles, shorter communications, and book reviews were tallied for a four year period (June 1960–June 1964). To provide some weighting, it was assumed that four short communications or eight book reviews were the equivalent of one substantive article.
Similarly, all books reviewed in the *American Economic Review*, the official journal of the American Economic Association, during the same four year period were tallied. A theoretical or research book was counted as the equivalent of six articles, a textbook as three articles, and an edited collection as two articles. Thus weighted, the publications originating in each department were aggregated and converted to an article equivalence index, the distribution ranging from a high of approximately 20 a year at Harvard to none for a few departments.

On the basis of confidential information collected by Francis M. Boddy, Cartter was also able to relate the graduate faculty quality ratings for 45 leading economics departments to the average salaries paid to their faculty members of each professorial rank. Within each rank (professor, associate professor, and assistant professor) averages were available for the upper third and for the lower two-thirds of salaries within the rank. The adjective "superior" was used to designate the upper third of the salaries in each rank.

Cartter found that the quality index correlated 0.794 with the mean salaries of "superior full professors"; the correlation with mean salaries of all full professors was 0.754. In sharp contrast, the quality index correlated 0.470, 0.357, and 0.181, respectively, with the mean salaries of "superior associate professors," all associate professors, and all assistant professors.

Cartter comments as follows on these results (1966, p. 84):

> These findings support the impression that the scholarly reputation of a department rests heavily on its distinguished full professors. The less prestigious universities compete more evenly for young assistant professors; thus the low coefficient. This would seem to be true for two reasons: (a) the poorer institutions can better afford to compete for promising young scholars in the $6,000–$9,000 range than they can in the $15,000–$25,000 range, and (b) the universities near the top can rely to a considerable extent on their prestige rather than pecuniary rewards in attracting the aspiring young scholar. Thus scholarly talent is somewhat more evenly distributed among universities in the lower ranks, but tends to become more highly concentrated at the highest ranks in a few institutions which have preferred environments and resources.

B. *Effectiveness of graduate program.* Cartter's questionnaire included the following instructions for assigning ratings of graduate faculty quality (1966, p. 127): "Which of the terms below best describe your judgment of the *quality of the graduate faculty* in your field at each institution listed? Consider only the scholarly competence and achievements of the present faculty. Limit the number of "Distinguished" ratings to no more than 5."

The instructions for rating the effectiveness of a graduate program were as follows (1966, p. 127): "How would you rate the institutions below if you were selecting a graduate school to work for a doctorate in your field today? Take into account the accessibility of faculty and their scholarly competence, curricula, educational and research facilities, the quality of graduate students and other factors which contribute to the *effectiveness of the doctoral program.*"

Each respondent was asked to rate the doctoral program of each economics department in a list of 71 as "extremely attractive," "attractive," "acceptable," or "not attractive," or to indicate that he had insufficient information to give a rating.

In principle, it appears that quality of the graduate faculty is primarily a "stock" and effectiveness of the doctoral program primarily a "flow." There is some evidence that the respondents made this distinction; for example, although there was a very high correlation between the ranks of leading departments on the two measures, there were cases in which a department was four or five ranks lower on rated effectiveness of its graduate program than on rated quality of its graduate faculty.

There are good reasons for expecting greater errors of measurement in rating doctoral program effectiveness than in rating graduate faculty quality. The "superior full professors" are usually more than forty years old and have been cumulatively productive and visible in their profession for a good many years. Their journal articles and advanced monographs are available in every university library and appear on the reading lists of appropriate graduate courses in nearly all economics departments.

In contrast, few economists have an accurate perception of the "effectiveness" of the current graduate programs of any large number of departments. Some departments maintain a good reputation for quality control with respect to the graduate students admitted to their programs, the training they receive, and the percentage who actually receive the doctorate within a period of four or five years. Other departments may undergo periods of turbulence or carelessness, during which the scholarly competence of the faculty is maintained but some of the doctoral candidates are inadequately supervised.

Thus, while there may be no need to remind members of a scientific community that the faculty of a given department continues to be distinguished, it might be helpful to make available statistics on the number of full-time graduate students enrolled in each department annually over a period of, say, ten years, together with figures for a similar period on the number of Ph.D. degrees (and, separately, M.S. degrees) actually awarded. If a department has 200 full-time graduate students and awards 5 or 6 Ph.D.s a year, it is almost certainly less effective than a department with 200 full-time graduate students which awards 20 or 25 Ph.D.s a year. Few department chairmen, and still fewer senior and junior scholars who are not department chairmen, carry such figures in mind for more than a handful of departments.

C. *Workloads and performance.* In the first part of this chapter we discussed problems of comparing workloads and performance among departments within a given university. Such comparisons should have greater validity for departments in the same discipline in different universities. We will leave open for the moment the purposes for which, and the auspices under which, such data might appropriately be collected.

Suppose that an agency, sworn to confidence concerning information below an agreed-upon level of aggregation, were to collect from each department information on student credit hours of instruction taught at the lower division, upper division, and graduate levels respectively. (These three levels, incidentally, could accommodate information from junior colleges and four-year colleges as well as from universities.)

This agency might also collect information concerning full-time equivalent instructors—by rank or category, according to agreed upon definitions—used at each of the three levels of instruction. The raw data, giving full-time equivalent man-years by ranks by levels of instruction along with the student credit hour teaching load, should be useful and not highly confidential information for the relevant department, college, and university level administrators in the institutions surveyed. Alternatively, or in addition, man-years of different categories of personnel could be converted into equivalent professorial man-years, using a set of agreed upon weights roughly proportional to average salaries for the various categories of personnel.

Additional information relevant to teaching workloads and performance might include (1) the number of undergraduate majors advised in the department; (2) the number of full-time equivalent graduate students enrolled; and (3) the numbers of B.A. and B.S., M.A. and M.S., and Ph.D. degrees awarded per year. Perhaps the undergraduate majors advised should be listed according to freshman, sophomore, junior, and senior standing, and the graduate students according to first, second, third, and fourth or higher years of graduate work. Estimates of man-years of different categories of personnel used in the undergraduate advising function and in all aspects of the graduate program in addition to classroom teaching would also be of value in appraising performance.

Such information for all departments might be useful to administrators as a basis of comparison for the workloads and performance measures of the various segments of departmental programs for which they were responsible. If it were thought that a completely integrated set of data for each department (even though the names of departments were not revealed) would permit an undesirable degree of certainty as to identification, it might be possible to array the information for each level of instruction, and for each of the other major program conponents, in separate tabulations. Thus, the lower division program of a particular department would appear in its appropriate rank in a tabulation for lower division programs; the upper division program of the same department would almost certainly have a different rank in a display limited to upper division programs.

Administrators interested in modifying the programs of a particular department could synthesize alternative departmental structures by combining what they regarded as desirable staffing patterns and student credit hour workloads for each level of instruction taken separately from the respective arrays. The local administrators would then have to appraise the suitability of alternative synthetic models for their own situation at a much greater level of detail, to be sure that their proposed patterns of instruction at different levels were complementary with one another and constituted a viable organization for a real department.

*Comparisons among colleges or professional schools of a given type*

Deans of professional schools, together with associate and assistant deans and perhaps department chairmen, should become connoisseurs of curricula, staffing patterns, and performance standards for the full range of departments normally included in such a school. Thus, the deans of colleges of engineering should understand both the similarities and the differences between departments of chemical, civil, electrical, and mechanical engineering. Engineering deans might benefit from studying arrays of workloads and apparent performance for major program segments within each kind of engineering department. A dean might be interested in alternative synthetic models of individual departments, and he might want to consider the staffing patterns and salary requirements implied in restructuring two or more departments or in making even more sweeping changes. Here again, before any major reorganizations were implemented their implications should be worked out in considerable operational detail.

At the college level, budgets of several million dollars a year are frequently involved. It seems reasonable to require high standards of administrative competence for college deans in addition to broad acquaintance with the subject matter and standards of scholarship in the disciplines under their stewardship.

*Comparisons involving entire universities*

University presidents are responsible for budgets ranging from perhaps $20,000,000 to $100,000,000 or more per year. University presidents, with their associated vice presidents and supporting staff, should be capable of making comparisons between alternative structures and workloads at the levels of departments, colleges, and entire universities.

**Workload, cost, and quality estimates for a given department**

This section can be brief, as most of the points which logically belong in it have already been touched upon.

*Elements involved in rating individual faculty members*

Few people like to work under close surveillance. Supervision is a different matter; most workers are accustomed to a certain amount of direction and co-ordination to facilitate the direct output-oriented objectives of their work. By "surveillance" we mean here deliberate observation for purposes of evaluation for salary increases, promotions, and the like.

In a typical university department, each faculty member is evaluated, implicitly or explicitly, for a number of purposes. One kind of evaluation (which often remains implicit) is made each year for purposes of salary increases. Other evaluations are made at less frequent intervals for purposes of promotion to tenure rank or from associate professor to full professor. Some universities have special screening procedures for admitting faculty members to full membership on the graduate faculty, which conveys the privilege of supervising doctoral dissertations. Evaluations may also be called for in connection with special awards and honors, some of which are intended to recognize outstanding performance in some particular aspect of a faculty member's duties.

It should be possible to organize a flow of information concerning the professional performance of faculty members, such that department chairmen, deans, vice presidents, and president will all have access, when they desire it, to the same factual information and at least a certain minimum amount of evaluative comment.

In principle, the basic data for such a system should be based on a checklist of all activities to which any faculty member may be assigned by his administrative superiors and which are regarded as official duties on behalf of the university. Thus, if five or six activities are regarded as exhausting a faculty member's professional responsibilities to the university, a summary measure of his performance during a stated year or sequence of years should include an approximate percentage breakdown of his working time (adding up to 100 percent) and an adjective or numerical rating of his performance with respect to each of those activities. These measures could, of course, be converted into a weighted average numerical rating or grade.

When department, college, and university administrators are confronted by a tabulation of this sort, gross injustices are less likely to occur. Thus, a heavy classroom teaching and advising load may be recognized as accounting for, or justifying, a below average rate of publication. At some institutions, teaching is alleged to be a "free good"; at others the volume and quality of a faculty member's research output may be undervalued.

Subdepartment administration, student advising, and committee work may also be undervalued by some administrators, in the sense that they are not regarded as relevant to salary determination or promotion. If this is the case, inequities can arise when an accommodating faculty member takes on considerably more than his share of committee work, advising, or co-ordination.

In principle, a faculty member's time should be allocated in such a way as to maximize the value of his services to the university. Hopefully, the pattern of activities which optimizes the faculty member's performance in terms of his own ego ideal is also the pattern which constitutes his maximum contribution to the university. Over the course of a year, or at least over a period of three to five years, the marginal value product of a given faculty member's time should be the same in each of the official activities he pursues.

Perhaps the omnipresence of opportunity cost could be dramatized by converting committee work and advising or co-ordinating time into equivalent journal articles forgone, the only recognized output of a true "publish or perish" system!

Evaluation of the quality of particular aspects of a faculty member's performance could draw upon student feedback (as described in the case of our small college model), upon a publication index, and perhaps upon less tangible characterizations of his effectiveness in advising, co-ordination, or committee work.

*Workload estimates based on standard coefficients*

It would certainly be possible to develop worksheets on which a faculty member could record daily or weekly the number of hours he had spent on each of a specified array of activities. Maintaining such a record for a week or a month may give the faculty member himself some insights into the effectiveness and appropriateness of his *de facto* allocation of time.

However, recording the actual allocation of time by individual faculty members may have two disadvantages: (1) It may overemphasize the reporting function relative to a desirable sense of personal freedom and creativeness and (2) some faculty members may spend more hours on an activity than their colleagues do simply because they are inefficient in that activity. It is more important to have a measure of outputs than a measure of inputs.

Workload estimates based on standard coefficients offer a less personal, less time-consuming, and more output-oriented alternative. Thus, records might be kept by all faculty members, for a limited period of time, and be compiled into arrays and averages. Also, some activities in a given department may require quite specific numbers of hours (for example, certain types of oral examinations for M.S. and Ph.D. candidates).

In this latter case, expected numbers of graduate students at specified stages in their programs can be translated into requirements for a certain number of man-years of faculty time and even to standardized estimates of the time likely to be required by the dissertation supervisors for particular students.

Workload estimates based on standard coefficients may also focus attention on activities which use time in small lumps but recur so frequently during a year as to require a very significant amount of faculty time. For example, in a department with 22.5 man-years of faculty time budgeted, 25 Ph.D. candidates were writing dissertations, involving an estimated input of about 1.4 academic years of time by their major professors. However, it turned out that the same faculty was performing 299 other roles involving the supervision, advising, and examination of graduate students. Each of these roles was estimated to require an average of 5 hours a year in one category, 4 hours a year in another, and 3 hours a year in a third. Thus, in total, the supervision of graduate students required about 2.4 faculty man-years rather than 1.4, and the system of workload reporting at the university level reflected only the direct supervision of the 25 dissertations. The prestige system in the department and in the graduate college also focused on the "major professor" role of supervising doctoral dissertations and gave little or no consideration to the other 299 roles which were required (for the most part) by graduate college rules.

As a result of these tabulations of roles and standardized workload estimates, it seems likely that the minor roles will be substantially reduced in number; also, the duration of certain committee meetings will be reduced and certain others may be eliminated entirely.

The exercise of making out workload estimates for a department for the academic year just ahead, using standardized coefficients, may be useful in other ways also. For example, it is generally recognized by faculty members that a graduate course requires more preparation time than an undergraduate course, that more preparation time is required for teaching two different courses in the same quarter than for teaching two sections of the same course, and that a teaching load which includes five repetitions of the same course during the academic year, plus one graduate course, is less demanding than a six-course load which involves, say, six different preparations.

Presentations on the estimated time required to do a high quality teaching job with different course-load compositions might very well lead a department to recognize that different numbers of courses per academic year would indeed be more equitable than equal numbers of courses for all faculty members, when such factors as level of instruction and number of preparations during the academic year are taken into account.

*Quality of teaching performance: Motivation and evaluation*

Most faculty members would rather do a good job of teaching than an average or poor one with any given input of time. The most important flow of student feedback concerning teaching performance is directly to the instructor involved. Such private feedback (which the faculty member may discuss with a trusted colleague if he wishes) provides the faculty member with an opportunity to improve his performance as it was perceived by his most recent classes.

Requiring that copies of such student evaluations be filed with the department chairman (or higher university administrator) may put an undue burden on the reporting system; suspicious faculty members might regard compulsory invitations for student feedback as compulsory invitations to solicit testimony against themselves. If there is a basic atmosphere of trust within a department, some aspects of the student feedback (such as averages, arrays of ratings, and profiles of various sorts) may be useful information for all faculty members in the department.

*Volume and quality of publications*

This is a relatively uncharted area. For the present, rough and ready methods such as those used by Cartter in constructing a publications index for economics departments are better than nothing, and a moderate amount of elaboration may make them very useful indeed.

A. *Styles of publication in different disciplines.* Cartter (1966) obtained from each of his respondents in 29 academic disciplines a statement as to the number of books and the number of articles he had published since receiving his highest academic degree. We will consider here only the information supplied by "senior scholars," whose average ages ranged from 46.2 years to 53.5 years in the various disciplines. The cumulative publication figures reported by them as of April 1964 must have represented on the average something like 20 years of professional work. The publication figures are presented in Table 8.1.

There are striking systematic differences among disciplines in the relative numbers of books and of articles published. The social sciences and humanities run quite heavily to books; the biological and physical sciences run quite heavily to articles.

We recall that Cartter used weights of one for articles and six for books in his publication index for economics departments. The publication index in column (3) also employs these weights. Column (4) lists the average percentages of their professional time reported by senior scholars in each discipline as spent on research and writing, and column (5) presents the ratio of the publication index to the percentage of research and writing time in each field.

The dispersion of the publication indexes in column (3) is much less percentage-wise than the dispersion of the numbers of articles in column (2). For example, pharmacology shows 4.3 times as many articles as classics (73/17) but pharmacology's publication index is only 2.4 times as high (80/34). Column (5) in effect standardizes the publication index figures by converting them to publication points per each one percent of professional time devoted to research and writing. Dispersion is further reduced by this standardization, so that pharmacology rates only 1.6 times as high as classics (2.76/1.48).

Table 8.2 compares broad groups of disciplines in terms of averages of actual responses (Section A) and of actual responses adjusted to equal percentages of research and writing time (Section B). The latter adjustment does not modify the sharp difference between groups in the relative emphasis placed on books versus articles, but it does bring the publication indexes for social sciences and humanities and engineering up to within 6 percent and 10 percent, respectively, of that for biological and physical sciences. The adjusted trade-off of articles for books is 7.2, if we compare the biological and physical sciences in Section B with the social sciences and humanities (2.9 fewer books and 21 more articles); this is not far from the six to one ratio used in constructing our publication index.

This exercise suggests that reasonable measures of volume of publica-

Table 8.1. Publication styles in different disciplines, based on responses by senior scholars to the Cartter–American Council on Education Survey of Graduate Education in the United States, April 1964

| Discipline | (1) Books | (2) Articles | (3) Publication index[a] | (4) Percent of time spent on research and writing | (5) Col. (3) divided by Col. (4) |
|---|---|---|---|---|---|
| **Humanities (6):** | **3.2** | **21** | **40** | **23** | **1.74** |
| Classics | 2.8 | 17 | 34 | 23 | 1.48 |
| English | 3.8 | 20 | 43 | 23 | 1.87 |
| French | 2.9 | 18 | 35 | 23 | 1.52 |
| German | 3.2 | 18 | 37 | 19 | 1.95 |
| Philosophy | 3.2 | 26 | 45 | 28 | 1.61 |
| Spanish | 3.3 | 29 | 49 | 23 | 2.13 |
| **Social sciences (6):** | **3.2** | **22** | **41** | **23** | **1.78** |
| Anthropology | 3.3 | 30 | 50 | 23 | 2.17 |
| Economics | 2.8 | 21 | 37 | 23 | 1.61 |
| Geography | 2.2 | 21 | 34 | 24 | 1.42 |
| History | 3.8 | 18 | 41 | 20 | 2.05 |
| Political Science | 3.2 | 19 | 38 | 19 | 2.00 |
| Sociology | 3.7 | 25 | 47 | 27 | 1.74 |
| **Biological sciences (8):** | **0.9** | **48** | **54** | **28** | **1.93** |
| Bacteriology/Microbiology | 0.9 | 46 | 51 | 27 | 1.89 |
| Biochemistry | 0.5 | 58 | 61 | 30 | 2.03 |
| Botany | 0.7 | 33 | 37 | 25 | 1.48 |
| Entomology | 0.5 | 47 | 50 | 35 | 1.43 |
| Pharmacology | 1.1 | 73 | 80 | 29 | 2.76 |
| Physiology | 0.8 | 48 | 53 | 28 | 1.89 |
| Psychology | 1.5 | 39 | 48 | 27 | 1.78 |
| Zoology | 1.2 | 44 | 51 | 26 | 1.96 |
| **Physical sciences (5):** | **1.0** | **44** | **50** | **25** | **2.00** |
| Astronomy | 1.2 | 58 | 65 | 35 | 1.86 |
| Chemistry | 0.7 | 58 | 62 | 19 | 3.26 |
| Geology | 1.1 | 37 | 44 | 22 | 2.00 |
| Mathematics | 1.2 | 30 | 37 | 28 | 1.32 |
| Physics | 0.8 | 37 | 42 | 23 | 1.83 |
| **Engineering (4):** | **1.2** | **24** | **31** | **18** | **1.72** |
| Chemical engineering | 0.8 | 34 | 39 | 16 | 2.44 |
| Civil engineering | 0.8 | 25 | 30 | 20 | 1.50 |
| Electrical engineering | 2.2 | 19 | 32 | 18 | 1.78 |
| Mechanical engineering | 0.8 | 19 | 24 | 19 | 1.26 |
| **All disciplines surveyed (29):** | **1.9** | **33** | **45** | **24** | **1.88** |

*Source:* Columns (1), (2), and (4) for individual disciplines are taken from Cartter (1966, various pages from 20 through 76). Columns (3) and (5), and means for groups of departments, were computed by Karl A. Fox.

[a] Publication index equals number of articles plus six times the number of books.

Table 8.2. Publication styles in major groups of disciplines based on responses by senior scholars in April 1964: (A) actual responses and (B) actual responses adjusted for differences in percentages of time spent on research and writing

| Major groups of disciplines | (1) Average number of publications since highest degree — Books | (2) Articles | (3) Publication index[a] | (4) Percent of time spent on research and writing | (5) Col. (3) divided by Col. (4) |
|---|---|---|---|---|---|
| A. BASED ON ACTUAL RESPONSES ||||||
| All disciplines surveyed (29): | 1.9 | 33 | 45 | 24 | 1.85 |
| Biological and physical sciences (13): | 0.9 | 47 | 52 | 27 | 1.93 |
| Social sciences and humanities (12): | 3.2 | 22 | 41 | 23 | 1.78 |
| Engineering (4): | 1.2 | 24 | 31 | 18 | 1.72 |
| B. ACTUAL RESPONSES ADJUSTED FOR DIFFERENCES IN PERCENTAGES OF TIME SPENT ON RESEARCH AND WRITING[b] ||||||
| All disciplines surveyed (29): | 2.1 | 37 | 50 | 27 | 1.85 |
| Biological and physical sciences (13): | 0.9 | 47 | 52 | 27 | 1.93 |
| Social sciences and humanities (12): | 3.8 | 26 | 49 | 27 | 1.81 |
| Engineering (4): | 1.8 | 36 | 47 | 27 | 1.75 |

*Source:* Further aggregations and adjustments of data presented in Table 8.1; basic data underlying columns (1), (2), and (4) are taken from Cartter (1966).

[a] Publications index equals number of articles plus six times the number of books.

[b] Adjustment consists of multiplying figures in columns (1) and (2) of Section A by the ratio of 27 to the percentage of research and writing time reported in column (4) of Section A, rounding the results, and using them in the recomputation of columns (3) and (5).

tion can be developed for comparisons across disciplines, just as Cartter's exercise suggested that reasonable volume measures could be developed for comparing departments in the same discipline.

Although we have stressed similarities here, great significance may attach to certain differences in publication styles among disciplines and among special fields in the same discipline. Publication styles may change in a given discipline as it emerges from a prescientific to a scientific stage or as it undergoes a major change in its basic model or *paradigm* for explaining certain categories of phenomena. We cannot pursue these questions here.

B. *Allowing for lengths as well as numbers of articles.* A department's volume of publication in refereed professional journals, in research monographs, in conference volumes of quality comparable to refereed journals, and in graduate level texts might be appraised in the following light:

   a. If editors of refereed journals and of commercial and university presses are "rational," they are allocating space and/or expected reader time and interest (as evidenced by willingness to subscribe to journals and buy books) to authors who have "supramarginal" things to say to their fellow Ph.D.s and to Ph.D. candidates;

   b. If this publication system is working well, it strikes a balance between the supply of things worth writing and the demand for things worth reading within the Ph.D. level community internationally (and on some issues nationally or within language areas); and

   c. The number of pages published within each of several categories of journals, conference volumes, monographs, and graduate level texts is probably the best crude measure of that part of academic research output which takes written form. Pages in different categories could be weighted differently, given appropriate rationales.

Editors of professional journals are usually under sufficiently severe space limitations that they urge (or force) authors to compress long articles as a precondition for publication. Hence, it seems reasonable to assume that an article of 20 pages in a given journal is worth twice as much on the average as an article of 10 pages in the same journal.

C. *Estimating the quality of individual publications.* There are many circumstances under which individual publications are evaluated. One of these is the decision of an editor to reject a manuscript or to accept it for publication. Frequently an acceptance for publication is conditioned upon making certain improvements by way of clarification, qualification, or extension to bring the original manuscript up to what the editor regards as a fully acceptable standard for his journal or press.

Another context for evaluation occurs in connection with prizes and competitions. For example, an individual department may give an award for the best doctoral dissertation completed in a given year, or a national professional association may give annual awards for outstanding doctoral dissertations or outstanding published research.

It may be quite difficult for the judges in such competitions to verbalize concerning their selections, or to assign weights to different characteristics of the publications being compared. However, in the field of science with which the editor is most familiar, there appears to be considerable consistency in such evaluations.

Byron T. Shaw, a former administrator of the Agricultural Research Service of the U.S. Department of Agriculture, worked out a proposed scheme for ranking publications by agricultural scientists (1967). His primary object was to improve the reliability and equity of evaluations made of some 3,500 scientists in the Agricultural Research Service for salary increases and promotions in grade.

Shaw proposed that original research papers be given ratings of from 100 down to 1. Ratings of 100 to 81 would imply *very great impact* on science, agriculture, or general welfare; ratings of 80 to 61 would imply *great impact;* and ratings of 60 to 1 would imply *moderate to limited impact.*

Shaw characterizes these three broad categories as follows:

*Rank Orders 100 to 81:* . . .

Papers falling in this range would be discussed in all histories of science pertaining to the given field. Also, the research would be cited in the writing of most, if not all, other scientists doing related research.

*Rank Orders 80 to 61:* . . .

These papers are frequently cited in histories of science and in the writing of other scientists doing related research. Authors of these papers will be invited to present their work at scientific symposiums and in scientific review publications and will often be cited for awards for outstanding work.

*Rank Orders 60 to 1:* . . .

Papers in the top of this range would be cited frequently in the writings of other scientists. Papers at the bottom of the range would be cited infrequently. Most research reports of original work will fall in this range—from good to run-of-the-mill.

Shaw also recommended the use of rank orders 50 to 1 for rating reviews of research for scientists and 40 to 1 for rating reviews of research for laymen.

Shaw made the following tentative classification of the 3,545 research publications issued by Agricultural Research Service scientists in 1964:

| | |
|---|---|
| Total, all publications: | 3,545 |
| Original research, all: | 2,548 |
|   Very great impact | 2 |
|   Great impact | 82 |
|   Moderate to limited impact | 2,464 |
| Reviews of research for scientists: | 507 |
| Reviews of research for laymen: | 490 |

As an aid to practical implementation of his system, Shaw appended a list of about 240 publications in fields of interest to Agricultural Research Service scientists, with a point rating assigned to each. He gave a rating of 100 to a classic paper by J. Willard Gibbs (1878) which founded a new branch of chemical science; a rating of 95 to a paper by George W. Beadle and Edward L. Tatum (1941) which won them a Nobel prize; and so on down to some run-of-the mill publications with ratings of 5 to 15.

Publications of the caliber of those by Gibbs (1878) and by Beadle and Tatum (1941) evoke Thomas S. Kuhn's (1962) concept of paradigm change—a sharp change in the conceptual framework accepted as explaining a certain class of phenomena. If there exists a hierarchical structure of scientific concepts which extends from the most general to the most specific, it may be possible to rank scientific discoveries according to the level in this hierarchy at which they replace accepted concepts with new ones.

*Direct costs of various activities, using average salaries for major categories of personnel*

If the faculty of a department wishes to analyze its present allocation of resources as a basis for possible modifications, discussion may be inhibited if information about salaries and workloads is displayed in full empirical detail. The important issues can probably be analyzed with sufficient accuracy if the allocation of resources is presented in terms of standardized workload factors and standardized salaries for each major category of personnel. Department-wide average salaries for each category may be stated with sufficient accuracy (though rounded) that the product of average salary and man-years comes within one or two percent of the official budget total for the category.

For example, in an exercise for a department one average salary figure was used for all members of the professorial ranks, another for all instructors who were Ph.D. candidates in the department, another for all teaching assistants, and another for all secretaries and stenographers. These figures were used in connection with standard workload factors recognized in the department for specific activities. Nearly all courses were for 3 credit hours and the quarter system was in effect. The total direct cost per student quarter was estimated at $24.27 for lower division, $48.52 for upper division, and $82.53 for graduate courses. Upper division instruction cost about twice as much and graduate level instruction about three and one-half times as much per student quarter as did lower division instruction. The cost of the other component of the graduate program (supervising dissertation research, special reading courses, preliminary and final examinations, admissions, advising, arranging assignments to major professors, and assisting in placement) per full-time graduate student in residence per quarter was estimated at $248.03, or about ten times as much as a student quarter of lower division instruction.

Estimates such as these provide a compelling introduction to the problem of specifying an objective function for a department. Suppose, as in our example, the department finds it is allocating twice as many dollars to a student quarter of upper division as to one of lower division instruction. Typically, this allocation pattern will have emerged from a long series of decisions by successive chairmen and recommendations by ad hoc faculty committees. The chances are that the dollar costs per unit of alternative ways of performing particular functions will have entered into the decisions only on a crude and intuitive basis.

In our example, this evolutionary process has resulted in the allocation of twice as many dollars per student quarter to upper division as to lower division instruction. If this allocation is regarded as optimal, the inference must be that the marginal value product per student quarter is perceived as being twice as large for upper division as for lower division instruction.

This suggests a possible approach to the allocation of resources by university and college level administrators to their various departments. As a first approximation, the same total salary bill per student credit hour of instruction might be assigned to each department, with separate but standard salary cost allocations for each level of instruction. The department chairmen and deans could then be asked to compare these norms with their current allocations of resources to each level of instruction. The differences among departments in resource allocation patterns would provide a starting point for clarifying differences in value systems and for isolating such convincing reasons as may exist for using more expensive combinations of personnel at the same level of instruction in one department than in another.

**Problems of aggregation**

We have commented earlier that the most difficult measurement problems in the educational process are found at the level of the individual student and the particular class. If we could agree upon terminology and units of measure for specifying the outputs of a particular classroom "behavior setting" over an academic quarter or semester, the problem of aggregating such measures of output might be tackled with a reasonable prospect of success. Some extensions of the principles of national income accounting (which in turn flow from the theory of general economic equilibrium) may be helpful.

In the case of an economic system, we require that the gross product be precisely and exhaustively allocated among the various actors (consumers, producers, and resource holders). It seems that a similar approach might be applied to the task of estimating the annual output of, say, a four-year college and the allocation of that output among categories of students and perhaps among individual students. Further, it should be possible to develop reasonable procedures for attributing the total output of the college to clusters of departments, individual departments, and individual classes.

If this could be done in a crude fashion for a four-year college, it could presumably be done for each of the various colleges which form a university. An analogy with regional economic accounting should apply.

The policy implications of a regional economic model are clearer and the estimates of gross product more precise if the region is very nearly closed or self-contained with respect to some major categories of activities, such as home-to-work commuting, services, and retail trade.

Professionally oriented colleges at the graduate level, such as law and medicine, have a high degree of closure in that their students take few or no courses in other colleges of the university. Undergraduates in a college of engineering take a moderate number of courses in the college of arts and sciences, but the reverse flow is negligible; the same tends to be true of other professional schools with undergraduate programs (such as agriculture, business, and home economics). Doctoral programs have a considerable degree of closure at the departmental level. The university as a whole has a high degree of closure relative to other universities. The same principle that simplifies the derivation of regional accounts also simplifies the derivation of output measures for relatively self-contained units at various levels in an educational system.

Ultimately, the people of a nation allocate their resources, most notably their time and energy, between the educational system and other social systems. The broad outlines of an approach to measuring all outputs of a social system have been put forward by the editor in another place (Sengupta and Fox 1969). The approach leads in principle to a comprehensive measure, the gross social product, which includes the gross economic product (GNP) symmetrically with all noneconomic outputs of a society.

CHAPTER 9

# Objective Functions and Optimization Models for Institutions of Higher Education

*Karl A. Fox*

In this chapter we first consider briefly those components of the higher educational system which lend themselves to optimization at the level of a multicounty functional economic area (FEA). Next we present a general discussion of optimization problems in the context of a state university. We then summarize Melichar's analysis of the national salary structure for scientists in the United States both within and among fields (1968); this analysis has implications for the "human capital" aspects of graduate education in the sciences. A recent publication by Hartman (1969) provides useful quantitative information on "correlates of quality" in graduate education, also on a national basis; these correlates are summarized later in this chapter.

We also present some elements of practical modeling for university departments on a highly specific and operational level. A consistency model for medium-range departmental planning is discussed in detail; so is a related model for short-term (year-to-year) planning of a major component of the same department. Special attention is given to the rationales for specifying prices of inputs and outputs.

**Educational institutions in a multicounty functional economic area framework**

The boundaries of a university extension service as a social system can be defined without reference to any particular territory. However, an agency devoted to continuing education (or adult education) must relate itself to the communities in which adults live and work. Particularly in nonmetropolitan areas, the deployment of extension service field personnel and activities to serve the people of a state must adapt to the spatial organization of other human activities.

The term "community college" seems to imply a real territorially based community. For most of its students a community college is also a commuters' college, with some driving in daily from homes as much as 40 or 50 miles away.

*The outer and inner boundaries of a university extension service*

A typical state-supported land grant university in the United States includes among its components a cooperative extension service. For brevity we will refer to it simply as the extension service.

The extension service maintains a presence throughout the state. For example, Iowa State University has an extension office in each of Iowa's 99 counties. In principle, the "outer boundary" of the extension service is easy to delineate. It includes the inputs of personnel and facilities from the university's extension budget and the inputs of members of extension audiences.

The "inner boundary" between extension and research is less easily drawn. The extension faculty of a state university is expected to deliver its outputs to residents of the state. If an extension faculty member is teaching the general principles of his discipline, the time he spends preparing for his presentation can hardly be regarded as research. However, sometimes it may be necessary to develop facts and relationships which are specific to his own state or to a subarea within it. The procedures needed to collect and organize these specific data and establish the specific relationships are research procedures.

Typically, the procedures required for extension-oriented research have been long established in the professional literature and in graduate level textbooks. As a rule, neither the methods nor the results will be of interest to national and international scientific journals; the costs of the research must justify themselves in terms of service to residents of the given state. Hence, adaptive or special purpose research in support of extension programs should probably be included within the boundary of the extension subsystem, along with other inputs required to achieve the results sought for the benefit of extension audiences in the state.

*The objective function for a university extension service under nonmetropolitan conditions*

The spatial organization of the Iowa economy and society is replicated in many other nonmetropolitan regions. Iowa was settled during 1830–70 in a pattern of dispersed farmsteads. By 1910, the state was organized *de facto* into a thousand or more communities, each consisting of a village or small town and a trade and service area covering perhaps 50 square miles—about one-tenth the size of an average county.

Since 1910, Iowa has been transformed by the automotive revolution. The passenger automobile is now the almost universal form of personal transportation. More than 90 percent of Iowa's population lives within 50 miles, or about one hour's commuting time, of one of 12 central cities. Newspapers, radio and television stations, department stores, community colleges, vocational and technical schools, and specialized medical, legal, and business services are located in or near the central cities; hence, the commuting field is not only a relatively self-contained labor market in the short run but also a trade and service area. Each commuting field, covering an average of about 5,000 square miles, may be viewed as a low density city containing farm, small town, and central city populations. We call such a low-density city a *functional economic area* (FEA).

Figures 9.1 through 9.5 should illustrate this concept sufficiently for our purposes. Fuller presentations can be found in Fox and Kumar (1965, 1966), Fox (1967, 1969), and Berry (1968).

Figure 9.1 shows the pattern of towns and cities of different sizes in a nonmetropolitan FEA centered on Fort Dodge, Iowa. Given the rectangular road grid in this and other parts of Iowa, we must travel 50 highway miles from the center of Fort Dodge to reach any point on the perimeter of the square. If we can average 50 miles per hour over all possible routes, the 50-mile square is a proxy for a 60-minute circle of commuting time. Other evidence indicates that the perimeter of this square closely approximates the actual commuting field.

Figure 9.2 shows similar squares centered on the seven Iowa cities which had more than 50,000 people in 1960. Figure 9.3 includes the same seven squares plus five more centered on FEA central cities of less than 50,000 people. The area within the squares contained 80 percent of Iowa's area and 90 percent of its population as of 1960.

Figure 9.4 depicts the 1960 commuting fields of all FEA central cities in the United States. Figure 9.5, "Functional Economic Areas of the United States," approximates these commuting fields with clusters of contiguous whole counties. Figures 9.4 and 9.5 were prepared in 1967 by Brian J. L. Berry (1968).

Iowa State University's extension service has taken advantage of this new spatial pattern to reorganize its traditional 99 county extension units into 12 multicounty areas. The more highly trained and specialized

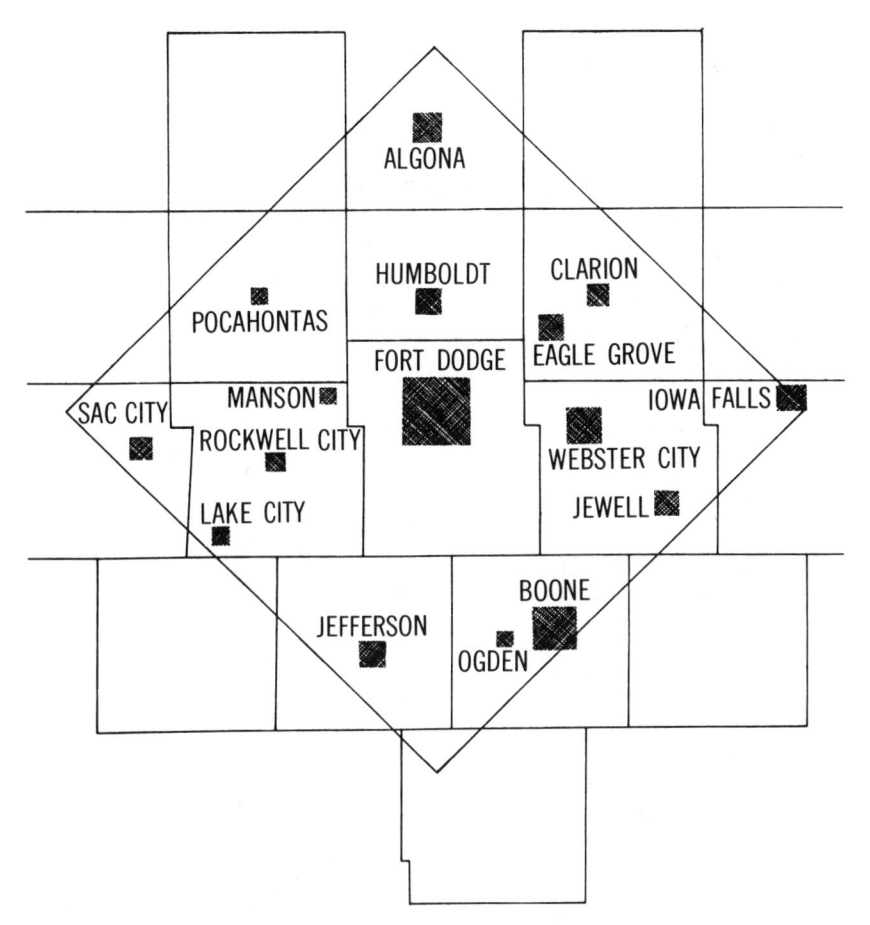

Fig. 9.1. Distribution of town population sizes in the Fort Dodge area. Areas of squares are proportional to 1960 town populations. Only towns with retail sales of $2.5 million or more for year ending June 30, 1964 are shown.

members of the area extension staff are concentrated in the area office located (typically) in the central city of the functional economic area. To the extent that the residents of this area form a relatively self-contained community, the task of the area extension staff can be defined quite clearly.

For simplicity, suppose that a functional economic area has a population of 100,000 people. The extension service in any given year offers a specified array of behavior settings, including short courses and special-purpose meetings of various types. Residents of the community allocate

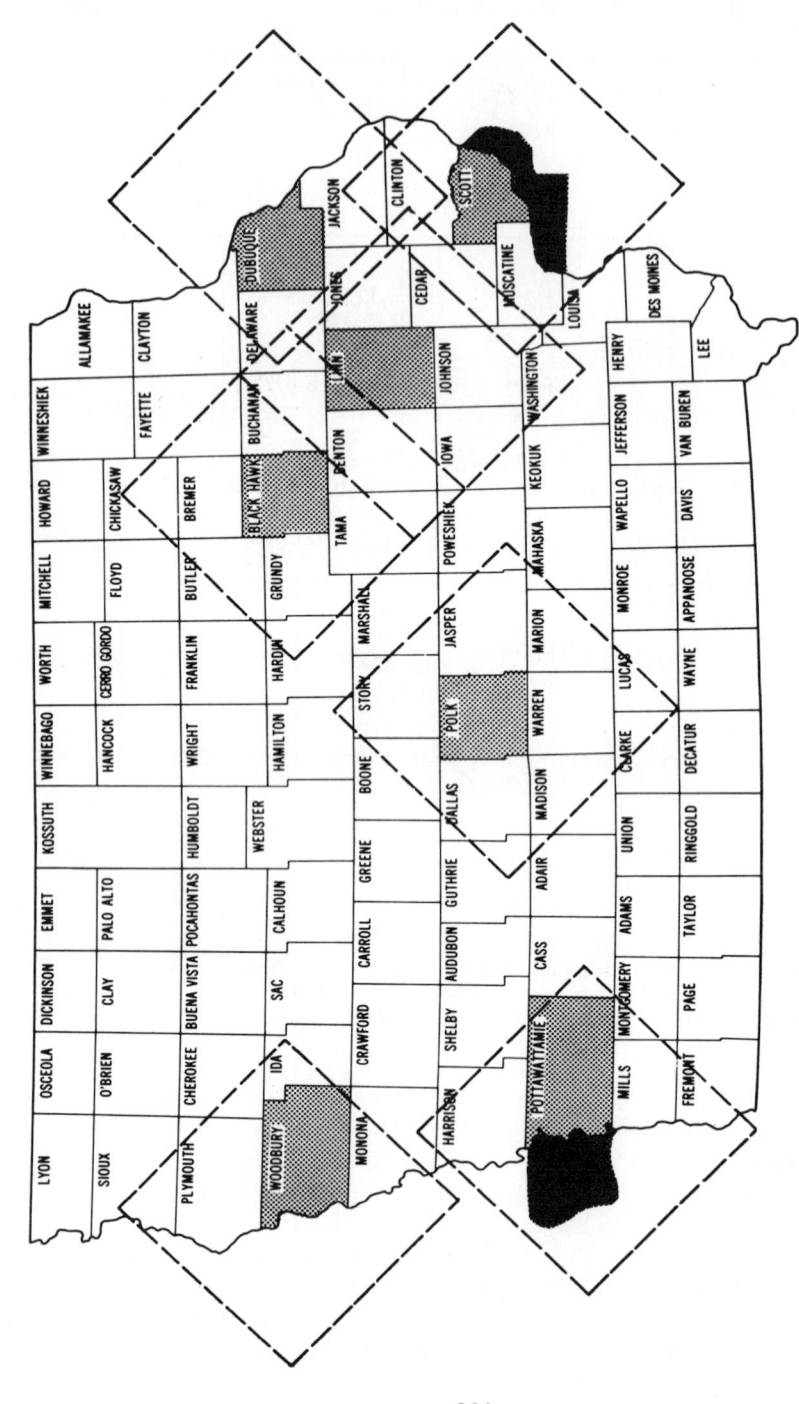

Fig. 9.2. Fifty-mile commuting distances from the central business districts of Iowa SMSA central cities. Central cities of 50,000 people or more in 1960. Each shaded county or pair of shaded contiguous counties are SMSA's.

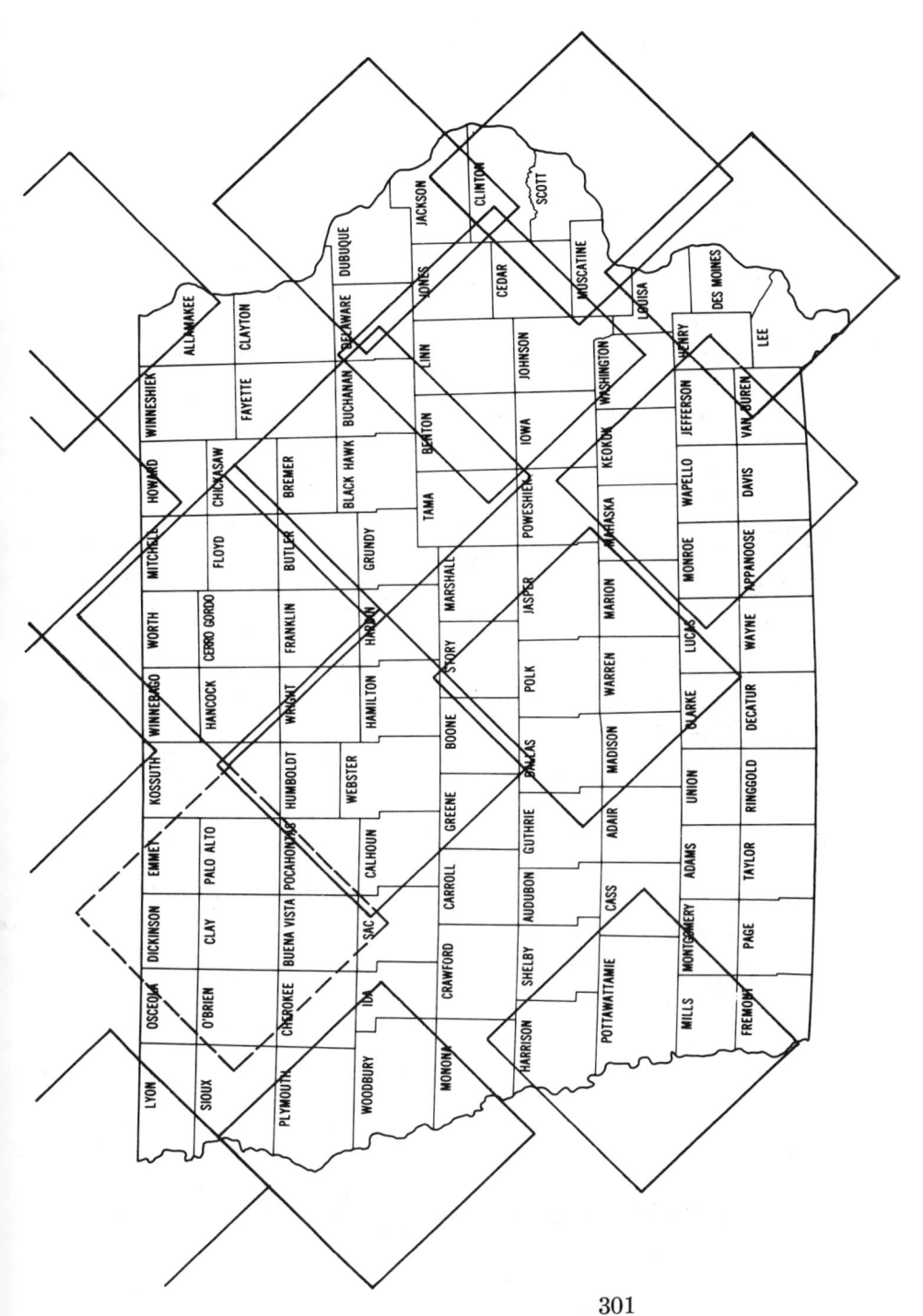

Fig. 9.3. Fifty-mile commuting distances from the central business districts of all FEA (including SMSA) central cities in or near Iowa. Central cities selected on the basis of range of economic activities performed and relationships to surrounding area.

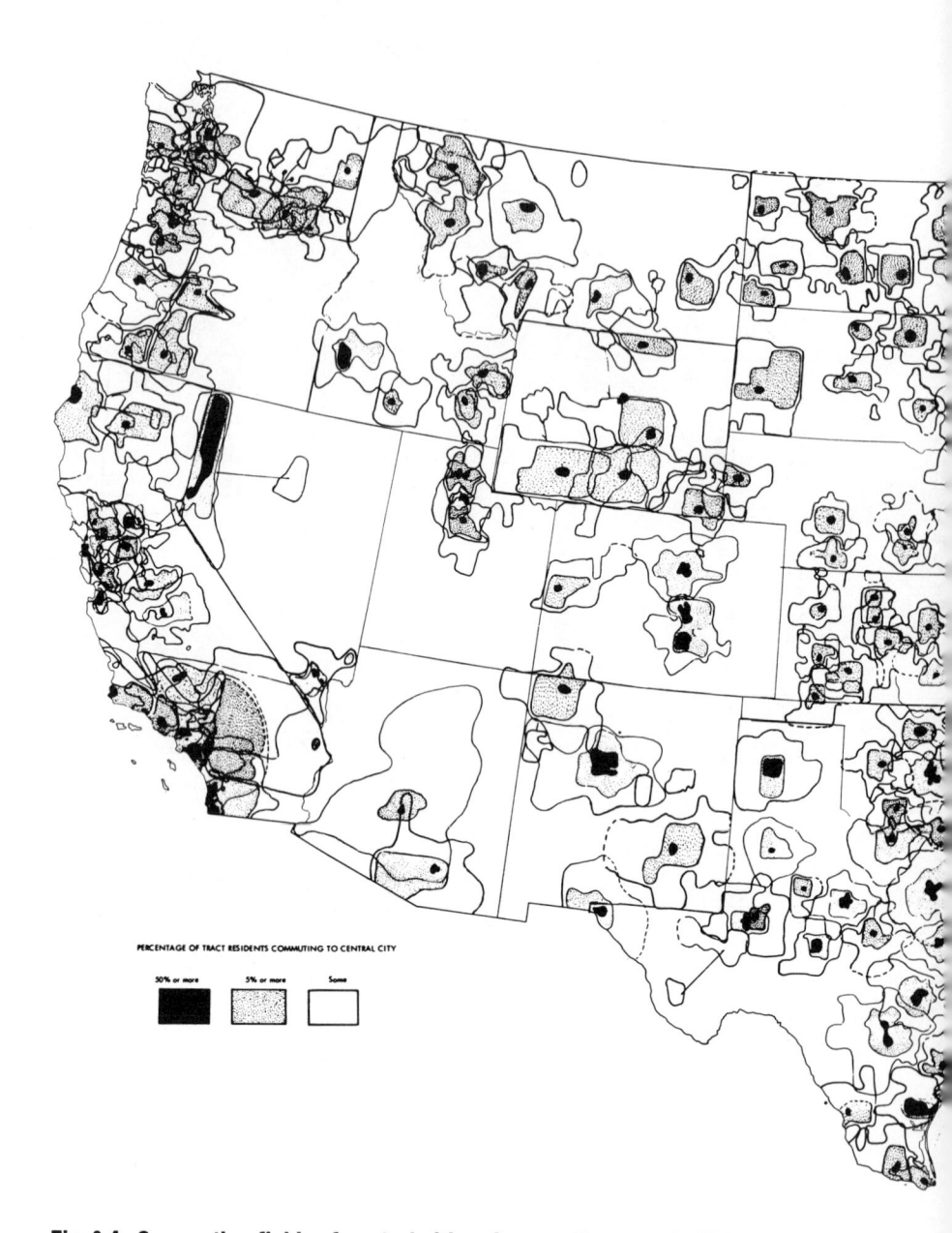

Fig. 9.4. Commuting fields of central cities. Source: Berry et al. (1968), pp. 30–31.

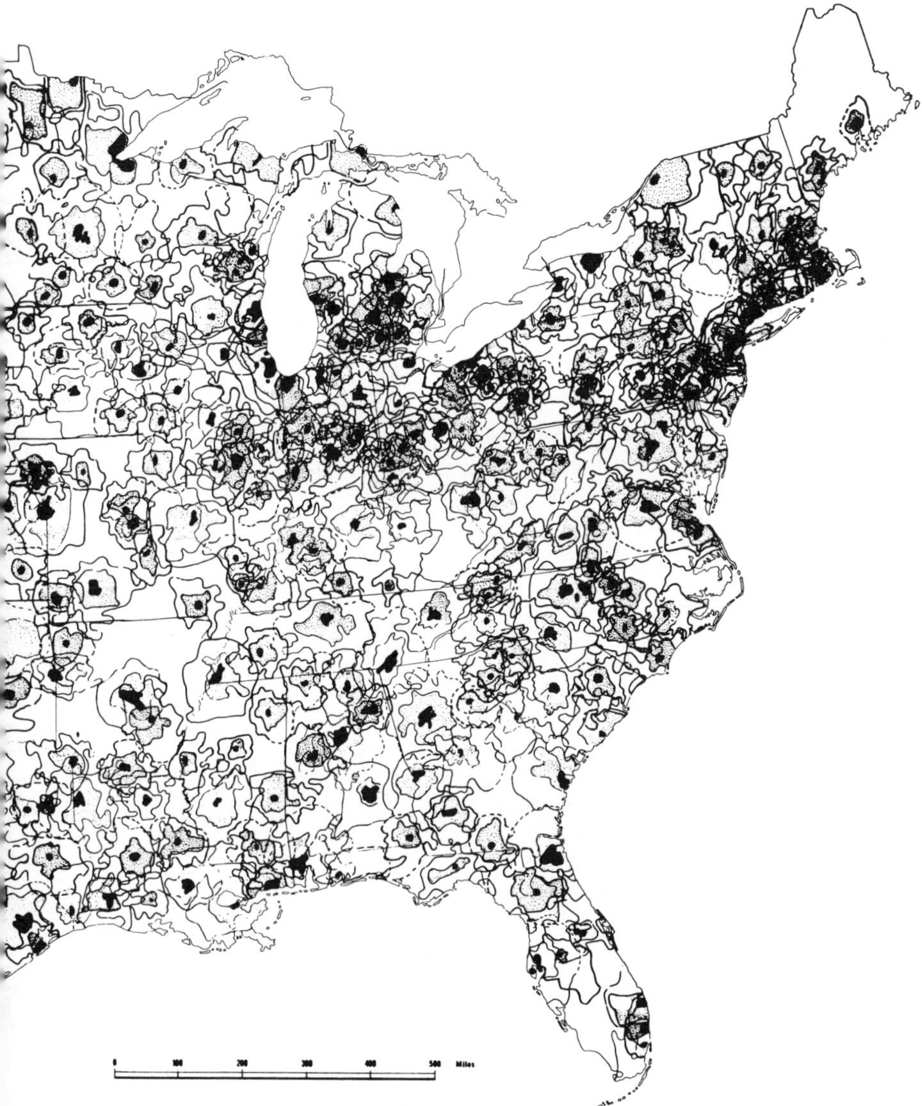
0
100
200
300
400
500 Miles

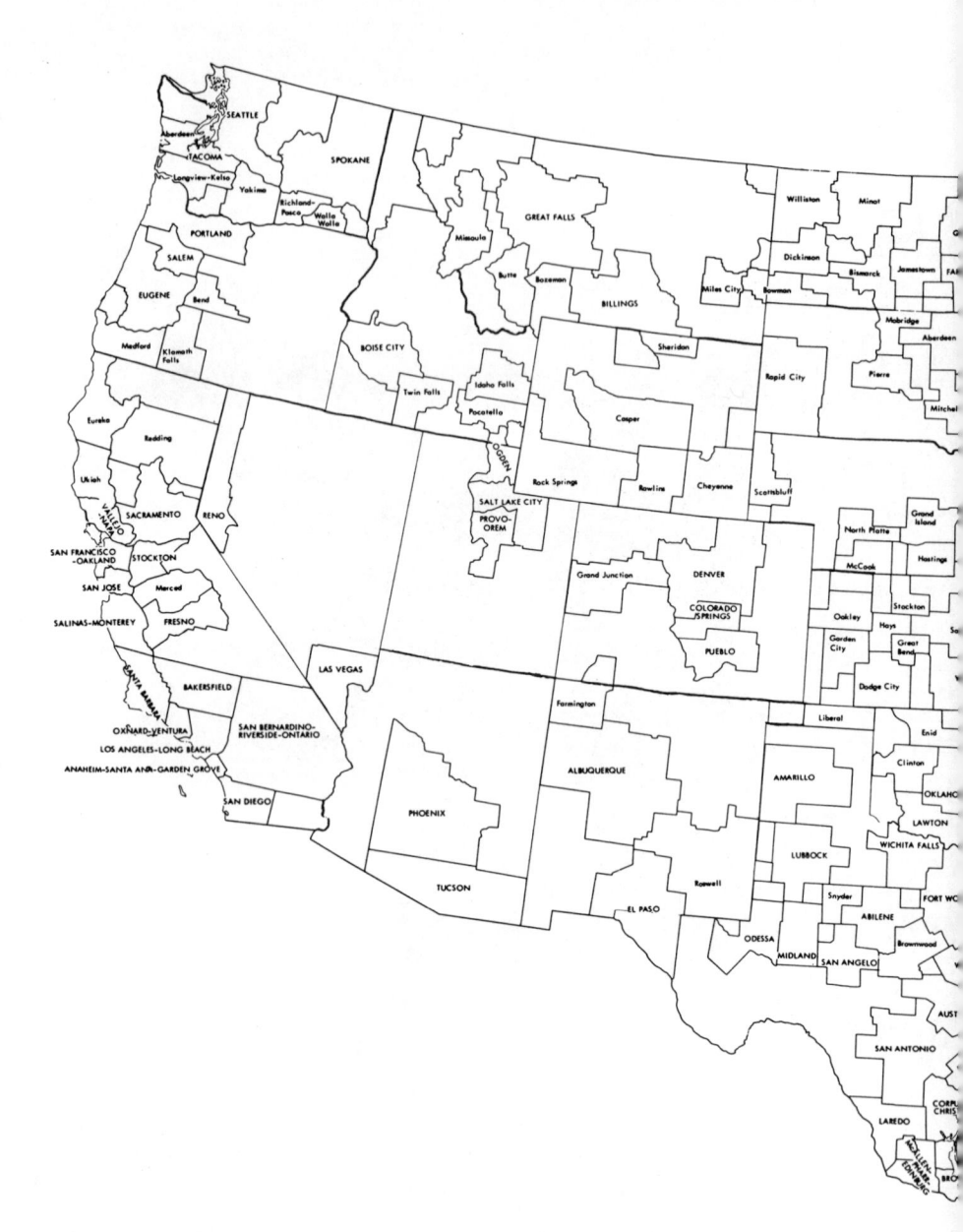

Fig. 9.5. Functional economic areas of the United States. Source: Berry et al. (1968), pp. 28–29.

OBJECTIVE FUNCTIONS AND OPTIMIZATION MODELS 305

their time between behavior settings controlled by the extension service and all other behavior settings.

As participation in the extension settings is always voluntary (though sometimes requiring a registration or enrollment fee), each resident of the community is free to allocate his time between extension and other behavior settings in what he perceives or expects to be an optimal manner. In the aggregate, the 100,000 residents of the community allocate 876 million hours of living time per year between extension and other settings. The extension settings should be regarded as including travel to and from the extension courses or meetings, plus any homework directly required for or induced by these extension activities.

The opportunity cost of spending more hours per year in extension settings is the utility of rewards forgone because of reduced participation in other settings. If the perceived quality of the extension service "offer" in the area increases, community residents will allocate more hours to participation in extension settings. Participation in some other settings (home and family, commercial recreation, and others) will be reduced.

The community demand curve for any fixed array of extension service offerings is downward sloping. As the extension service reaches out beyond its traditional agricultural and rural orientation to provide new programs for urban residents, the total man-hours of occupancy of extension settings may increase; fuller information about the new opportunities available may also shift the demand curve to the right.

The boundaries between the extension service and other educational systems in the area must be recognized. In principle, an optimal allocation of resources and enrollment should be achieved within and between all educational and training facilities in the delineated multicounty area.

Thus, an objective function could be specified for university extension activities in each of the 12 multicounty areas of Iowa. The extension service also include faculty members and other resources located on the Iowa State University campus in Ames. The duties of the Ames staff include training and advising the area specialists, providing them with certain kinds of teaching materials, and doing some teaching and advising that require Ph.D.-level training and experience. (Most members of the area staffs have M.S. or equivalent training.) In principle, the Ames resources should be allocated among the 12 areas in such a way as to equalize their marginal social value products in all areas. This is a special and obvious case of the decentralization problem which has been discussed in earlier chapters.

*The role of the community college*

The role of the community college is a logical extension of the historical trend of rising educational standards for the entire population. The economies of size associated with a community college and the age of its student body are favorable to its serving a multicounty area in most nonmetropolitan settings.

Each FEA contains a wide range of occupational and other roles to which children and young adults can be introduced; most of these roles are replicated in every FEA. The FEA itself represents a synthesis of rural and urban societies into what is, economically and culturally speaking, a low-density city. The community college should be able to help young adults prepare themselves for the roles to which they aspire within the FEA. Some of these roles require upper division, graduate, or professional school educations; in general, these must be pursued in the universities and four-year colleges. Hence, the arts and sciences programs of the two-year community colleges should be compatible with the junior and senior programs of the corresponding state universities.

## Optimization models for university planning

So far, optimization models have not been widely used in university planning. Techniques of optimization are not the limiting factor; many such techniques are available (see, for example, Sengupta and Fox 1969). The obstacle lies in the specification of objective functions that will carry conviction (a) to one analyst and/or one university president; (b) to two or more analysts and/or university presidents; (c) to the scientific community at large; (d) to university students; and (e) to legislators, parents, alumni, and other taxpayers upon whom universities depend for financial support.

We will, therefore, devote the first part of this section to the problem of specifying objective functions for university planning.

*Objective functions and pricing systems*

Sengupta and Fox (1969, Chapter 1) briefly review three kinds of optimizing models that have been developed and used by economists. The *theory of the firm* employs a cardinal objective function and the weights applied to its various outputs are market prices. The *theory of consumption* employs an ordinal utility function; in equilibrium the marginal utilities of different commodities are proportional to their prices:

$$\frac{\frac{\partial U}{\partial q_i}}{\frac{\partial U}{\partial q_j}} = \frac{\lambda p_i}{\lambda p_j} = \frac{p_i}{p_j}, \text{ where } \lambda,$$

a Lagrangean multiplier, corresponds to the shadow price of the consumer's income constraint. If his income were increased by one dollar, the value of his utility function, $U$, would be increased by $\lambda$ units of his own internal and unspecified currency. The *theory of economic policy* as presented by Theil (1961) ascribes an ordinal utility function to a national policymaker. The ratio of the marginal "utilities" of any two policy instruments $x_j$ and $x_k$ can be expressed as:

$$\frac{\frac{\partial W}{\partial x_j}}{\frac{\partial W}{\partial x_k}} = \frac{(\lambda_1 r_{1j} + \lambda_2 r_{2j} + \ldots + \lambda_n r_{nj})}{(\lambda_1 r_{1k} + \lambda_2 r_{2k} + \ldots + \lambda_n r_{nk})},$$

where the $r_{ij}$'s and $r_{ik}$'s reflect the real structure of the economy (net effects of a unit change in each instrument upon each target variable) and $\lambda_i$ is the increase in utility (as perceived by the policymaker) which would result if the $i$th restriction were relaxed by one unit. The ratio of $\partial W/\partial x_j$ to $\partial W/\partial x_k$ will not be affected if we multiply both numerator and denominator by the same scalar. This means, for example, that there is no unique way of converting utilities into dollars.

In the theory of the firm we assume that satisfactory cardinal measures exist for all quantities of outputs and inputs, all technical coefficients, and all prices. Nearly all members of an industrial society have direct experience of prices, of budget constraints, and of some kinds of production processes in which inputs are transformed into outputs, so the assumption of measurability commends itself to common sense in such a society.

*A university's contribution to the gross social product*

In Chapter 10 we suggest a tentative generalization of economic theory to all outputs of a social system. This suggestion might be adapted to a university. First, assume that a university president understands the internal "technology" of the university very well and can compute rather accurately what would happen to various measurable outputs (such as numbers of B.S., M.S., and Ph.D. graduates in specific fields, numbers of research publications in specific fields, and so on) if a million dollars a year were withdrawn from one cluster of activities and added to another cluster. For simplicity, assume that all outputs are aggregated into two and that all limiting resources are converted into two, say, funds for current operations (mostly salaries for professors and supporting staff) and physical plant (classrooms, office space, laboratories, library facilities, and the like). Given these two constraints, he chooses to operate the two activities $Q_1$ and $Q_2$ at the levels $q_1$ and $q_2$.

We infer a utility function and an optimizing model:

$$\max W = f(Q_1, Q_2)$$

subject to the nonlinear production functions:

$$Q_1 = f_1(F, B),$$
$$Q_2 = f_2(F, B),$$

the production transformation curve

$$g(Q_1, Q_2) = 0,$$

and the constraints

$$F \leq F_0,$$
$$B \leq B_0.$$

We assume that the president's utility function (like the consumer's) is simply ordinal but has the property of diminishing marginal rates of substitution of $Q_i$ for $Q_j$ ($i, j = 1, 2, i \neq j$); also, that the production possibilities frontier has the property of diminishing marginal rates of transformation of $Q_i$ into $Q_j$.

If the point $(q_1, q_2)$ is optimal under the specified restrictions, it is a point of tangency between the president's utility function and the transformation function. Assume that the (continuous) transformation function is specified numerically over a reasonable range of values of $Q_1$ and $Q_2$; then the slope $-r$ of the tangent at $(q_1, q_2)$ is:

$$-r = \frac{\partial Q_1}{\partial Q_2} = \frac{\dfrac{\partial g(Q_1, Q_2)}{\partial Q_2}}{\dfrac{\partial g(Q_1, Q_2)}{\partial Q_1}}.$$

If a vice-president agrees with the specification of the transformation function, but believes that the (constrained) optimal point at which to operate would be $(q_1', q_2')$, at which the absolute value of the slope of the tangent is $|r'| > |r|$, we infer that he sets a higher value on $Q_2$ relative to $Q_1$ than does the president. If both utility functions are ordinal and no market-like prices are available for $Q_1$ and $Q_2$, there is no objective way to choose between the two views. Quantification of the ratios determined from the transformation function as, say, $r = 1.5$ and $r' = 2.0$ might provoke a clarifying exchange of "reasons why." If $Q_1$ and $Q_2$ are disaggregated into more sharply defined components, such as Ph.D. degrees in biological sciences versus Ph.D. degrees in social sciences, each party can specify his "barter terms of trade" at this more detailed level. Different assumptions about facts can be checked against facutal data, and the areas of disagreement over as yet unmeasurable values can be more clearly delimited. The result might lead to some changes in both objective functions and the selection of a point $(q''_1, q''_2)$ as optimal.

If the detailed components of $Q_1$ can be assigned market-like prices, such as the net increases in expected career earnings associated with taking B.S. degrees rather than starting work with high school diplomas, we can compute a "market" price $P_1$ and infer an implicit price, $P_2 = rP_1$, for $Q_2$. The next challenge would be to analyze the suboutputs of $Q_2$ in more detail, as inputs into various subsystems of the society; determine the media of exchange (in Talcott Parsons' sense) in which these inputs should be priced; and probe more deeply into the measurement of exchange rates between media. We have made some conjectures about such exchange rates for an individual in (Sengupta and Fox 1969, Chapter 9).

The analogy of GNP calculations based on market prices seems to be the logical starting point. Many problems of measurement and aggregation are involved in computing gross national product. Yet the development of national income and product accounts in the 1930's and 1940's was prerequisite to the development and implementation of rational macroeconomic policies and the theory of quantitative economic policy in general. We should regard the prices of some university outputs not as unmeasurable but simply as not yet measured.

*The boundary between the university and the rest of society*

A university may be regarded as an array of behavior settings, including classes and seminars, extension service meetings, research activities in laboratories, offices, and libraries, and so on. Each of these behavior settings involves some personnel and facilities that are paid for from the university budget. Inputs of faculty members in preparing for classes (whether the preparation is done at home or not), and inputs of students in doing homework (whether done in the university library, a university-controlled dormitory or a private home) are also inputs into the university as here defined. Time spent by participants in traveling to and from extension meetings and doing homework in connection with them is also an input into the university.

Every person who provides any inputs to the university in this extended sense is allocating his total time between university behavior settings and all others. The allocation of a student's time between university and other settings may not be optimal in a static sense (within the current year); however, the forgoing of current money income and other potential rewards should be compensated by an expected flow of more income and/or other rewards in later years after leaving the university.

*The university's objective function and the purpose of internal administrative organization*

All administrative structures below the level of the president in a state university may be regarded as auxiliary to the central problem of optimizing an objective function that can be ascribed to the university as a whole. If each faculty member and administrator in the university accepted the same explicit set of prices of all university outputs and inputs, and if each faculty member clearly recognized his own comparative advantages in different functional and subject matter areas, optimal allocation of resources within the university could *in theory* be achieved through a pricing mechanism and with no administrative layers between the individual faculty member and the president.

In this theoretical framework, the only necessary costs of administration within the university would be the costs of collecting input and output prices from markets or quasi markets outside the university, costs of calculating shadow prices for resources and intermediate goods within the university, and costs of disseminating and interpreting these prices to all members of the faculty. However, these prices will change over time for reasons both external and internal to the university, so faculty members must cope with problems of forecasting, discounting, and uncertainty.

One function of an administrator is to absorb some of the uncertainty as to what prices will be paid for various kinds and qualities of outputs, some of which require long-term investments on the part of faculty members. A major function of recruitment interviews is to determine whether the things a potential faculty member is most eager to do are the things that will bring him the greatest rewards within the university; when a mismatch is avoided, the angels sing!

*The structure of knowledge, the boundaries of scientific communities, and principles for clustering courses and fields*

Departmental organization within a university reflects several different considerations, three of which are mentioned in this section.

A. *The boundaries of scientific communities.* Information about salaries, working conditions, prestige gradients, and opportunities for social service relevant to, say, economists seems to flow into "containers" roughly coextensive with economics departments. Another way of putting it is that this sort of information flows within *scientific communities* nationally and even internationally, and the *de facto* boundaries between scientific communities are replicated in the pattern of information flows within the university.

From a sociology-of-science viewpoint, scientific communities could be delineated by observing patterns of communication, travel, conferences, association memberships, journal subscriptions, and journal publication patterns. If these patterns indicate intense communication and mutual visibility among relatively small groups of scientists, we may be dealing with "first-order communities" (our terminology); somewhat less intense patterns of communication among members of different "first-order communities" may define "second-order communities," and so on. These patterns might support commonly used terms such as labor economics (field of specialization); economics (department); social sciences (division); sciences and humanities (college), and so on.

B. *The structure of knowledge.* It seems intuitively clear that the structures of scientific communities will lag behind what might be called the structure of knowledge. The structure of knowledge as of January 1, 1972 must accommodate all discoveries made through December 31, 1971. This structure might be thought of as a least-cost network of concepts and proofs that "explains" all phenomena which (according to the best available evidence as of December 31, 1971) are considered to be explained in any and every discipline. It is hard to visualize this structure; however, it might consist of a set of words, concepts, equations, pictures, and diagrams that could be covered in, say, 300 courses instead of the 3,000 or so found in some university catalogs.

The basic concept of optimization might appear only once in this "structure of knowledge." However, good pedagogy might still require a college catalog with more than 1,000 courses, and the concept of optimization might be taught and/or reviewed at different levels and in different contexts in 50 of them.

The structure of knowledge could be regarded as a moving norm or frontier with respect to which such concepts as keeping up or catching up could be defined. In principle, all teaching of all subject matter involving science and technology, from the first grade through the advanced graduate level and in all types of informal or adult education, should be consistent (or not inconsistent) with this moving norm.

Every day a few elements of the structure of knowledge are seen in a new perspective and rearranged. "Keeping up" within a particular field or in teaching a certain course means being almost immediately perceptive of, and receptive to, those rearrangements in the structure of knowledge which have implications for the field or course.

Major scientific breakthroughs may involve rearranging a substantial portion of the structure of knowledge. Disciplines or specialities such as physical chemistry, biochemistry, and molecular biology probably reflect a limited number of major rearrangements in the structure of knowledge and a good many minor ones.

It seems to us that the role of a department in a university should be conceived in this dynamic and swiftly adaptive context. There is room in the university community for a variety of talents and enthusiasms. Some faculty members are most successful at rearranging the structure of knowledge, some at adapting new knowledge to specific situations, and some at transmitting new knowledge and explaining the structure of existing knowledge in resident teaching and extension settings.

C. *Principles for clustering courses and fields.* T. W. Schultz (1968) attributes three functions to universities; (1) teaching; (2) research; and (3) the discovery of talent. Requiring the student to select courses from a wide range of disciplines during his first two undergraduate years should increase the probability that he will select a field of specialization for which he is well suited and motivated (i.e., which matches his talents).

At Iowa State University, as of 1971, a B.S. degree requires the completion of 192 credit hours, equivalent to 64 courses of 3 credit hours each; completion normally requires four academic years. A major subject must be chosen, involving a cluster of 10 or more such courses; one or more minor subjects, involving smaller clusters of courses, must also be chosen.

The advantage of clustering related courses presumably consists of the internalization of external economies; otherwise, 64 courses chosen at random would serve just as well. We may write:

$$V = p'Bq, \quad p: n.\ 1 \tag{1}$$
$$q: n.\ 1$$
$$B: n.\ n,$$

where $p_i$ is the expected value of course $i$ taken in isolation; $q_i = 1$ if course $i$ is taken, and zero otherwise; $B$ is a square matrix with diagonal elements $b_{ii} = 1$ or 0 and off-diagonal elements $0 \leq b_{ij} \leq 1$, $i \neq j$. Let $p^*$ be a 64 element vector of courses actually taken by a specified B.S. candidate; $q^*$ is a 64 element vector with $q_i = 1$, $i = 1, 2, \ldots, 64$; and $B^*$ is a 64 times 64 matrix with $b_{ii}^* = 1$ for all $i$ and $0 \leq b_{ij}^* \leq 1$ for all $i \neq j$. We may rewrite (1) as:

$$V^* = p^{*\prime} B^* q^*. \tag{2}$$

If courses $i$ and $j$ are complementary, then $b_{ij} > 0$, $b_{ji} > 0$, $b_{ii} = 1$, $b_{jj} = 1$, and the value of the two courses combined is:

$$V_{(i+j)} = p_i + p_j + (b_{ij}p_i + b_{ji}p_j). \tag{3}$$

If the complementary courses are vocationally oriented, they jointly enhance the capacity of the student to perform some vocational role; if they are "student expressive," they jointly enhance the student's capacity to, say, play a musical instrument or speak a foreign language.

Similarly, suppose a Ph.D. program in, say, Economics is stated in terms of several optional fields of three courses each. Presumably each field contains courses with a high degree of complementarity; in fact, complementarity among three courses might be measured as the value of $c$ in the following equation:

$$1 + c = \frac{(1 + b_{12} + b_{13}) + (b_{21} + 1 + b_{23}) + (b_{31} + b_{32} + 1)}{3} \tag{4}$$

or

$$1 + c = 1 + (1/3)[(b_{12} + b_{13}) + (b_{21} + b_{23}) + (b_{31} + b_{32})].$$

For three courses selected at random, $c = 0$. At the next level of aggregation, the value of a particular Ph.D. program could be expressed in terms of complementarities among fields.

### National salary differentials for scientists within and among scientific fields

Salary is only one of the rewards of a scientist, but reputation and influence are no doubt strongly correlated with salary when other factors (notably type of employer) are held constant.

Emanuel Melichar (1968) has published a multiple regression analysis of salaries of 196,428 scientists who were on the U.S. National Register of Scientific and Technical Personnel for 1966. His multiple regression equation included 58 independent variables, all of the zero-or-one type.

Table 9.1. Importance of selected characteristics in explaining variation in professional salaries: All professions, 1966 National Register

| Characteristic | Net relationship Partial $R^2$ | $F$-ratio | Number of variables used |
|---|---|---|---|
| Highest academic degree | .159 | 9260 | 4 |
| Years of experience and type of employer | .149 | 1185 | 29 |
| Profession | .066 | 1062 | 13 |
| Primary work activity | .065 | 3417 | 4 |
| Sex | .024 | 4923 | 1 |
| Age | .019 | 555 | 7 |

Source: (Melichar 1968, p. 60).

The original salaries were converted into logarithms prior to running the regression.

Melichar's regression equation explained 54 percent of the variance of the logarithms of salaries around their mean. Table 9.1 indicates the nature of the explanatory variables used. The highest academic degree was most important; a combination of years of experience and type of employer was almost equally important; profession (to be defined later) made a substantial contribution, as did the primary work activity; sex and age made smaller contributions to explaining the total variance of scientists' salaries. (Age is, of course, highly correlated with years of experience; the partial $R^2$ of 0.019 represents the contribution of age over and above the estimated contribution of years of experience.)

With 196,428 observations, the $F$-ratios in Table 9.1 are astronomical; the smallest is 555 and the others range from 1,062 to 9,260! All the relationships are significant far beyond the 0.01 probability level.

Table 9.2 shows the net relationship between professional salaries and various combinations of years of experience and type of employer. The multiple regression equation yields separate estimates for salaries on an academic year base and those on a calendar year base. The percentage rates of salary progression with years of experience appear to be broadly similar for the various types of employer.

Table 9.3 shows the net effects of the other 29 variables included in Melichar's multiple regression analysis. The figures in the left-hand column are net percentage differences which are to be added to or subtracted from the national geometric mean salary for all professions ($12,050 as of January 1966).

On the average, the net effect of the Ph.D. degree was to raise salary by 26.2 percent (1.155/.915) above the Master's degree, while the Mas-

Table 9.2. Net relationships between professional salaries and employer-experience characteristics: All professions, 1966 National Register

|   | Years of experience ||||||
|---|---|---|---|---|---|---|
|   | 1 or less | 2 to 4 | 5 to 9 | 10 to 14 | 15 to 19 | 20 to 29 | 30 and over |
| Type of employer | Percentage difference from national geometric mean ||||||
| Educational institutions: | | | | | | | |
| Academic year base | −36.6 | −31.9 | −25.7 | −17.6 | −11.5 | −4.3 | 0.0 |
| Calendar year base | −28.8 | −23.4 | −16.5 | −7.3 | −0.5 | 7.6 | 12.4 |
| Government: | | | | | | | |
| Federal | −26.0 | −15.8 | −5.7 | 0.9 | 7.2 | 16.0 | 24.7 |
| Other | −36.5 | −27.8 | −19.1 | −13.5 | −8.0 | −0.5 | 7.0 |
| Other employer: | | | | | | | |
| Nonprofit organization | −20.9 | −16.7 | −9.0 | −1.2 | 6.5 | 15.6 | 24.8 |
| Industry or business | −10.8 | −6.0 | 2.7 | 11.5 | 20.2 | 30.5 | 40.8 |
| Self-employed | 0.7 | 6.1 | 15.9 | 25.9 | 35.7 | 47.4 | 59.0 |

*Source:* (Melichar 1968, p. 62.)

ter's tended to raise salary by 5.9 percent (0.915/0.864) above the Bachelor's degree.

Among scientists employed by educational institutions, those who listed teaching as their primary work activity most frequently listed research and development as their secondary activity; those who listed research and development as their primary activity most frequently listed teaching as their secondary activity. Those who listed research and development in educational institutions as their primary work activity presumably included most faculty members who were heavily involved in research and graduate teaching. It seems likely that those scientists in educational institutions who listed teaching as their primary activity were mainly engaged in undergraduate teaching and extension.

After years of experience had been taken into account, age made only a moderate contribution to the explanation of salary differences. The peak positive effect for age was experienced by the age group 45–54.

More than 90 percent of the scientists in the 1966 National Register were male; the net effect estimated for sex was a salary premium of 18.9 percent (1.011/0.850) for men over women.

The net relationships between field of science and salary received are of great interest. These results are indeed the primary purpose for which Melichar's analysis was designed. Scientists in all the fields listed were treated symmetrically in the analysis so far as all of the explanatory

Table 9.3. Net relationships between professional salaries and specified characteristics: All professions, 1966 National Register

| Characteristic | Percentage difference from national geometric mean, 1966 | Percentage of respondents in class |
|---|---|---|
| Highest academic degree: | | |
| Professional medical | 38.9 | 2.5 |
| Ph.D. | 15.5 | 41.5 |
| Master's | −8.5 | 25.1 |
| Bachelor's | −13.6 | 28.8 |
| Other or not reported | −18.3 | 2.1 |
| Primary work activity: | | |
| Management | 14.9 | 23.0 |
| Research and development | −1.5 | 35.4 |
| Production and inspection | −5.5 | 7.9 |
| Teaching | −9.4 | 19.9 |
| Other or not reported | −2.3 | 13.8 |
| Age: | | |
| Under 30 | −12.8 | 13.8 |
| 30–34 | −4.2 | 17.6 |
| 35–39 | 1.9 | 19.2 |
| 40–44 | 4.7 | 17.0 |
| 45–54 | 5.9 | 22.0 |
| 55–64 | 2.7 | 8.8 |
| 65 and over | −2.8 | 1.4 |
| Not reported | −1.5 | .2 |
| Sex: | | |
| Male | 1.1 | 93.4 |
| Female | −15.0 | 6.6 |
| Field of science: | | |
| Mathematics | 13.3 | 9.6 |
| Economics | 11.6 | 5.7 |
| Statistics | 8.5 | 1.3 |
| Physics | 7.9 | 11.0 |
| Anthropology | 1.0 | 0.4 |
| Meteorology | −0.4 | 1.7 |
| Sociology | −0.6 | 1.5 |
| Psychology | −1.4 | 8.2 |
| Earth sciences | −2.7 | 7.9 |
| Chemistry | −4.7 | 27.2 |
| Biological sciences | −4.9 | 12.4 |
| Linguistics | −6.7 | 0.5 |
| Agricultural sciences | −15.5 | 4.8 |
| Other | 3.7 | 7.7 |

*Source:* (Melichar 1968, p. 66.)

variables previously discussed are concerned. The results indicate that, among scientists identical with respect to years of experience, type of employer, age, sex, primary work activity, and highest academic degree, salaries ranged from 13.3 percent above the all-scientists average in the case of mathematicians to 15.5 percent below the all-scientists average in the case of agricultural scientists.*

*Interpreting the deviations of individual salaries from the multiple regression estimates*

We have noted that Melichar's multiple regression equation explained 54 percent of the variance of the logarithms of scientists' salaries around the logarithm of the all-sciences geometric mean salary. Conversely, 46 percent of the variance in scientists' salaries was not explained; the standard error of estimate of these deviations from regression, in terms of logarithms, was approximately 0.114. If we assume that the logarithmic salary deviations are normally distributed, we can use a table of areas under the normal curve to determine the logarithms associated with specified percentile ranks of salaries within any sharply defined category (for example, male Ph.D.'s in mathematics, age 30–34 with 5–9 years of experience, employed by educational institutions on an academic year basis with teaching as their primary work activity). The regression estimate for the category is the 50th percentile or median salary.

Figure 9.6 shows the results of this approach for selected percentile ranks and for specified degree levels and primary work activities in a particular science. The contours assume that the general level of all salaries is frozen at the 1968–69 level.

The percentile contours are only a description and not an explanation of salary variations within experience-age-degree-activity categories. The salary distribution for Ph.D.'s in any age group includes essentially all Ph.D.'s of that cohort nationally in economics and agricultural economics.

Quality of training and selectivity of admission policies into the Ph.D. programs of different departments have systematic effects. Many other factors affect individual salaries after the Ph.D. is completed, some potentially within the individual's control and some not. Some are potentially within the control of individuals and an enlightened university administration working together.

To a large extent, salary differences reflect what are perceived or interpreted as differences in productivity relative to the goals of the

* See Fox (1966a) for suggestions toward a more detailed analysis of the 1966 National Register data.

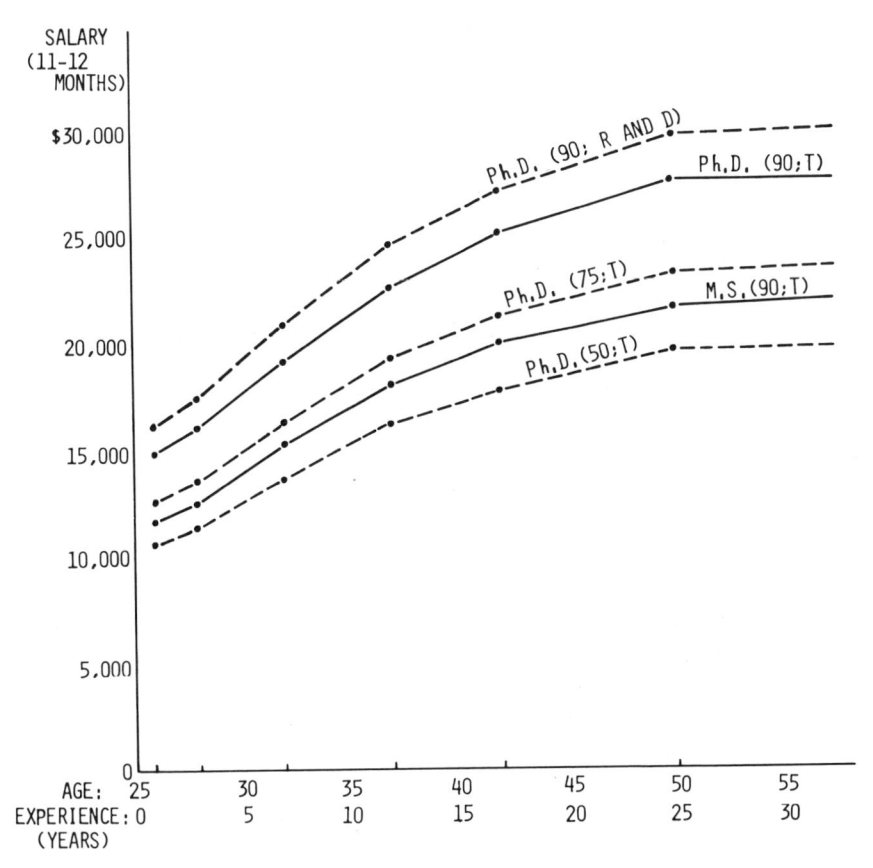

OBJECTIVE FUNCTIONS AND OPTIMIZATION MODELS    319

**Fig. 9.6. Estimated 1968–69 national salary structure for economists employed by educational institutions on an 11–12 month basis.**

institutions by which economists are employed. It is almost impossible to judge the accuracy of these perceptions unless we are prepared to measure the outputs of the activities in which economists are engaged. Some of these outputs can at least be counted (B.S., M.S., and Ph.D. degrees completed; student quarters of enrollment; pages published in specified categories of journals and conference volumes or prepared for extension and resident teaching purposes, and the like).

*Salary differentials and adjustments in the supply of scientists as between fields*

The net differentials among salaries in the various scientific fields may be viewed as a price vector with considerable potential significance (Fox 1966b):

$$\log p_t = a + B \log q_t + c \log y_t, \quad p\colon 14.1$$
$$q\colon 14.1$$
$$a\colon 14.1$$
$$c\colon 14.1$$
$$B\colon 14.14,$$

where $y$ is a vector of demand for scientists, similar to a wage fund vector in any given year; $q$ is a vector of numbers of scientists in 14 different fields or of numbers adjusted for apparent effectiveness given their distribution by age, experience, highest academic degree, and so on.

If scientists in all fields are, on the average, of equal ability, the situation in Table 9.3 should lead to a lagged supply response, so that the current inflow of new scientists to high-salaried fields would increase and the inflow to low-salaried fields would slow down:

$$\log q_{t+1} = \alpha + S \log p_t. \tag{6}$$

Equilibrium, on the equal ability assumption, would involve approximately equal salaries in all scientific fields. Part of the supply response might involve moderate shifts of emphasis by many existing scientists, with or without additional formal training.

Finally, there would be the question of equilibrium between salaries of all scientists and those of engineers, doctors, lawyers, teachers, and other professionals with M.S. and equivalent (or higher) degrees and equilibrium in the national labor market as a whole.

### Correlates of quality in graduate education

A 1969 study prepared by Lawton M. Hartman of the National Science Foundation, for the National Science Board, presents interesting evidence of the association of a number of measurable variables with subjective evaluations of the quality of graduate faculties at 106 universities in the United States. The quality measure was based on data underlying Allan M. Cartter's 1966 study.

The 106 doctorate-granting universities were, for the purposes of Chapter II ("Correlates of Quality") in the 1969 report, grouped into seven quality classes A, B, C, D, E, F, and G in descending order of the perceived quality of their graduate faculties as of April 1964. The ratings were based on the combined judgments of 4,008 respondents who had been selected by the graduate deans of the 106 universities. Each respondent rated departments in his own specialty; 29 disciplines were rated, so there was an average of about 140 respondents (department chairmen, senior scholars, and junior scholars) rating each discipline. The ratings of individual departments in each university were combined to produce an approximate quality rating for the graduate program of the university as a whole.

Most of the comparisons reported are in terms of the median value of some specified attribute among the universities in each of the seven quality classes. We have summarized twelve of these attributes and performance measures in Table 9.4. We have limited our comparisons to the top four quality classes, which comprise 70 percent of the universities in the sample under review (Hartman 1969, p. 57). Evidently, these four classes include about 74 universities. The "score or more great universities," which according to Kaysen (1969, p. 14), form the core of the higher educational system so far as science and learning are concerned, presumably include those in Class A plus, perhaps, some of those in Class B.

The twelve measures in Table 9.4 present a consistent and logical picture. The Class A institutions demonstrate a commitment to science and learning by retaining a large absolute number of full professors.

Table 9.4. Correlates of quality in graduate education in the United States: Attributes and performance measures as of 1963–64 to 1967–68

| Quality attribute or performance measure | Quality class of university's graduate faculty, 1963–64: A | B | C | D |
|---|---|---|---|---|
| 1. Years since award of first doctorate[a] | 82 | 66 | 45 | 30 |
| 2. Index of library resources[a] | over 2.00 | 1.00–1.49 | 0.75–0.99 | 0.50–0.74 |
| 3. Number of doctoral awards per year[a] | 316 | 205 | 102 | 56 |
| 4. Federal obligations for academic research and development (1,000) | $22,878 | $10,898 | $ 6,479 | $ 3,447 |
| 5. Selection of institutions by recipients of graduate fellowships (number)[b] | 362 | 62 | 26 | 10 |
| 6. Postdoctoral students in science and engineering (number)[c] | 174 | 84 | 47 | 22 |
| 7. Ratio of doctorates to baccalaureates[a] | 0.202 | 0.110 | 0.070 | 0.055 |
| 8. Graduate student-faculty ratio[d] | 4.24 | 3.64 | 3.26 | 2.64 |
| 9. Doctoral awards per graduate student[d] | 0.102 | 0.096 | 0.087 | 0.074 |
| 10. Doctoral awards per member of graduate faculty[d] | 0.429 | 0.353 | 0.283 | 0.239 |
| 11. Number of full professors[e] | 375 | 308 | 210 | 160 |
| 12. Average compensation of full professors (nine months)[f] | $18,838 | $17,616 | $16,600 | $15,200 |

Source: (Lawton M. Hartman 1969. See especially Chapter II, "Correlates of Quality," pp. 49–121.)

[a] As of 1963–64.
[b] Total, 1963–67.
[c] Fall of 1966.
[d] Fall 1966 (science and engineering).
[e] As of 1967–68.
[f] As of 1967–68 (salary plus employee benefits, adjusted to a nine-month basis).

On the average, they pay higher salaries to their full professors than do other universities. A large percentage of the most promising students (as suggested by Items 5 and 6 in Table 9.4) choose these institutions for their doctoral and postdoctoral training. The prestige of their faculties attracts large amounts of federal (and other) funds for academic research and development. Their commitment to science and learning is further reflected in their library resources. Given favorable selectivity with respect to faculty, students, research funds, and library resources, the Class A universities show favorable ratios of doctoral awards per graduate student and per member of the graduate faculty as well as large absolute numbers of doctoral awards per year.

Table 9.5, adapted from the notes to Figure 2.19 in Hartman (1969, p. 100), is based on departments rather than universities. The quality ratings of departmental graduate faculties as of April 1964 (Cartter 1966, pp. 15–16) were classed as "distinguished," "strong," "good," "adequate," and "other."

Table 9.5 shows that, on the average, "distinguished" departments had considerably larger numbers of full-time graduate faculty members (in fall 1966) than did "strong," "good," "adequate," and "other" departments, the median numbers ranging from 28.5 down to 11.0. As in most disciplines only 5 or 6 departments were rated "distinguished" and only 10 to 15 or 20 were rated "strong" in the 1966 report, it seems probable that most of the departments in these two categories are to be found among the Class A universities, as these are defined relative to Table 9.4.

Table 9.5. Number of graduate faculty members per department, fall, 1966[a]

| Quality class of departments | No. of faculty per department – Minimum | No. of faculty per department – Median | Percent of departments with more than 30 faculty members | Total no. of departments |
|---|---|---|---|---|
| Distinguished | 7 | 28.5 | 42.7 | 68 |
| Strong | 5 | 20.0 | 28.1 | 192 |
| Good | 4 | 16.0 | 9.2 | 152 |
| Adequate | 4 | 13.0 | 5.3 | 152 |
| Other | 2 | 11.0 | 0.7 | 439 |
| | | | | 1,003 |

*Source:* (Hartman 1969, p. 100.)

[a] The number of departments of each quality class in 20 disciplines combined considered as a function of the number of full-time graduate faculty members. Quality classes refer to the departmental ratings in Cartter (1966). The 20 disciplines are included among the science and engineering disciplines of the Cartter study.

OBJECTIVE FUNCTIONS AND OPTIMIZATION MODELS    323

### Some elements of practical modeling for university departments

This section is based on an actual planning activity carried out under the supervision of the editor during 1968–70. As the department involved is a large and unusually complex one, the concepts and techniques used may at least be suggestive with respect to university departments within the usual range of size and functional diversity.

*A consistency model for departmental planning*

Table 9.6, originally prepared by the editor in 1968, was designed to provide a framework for appraising the consistency of 1972–73 plans for various program areas within X-department. We will emphasize here those ideas which might be transferable to other university departments. To save space, we have omitted activities 13 through 66.

Some broad aspects of the complete Table 9.6 matrix are as follows:

1) *Coverage:* The resources required by the 68 activities in the matrix were intended to cover all regular programs of the X-department as such, including committees and public service activities, faculty development and administration, in addition to teaching, research, and extension. No allowance was made for long-term assignments of X-department faculty members as part-time directors of centers or contract programs.

The matrix was based on 1972–73 enrollment projections and rough interpretations of other department plans and needs. If part of a faculty member's time were transferred to nondepartmental assignments, some reduction in output would be sustained in the X-department as such. The matrix could help us to estimate the nature and the magnitude of the reduction in X-department outputs (a) without internal readjustment and (b) with the best internal readjustments that could be made with its remaining resources. This would provide us with a tangible basis for determining what the real costs of proposed transfers would be (to regular X-department outputs) unless compensated by planned uses of a corresponding number of dollars.

2) *Prices of outputs and inputs:* The prices of outputs were specified in simple rounded numbers. For example, we ascribed gross benefits per student quarter of $400 for freshman and sophomore courses, $800 for junior and senior courses, $1,600 for M.S. level instruction, and $3,200 for the last two years of a Ph.D. program. If we believed that the ratios were reasonable, but that the absolute level was too high or too low, we could easily shift the entire structure upward or downward by a common percentage. We could also test the implications of changing the esti-

Table 9.6. Preliminary estimates of 1972–73 output levels and input requirements for X-Department programs: Approximation I[a]

| A. OUTPUTS | | | | | | |
|---|---|---|---|---|---|---|
| Value of output per unit of activity ($1,000): | 112 | 14 | 112 | 56 | 56 | 63.2 |
| Activity level (units): | 12 | 110 | 9 | 20 | 28 | 48 |
| Activity number: | $x_1$ | $x_2$ | $x_3$ | $x_4$ | $x_5$ | $x_6$ |
| Identification: | EPL | EPS | L1I | M1I | M1I | MAB |
| 1. Ep | −280 | −35 | | | | |
| 2. EuSL | | | −140 | −70 | | |
| 3. EuSM | | | | | −70 | |
| 4. EuA | | | | | | −79 |
| 5. AdvS | | | | | | |
| 6. AdvA | | | | | | |
| 7. EgT | | | | | | |
| 8. EgS | | | | | | |
| 9. EgA | | | | | | |
| 10. Tad | | | | | | |
| 11. Et | | | | | | |
| 12. Edi | | | | | | |
| 13. MSTS | | | | | | |
| 14. MSTA | | | | | | |
| 15. DISS | | | | | | |
| 16. DISA | | | | | | |
| 17. Pub-2 | | | | | | |
| 18. Pub-1 | | | | | | |
| 19. Pub-1SO | | | | | | |
| 20. RCO | | | | | | |
| 21. GRad | | | | | | |
| 22. Ec | | | | | | |
| 23. Ea | | | | | | |
| 24. Es | | | | | | |
| 25. Eca | | | | | | |
| 26. Ecs | | | | | | |
| 27. Etr0 | | | | | | |
| 28. Pub-4 | | | | | | |
| 29. Pub-4SO | | | | | | |
| 30. Pub-3 | | | | | | |
| 31. Pub-3SO | | | | | | |
| 32. ERad | | | | | | |
| 33. Had | | | | | | |
| 34. CPS | | | | | | |
| 35. FDO | | | | | | |

mates of *relative* gross benefits resulting from different levels of instruction.

In Table 9.6, we made no allowance for variations in quality. Implicitly, a quality index of 1 was assigned to each of the 68 columns. (In more detailed submodels the editor specified 14 different patterns of instruction using faculty members, instructors, and teaching assistants in various combinations and tentatively associated explicit quality factors with each pattern.)

The prices ascribed to inputs were also simple, rounded, and impersonal. The salary pattern for 1972–73 was intended to reflect primarily a maturing of existing faculty members within the 1968–69 national salary structure. That is, the salary levels did not include estimates of

# OBJECTIVE FUNCTIONS AND OPTIMIZATION MODELS 325

| 20 | 7 | 20 | 7 | 40 | 80 | ... | 284.85 | 189.90 | | |
|---|---|---|---|---|---|---|---|---|---|---|
| 1 | 5.6 | 4 | 7.3 | 9 | 6 | ... | 1 | 1 | | |
| $x_7$ | $x_8$ | $x_9$ | $x_{10}$ | $x_{11}$ | $x_{12}$ | ... | $x_{67}$ | $x_{68}$ | | Restrictions |
| AVPS | AVIS | AVPA | AVIA | GTM | GTD | ... | CPS | FD | | |
| | | | | | | ... | | | = | −7,210 |
| | | | | | | ... | | | = | −2,660 |
| | | | | | | ... | | | = | −1,960 |
| | | | | | | ... | | | = | −3,790 |
| −50 | −35 | | | | | ... | | | = | −245 |
| | | −50 | −35 | | | ... | | | = | −455 |
| | | | | −25 | −25 | ... | | | = | −375 |
| | | | | | | ... | | | = | −660 |
| | | | | | | ... | | | = | −340 |
| | | | | | | ... | | | = | −1 |
| | | | | | | ... | | | = | −100 |
| | | | | | | ... | | | = | −400 |
| | | | | | | ... | | | = | −10 |
| | | | | | | ... | | | = | −15 |
| | | | | | | ... | | | = | −33 |
| | | | | | | ... | | | = | −17 |
| | | | | | | ... | | | = | −356.5 |
| | | | | | | ... | | | = | −44.45 |
| | | | | | | ... | | | = | −33 |
| | | | | | | ... | | | = | −42 |
| | | | | | | ... | | | = | −1 |
| | | | | | | ... | | | = | −420 |
| | | | | | | ... | | | = | −1,000 |
| | | | | | | ... | | | = | −500 |
| | | | | | | ... | | | = | −100 |
| | | | | | | ... | | | = | −100 |
| | | | | | | ... | | | = | −50 |
| | | | | | | ... | | | = | −21 |
| | | | | | | ... | | | = | −13.5 |
| | | | | | | ... | | | = | −47.7 |
| | | | | | | ... | | | = | −51.0 |
| | | | | | | ... | | | = | −1 |
| | | | | | | ... | | | = | −1 |
| | | | | | | ... | −1 | | = | −1 |
| | | | | | | ... | | −1 | = | −1 |

price inflation or of movements in the entire national salary structure for university professors between 1968 and 1972–73. In ascribing values to the time-inputs of students, extension audiences, and others outside of the university budget we used rounded figures, generally on what we believed to be the liberal side.

This feature of the matrix should perhaps be stressed: The time-inputs of students, extension audiences, and readers of department publications were explicitly listed and included in the matrix. Thus, in one calculation we could optimize X-department outputs with respect only to inputs included in the university budget. Alternatively, we could consider the implications of trying to optimize gross benefits received by undergraduate or graduate students (this would occur through increasing the

Table 9.6. (*continued*)

| B. INPUTS | | | | | | |
|---|---|---|---|---|---|---|
| Estimated cost of inputs per unit of activity ($1,000): | 62.000 | 7.672 | 59.328 | 30.688 | 30.688 | 34.151 |
| Activity levels (units): | 12 | 110 | 9 | 20 | 28 | 48 |
| Activity number: | $x_1$ | $x_2$ | $x_3$ | $x_4$ | $x_5$ | $x_6$ |
| *Identification:* | EPL | EPS | L1I | M1I | M1I | MAB |
| 1. P-2 | 0.125 | | 0.088 | 0.083 | 0.083 | |
| 2. P-1 | | | | | | 0.083 |
| 3. A-1 | | | | | | |
| 4. D-2 | | | | | | |
| 5. I-1 | | 0.083 | 0.167 | 0.083 | 0.083 | 0.099 |
| 6. T-1 | 0.500 | | | | | |
| 7. R-2 | | | | | | |
| 8. C-2 | | | | | | |
| 9. P-34 | | | | | | |
| 10. A-34 | | | | | | |
| 11. M-34 | | | | | | |
| 12. Pub-1SI | | | | | | |
| 13. RCI | | | | | | |
| 14. Pub-3SI | | | | | | |
| 15. EtrI | | | | | | |
| 16. FDI | | | | | | |
| 17. Sp | 17.500 | 2.190 | | | | |
| 18. Su | | | 8.750 | 4.380 | 4.380 | 4.940 |
| 19. Sm | | | | | | |
| 20. Sd | | | | | | |
| 21. St | | | | | | |
| 22. Sdi | | | | | | |
| 23. RPub2 | | | | | | |
| 24. RPub1 | | | | | | |
| 25. Ac | | | | | | |
| 26. Aa | | | | | | |
| 27. As | | | | | | |
| 28. Fea | | | | | | |
| 29. Fec | | | | | | |
| 30. RPub4 | | | | | | |
| 31. RPub3 | | | | | | |
| 32. ADM | | | | | | |
| 33. SCL | | | | | | |
| 34. CES | | | | | | |
| 35. CEO | | | | | | |
| 36. Sadv | | | | | | |
| 37. Pub-4SI | | | | | | |

[a] This is one of many feasible patterns and is intended only as a starting point for discussion.

average quality level of instruction in a specified number of student quarters). Similarly, we could consider the implications for budget costs and staffing patterns of trying to optimize the gross benefits received by extension audiences for a specified number of man-years of their time.

3) *Input-output coefficients:* The input-output coefficients for resident teaching activities were based upon standard department allowances. For example, teaching one three-hour course for one quarter was considered to be one-twelfth of an academic year's load for a faculty member. Thus, the figure 0.083 appears frequently in the first five input rows.

# OBJECTIVE FUNCTIONS AND OPTIMIZATION MODELS

| 15.998 | 5.499 | 15.248 | 5.499 | 21.989 | 31.987 | ... | 142.445 | 94.950 | | |
|---|---|---|---|---|---|---|---|---|---|---|
| 1 | 5.6 | 4 | 7.14 | 9 | 6 | ... | 1 | 1 | | |
| $x_7$ | $x_8$ | $x_9$ | $x_{10}$ | $x_{11}$ | $x_{12}$ | ... | $x_{67}$ | $x_{68}$ | | Restrictions |
| AVPS | AVIS | AVPA | AVIA | GTM | GTD | ... | CPS | FD | | |
| 0.250 | | | | 0.083 | 0.083 | ... | 3.370 | 2.250 | = | 33.72 |
| | | 0.250 | | | | ... | 0.820 | 0.550 | = | 8.22 |
| | | | | | | ... | | | = | 0 |
| | | | | | | ... | | | = | 15.00 |
| | 0.250 | | 0.250 | | | ... | | | = | 22.60 |
| | | | | | | ... | | | = | 6.00 |
| | | | | | | ... | | | = | 50.00 |
| | | | | | | ... | | | = | 33.50 |
| | | | | | | ... | 1.810 | 1.200 | = | 18.05 |
| | | | | | | ... | | | = | 0 |
| | | | | | | ... | | | = | 3.50 |
| | | | | | | ... | | | = | 33 |
| | | | | | | ... | | | = | 42 |
| | | | | | | ... | | | = | 51 |
| | | | | | | ... | | | = | 4.17 |
| | | | | | | ... | | | = | 4.00 |
| | | | | | | ... | | | = | 450.62 |
| | | | | | | ... | | | = | 525.63 |
| | | | | 2.083 | | ... | | | = | 65.58 |
| | | | | | 2.083 | ... | | | = | 49.00 |
| | | | | | | ... | | | = | 4.17[a] |
| | | | | | | ... | | | = | 16.67[a] |
| | | | | | | ... | | | | 44.56 |
| | | | | | | ... | | | = | 5.56 |
| | | | | | | ... | | | = | 26.25 |
| | | | | | | ... | | | = | 83.33 |
| | | | | | | ... | | | = | 41.67 |
| | | | | | | ... | | | = | 4.17 |
| | | | | | | ... | | | ≥ | 0 |
| | | | | | | ... | | | = | 2.62 |
| | | | | | | ... | | | = | 5.96 |
| | | | | | | ... | | | = | 1 |
| | | | | | | ... | | | ≤ | 30.00 |
| | | | | | | ... | | | ≤ | 140.00 |
| | | | | | | ... | | | ≤ | 260.00 |
| 2.083 | 0.729 | 2.083 | 0.729 | | | ... | | | = | 4.46 |
| | | | | | | ... | | | = | 13.5 |

4) *Intermediate goods:* An interesting and potentially useful feature of the attached matrix is its inclusion of several "intermediate goods." For example, one intermediate good is the value of the training gained by experience as a research assistant, the pay-off coming in terms of increased research output per man-year when the former research assistant becomes a dissertation-stage research associate. Also, the outputs of research conducted as a basis for extension programs are listed as "publications" outputs of one set of research activities and included as inputs in a corresponding set of extension activities.

We will now identify the various outputs, inputs, and activities and their units of measure and comment briefly on some of them.

A. *Outputs.* There are 35 outputs listed in Table 9.6. The minus signs in front of the outputs, such as −280 student quarters of instruction in a large sophomore lecture group, indicate that the outputs are moving out of the production activities. The inputs have positive signs, as they are moving into the production activities.

Outputs 1–21 are products of the resident instruction program and of research conducted in conjunction with graduate training and the preparation of M.S. theses and doctoral dissertations.

The nature of these outputs can best be seen by looking at the numbers on the right-hand side of the equality signs. Thus, the figure at the top of this column, −7,210, represents an enrollment projection of 7,210 student quarters of instruction in the basic sophomore course in 1972–73.

Rows 2, 3, and 4 are estimated student quarters of instruction in three categories of undergraduate courses. Rows 5 and 6 imply, as of 1972–73, 245 undergraduate majors in Curriculum $S$ and 455 in Curriculum A. Rows 7, 8, and 9 are student quarters of three categories of graduate level course work. Row 10, one unit of teaching administration, claims the 0.500 man-years of faculty time assigned to this function. Rows 11 and 12 are expressed as student quarters, allowing 4 student quarters of credit for a Master's thesis and 8 student quarters of credit for a doctoral dissertation. Rows 13, 14, 15, and 16 are in terms of numbers of Master's theses and doctoral dissertations completed during the year.

Rows 17, 18, and 19 are in terms of publication units. This is a concoction of our own; the empirical basis for it is not nearly as clear as that for the resident teaching outputs. Provisionally, we defined a "publication unit" as twenty double-spaced manuscript pages or twelve printed pages of material of the appropriate professional kind and level. Row 17, Publication-2, signifies publication or communication at the intellectual level usually associated with professional journal articles, advanced research monographs, and graduate level textbooks. Thus, a 600-page graduate level textbook would be assigned 50 publication units; a 12-page article in an appropriate professional journal would count as 1 publication unit. We would include presentations made at national professional association meetings in our concept of publication, whether or not the presentation subsequently appeared in print.

Row 18 would include publication useful primarily in connection with undergraduate teaching. Row 19 would represent undergraduate teaching materials which are fed back into the undergraduate teaching program in X-department.

Row 20 is measured in terms of units of training of research assistants, with one year of experience as a half-time research assistant counting as one unit. This training output reappears as an input in activities which involve dissertation-stage research associates who have had previous experience as research assistants. Row 21 is graduate program administration.

Rows 22 through 26 deal with outputs of the extension program; the factual basis for these figures as of 1968 was very weak. In concept, Rows 22, 23, and 24 are expressed in units *equivalent to* student quarters of enrollment in resident instruction. Row 22 represents instruction given to "county level" extension audiences, to which we ascribe gross benefits per student quarter of $800, the same as for senior undergraduate teaching in the resident program. Row 23 represents multicounty area level extension audiences, with gross benefits per student quarter estimated at $1,600, the same as for Master's level teaching in the resident program. Row 23 is concerned with state level extension audiences, with gross benefits ascribed at $3,200 per student quarter, the same as in the final two years of a Ph.D. program.

Row 25 is in student quarters, and reflects consultation and discussion with small groups of multicounty area level leaders; Row 26 reflects similar consultation and discussion with small groups (say, three to ten persons) of state level leaders. The gross benefits and the inputs ascribed to these small-group consulting and discussion activities are equivalent to those associated with M.S. (area level) and Ph.D. (state level) seminars conducted for groups of seven graduate students.

Row 27 represents the outputs of training given by extension faculty members to multicounty area extension specialists; the output is measured in terms of student quarters and priced at $3,200 per student quarter, the same as three hours of resident instruction credit in the final two years of a Ph.D. program.

Rows 28, 29, 30, and 31 are in terms of publication units. Rows 28 and 29 are extension publications and Rows 30 and 31 are state-oriented research publications. Row 29 produces an intermediate good (for example, material prepared by extension faculty members in fairly rough form for use by area extension specialists in their teaching presentations). Row 31 represents the results of research conducted for extension use; the research outputs may be in rather rough form so far as write-up is concerned, and final publication could take the form of oral presentations and/or write-ups designed for specific extension audiences.

Row 32 is administration of extension and state-oriented research programs, and Row 33 is the administrative contribution of the department head across the entire department. Row 34 is committees and public service, and Row 35 is faculty development (faculty improvement leaves and the like).

B. *Inputs.* The inputs can also be best described in terms of the totals on the right-hand side of the equality signs in Table 9.6. In the great majority of cases the inputs are measured in terms of man-years. The exceptions are Rows 12, 14, and 37, which are measured in publication units, Row 13 which is measured in units of one year's experience by research assistants prior to their becoming research associates at dissertation stage, and Rows 34 and 35, which are measured in thousands of dollars of current expense funds.

Rows 1–11 are concerned with faculty members, instructors and research associates, teaching and research assistants, and related personnel. Row 1 consists of full professors in teaching and research who are full members of the graduate faculty. Row 2 includes full professors in teaching and research who are not full members of the graduate faculty. The full professors represented in both Row 1 and Row 2 are concerned with the resident teaching program and with research which is complementary with the training of M.S. and Ph.D. candidates at thesis and dissertation stages.

Row 3 is essentially an associate professor category in terms of the ascribed salary level. Row 4 includes postdoctorals and/or temporary assistant professors; the assumed salary is at the beginning assistant professor or new Ph.D. level.

Row 5 consists of instructors who are also graduate students, and Row 6 consists of teaching assistants.

Row 7 includes dissertation-stage research associates. Row 8 includes research assistants who may be working toward M.S. degrees or simply serving as research assistants during one or more of the first two or three years of their Ph.D. programs.

Row 9 includes full professors involved in extension and state-oriented research. Row 10 includes associate professors (and others, perhaps, on a similar salary level) who are engaged in extension or complementary research (in contrast with Row 3, which refers to associate professors or persons of similar salary primarily engaged in resident instruction). Row 11 includes temporary extension and state-oriented research associates who are not working toward doctoral degrees but have completed Master's degrees.

Rows 12, 14, and 37 are "publications" in the sense of research results or rough research manuscripts which are intended for use in the extension program, in resident instruction, or in presentations to appropriate groups in the state.

Rows 13, 15, and 16 are all conceptually similar. With respect to Row 12, if a research project includes a research associate who has had previous experience as a research assistant, we assume that the research output is $5,000, or one publication unit, larger than if the research associate has had no previous training as a research assistant. (This training could be in the form of summer appointments as research assistants for graduate students who serve as teaching assistants or instructors during the academic year.)

In Row 15, the training given to multicounty area extension specialists by the X-department faculty is treated as an input.

Row 16 treats the man-years of faculty development activities as feeding back into the directly productive activities of the department.

Rows 17 through 22 describe student inputs. The students in Rows 17 and 18 are undergraduates; as 16 three-credit-hour courses per year are required to graduate in four years, we assume that each undergraduate student applies one-sixteenth of a man-year to a three-hour course. On this basis, the student inputs associated with the basic sophomore course in 1972–73 would be approximately 450 man-years, and the student inputs associated with other undergraduate courses would be around 525 man-years.

In Rows 19 and 20, we assume that a graduate student allocates one-twelfth of a man-year to each of his three-hour courses, as 12 such courses represent the maximum he is permitted to take during an academic year even if he does not have obligations as a teaching or research assistant or associate.

Rows 21 and 22 are thesis and dissertation credits converted into equivalent student quarters of course work and thence into graduate student man-years.

Rows 23, 24, 30, and 31 represent a concept that we have not seen elsewhere, though others may indeed have used similar concepts with more sophistication and empirical support.

Row 23 involves the time, in man-years, spent by readers of publications in the forms of professional journal articles, research monographs and graduate textbooks. We believe that few professional journals in X-discipline have more than 5,000 subscribers. If 10 percent of the subscribers, or 500 persons, spend an average of 30 minutes reading a particular 12-page article, the time thus spent amounts to 250-man hours or one-eighth of a man-year. The relationship between author and reader is thus regarded as a teacher and student (or lecturer and audience) relationship, with teacher and student (or lecturer and audience) separated from one another in time and space. If a faculty member delivers a 30-minute paper to an audience of 500 colleagues at a professional meeting, the audience collectively invests 250 man-hours (one-eighth of a man-year) on the receiving end of the speech or paper; we would regard this transaction as one publication unit.

We believe the idea of using time as an input will help to dispel some of the vagueness and even mysticism which stands in the way of ascribing values to the outputs of research.

Some other rough estimates may serve to indicate that the potential readership of professional publications is finite and quite possibly measurable. There are about 12,000 members of X-discipline listed in the 1966 National Register of Scientific and Technical Personnel. These people have received questionnaires to fill out, based on their subscriptions to professional journals, their memberships in national professional associations, and so on, and the returned questionnaires have also been screened by representatives of the relevant national professional association to see, so far as possible, that they have had formal training at the M.S. level or higher in X-discipline or have had equivalent experience.

Of the approximately 12,000 professionals in X-discipline under this definition, we believe roughly half, or 6,000, are employed in educational institutions and the remainder in government and industry. If graduate level teachers spent 20 percent of their time reading graduate level material and if the undergraduate teachers, government, and industry members spent an average of 5 percent of their time reading such material, the total would come to about 800 man-years.

We do not have figures at hand on the number of graduate students currently enrolled in X-discipline and closely related applied fields, but we believe that 12,000 would be a liberal estimate. If these assumed 12,000 graduate students spent half of their time reading graduate level material, the readership would amount to 6,000 man-years, or several times as large as the number of man-years we assumed for the professionals who are no longer engaged in graduate work.

Applying our conversion factor of 0.125 man-years of readers' time per publication unit, the reading capacity of 12,000 professionals and 12,000 graduate students would be on the order of 54,000 publication units. The particular activity levels used in the 1972–73 matrix would result in about 350 graduate level publication units per year from X-department. This would amount to about 0.65 percent of the total annual reading capacity of the assumed audiences.

Some well-known graduate textbooks have a much larger readership than the 500 used in our definition of a publication unit; on the other hand, some highly specialized articles and reports may have a smaller readership. At this point we can only open a discussion and make no attempt to close it.

Rows 25 through 27 are in terms of man-years of extension audiences, including small discussion groups and informal consultations with area level and state level leaders. To the extent that extension activities involve teacher and student relationships, it seems reasonable to assume about the same level of gross benefit per equivalent student quarter as in the resident teaching program. We have estimated the opportunity cost of the time of extension audiences at a considerably higher level than for resident students, and we have assumed that area level and state level audiences use up a significant amount of time getting to and from the meeting places.

Rows 33–35 include secretarial and clerical time in man-years, current expense funds from state sources, and current expense funds from other sources which are used in supporting the 68 activities provided in the matrix.

Row 36, time spent by students in connection with the undergraduate advising program for B.A. and B.S. majors, cannot be valued only at the number of hours the student spends talking with his advisor. Presumably, the conversations between student and advisor center on problems which are unusually important to the student.

One way of looking at this activity is as follows: We ascribe an average gross benefit per undergraduate course of $600 per student quarter over the four years of a B.A. or B.S. program; 64 three-hour courses times $600 is $38,400. If we ascribe a gross benefit of $400 per year for four years to the counsel received by a student from a regular faculty advisor, the gross benefit of this activity for four years is $1,600. If we add this to the gross benefits from classroom instruction, we have a total of $40,000, of which 96 percent is ascribed to course work and 4 percent is ascribed to the advising function. This 4 percent might be thought of as a management or consulting cost for helping the student to manage his academic affairs.

C. *Prices of outputs and inputs.* There is no point in reproducing the assumed prices of outputs and inputs, as Table 9.6 contains only a few of the activities in which these 72 prices appear. We have already indicated the principles on the basis of which these prices were selected.

The prices assigned to career income benefits per student quarter in the resident instruction program are reasonably well in line with the values of the expected increases in 39-year income streams capitalized into present values at an interest rate of 5 percent, as shown in Table 9.7.

Table 9.7. Some implications of the gross benefit figures per student quarter ascribed to the resident instruction program

A. Income streams implied by the gross benefit figures

| Level and kind of resident program | (1) Gross benefit ascribed per student quarter | (2) Number of courses (3 credit hours) | (3) Total gross benefit ascribed | (4) Equivalent income stream (39 years, capitalized at 5 percent)[a] |
|---|---|---|---|---|
| 1. Freshman–sophomore courses (required) | $ 400 | 32 | $12,800 | $ 750 |
| 2. Junior–senior courses (elective) | 800 | 32 | 25,600 | 1,500 |
| 3. M.S. courses, M.S. thesis credits (12 hours), and first 54 credits of Ph.D. programs | 1,600 | 18 | 28,800 | 1,700 |
| 4. Last 54 credits of Ph.D. program, including 24 hours for dissertation | 3,200 | 18 | 57,600 | 3,400 |

B. Multiple regression estimates of 1968–69 average salaries of U.S. economists in 1966 National Register (all ages and kinds of employer, etc.).[b]

Percentile rank in income distribution

| | 50 | 75 |
|---|---|---|
| Ph.D. | $17,300 | $20,500 |
| M.S. | 14,000 | 16,300 |
| B.S. | 13,300 | 15,300 |

[a] We are interested here only in rough estimates and do not bother to vary the lengths of the income streams or the level of the discount rate.
[b] Based on analysis by Melichar (1968) with projections and elaborations by Fox.

They are at least in the same ball park with the estimates of T. W. Schultz (1963), Gary Becker (1964) and others. The teaching and learning components of the extension program, it seems to us, might reasonably be estimated on a similar basis.

D. *The nature of the activity levels, total output, and total input estimates in the matrix.* Table 9.6 is laid out in activity analysis form. However, the activity levels at the tops of the columns (immediately above the $X_i$'s) simply represent judgment estimates on the editor's part to get an initial rough balance between outputs and inputs. For example, given our estimate of 7,210 student quarters of enrollment in the basic sophomore course in 1972–73, we assumed a reasonable number of large lectures, namely 12, and added enough sections of 35 students taught by instructors to account for the rest of the 7,210 student quarters. Similarly, we assigned the 25 M.S. theses per year to a limited number of reasonable and relatively efficient looking activities for this purpose, and so on.

As of 1968, X-department had about 50 man-years of faculty time budgeted, with approximately 30 full professors, 15 associate professors, and 5 assistant professors. The inputs in the 1972–73 matrix include 60 man-years of faculty time, all at the full professor rank (Rows 1, 2, and 9). The increase in faculty man-years was predicated largely on a projected increase of 25 percent or so in university enrollment from 1968–69 to 1972–73.

The assumption of 60 full professors in 1972–73 was intended more as a challenge than as a forecast. The challenge was, could a department consisting of 60 full professors with correspondingly high average salaries operate so efficiently and creatively as to justify its staffing pattern in terms of productivity and hence costs per unit of output, both quantity and quality considered? By adding some alternative activities to the 68 in the present matrix, we could at least check our judgments as to whether lower costs per unit (quality considered) could be achieved by reducing the number of full professors and increasing the number of associate professors (Rows 3 and 10) on a continuing basis. Inadvertently, we provided no activity in this matrix which used postdoctorals or temporary assistant professors partly in the teaching program. Some postdoctoral time might well be used in the teaching program as a substitute for either professorial or instructor inputs.

The Table 9.6 matrix has the virtues of specificity, reproducibility, and comprehensiveness as compared with the specialized reports which were also prepared for particular segments of X-department's activities, such as undergraduate teaching, extension, graduate programs, and research. Also, complementarities among the various programs can be identified and (within reasonable limits) estimated with the help of the matrix.

The activity mix shown in Table 9.6 results in estimated total gross benefits of approximately $23,000,000 a year for the 68 activities listed in the matrix (some of these are used at zero levels). Nearly $10,000,000 would be ascribed to the outputs of the undergraduate teaching and advising programs (Rows 1 through 6 in the output matrix). Somewhat less than $8,000,000 of gross benefits would be ascribed to the graduate programs and complementary research and publication. About $5,-000,000 of gross benefits would be ascribed to the extension and state-oriented research programs, and about $500,000 to other activities (department, college, and university committees; professional association

Table 9.8. Component $S$ of X-department: Planned activities and budget restrictions for 1970–71

| Value per unit ($1,000): | 112 | 14 | 52 | 27.2 | 54.4 | 96 | 72 | 48 | 36 | 24 |
|---|---|---|---|---|---|---|---|---|---|---|
| Level: | 8 | 94 | 9 | 34 | 29 | 8 | 6 | 10 | 6 | 11 |
| Activity no.: | $X_1$ | $X_2$ | $X_3$ | $X_4$ | $X_5$ | $X_6$ | $X_7$ | $X_8$ | $X_9$ | $X_{10}$ |
| A. OUTPUTS | | | | | | | | | | |
| 1. Ep | −280 | −35 | −130 | | | | | | | |
| 2. Eu | | | | −34 | −68 | | | | | |
| 3. Eg | | | | | | −40 | −30 | −20 | −15 | −10 |
| 4. GSY | | | | | | | | | | |
| 5. Adv | | | | | | | | | | |
| 6. Admin | | | | | | | | | | |
| 7. EcComm | | | | | | | | | | |
| 8. NPAssoc | | | | | | | | | | |
| 9. PRtr | | | | | | | | | | |
| 10. Pub | | | | | | | | | | |
| B. INPUTS (man-years)[a] | | | | | | | | | | |
| 1. P | 0.125 | | 0.083 | 0.083 | 0.083 | 0.083 | .083 | .083 | .083 | .083 |
| 2. I | | 0.083 | | | | | | | | |
| 3. T | 0.500 | | 0.167 | | 0.083 | | | | | |
| 4. E | 0.125 | 0.0042 | 0.05 | 0.0042 | 0.0083 | .04 | 0.03 | 0.02 | 0.015 | 0.01 |
| 5. AA | | | | | | | | | | |

[a] Nine months (September 1 through May 31).

activities; advisory committees, etc.; formal and informal faculty development activities; and the administrative input of the department head).

It should be emphasized that the inputs required to produce the estimated $23,000,000 of gross benefits are not limited to items in the university budget. They also include about 1,000 man-years of the time of undergraduate students and several hundred man-years of the time of graduate students, extension audiences, and readers of the department's research and extension publications.

*A model for short-term (year-to-year) planning*

Table 9.8 relates to a major component of X-department for a specified academic year. The symbols are similar in meaning to those in Table 9.6. However, all professorial ranks have been combined (input Row 1).

A. *Activities, inputs and outputs.* Activities 1, 2, and 3 are different patterns of instruction used in the basic sophomore course, which is taken by a large proportion of all students in the university. Activities 4 and 5 are alternatives used in junior and senior level courses. Activities 6, 7, 8, 9, and 10 are graduate courses, grouped according to expected enrollments. Activity 11 includes supervision of graduate student theses and dissertations and related consultations and examinations. Activity 12 is academic advising of undergraduate majors. Activity 13 is administration; Activity 14 is committee work at department, college, and university levels; and Activity 15 is time spent on national professional association activities.

OBJECTIVE FUNCTIONS AND OPTIMIZATION MODELS 337

| 8.9 | 0.5 | 76 | 35 | 26.5 | 0 | 0 | 0 | 5 | 5 | 5 | | |
|---|---|---|---|---|---|---|---|---|---|---|---|---|
| 90 | 130 | 1 | 1 | 1 | 2.142 | 1.033 | 0.459 | 16 | 16 | 4.91 | | |
| $X_{11}$ | $X_{12}$ | $X_{13}$ | $X_{14}$ | $X_{15}$ | $X_{16}$ | $X_{17}$ | $X_{18}$ | $X_{19}$ | $X_{20}$ | $X_{21}$ | | |
| | | | | | | | | | | | = | −6,700 |
| | | | | | | | | | | | = | −3,128 |
| | | | | | | | | | | | = | −900 |
| −1 | | | | | | | | | | | = | −90 |
| | −1 | | | | | | | | | | = | −130 |
| | | −1 | | | | | | | | | = | −1 |
| | | | −1 | | | | | | | | = | −1 |
| | | | | −1 | | | | | | | = | −1 |
| | | | | | −1 | −1 | −1 | | | | ≥ | −3.634 |
| | | | | | | | | −1 | −1 | −1 | ≤ | 0 |
| .0244 | | 1.30 | 0.90 | 0.67 | 1.00 | 1.00 | 1.00 | 0.111 | 0.222 | 0.333 | ≤ | 22.45 |
| | .0050 | | | | −2.325 | | | | | | ≥ | 3.50 |
| | | | | | | −2.894 | | | | | ≥ | 4.93 |
| .0122 | .0025 | 1.95 | 0.15 | 0.167 | | | −3.957 | 0.02 | 0.03 | 0.04 | ≥ | 6.00 |
| | | 0.30 | | | | | | | | | ≤ | 0.30 |

Activities 16, 17, and 18 reflect the use of a particular budgetary technique. The positions budgeted for this component of X-department are indicated by the input vector in the extreme right-hand column. However, the established instructional pattern requires more instructors (I) and teaching assistants (T) and fewer man-years of professorial time (P) than are budgeted. As some professors are on leaves of absence or on contract programs in any given year, salary savings from these positions are converted into the required junior (I and T) positions. The coefficients in input Rows 2, 3, and 4 of Activities 16, 17, and 18 represent the numbers of man-years of instructor, teaching assistant, and secretarial time respectively which could be purchased (on the average) with one man-year of salary savings from the professorial ranks. Activities 19, 20, and 21 are faculty research activities. Research grants and contracts are not included in Table 9.8; in practice, much of the faculty time used in these activities is combined with that of research assistants and associates.

The outputs include 6,700 student quarters of the basic sophomore course; 3,128 student quarters of junior and senior courses; 900 student quarters of graduate courses or seminars; the thesis and dissertation outputs per year of 90 graduate students; the academic advising of 130 undergraduate majors; prespecified contributions to administration, committee work, and national professional association activities; the release of not more than 3.634 man-years of professorial time; and an unspecified number of publication units. Most of the output restrictions must hold with equality, as they represent close estimates of actual student demands for courses in the year immediately ahead.

B. *Special features of the model.* The activities in Table 9.8 are clustered for administrative purposes as follows:

I. Activities 1, 2, 3: Basic sophomore course
II. Activities 4, 5, 12: Other undergraduate teaching and advising
III. Activities 6, 7, 8, 9, 10, 11: Graduate teaching and advising
IV. Activities 13, 14, 15: Administration, committee work, and national professional association activities
V. Activities 19, 20, 21: Faculty research
VI. Activities 16, 17, 18: Resource transfer activities

The dollar values attributed to the particular output mix shown in Table 9.8 are as follows:

| | |
|---|---|
| Group I: | $2,680,000 |
| Group II: | 2,567,000 |
| Group III: | 2,961,000 |
| Group IV: | 137,500 |
| Group V: | 184,550 |
| Group VI: | 0 |
| Total: | $8,530,050 |

The same output prices are used in these calculations as in Table 9.6.

The use of dollar values supplies a common unit of account for the different programs and reminds those with co-ordinating responsibility of the approximate magnitudes of the potential gains to students which are at stake.

The Group I co-ordinator can then attempt more refined estimates of the output values of alternative patterns of instruction, run experimental sections to get student feedback, and generally try to maximize the student gain from any specified dollar value of budget resources. The dollar estimates are not a substitute for intuition and should not inhibit creative innovation. They should, however, help to keep expectations within reasonable bounds and to limit the duration of faculty arguments about the merits of alternative patterns of instruction which (when tested) do not show significantly different outcomes.

The co-ordinator for Group II has opportunities for feedback from undergraduate majors in X-discipline, from nonmajors, and from colleagues. The co-ordinator for Group III has similar opportunities for feedback from graduate students and colleagues. In these areas, too, the dollar estimates should encourage introspection and small-scale experiments to estimate the quantitative importance of proposed changes.

To some extent, the co-ordinators of Groups I, II, and III are rival claimants for the same resources. However, if they all have current involvements with, or past experience in, all three levels of teaching, their interactions should lead toward a near-optimal allocation of total resources among the three levels.

Another device for encouraging balance between graduate and undergraduate programs is the use of much more detailed models of subdepartments, such as the Y-subdepartment shown in Table 6.1. With such submodels, the two or three faculty members identified with a special field can explore the implications of changes in the instructional pattern of any course, the addition of a course, an increase in enrollment in any course, or a change in the number of graduate students writing dissertations in the field.

The process of revising the university curriculum every two years should in principle result in a general equilibrium solution for the teaching programs of the entire university, subject to traditional, inertial, or imposed constraints. The use of quantitative models within some departments as adjuncts to their curriculum discussions should improve the efficiency of the process even if it did not change the "negotiated equilibrium" for the university as a whole.

C. *Some estimates for other components of X-department.* In the same year to which Table 9.8 relates, dollar output estimates for some other groups of activities in X-department were as follows:

| | | |
|---|---|---:|
| Group VII. | Other undergraduate programs: | $2,265,000 |
| Group VIII. | Other graduate programs: | 1,593,000 |
| Group IX. | Extension programs: | 5,127,000 |
| | Subtotal: | $8,985,000 |

These figures do not include administration, committee work, or national professional association activities. The same principles and kinds of submodels may be applied to Groups VII and VIII as to Groups I, II, and III. Within Group IX there are a number of special fields, each engaging the primary attention of two or three faculty members. Each field can be programmed as a set of elements comparable to resident courses or to subunits within courses. Dollar estimates can help to sharpen judgments concerning allocation of time and effort both within and between extension fields.

We did not try to estimate the volume and value of expected research outputs in this exercise.

CHAPTER 10

# The Areas of Potential Application

*Karl A. Fox*

Educational systems exist to help people prepare themselves for the roles they aspire to play in society and to improve their performance in the roles they are actually playing. At any given time in a society, a certain array of roles is being performed and a certain array of rewards is being received by the persons performing them. The joint array of role-and-reward pairs may be regarded as points of intersection of a set of demand functions for roles to be performed and a set of supply functions for persons ("personalities") willing and able to perform them. This is a generalization of the situation prevailing in the labor market, in which the roles to be performed are jobs and the persons willing and able to perform them are workers. Jobs are one subset (a very important one) of the set of roles.

Schools are not the only settings in which roles are learned; furthermore, the roles performed by students are a subset of the set of roles. The time-flow encompassed by the complete set of roles is 24 hours a day for all members of the society.

Thus, educational systems are integral components of the society; their outputs are part of the total output of the society; and the values of their outputs are determined as part of the general reward system of the society, which includes prestige, power, and other noneconomic media in addition to money income.

### Extending economic analysis to nonmarket systems

As economists, we have quite properly tried to extend and adapt economic theory to the resource allocation problems of educational institutions. Where market prices in the conventional sense are not available, we have suggested that relative weights assigned to units of various outputs by the administrators of, say, a university may substitute for a pricing system; if so, well-known techniques can be used to compute an allocation of resources within the university which is optimal under the specified weighting scheme.

It is possible to conceive of an economic system which operated without prices. The gross product would be allocated exhaustively among the actors; housing could be assigned and bundles of consumer goods delivered on the basis of rank, occupation, family size, party loyalty, or any other criteria whatsoever. A person might conclude that his neighbor had received a larger share than his own; without a pricing system for final goods, he could not begin to say how much larger. Or, he might conclude that his neighbor had received more than he (the neighbor) deserved; without a pricing system for factors of production as well as for final goods he could not begin to say how much more.

We find ourselves similarly inhibited at times in describing the production processes that take place in an educational institution. There is need for a terminology that will encompass noneconomic as well as economic inputs and outputs not only of educational systems but of all other organizations and systems in a society.

The concept of exchange or reciprocity permeates all social relations. At the micro level, Berne's *transactional analysis* (1961, 1964) offers an approach to describing (and possibly to quantifying) exchanges between persons. Roger Barker's concept of *behavior settings* (1968) provides an exhaustive spatial-temporal framework for recording and describing human behavior. His terminology has been developed particularly for public behavior settings (stores, school classes, meetings of voluntary organizations, restaurants, plays, athletic events, and the like) rather than for home and family situations.

The level of activity in any particular behavior setting (e.g., a university economics class) is kept within fairly narrow limits by homeostatic forces of various kinds. If the students spend more time on homework for this class they must spend less time on other classes or on outside activities. If the professor spends more time preparing for this class he must spend less time on other professional or nonprofessional activities. The awareness of opportunity cost seems to permeate decisions on class attendance and preparation; the most limiting resource is time.

The output of a classroom behavior setting involving a professor and some students can be increased by using a given amount of time more productively or by investing a larger amount of time. The university as a whole is a general equilibrium system in which each actor allocates his time among behavior settings in such a way as to equalize its marginal value product (as he perceives it) in the different settings.

Talcott Parsons (1968) states that each person experiences the outputs he receives from the social system as *rewards* and the inputs he provides to the social system as *contributions*. By an extension of economic theory, each person may be viewed as contributing up to the point at which the diminishing marginal utility of further rewards is equal to the (increasing) marginal disutility of further contributions.* For the society as a whole, total rewards equal total contributions, just as gross national income equals gross national product. The gross social product includes the gross economic product and a great deal more besides.

Considerable experimentation will be necessary to arrive at convincing definitions of the various nonmonetary rewards and plausible measures of the implicit exchange rates between them and money. The logical outcome would be a measure of gross social product (GSP) in equivalent dollar terms. (Dollars would be used as a unit of account, with no implications as to the importance of money as an object of human endeavor).

An explicit set of exchange rates relating nonmonetary to monetary rewards would permit us to treat economic and noneconomic outputs of, say, a university symmetrically in objective functions and to generate shadow prices for university resources in dollar terms. In their absence, the actual allocations of budget and nonbudget resources among alternative activities provide implicit evidence of the value systems of the decisionmakers involved.

### Optimization models at many levels

Although glamor may attach to models of whole universities and of national educational systems, the optimizing approach may prove to be most valuable at department and subdepartment levels. Some modest but highly promising applications would include:

1) small-scale activity analysis models to aid choices between alternative class sizes and staffing patterns for a large service course or for the upper division program of a department; and

2) models of subdepartments consisting of two or three faculty members devoted primarily to undergraduate and graduate teaching and research in a special field, to clarify the implications of alternative class

---

* This extension has been made explicitly by the editor; see Chapter 9 of Sengupta and Fox (1969).

sizes, staffing patterns, schedules, and teaching loads for the courses in that field (see, for example, the model of Y-subdepartment presented in Chapter 6).

These models should focus considerable attention on the problem of measuring the quality (i.e., value of output per student quarter) of instruction under different class sizes and staffing patterns. Such attention might disclose means by which the performance of a faculty member could be improved relatively more in one class size than in another, thus changing the initial prices attributed to alternative activities and perhaps changing the optimal solution. Sensitivity analysis could be applied to determine the effects upon the optimal solution of changing the relative prices of different outputs or of changing the quantities of particular categories of personnel assigned to a subdepartment.

The objective function and constraints applied to small-scale models could be varied in a more fundamental sense. In a subdepartment, for example, what would be the optimal allocation of faculty and other budget resources from the standpoint of (a) undergraduates only; (b) graduate students only; and (c) faculty members only? Could a "community objective function" be specified which would give appropriate weights to the interests of the three groups? The questions raised by these small-scale models are replicated in many departments and many universities; the answers should have considerable transferability from one unit to another.

An advantage of the very small-scale models is that they can be used in a participatory manner by small groups of faculty members and students. The reasonableness of the optimal solutions can be checked to some extent by direct reasoning or by side calculations with pencil and paper. The sensitivity analyses would have common-sense interpretations (e.g., what differences in the means and distributions of test scores of students in different-sized classes would be accepted as evidence that the quality of instruction was significantly affected by class size?).

Optimization models of entire departments of moderate size and complexity might also be used in a participatory context. Models of the entire graduate program of a department might be illuminating for both faculty and graduate students, and the probable consequences of modifying various requirements could be studied by, and for the benefit of, both groups. Undergraduate majors could react constructively to proposed modifications in class sizes and staffing patterns in the upper division program. The question of balance between graduate, upper division, and lower division teaching and research might then be left to faculty and administrative judgment.

*The resolving power of optimization models*

Activity analysis models of two subdepartments within a department should put to the test our quantitative knowledge concerning each element in the comparison. For example, what evidence is required to justify a more expensive pattern of instruction (in terms of budget resources) in one subdepartment than in another?

The same question could be posed concerning models of two departments: What evidence is required to justify a smaller number of student credit hours per man-year or per budget dollar in one than in another? Is the full difference justified by a difference in the distribution of total credit hours by levels of instruction? Is the dean justified in withdrawing a position from one department on the grounds that its resources are underemployed?

After considerable experience with such models, the administrators of a university might arrive at reasonable workload factors for various activities and levels of instruction which would account for, say, 80 percent of the variance among its nationally recognized departments with respect to student credit hours per full-time instructor and/or per dollar of instructional salaries. What are the components of the remaining 20 percent of the variance? Would attempts at "finer tuning" undermine morale and suppress differences in departmental style that are inherently productive? Does the apparent overemphasis of graduate training in one department signal the presence of an incipient Nobel laureate? It is possible that "80 percent of variance explained" represents an optimal degree of quality control for that set of departments. The same set of workload factors by levels of instruction applied to other departments on the campus might, however, lead to better quality control, with marked improvements in staffing patterns, curricula, and teaching performance.

*Optimization models at college and university levels*

McCamley's model (1967) of three department chairmen interacting with a dean to arrive at an optimal allocation of the dean's "central" resources expresses the logic of budget negotiations at this level. The same model and logic evidently apply to budget negotiations between college deans and the university president. The president is responsible for allocating the resources of the university in an optimal manner within the limits of his perception, judgment, and influence.

If the same pricing system is recognized by president, deans, and chairmen, each administrator can use his steering capacity to approximate a near optimal response to the same set of price signals. The market analogy is obvious.

**Concluding remarks**

Chapters 2 through 7 repeatedly demonstrate the importance of decomposition techniques for resource allocation in nonmarket institutions. As economists, we have a preference for price-guided allocation procedures whenever possible. For nonmarket institutions at present, some (perhaps all) of the required prices may have to be based on the subjective judgments of their key administrators. Similar subjective prices and barter terms of trade between policy targets have been used effectively to clarify the implications of alternative economic stabilization policies; for this reason, Jan Tinbergen's theory of economic policy provides a useful introduction to the problem of objective functions and optimization models for nonmarket institutions.

Computational techniques are available for implementing many different kinds of optimization models of universities and their subdivisions. Experimentation with such models will be instructive to university policymakers, even if the objective function weights or prices are supplied somewhat arbitrarily by the policymakers themselves. However, the usefulness of optimization models for communication between officials of different universities or between university officials and regents, legislators and lay leaders will be enhanced if and when social scientists come forward with provisional measures of the gross social product which are compatible with accepted measures of the GNP. Even today we can assign prices to the outputs of a university's teaching program which approximately reflect the national salary and income structure for university graduates in various fields.

Publication of uniform data on workloads, staffing patterns, and outputs at lower division, upper division, and graduate levels in a large number of departments should be useful to university administrators in appraising the performance of departments in their own institutions. The identities of individual departments could be disguised, if need be, by publishing data for the different levels of instruction in different arrays, where they would, in general, occupy different rank orders.

The models presented in this book reflect the conventional organization of a university curriculum into courses, with specified numbers of hours of class meetings and of credits toward graduation. A more flexible program would change the detailed technical coefficients and some of the output measures. However, the learning process would still involve the performance of roles in behavior settings which require contributions (inputs) and yield rewards (outputs). An appraisal of the effectiveness of a more flexible program would logically require application of the same measures of learned capacities (i.e., behavior modifications) to students following each kind of régime.

Finally, concepts are at hand for studying the higher educational system as one which interpenetrates the economic and other subsystems of our society. The primary and secondary schools are embedded in relatively small territorially-based communities. The junior (or community) colleges and area vocational-technical schools in nonmetropolitan regions often are embedded in functional economic areas extending over several counties. Schools of medicine, law, engineering, and business are embedded in professional communities on a state, regional, or national basis. The graduate college represents the intersection of the university with a number of scientific communities (and humanistic ones) organized along disciplinary or departmental lines and of national or international scope.

Its interpenetration with the economy has encouraged us to apply price theory and optimization models to the educational system. Its interpenetration with the rest of society encourages us to believe that economic theory and optimization techniques can be extended to nonmarket systems in general. In the process, however, the economists' repertoire must expand to include concepts (such as transactions, roles, and behavior settings) that have originated in other behavioral sciences.

# References

Abadie, J. M., and Williams, A. C. 1963. Dual and parametric methods in decomposition. In *Recent advances in mathematical programming*, ed. R. L. Graves and P. Wolfe, pp. 149–58. New York: McGraw–Hill.

Adelman, I. 1966. A linear programming model of educational planning: A case study of Argentina. In *The theory and design of economic development*, ed. I. Adelman and E. Thorbecke, pp. 385–412. Baltimore: The Johns Hopkins Press.

Alper, P. 1966. Introduction of control concepts in educational planning models. Paper presented at the Organization for Economic Cooperation and Development Conference on Systems Analysis Techniques in Educational Planning, Paris, March 1966. Paris: Organization for Economic Cooperation and Development.

———. 1968. A critical appraisal of the application of systems analysis to educational planning. *IEEE Transactions on Education* E–11:94–98.

Alper, P., and Smith, C. S. 1967. An application of control theory to a problem in educational planning. *IEEE Transactions on Automatic Control* AC–12:176–78.

Aoki, M. 1971. A planning process for an economy with increasing returns. Discussion Paper No. 168, February 1971, Harvard Institute of Economic Research.

Aris, R. 1963. *Discrete dynamic programming*. New York: Ginn and Co.

Armitage, P.; Smith, C. S.; and Alper, P. ca. 1970. *Models for educational decision making*. London: Penguin Book Company.

Arrow, K. J. 1951. An extension of the basic theorems of classical welfare economics. *Proceedings of the Second Berkeley Symposium on Mathematical Statistics and Probability*, ed. Jerzy Neyman, pp. 507–32. Berkeley: University of California Press.

———. 1959. Optimization, decentralization, and internal pricing in business firms. In *Contributions to scientific research in management*. Los Angeles: University of California.

―――. 1964. Control in large organizations. *Management Science* 10:397–408.
―――. 1969. The organization of economic activity: Issues pertinent to the choice of market versus nonmarket allocation. In *The analysis and evaluation of public expenditures: The PPB system*, vol. 1, part 3, pp. 47–64. A compendium of papers submitted to the subcommittee on Economy in Government. Washington, D.C.: Joint Economic Committee, U.S. Congress.
Arrow, K. J., and Enthoven, A. C. 1961. Quasi-concave programming. *Econometrica* 29:779–800.
Arrow, K. J., and Hurwicz, L. 1960. Decentralization and computation in resource allocation. In *Essays in economics and econometrics*, ed. R. W. Pfouts, pp. 34–104. Chapel Hill: University of North Carolina Press.
Arrow, K. J.; Hurwicz, L.; and Uzawa, H. 1958. *Studies in linear and non-linear programming*. Stanford: Stanford University Press.
Arrow, K. J., and Kurz, M. 1970. *Public investment, the rate of return and optimal fiscal policy*. Baltimore: The Johns Hopkins Press.

Balderston, F. E. 1964. Two problems in the study of multiple-branch organizations: Goal configurations and strategies of branch location. In *Management controls: New directions in basic research*, ed. C. P. Bonini, R. K. Jaedicke, and H. M. Wagner, pp. 75–80. New York: McGraw-Hill.
Balinski, M. L., and Baumol, W. J. 1968. The dual in nonlinear programming and its economic interpretation. *Review of Economic Studies* 35:237–56.
Balogh, T. 1967. The economics of educational planning: Sense and nonsense. In *The teaching of development economics*, ed. K. Martin and J. Knapp, pp. 85–105. London: Frank Cass & Co.
Balogh, T., and Streeten, P. P. 1968. The planning of education in poor countries. In *Economics of education, 1*, ed. M. Blaug, pp. 383–95. Baltimore: Penguin Books.
Barker, R. G. 1968. *Ecological psychology: Concepts and methods for studying the environment of human behavior*. Stanford: Stanford University Press.
Barone, E. 1938. The ministry of production in the collectivist state. In *Collectivist economic planning*, ed. F. A. Hayek, pp. 245–93. London: Routledge.
Barson, J. 1965. A procedural and cost analysis study of media in instructional systems development. Final report, Grant no. OE–16–030, September 1, 1965. Office of Education, U.S. Department of Health, Education, and Welfare.
Bator, F. M. 1957. The simple analytics of welfare maximization. *American Economic Review* 47:22–59.
―――. 1958. The anatomy of market failure. *Quarterly Journal of Economics* 72:351–79.
Baumol, W. J. 1959. *Business behavior, value and growth*. New York: Macmillan.
Baumol, W. J., and Fabian, T. 1964. Decomposition pricing for decentralization and external economies. *Management Science* 11:1–32.
Beadle, G. W., and Tatum, E. L. 1941. Genetic control of biochemical reactions in neurospora. *Proceedings of the National Academy of Science* 27:499–506.
Beale, E. M. L. 1961. *The use of quadratic programming in stochastic linear programming*. Rand Corporation Report P–2404–1, August 15, 1961.
―――. 1963. The simplex method using pseudo-basic variables for structured

## REFERENCES

linear programming problems. In *Recent advances in mathematical programming*, ed. R. L. Graves and P. Wolfe, pp. 133–48. New York: McGraw-Hill.

Becker, G. S. 1964. *Human capital: A theoretical and empirical analysis with special reference to education*. New York: Columbia University Press.

Becker, G. S., and Chiswick, B. R. 1966. Education and the distribution of earnings. *American Economic Review* 56:358–69.

Bellman, R. 1957. *Dynamic programming*. Princeton: Princeton University Press.

Benard, J. 1967. General optimization model for the economy and education. In *Mathematical models in educational planning*, pp. 267–344. Paris: Organization for Economic Cooperation and Development.

Berkowitz, L. D. 1961. Variational methods in problems of control and programming. *Journal of Mathematical Analysis and Applications* 3:145–69.

Berne, E. 1961. *Transactional analysis in psychotherapy*. New York: Grove Press, Inc.

———. 1964. *Games people play: The psychology of human relationships*. New York: Grove Press, Inc.

Berry, B. J. L. (with P. G. Goheen and H. Goldstein). 1968. *Metropolitan area definition: A re-evaluation of concept and statistical practice*, U.S. Bureau of the Census *Working Paper 28*, June 1968; reissued, slightly revised, July 1969.

Blaug, M. 1965. The rate of return on investment in education in Great Britain. *Manchester School* 33:205–51.

———. 1966. An economic interpretation of the private demand for education. *Economica* 33:166–82.

———. 1968a. The rate of return on investment in education. In *Economics of education 1: Selected readings*, ed. M. Blaug, pp. 215–59. Baltimore: Penguin Books.

———. 1968b. *Economics of education*, vol. 1. Baltimore: Penguin Books.

———. 1969. *Economics of education*, vol. 2. Baltimore: Penguin Books.

Bohm, P. 1967. On the theory of "second best." *Review of Economic Studies* 34:301–14.

Boiteux, M. 1949. La tarification des demandes en pointe. *Revue Générale de l'Electricité* 58:321–40; translated as "Peak load pricing," *Journal of Business*, vol. 33, no. 2 (1960): 157–79.

———. 1956. Sur la question des monopoles publics astreints à l'équilibre budgétaire. *Econometrica* 24:22–40.

Bolt, R. H., et al. 1965. Doctoral feedback into higher education. *Science* 148:918–28.

Bose, D. K. 1968. On shadow prices for free goods in linear programming. Discussion paper, author, September 1968.

Bowen, W. G. 1963. Assessing the economic contribution of education: An appraisal of alternative approaches. In *Higher education: Report of the committee under the chairmanship of Lord Robbins, 1961–63*, appendix 4, pp. 73–96. London: H.M.S.O.

Bowles, S. 1965. A planning model for the efficient allocation of resources in education. Unpublished paper presented at the annual meeting of the Allied Social Sciences Association, New York, December 1965. Mimeo-

graphed. Department of Economics, Harvard University, Cambridge, Mass. Also unpublished Ph.D. thesis, Harvard University Library.
———. 1967. The efficient allocation of resources in education. *Quarterly Journal of Economics* 81:189–219.
Brink, E. L. 1966. Decision-making in a university system. In *Operational research and the social sciences*, ed. J. R. Lawrence, pp. 225–36. London: Tavistock Publications.
Buchanan, J. M. 1966. Joint supply, externality and optimality. *Economica* 33:404–15.
Buchanan, J. M., and Stubblebine, W. C. 1962. Externality. *Economica* 29:371–84.
Buchanan, J. M., and Tullock, G. 1962. *The calculus of consent*. Ann Arbor: University of Michigan Press.
Buffa, E. S.; Armour, G. C.; and Vollman, T. E. 1964. Allocating facilities with CRAFT. *Harvard Business Review* 42:136–47.

Carresse, L. M., and Barker, C. 1967. The convergence technique: A method for planning and programming of research efforts. *Management Science* 13:B420–38.
Cartter, A. M. 1965. Economics of the university. *American Economic Review* 55:481–94.
———. 1966. *An assessment of quality in graduate education*. Washington: American Council on Education.
Cass, D. 1965. Optimum growth in an aggregative model of capital accumulation. *Review of Economic Studies* 32:233–40.
Cass, D., and Yaari, M. E. 1967. Individual saving, aggregate capital accumulation and efficient growth. In *Essays on the theory of optimal economic growth*, ed. K. Shell, pp. 233–68. Cambridge, Mass.: MIT Press.
Caswell, W. C. 1956. Taking stock of divisionalization. *Journal of Business* 29:160–71.
Charnes, A.; Clower, R. W.; and Kortanek, K. D. 1967. Effective control through coherent decentralization with preemptive goals. *Econometrica* 35:294–320.
Charnes, A., and Cooper, W. W. 1960. On the theory and computation of delegation models: K-efficiency, functional efficiency and goals. In *Management science: Models and techniques*, ed. C. W. Churchman and M. Verhulst, vol. 1, pp. 56–91. London: Pergamon Press.
———. 1961. *Management models and industrial applications of linear programming*, vol. 1. New York: John Wiley.
Contini, B. 1968. A stochastic approach to goal programming. *Operations Research* 16:576–86.
Cook, D. L. 1966. *Program evaluation and review techniques: Application to education*. Washington, D.C.: U.S. Office of Education, O.E. 12024.
Cook, P. W., Jr. 1955. Decentralization and the transfer-price problem. *Journal of Business* 28:87–94.
Corlett, W. J., and Hague, D. C. 1953–54. Complementarity and excess burden of taxation. *Review of Economic Studies* 21:21–30.
Correa, H. 1963. *The economics of human resources*. Amsterdam: North–Holland Publishing Co.

———. 1967. *A survey of mathematical models in educational planning.* Paris: Organization for Economic Cooperation and Development.
Correa, H., and Tinbergen, J. 1962. Quantitative adaptation of education to accelerated growth. *Kyklos* 15:776–85.
Cyert, R. M., and March, J. G. 1959. A behavioral theory of organizational objectives. In *Modern organization theory*, ed. Mason Haire. New York: John Wiley.

Dantzig, G. B. 1963. *Linear programming and extensions.* Princeton: Princeton University Press.
Dantzig, G. B., and Madansky, A. 1961. On the solution of two-stage linear programs under uncertainty. In *Proceedings of fourth Berkeley symposium on mathematical statistics and probability*, vol. 1, ed. Jerzy Neyman, pp. 165–76. Berkeley: University of California Press.
Dantzig, G. B., and Wolfe, P. The decomposition principle for linear programs. *Operations Research* 8:101–11.
Davis, O. A., and Kamien, M. I. 1969. Externalities, information and alternative collective action. In *The analysis and evaluation of public expenditures: The PPB system*, vol. 1, part 1, pp. 67–86. A compendium of papers submitted to the subcommittee on Economy in Government. Washington, D.C.: Joint Economic Committee, U.S. Congress.
Davis, O. A., and Whinston, A. B. 1962. Externalities, welfare and the theory of games. *Journal of Political Economy* 70:241–62.
———. 1965. Welfare economics and the theory of second best. *Review of Economic Studies* 32:1–14.
———. 1967. On the distinction between public and private goods. *American Economic Review* 57:360–73.
Day, R. H. 1963a. On aggregating linear programming models of production. *Journal of Farm Economics* 45:797–813.
———. 1963b. *Recursive programming and production response.* Amsterdam: North-Holland Publishing Company.
Dean, J. 1955. Decentralization and intra-company pricing. *Harvard Business Review* 33:65–74.
Debreu, G. 1959. *Theory of value.* New York: John Wiley.
Denison, E. F. 1962. *The sources of economic growth in the United States and the alternatives before us.* Committee for Economic Development, supplementary paper no. 13, New York.
———. 1964. Measuring the contribution of education and the residual to economic growth. In *The residual factor and economic growth*, pp. 13–55. Paris: Organization for Economic Cooperation and Development.
Dhrymes, P. 1964. On the theory of the monopolistic multiproduct firm under uncertainty. *International Economic Review* 5:239–57.
Dorfman, R.; Samuelson, P. A.; and Solow, R. 1958. *Linear programming and economic analysis.* New York: McGraw-Hill.
Duesenberry, J. S.; Fromm, G.; Klein, L. R.; and Kuh, E., eds. 1965. *The Brookings quarterly econometric model of the United States*, pp. 24–25. Chicago: Rand McNally; and Amsterdam: North-Holland Publishing Company.

Duffin, R. J.; Peterson, E. L.; and Zener, C. 1967. *Geometric programming: Theory and application.* New York: John Wiley.

El-Hodiri, M. A. 1966. Optimality criteria of economic growth as examples of optimal resource allocation over time. Ph.D. dissertation. Minneapolis: University of Minnesota Library.

Ellman, M. 1969. Aggregation as a cause of inconsistent plans. *Economica* 36:69–74.

Feinstein, C. H., ed. 1967. *Socialism, capitalism and economic growth: Essays presented to M. Dobb.* Cambridge: Cambridge University Press.

Firmin, P. A.; Goodman, S. S.; Hendricks, T. E.; and Linn, J. J. 1967. *University cost structure and behavior.* New Orleans: Tulane University.

Forrester, J. W. 1961. *Industrial dynamics.* Cambridge, Mass.: MIT Press.

Fox, K. A. 1953. A spatial equilibrium model of the livestock-feed economy in the United States. *Econometrica* 21:547–66.

———. 1963. Spatial price equilibrium and process analysis in the food and agricultural sector. In *Studies in process analysis,* ed. A. Manne and H. M. Markowitz, chapter 8, pp. 215–33. New York: John Wiley.

———. 1964. On the current lack of policy orientation in regional accounting. In *Elements of regional accounts,* ed. W. Z. Hirsch, pp. 80–85. Baltimore: The Johns Hopkins Press.

———. 1966a. Economists' salary and income relationships. Unpublished memorandum dated May 25, 1966, Department of Economics, Iowa State University, Ames.

———. 1966b. In unpublished letter to Study Director, National Register of Scientific and Technical Personnel, National Science Foundation, September 22, 1966.

———. 1967. Functional economic areas and consolidated urban regions of the United States. *Social Science Research Council ITEMS* 21(4):45–49.

———. 1968. A framework for appraising the consistency of 1972–73 plans for various department programs. Unpublished memorandum dated November 15, 1968, Department of Economics, Iowa State University, Ames.

———. 1969. The new synthesis of rural and urban society in the United States. In *Economic problems of agriculture in industrial societies,* proceedings of a conference held by the International Economic Association, September 1965, ed. U. Papi and C. Nunn, chapter 28, pp. 606–28. London: Macmillan; and New York: St. Martin's Press.

———. 1970. Discussion of papers presented at the session on Economics of Education, annual meetings of the American Economic Association, New York, December 29, 1969. *American Economic Review* 40:349–50.

Fox, K. A., and Kumar, T. K. 1965. Functional economic areas: Delineation and implications for economic analysis and policy. *Regional Science Association PAPERS* 15:57–85.

———. 1966. Delineating functional economic areas. In *Research and education for regional and area development,* ed. W. R. Maki and B. J. L. Berry, pp. 13–55. Ames: Iowa State University Press.

Fox, K. A.; McCamley, F. P.; and Plessner, Y. 1967. *Formulation of management science models for selected problems of college administration.* Final report submitted to U.S. Office of Education, November 10, 1967.

Fox, K. A., and Sengupta, J. K. 1968. The specification of econometric models for planning educational systems: An appraisal of alternative approaches. *Kyklos* 21:665-94.

Fox, K. A.; Sengupta, J. K.; and Sanyal, B. C. 1969. On the optimality of resource allocation in educational systems: Problems posed by fixed, semi-fixed, divisible or semi-divisible resources. Paper presented at the 36th national meeting of Operations Research Society of America, Miami Beach, Florida, November 10-12, 1969.

Fox, K. A.; Sengupta, J. K.; and Thorbecke, E. 1966. *The theory of quantitative economic policy: With applications to economic growth and stabilization.* Amsterdam: North-Holland Publishing Co.; and Chicago: Rand McNally.

Fox, K. A., and Taeuber, R. C. 1955. Spatial equilibrium models of the livestock-feed economy. *American Economic Review* 45:584-608.

Frank, C. R. 1969. *Production theory and indivisible commodities.* Princeton: Princeton University Press.

Frisch, R. 1959. On welfare theory and Pareto regions. *International Economic Papers* no. 9, pp. 39-92.

———. 1960. *Planning for India: Selected explorations in methodology.* Calcutta: Asia Publishing House.

Froomkin, J. 1968. Allocation of resources to education: Towards a theory of subsidy. In *Budgeting, programme analysis and cost-effectiveness in educational planning.* Paris: Organization for Economic Cooperation and Development.

Furuya, H., and Inada, K. 1962. Balanced growth and intertemporal efficiency in capital accumulation. *International Economic Review* 3:94-107.

Gale, D. 1960. *The theory of linear economic models.* New York: McGraw-Hill.

Geoffrion, A. M. 1971. Primal resource-directive approaches for optimizing non-linear decomposable systems. In *Optimization methods for large scale systems,* ed. D. Wismer. New York: McGraw-Hill.

Gibbs, J. W. 1878. On the equilibrium of heterogeneous substances. *Conn. Acad. Trans.* 3:108-248, 343-524.

Glasserman, J. 1968. *Organizational strategies in schools: A computer model for their analysis.* Yorktown Heights, New York: IBM-ASDD.

Goldman, A. J. 1956. Resolution and separation theorem for polyhedral convex sets. In *Linear inequalities and related systems. Annals of mathematics studies no. 38,* ed. H. W. Kuhn and A. W. Tucker, pp. 41-51. Princeton: Princeton University Press.

Gordon, M. J. 1964. The use of administered price systems to control large organizations. In *Management controls: New directions in basic research,* ed. C. P. Bonini, et al., pp. 1-26. New York: McGraw-Hill.

Grambsch, P. V., and Gross, E. 1967. *Academic administrators and university goals: A study in conflict and cooperation.* Final report to the U.S. Office of Education, University of Minnesota, Minneapolis.

Grossman, G., ed. 1960. *Value and plan: Economic calculation and organization in Eastern Europe.* Berkeley: University of California Press.

Hahn, F. H. 1966. Equilibrium dynamics with heterogeneous capital goods. *Quarterly Journal of Economics* 80:633-46.

Hahn, F. H., and Negishi, T. 1962. A theorem on non-tâtonnement stability. *Econometrica* 30:463–69.

Hansen, W. L. 1963. Total and private rates of return to investment in schooling. *Journal of Political Economy* 81:128–41.

———. 1970. Income distribution effects of higher education. *American Economic Review* 40:335–40.

Hansen, W. L., and Weisbrod, B. A. 1969. *Benefits, costs and finance of public higher education.* Chicago: Markham.

Harbison, F., and Myers, C. A. 1964. *Education, manpower and economic growth.* New York: McGraw-Hill.

Harsanyi, J. C. 1956. Approaches to the bargaining problem before and after the theory of games: A critical discussion of Zeuthen's, Hicks', and Nash's theories. *Econometrica* 24:147–57.

———. 1963. A simplified bargaining model for the n-person cooperative game. *International Economic Review* 4:194–220.

Hartley, H. J. 1968. *Educational planning—programming—budgeting: A systems approach.* Englewood Cliffs, New Jersey: Prentice-Hall.

Hartman, Lawton M. 1969. *Graduate education: parameters for public policy*, Washington, D.C.: National Science Board, National Science Foundation.

Hass, J. E. 1968. Transfer pricing in a decentralized firm. *Management Science* 14:B310–31.

Heal, G. M. 1969. Planning without prices. *Review of Economic Studies* 36: 347–61.

Hicks, J. R. 1939. The foundations of welfare economics. *Economic Journal* 49:696–712.

Hirshleifer, J. 1956. On the economics of transfer pricing. *Journal of Business* 29:172–84.

———. 1957. Economics of the divisionalized firm. *Journal of Business* 30: 96–108.

———. 1958. Peak loads and efficient pricing: Comment. *Quarterly Journal of Economics* 72:451–62.

———. 1964. Internal pricing and decentralized decisions. In *Management controls: New directions in basic research*, ed. C. P. Bonini, et al., pp. 27–37. New York: McGraw-Hill.

Hoggatt, A. C., and Balderston, F. E., eds. 1963. *Symposium on simulation models: Methodology and applications to behavioral sciences.* Cincinnati, Ohio: South-Western Publishing Co.

Hohenbalken, B. von, and Fox, K. A. 1967. A policy model to maximize the excellence of an academic department. Unpublished manuscript, June 1967, Department of Economics, Iowa State University, Ames.

Hollister, R. G. 1968. An evaluation of a manpower forecasting exercise. In *Economics of education, 1*, ed. M. Blaug, pp. 338–48. Baltimore: Penguin Books.

Hotelling, H. 1938. The general welfare in relation to problems of taxation and of railway and utility rates. *Econometrica* 6:242–69.

Howard, R. 1960. *Dynamic programming and Markov processes.* Cambridge, Mass.: MIT Press.

Hurwicz, L. 1960. Conditions for economic efficiency of centralized and decentralized structures. In *Value and plan*, ed. G. Grossman, pp. 162–75. Berkeley: University of California Press.

Ijiri, Y. 1965. *Management goals and accounting for control*. Amsterdam: North-Holland Publishing Co.

Intriligator, M., and Smith, B. 1966. Some aspects of the allocation of scientific effort between teaching and research. Rand Memorandum RM–4339–PR.

Isaac, R. 1962. *Differential games*. New York: Interscience.

James, E. 1969. Resource allocation and costs in higher education: A case study of State University of New York at Stony Brook. A paper presented at the Southern Economic Association meetings on November 14, 1969.

Jasny, N. 1951. *The Soviet price system*. Stanford: Stanford University Press.

Johansen, L. 1960. *A multisectoral study of economic growth*. Amsterdam: North-Holland Publishing Co.

———. 1965. *Public economics*. Chicago: Rand McNally.

Joint Economic Committee, U.S. Congress. 1969. *An analysis and evaluation of public expenditures: The PPB system*, vol. 1. Washington, D.C.: U.S. Government Printing Office.

Judy, R. W. 1969. Simulation and rational resource allocation in universities. In *Efficiency in resource utilization in education*, pp. 255–85. Paris: Organization for Economic Cooperation and Development.

Judy, R. W., and Levine, J. B. 1967. Systems analysis and university planning. Paper presented at the Symposium on Operations Analysis of Education, Washington, D.C., November 1967.

Judy, R. W.; Levine, J. B.; Wilson, R.; and Walter, J. 1968. Systems analysis of alternative designs of a faculty. In *Budgeting, programme analysis and cost effectiveness in educational planning*. Paris: Organization for Economic Cooperation and Development.

Kahn, R. F. 1935. Some notes on ideal output. *Economic Journal* 45:1–35.

Kaldor, N. 1939. Welfare propositions in economics. *Economic Journal* 49: 549–52.

———. 1956. Alternative theories of distribution. *Review of Economic Studies* 23:83–100.

Kaldor, N., and Mirrlees, J. A. 1962. A new model of economic growth. *Review of Economic Studies* 29:174–92.

Kaysen, C. 1969. *The higher learning, the universities, and the public*. Princeton: Princeton University Press.

Keeney, M. G.; Koenig, H. E.; and Zemach, R. 1967. *A systems approach to higher education*. Final report of the Division of Engineering Research, March 27, 1967. Michigan State University, East Lansing.

Kemeny, J. G.; Morgenstern, O.; and Thompson, G. L. 1956. A generalization of the von Neumann model of an expanding economy. *Econometrica* 24: 115–35.

Kershaw, J., and McKean, R. N. 1959. *Systems analysis and education*. Rand Corporation Memorandum RM 2473.

Kershaw, J. A., and Mood, A. M. 1970. Resource allocation in higher education. *American Economic Review* 40:341–46.

Keynes, J. M. 1936. *The general theory of employment, interest and money.* London: Macmillan Company.

Klein, L. R. 1946. Remarks on the theory of aggregation. *Econometrica* 14: 303–12.

Klinger, A. 1968. Logarithmic convexity and geometric programming. *Journal of Mathematical Analysis and Applications* 24:388–408.

Koopmans, T. C. 1951. Analysis of production as an efficient combination of activities. In *Activity analysis of production and allocation. Cowles Commission monograph no. 13,* ed. T. C. Koopmans, chapter 3, pp. 33–97. New York: John Wiley.

———. 1957. *Three essays on the state of economic science.* New York: McGraw-Hill.

Kornai, J., and Lipták, T. 1962. A mathematical investigation of some economic effects of profit sharing in socialist firms. *Econometrica* 30:140–61.

———. 1965. Two-level planning. *Econometrica* 33:141–69.

Kuhn, H. W. 1963. Locational problems and mathematical programming. In *Colloquium on applications of mathematics to economics,* ed. A. Prekopa, pp. 235–42. Budapest: Publishing House of Hungarian Academy of Sciences.

Kuhn, H. W., and Tucker, A. W. 1950. Nonlinear programming. In *Proceedings of the second Berkeley symposium on mathematical statistics and probability,* ed. Jerzy Neyman, pp. 481–92. Berkeley: University of California Press.

Kuhn, T. S. 1962. *The structure of scientific revolutions.* Chicago: University of Chicago Press.

Kulikowski, R. 1966. Optimum control of multidimensional and multilevel systems. In *Advances in control systems,* vol. 4, ed. C. T. Leondes, pp. 157–80. New York and London: Academic Press.

Kumar, T. K. 1969. The existence of an optimal economic policy. *Econometrica* 37:600–10.

Kushner, H. J. 1967. *Stochastic stability and control.* New York: Academic Press.

Kuznets, S. S. 1937. *National income and capital formation, 1919–1935.* New York: National Bureau of Economic Research.

———. 1948. On the valuation of social income: Reflections on Professor Hicks' Article. *Economica* 50:1–16; 58:116–31.

Lange, O. 1958. The role of planning in socialist economy. In *The political economy of socialism,* ed. O. Lange. The Hague: Institute of Social Studies.

———. 1960. Output-investment ratio and input-output analysis. *Econometrica* 28:310–24.

———. 1967. The computer and the market. In *Socialism, capitalism and economic growth: Essays presented to M. Dobb,* ed. C. H. Feinstein, pp. 158–61. Cambridge: Cambridge University Press.

Lange, O., ed. 1958. *The political economy of socialism.* The Hague: Institute of Social Studies.

Lange, O., and Taylor, F. M. 1938. *On the economic theory of socialism.* Minneapolis: University of Minnesota Press.

Lave, R. E., and Kyle, D. W. 1968. The application of systems analysis to educational planning. *Comparative Education Review* 12:39–56.

Lee, S. M., and Clayton, E. R. 1969. A mathematical programming model for academic planning. A paper presented at the Southern Management Association meeting, St. Louis, Missouri, November 15, 1969.

Leontief, W. W. 1941. *The structure of American economy, 1919–1929: An empirical application of equilibrium analysis.* Cambridge, Mass.: Harvard University Press.

Lerner, A. P. 1934. The concept of monopoly and the measurement of monopoly power. *Review of Economic Studies* 1:157–75.

———. 1944. *The Economics of control.* New York: The Macmillan Co.

LeVasseur, P. M. 1968. A study of interrelationships between education, manpower and economy. In *Proceedings of the symposium on operations analysis of education.* Washington, D.C.: U.S. Office of Education.

Levine, H. S. 1966. Pressure and planning in the Soviet economy. In *Industrialization in two systems*, ed. H. Rodobdky. New York: John Wiley.

Levine, S. N. 1967. Economic growth and development of educational facilities: A system analysis. *Socio-Economic Planning Sciences* 1:27–32.

Lind, G. 1959–65. *Statistics of land-grant colleges and universities.* U.S. Office of Education, annual issues 1956–57 through 1962–63. 7 vols. Washington, D.C.: U.S. Office of Education.

Lindsay, F. H. I. 1964. *Financial statistics of institutions of higher education, 1959–1960.* U.S. Office of Education circular no. 744. Washington, D.C.: U.S. Office of Education.

Lipsey, R. G., and Lancaster, K. 1956–57. The general theory of second best. *Review of Economic Studies* 24:11–32.

Little, I. M. D. 1957. *A critique of welfare economics.* 2nd ed. Oxford: Oxford University Press.

Luce, R. D. and Raiffa, H. 1957. *Games and decisions.* New York: John Wiley.

MacDonald, J. S. 1964. Employment programming and education programming. A paper presented at The Institute of Management Science/Operations Research Society of America Conference, 1964.

Mahalanobis, P. C. 1955. The approach of operational research to planning in India. *Sankhya* 16:3–62.

Malinvaud, E. 1967. Decentralized procedures for planning. In *Activity analysis in the theory of growth and planning*, ed. E. Malinvaud and M. O. Bacharach, pp. 170–208. New York: St. Martin's Press.

Manne, A. S., ed. 1967. *Investments for capacity expansion.* Cambridge, Mass.: MIT Press.

March, J. G. 1965. *Handbook of organizations.* Chicago: Rand McNally.

Marschak, J. 1955. Elements for a theory of teams. *Management Science* 1:127–37.

———. 1964. Problems in information economics. In *Management controls: New directions in basic research*, ed. C. P. Bonini, R. K. Jaedicke, and H. M. Wagner, chapter 3, pp. 38–74. New York: McGraw-Hill.

Marschak, T. A. 1964. Economic theory and management control. In *Management controls: New directions in basic research*, ed. C. P. Bonini, R. K. Jaedicke, and H. M. Wagner, pp. 81–87. New York: McGraw-Hill.

———. 1965. Economic theories of organization. In *Handbook of organization*, ed. J. G. March, chapter 10, pp. 423–50. Chicago: Rand McNally.

May, K. 1946. The aggregation problem for a one-industry model. *Econometrica* 14:285–98.
McCamley, F. P. 1967. Activity analysis models of educational institutions. Ph.D. dissertation. Iowa State University Library, Ames.
McKean, R. N. 1958. *Efficiency in government through systems analysis*. New York: John Wiley.
McKean, R. N. and Hitch, C. J. 1967. *The economics of defense in the nuclear age*. New York: Atheneum.
McManus, M. 1967. Private and social costs in the theory of second best. *Review of Economic Studies* 34:317–21.
Meade, J. E. 1952. External economies and diseconomies in a competitive situation. *Economic Journal* 62:54–67.
Melichar, E. 1968. Factors affecting 1966 basic salaries in the National Register professions. Study 2 in *Studies of the structure of economists' salaries and income*. Supplement 2 to *American Economic Review* 58:56–69.
Mesarovic, M. 1960. The control of multi-variable systems. New York: John Wiley.
Mincer, J. 1958. Investment in human capital and personal income distribution. *Journal of Political Economy* 66:281–302.
———. 1962. On-the-job training: Costs, returns and some implications. In a supplement on investment in human beings, *Journal of Political Economy* 70:50–79.
Mond, B. and Hanson, M. 1968. Duality for control problems. *SIAM Journal on Control* 6:114–20.
Montias, J. M. 1960. Producer prices in a centrally planned economy. In *Value and plan: Economic calculation and organization in Eastern Europe*, ed. G. Grossman, pp. 47–65. Berkeley: University of California Press.
Mood, A. M., and Stoller, D. S. 1967. Operations analysis in the U.S. Office of Education. Mimeographed report dated August 1967.
Morishima, M. 1964. *Equilibrium stability and growth*. Oxford: Clarendon Press.
———. 1969. *Theory of economic growth*. Oxford: Clarendon Press.
Morris, W. T. 1968. *Decentralization in management systems*. Columbus: Ohio State University Press.
Moser, C. A., and Layard, P. R. G. 1964. Planning the scale of higher education in Britain: Some statistical problems. *Journal of Royal Statistical Society*. Series A 127:493–513.
Moser, C. A., and Redfern, P. 1965a. A computable model of the educational system in England and Wales. Read at the 35th session of the International Statistical Institute in Belgrade in September 1965 and published in the *Bulletin of the International Statistical Institute*, 1967.
———. 1965b. Education and manpower: Some current research. In *Models for decision*. London: English Universities Press.
Mushkin, S. J., ed. 1962. *Economics of higher education*. Washington, D.C.: Dept. Health, Education, and Welfare, Office of Education.

Nance, P. K.; Robbins, L. F.; and Harvey, C. J. 1965. *Guide to college and university business management*. Washington, D.C.: U.S. Government Printing Office.

Naslund, B. 1967. *Decisions under risk: Economic applications of chance-constrained programming.* Stockholm: Stockholm School of Economics.
National Affairs, Inc. 1967. *The public interest,* no. 8, summer 1967. New York: Freedom House.
National Science Board, National Science Foundation. 1969. *Graduate education: parameters for public policy.* Washington, D.C.: U.S. Government Printing Office.
Nef, W. 1967. *Linear algebra,* chapter 9. Translated from the German by J. C. Ault. New York: McGraw–Hill.
Negishi, T. 1960. Welfare economics and existence of an equilibrium for a competitive economy. *Metroeconomica* 12(2 and 3):92–97.
Neumann, J. von. 1945–46. A model of general equilibrium. *Review of Economic Studies* 13:1–9.
Neumann, J. von, and Morgenstern, O. 1953. *Theory of games and economic behavior.* 3rd. ed. Princeton: Princeton University Press.
Nikaido, H. 1964. Monopolistic factor price imputation and linear programming. *Zeitschrift für National Okonomie* 24:298–301.
Nordell, L. 1965. A linear activity analysis model of primary and secondary education. *Internal working paper no. 35,* Space Sciences Laboratory, University of California, Berkeley.
Nyblen, G. 1951. *The problem of summation in economic science.* Lund, Sweden: C. W. K. Gleerup.

Oakford, A., and Chatterton, R. 1966–67. School scheduling practice and theory. *Journal of Educational Data Processing,* winter 1966–67.
Organization for Economic Cooperation and Development Research Group. 1962. *Policy conference on economic growth and investment in education: Report.* Proceedings of a conference held in Washington, D.C., October 16–20, 1961. Paris: Organization for Economic Cooperation and Development.
———. 1965. *Econometric models of education: Some applications.* Paris: Organization for Economic Cooperation and Development.
———. 1967. *Mathematical models in educational planning.* Paris: Organization for Economic Cooperation and Development.
———. 1968. *Budgeting, programme analysis and cost-effectiveness in educational planning.* Paris: Organization for Economic Cooperation and Development.
———. 1969. *Systems analysis for educational planning.* Paris: Organization for Economic Cooperation and Development.

Pareto, V. 1897. *Cours d'économie politique,* vol. 2, book 2, chapter ii, paras. 717–24, pp. 84–95. Lausanne: F. Rouge.
———. 1909. *Le manuel d'économie politique.* Paris: V. Giard and E. Briere.
Parnes, H. S. 1962. *Forecasting educational needs for economic and social development.* Paris: Organization for Economic Cooperation and Development.
———. 1964. Manpower analysis in educational planning. In *Planning education for economic and social development,* ed. H. S. Parnes, pp. 73–80. Paris: Organization for Economic Cooperation and Development.
Parsons, T. 1968. Systems analysis: Social systems. In *International encyclo-*

*pedia of the social sciences* 15:458–73. New York: The Macmillan Co. and the Free Press.

Passy, V., and Wilde, D. J. 1967. Generalized polynomial optimization. *SIAM Journal on Applied Mathematics* 15:1344–56.

Pearson, J. D. 1966. Duality and a decomposition technique. *SIAM Journal on Control* 4:164–72.

Pfouts, R. W. 1961. The theory of cost and production in the multi-product firm. *Econometrica* 29:650–58.

Phelps, E. S., and Pollack, R. A. 1968. On second-best national saving and game-equilibrium growth. *Review of Economic Studies* 35:185–99.

Pigou, A. C. 1932. *The economics of welfare*. 4th ed. London: The Macmillan Co.

Plessner, Y. 1967. Activity analysis, quadratic programming and general equilibrium. *International Economic Review* 8:168–79.

Plessner, Y.; Fox, K. A.; and Sanyal, B. C. 1968. On the allocation of resources in a university department. *Metroeconomica* 20:256–71.

Poignant, R. 1967. *The relation of educational plans to economic and social planning*. Paris: UNESCO, International Institute for Educational Planning.

Pollack, R. A. 1968. Consistent planning. *Review of Economic Studies* 35:201–8.

Pontryagin, L. S., et al. 1962. *The mathematical theory of optimal processes*. New York: Interscience Publishers.

Portes, R. D. 1969. The enterprise under central planning. *Review of Economic Studies* 36(2):197–212.

Radner, R. 1962. Team decision problems. *Annals of Mathematical Statistics* 33:857–81.

———. 1964. Mathematical specification of goals for decision problems. In *Human judgements and optimality*, ed. M. W. Shelly II and G. L. Bryan, chapter 2, pp. 178–216. New York: John Wiley.

———. 1968. Competitive equilibrium under uncertainty. *Econometrica* 36:31–58.

Radner, R., and Miller, L. S. 1970. Demand and supply in U.S. higher education. *American Economic Review* 40:326–34.

Radström, H. 1964. A property of stability possessed by certain imputations. In *Advances in game theory, annals of mathematics studies no. 52*, ed. M. Dresher, L. S. Shapley, and A. W. Tucker, pp. 513–29. Princeton: Princeton University Press.

Raiffa, H. and Schlaifer, R. 1961. *Applied statistical theory*. Division of Research, Graduate School of Business Administration, Harvard University, 1961; student edition MIT Press, April 1968.

Rath, G. 1968. Management science in university operation. *Management Science* 14:B373.

Reisman, A. 1966. Higher education: A population flow feedback model. *Science* 153:89–91.

Riew, J. 1966. Economies of scale in high school operation. *Review of Economics and Statistics* 48:280–87.

Robinson, J. 1951. An iterative method of solving a game. *Annals of Mathematics* no. 54:296–301. Princeton: Princeton University Press.

Robinson, Joan. 1964. *Essays in the theory of economic growth*. London: Macmillan Co.
Roose, K. D., and Andersen, C. J. 1970. *A rating of graduate programs*. Washington, D.C.: American Council on Education.
Rosen, J. B. 1963. Convex partition programming. In *Recent advances in mathematical programming*, ed. R. L. Graves and P. Wolfe, pp. 159–76. New York: McGraw-Hill.
Rosenfeld, J. L. 1964. Adaptive competitive decision. In *Advances in game theory*, annals of mathematics studies no. 52, ed. M. Dresher, L. S. Shapley, and A. W. Tucker, pp. 69–83. Princeton: Princeton University Press.
Roy, R. 1947. La distribution des revenus entre les divers biens. *Econometrica* 15:205–25.
Ryans, D. G. 1965. System analysis in planning. In *Long-range planning in higher education*, ed. O. A. Knorr, pp. 79–118. Boulder, Colorado: Western Inter-State Commission for Higher Education.

Samuelson, P. A. 1947. *Foundations of economic analysis*. Cambridge: Harvard University Press.
———. 1952. Spatial price equilibrium and linear programming. *American Economic Review* 42:294–303.
———. 1954. The pure theory of public expenditure. *Review of Economics and Statistics* 36:387–89.
———. 1969. Contrast between welfare conditions for joint supply and for public goods. *Review of Economics and Statistics* 51:26–30.
Sanders, J. L. 1965. Nonlinear decomposition principle. *Operations Research* 13:266–71.
Savage, L. J. 1954. *The foundations of statistics*. New York: John Wiley.
Scarborough, C. W., and Daniel, J. N. 1968. Management use of simulation in long-range planning for colleges and universities. A paper presented at The Institute of Management Science/Operations Research Society of America meeting, San Francisco, May 1, 1968.
Schotta, C., and Schotta, S. G. 1967. Optimal sequencing of second language instruction: An operations research approach. A paper presented at the 32nd national meeting of the Operations Research Society of America, November 3, 1967.
Schultz, T. W. 1961a. Investment in human capital. *American Economic Review* 51:1–17.
———. 1961b. The concept of human capital: A reply. *American Economic Review* 51:1035–39.
———. 1963. *The economic value of education*. New York: Columbia University Press.
———. 1968. Resources for higher education: An economist's view. *Journal of Political Economy* 76:327–47.
Scitovsky, T. A. 1941. A note on welfare propositions in economics. *Review of Economic Studies* 9:77–88.
Sengupta, J. K. 1964. Price stabilization under a Walrasian model. *Arthaniti* 7:37–50.
———. 1966a. The stability of truncated solutions of stochastic linear programming. *Econometrica* 34:77–104.

———. 1966b. Truncated decision rules and optimal economic growth with a fixed horizon. *International Economic Review* 7:42–64.
———. 1969. Safety-first rules under chance-constrained linear programming. *Operations Research* 17:112–32.
———. 1970a. A generalization of some distribution aspects of chance-constrained linear programming. *International Economic Review* 11:287–304.
———. 1970b. Stochastic linear programming with chance constraints. *International Economic Review* 11:101–16.
———. 1971a. Economics of decomposition and divisionalization under transfer pricing. *Zeitschrift für die Gesamte Staatswissenschaft* 127:50–71.
———. 1971b. A statistical reliability approach to linear programming. *Unternehmensforschung*, vol. 3.
Sengupta, J. K., and Fox, K. A. 1969. *Economic analysis and operations research: Optimization techniques in quantitative economic models*. Amsterdam: North-Holland Publishing Co.
———. 1970. A computable approach to optimal growth of an academic department. *Zeitschrift für die Gesamte Staatswissenschaft* 126:97–125.
Sengupta, J. K., and Sen, A. 1969. Models of optimal capacity expansion for the firm: An appraisal. *Metroeconomica* 21:1–27.
Sengupta, J. K., and Tintner, G. 1963. On some economic models of development planning. *Economia Internazionale* 16:34–50.
———. 1971. A review of stochastic linear programming. *Review of International Statistical Institute*, vol. 39, no. 2.
Sengupta, J. K.; Tintner, G.; and Millham, C. 1963. On some theorems of stochastic linear programming with applications. *Management Science* 10:143–59.
Sengupta, J. K.; Tintner, G.; and Morrison, B. 1963. Stochastic linear programming with applications to economic models. *Economica* 30:262–76.
Shackle, G. L. S. 1955. *Uncertainty in economics*. Cambridge: Cambridge University Press.
Shapley, L. S. 1953. The value of an n-person game. In *Contributions to the theory of games*, vol. 2, ed. H. W. Kuhn and A. W. Tucker, pp. 307–17. Princeton: Princeton University Press.
———. 1959. The solutions of a symmetric market game. In *Advances in game theory, annals of mathematics studies no. 40*, ed. A. W. Tucker and R. D. Luce, pp. 145–62. Princeton: Princeton University Press.
Shaw, B. T. 1967. *The use of quality and quantity of publication as criteria for evaluating scientists*. Washington, D.C.: U.S. Department of Agriculture, Agricultural Research Service Misc. Publication no. 1041.
Shell, K. 1967. A model of inventive activity and capital accumulation. In *Essays on the theory of optimal economic growth*, ed. K. Shell, pp. 67–85. Cambridge, Mass.: MIT Press.
Sheshinski, E. 1967. Optimal accumulation with learning by doing. In *Essays on the theory of optimal growth*, ed. K. Shell, pp. 31–52. Cambridge, Mass.: MIT Press.
Shubik, M. 1961. Extended Edgeworth bargaining games and competitive equilibrium. *Cowles Foundation discussion paper no. 107*.
———. 1962. Incentives, decentralized control, the assignment of joint costs and internal pricing. *Management Science* 8:325–43.

## REFERENCES

Sik, O. 1967. Socialist market relations and planning. In *Socialism, capitalism and economic growth*, ed. C. H. Feinstein, pp. 133–57. Cambridge: Cambridge University Press.

Simon, H. A. 1953. Birth of an organization: The economic cooperation administration. *Public Administration Review*, no. 4:227–36.

———. 1959. Theories of decision-making in economics and behavior science. *American Economic Review* 49:253–83.

———. 1960. *Administrative behavior.* New York: The Macmillan Co.

———. 1965. *The shape of automation for men and management.* New York: Harper and Row.

———. 1967. The job of a college president. *Educational Record* 48:68–78.

Smith, A. 1967. *The wealth of nations.* New York: Modern Library.

Smith, C. S., and Armitage, P. 1967. The development of computable models of the British educational system and their possible uses. OECD Conference proceedings on *Mathematical models in educational planning.* Paris: Organization for Economic Cooperation and Development.

Smith, V. L. 1963. Minimization of economic rent in spatial price equilibrium. *Review of Economic Studies* 30:24–31.

Solow, R. M. 1956. A contribution to the theory of economic growth. *Quarterly Journal of Economics* 70:65–94.

———. 1959. Competitive valuation in a dynamic input-output system. *Econometrica* 27:30–53.

Southwick, L. 1969. Cost trends in land-grant colleges and universities. *Applied Economics* 1:167–82.

Southwick, L., and Zionts, S. 1969. A control theory model of an education decision: Education, the negative income tax and public policy. A paper presented at the 36th national meeting of the Operations Research Society of America, Miami Beach, Florida, November 10–12, 1969.

Steindl, J. 1945. *Small and big business: Economic problems of the size of firms.* Oxford: Blackwell.

———. 1952. *Maturity and stagnation in American capitalism.* Oxford: Blackwell.

Steiner, P. 1957. Peak loads and efficient pricing. *Quarterly Journal of Economics* 71:585–610.

———. 1969. The public sector and the public interest. In *The analysis and evaluation of public expenditures: The PPB system*, vol. 1, part 3, pp. 13–45. A compendium of papers submitted to the subcommittee on Economy in Government. Washington, D.C.: Joint Economic Committee, U.S. Congress.

Stigler, G. 1951. Production and distribution in the short run. In *Readings in the theory of income distribution*, ed. W. Fellner and B. F. Haley, pp. 119–42. Philadelphia: American Economic Association.

Stigum, B. P. 1969. Competitive equilibrium under uncertainty. *Quarterly Journal of Economics* 83:533–61.

Stoikov, V. 1964. The allocation of scientific effort: Some important aspects. *Quarterly Journal of Economics* 78:307–23.

Stone, R. 1955. Model building and the social accounts. In *Income and wealth*, series 4, ed. M. Gilbert and R. Stone, pp. 27–77. London: Bowes and Bowes.

———. 1963. Models of the national economy for planning purposes. *Operational Research Quarterly* 14:51–59.
———. 1965. A model of the educational system. *Minerva* 3:172–86.
Stone, R., and Brown, A. 1962. *A programme for growth: A computable model of growth*. London: Chapman and Hall.
Swanson, J. E.; Arden, W.; and Still, H. E., Jr. 1966. *Financial analysis of current operations of colleges and universities*. Ann Arbor: Institute of Public Administration, University of Michigan.

Taft, M. I., and Reisman, A. 1967. Toward better curricula through computer sequencing of subject matter. *Management Science* 13:926–45.
Theil, H. 1954. *Linear aggregation of economic relations*. Amsterdam: North-Holland Publishing Co.
———. 1961. *Economic forecasts and policy*. 2nd rev. ed. Amsterdam: North-Holland Publishing Co.
———. 1964. *Optimal decision rules for government and industry*. Amsterdam: North-Holland Publishing Co.
Tinbergen, J. 1939. *Statistical testing of business cycle theories*, vol. 2: *Business cycles in the United States of America, 1919–1932*. Geneva: League of Nations, Economic Intelligence Service.
———. 1952. *On the theory of economic policy*. Amsterdam: North-Holland Publishing Co.
———. 1954. *Centralization and decentralization in economic policy*. Amsterdam: North-Holland Publishing Co.
———. 1956. *Economic policy: Principles and design*. Amsterdam: North-Holland Publishing Co.
———. 1958. *The design of development*. Baltimore: The Johns Hopkins Press.
———. 1967. Some suggestions on a modern theory of the optimum regime. In *Socialism, capitalism and economic growth*, ed. C. H. Feinstein. Cambridge: Cambridge University Press.
Tinbergen, J., and Bos, H. C. 1965. A planning model for the educational requirements of economic development. In *Econometric models of education: Some applications*, Organization for European Cooperation and Development, pp. 9–27. Paris: OECD Publications.
Tinbergen, J.; Bos, H. C.; Blum, J.; Emmerij, L.; and Williams, G. 1965. *Econometric models of education: Some applications*. Paris: OECD Publications.
Tisdell, C. A. 1968. *The theory of price uncertainty, production and profit*. Princeton: Princeton University Press.
Tullock, G., ed. 1966. *Papers on non-market decision-making*. Charlottesville, Virginia: Thomas Jefferson Center for Political Economy.
Turvey, R., ed. 1968. *Public enterprise*. Baltimore: Penguin Books.

Uzawa, H. 1961. The stability of dynamic processes. *Econometrica* 29:617–31.
———. 1966. An optimum fiscal policy in an aggregative model of economic growth. In *The theory and design of economic development*, ed. I. Adelman and E. Thorbecke, pp. 113–39. Baltimore: The Johns Hopkins Press.

Vaizey, J., ed. 1964. *The residual factor and economic growth*. Paris: Organization for Economic Cooperation and Development.

Van de Panne, C., and Whinston, A. 1964. The simplex and the dual method for quadratic programming. *Operational Research Quarterly* 15:355–88.

Van den Bogaard, P. J. M., and Theil, H. 1959. Macrodynamic policy making: An application of strategy and certainty equivalence concepts to the economy of the United States, 1933–36. *Metroeconomica* 11:149–67.

Van Eijk, C. J., and Sandee, J. 1959. Quantitative determination of an optimum economic policy. *Econometrica* 27:1–13.

Vickrey, W. S. 1969. Decreasing costs, publicly administered prices and economic efficiency. In *The analysis and evaluation of public expenditures: The PPB system*, vol. 1, pp. 119–48. Washington, D.C.: Joint Economic Committee, U.S. Congress.

Walden, L. J. 1964. Long term manpower problems: Research, education and economic development. *Ekonomisk Tidskrift* 66:113–60.

Ward, B. 1960. The planners' choice variables. In *Value and plan: Economic calculation and organization in Eastern Europe*, ed. G. Grossman, pp. 132–51. Berkeley: University of California Press.

Weathersby, G. 1967. *The development and applications of a university simulation model*. Graduate School of Business Administration and Office of Analytical Studies, University of California, Berkeley, June 15, 1967.

Weisbrod, B. A. 1962. Education and investment in human capital. *Journal of Political Economy*, vol. 70, no. 5, part 2, pp. 106–23.

———. 1964. *External benefits of public education: An economic analysis*. Princeton: Industrial Relations Section, Princeton University Press.

Whinston, A. 1964. Price guides in decentralized organizations. In *New perspectives in organizalional research*, ed. W. W. Cooper, H. J. Leavitt, M. W. Shelly II, pp. 405–48. New York: John Wiley.

———. 1966. Theoretical and computational problems in organizational decision-making. In *Operational research and the social sciences*, ed. J. R. Lawrence, chapter 14, pp. 191–207. London: Tavistock Publications.

Wilde, D. J., and Beightler, C. S. 1967. *Foundations of optimization*. Englewood Cliffs, New Jersey: Prentice-Hall.

Wilkinson, B. W. 1966. Present values of lifetime earnings for different occupations. *Journal of Political Economy* 74:556–72.

Williams, B. R. 1963. Capacity and output of universities. *Manchester School* 31:185–202.

Williams, H. 1966. *Planning for effective resource allocation in universities*. Washington, D.C.: American Council on Education.

Williams, R. L. 1961. The cost of educating one college student. *Educational Record* 42:322–29.

Williamson, O. E. 1963. Managerial discretion and business behavior. *American Economic Review* 53:1032–57.

———. 1964. *The economics of discretionary behavior: Managerial objectives in a theory of the firm*. Englewood Cliffs, New Jersey: Prentice-Hall.

Windham, D. M. 1969. State financed higher education and the distribution of income in Florida. Ph.D. dissertation, Florida State University, June 1969.

Winkelmann, D. 1965. A programming approach to the allocation of teaching resources. A paper presented at the 1965 meeting of the Midwest Economics Association, April 1965.

Wolfe, J. N. 1967. Planning by forecast. In *Price formation in various economies*, ed. D. C. Hauge, pp. 153–69. New York: St. Martin's Press.

Wolff, P. de. 1965. Models for manpower and educational planning. A paper presented at the annual meeting of the Econometric Society, New York, December 1965.

Zemach, R. 1967. *A state-space model for resource allocation in higher education*. East Lansing: Michigan State University.

———. 1968. A state-space model for resource allocation in higher education. *IEEE Transactions on Systems Science and Cybernetics* SSC–14:108–18.

Zielinski, J. G. 1968. *Lectures on the theory of socialist planning*. London and Ibadan: Oxford University Press.

Zoutendijk, G. 1960. *Methods of feasible directions*. Amsterdam: Elsevier Publishing Co.

Zukhovitskiy, S. I., and Avdeyeva, L. I. 1966. *Linear and convex programming*. Translated into English by Scripta Technica, Inc. Philadelphia: W. B. Saunders Co.

# Author Index

Abadie, J. M., 135
Adelman, I., 45, 51, 58, 226
Alper, P., 26, 65, 226
Andersen, C. J., 269
Aoki, M., 142, 190
Aris, R., 75
Armitage, P., 26, 51, 226
Arrow, K. J., 20, 21, 85, 86, 92, 115, 154, 161, 187, 210, 212, 213
Avdeyeva, L. I., 184

Balderston, F. E., 82, 252
Balinski, M. L., 120, 134
Balogh, T., 31, 44
Barker, C., 251
Barker, R., 16, 260, 341
Barone, E., 87
Barson, J., 227, 228
Bator, F. M., 84
Baumol, W. J., 106, 120, 134, 154
Beadle, G. W., 293
Beale, E. M. L., 135, 203
Becker, G., 9, 23, 43, 334
Beightler, C. S., 216
Bellman, R., 139
Benard, J., 45, 60
Berne, E., 341
Berry, B. J. L., 298
Blaug, M., 25, 44, 64, 212
Bohm, P., 217, 221
Boiteux, M., 86, 90
Bolt, R. H., 52
Bos, H. C., 51, 52
Bowles, S., 46, 56, 60, 226

Brink, E. L., 48, 229, 230, 231
Brown, A., 39
Buchanan, J. M., 156, 217, 239
Buffa, E. S., 251

Carresse, L. M., 251
Cartter, A. M., 69, 207, 277, 280, 287, 288, 290, 320, 322
Cass, D., 144, 211
Charnes, A., 179, 180, 192
Chatterton, R., 251
Clayton, E. R., 179
Clower, R. W., 180
Contini, B., 184
Cook, D. L., 251
Cook, P. W., Jr., 206
Cooper, W. W., 179, 192
Corlett, W. J., 86
Correa, H., 38, 39, 226
Cyert, R. M., 161

Daniel, J. N., 257
Dantzig, G. B., 17, 95, 122, 187, 191, 202
Davis, O. A., 20, 28, 81, 156, 217, 218, 220, 221, 222
Day, R. H., 194, 198
Dean, J., 115, 147, 206
Debreu, G., 85, 149
Denison, E. F., 40, 43
Dhrymes, P., 170
Duesenberry, J. S., 13
Duffin, R. J., 214

Ellman, M., 149, 190

## AUTHOR INDEX

Fabian, T., 106, 154
Feinstein, C. H., 21, 80, 149
Firmin, P. A., 253
Forrester, J. W., 41, 225
Fox, K. A., 9, 26, 27, 29, 32, 37, 38, 39, 40, 45, 49, 50, 52, 63, 68, 82, 88, 99, 116, 118, 127, 128, 139, 140, 153, 157, 166, 172, 173, 187, 191, 198, 210, 212, 225, 226, 227, 232, 238, 295, 298, 307, 310, 319
Frank, C. R., 213, 214, 215
Frisch, R., 40, 156
Froomkin, J., 50, 60

Gale, D., 99
Geoffrion, A. M., 133, 135
Gibbs, J. W., 293
Glasserman, J., 251
Gordon, M. J., 115
Grambsch, P. V., 249
Gross, E., 249
Grossman, G., 149
Gruver, G., 17, 179

Hague, D. C., 86
Hahn, F. H., 20, 149, 201, 202
Hansen, W. L., 23, 31, 40, 44, 50, 60
Hanson, M., 137
Harbison, F., 38
Harsanyi, J. C., 197, 202
Hartley, H. J., 26
Hartman, L. M., 320, 321, 322
Hass, J. E., 127, 128, 173
Heal, G. M., 190
Hicks, J. R., 84
Hirshleifer, J., 90, 115, 147, 153, 188, 205
Hitch, C. J., 239
Hoggatt, A. C., 252
Hohenbalken, B. von, 68
Hollister, R. G., 38
Hotelling, H., 90
Howard, R., 198
Hurwicz, L., 92, 143, 154, 161

Ijiri, Y., 115, 179, 184
Intriligator, M., 52, 226

James, E., 31, 71
Jasny, N., 205
Johansen, L., 39, 56, 92, 177
Judy, R. W., 46, 229, 257

Kahn, R. F., 90
Kaldor, N., 84, 86, 211
Kamien, M. I., 20

Kaysen, C., 321
Keeney, M. G., 26, 46, 48, 140, 230, 244, 257
Kemeny, J. C., 136, 201
Kershaw, J. A., 71, 73, 230
Keynes, J. M., 150
Klein, L. R., 193
Klinger, A., 214
Koenig, H. E., 244, 257
Koopmans, T. C., 85, 93, 99, 117, 192, 243
Kornai, J., 17, 29, 90, 110, 113, 114, 119, 156, 171, 172, 191
Kortanek, K. D., 180
Kuhn, H. W., 203
Kuhn, T. S., 293
Kulikowski, R., 94
Kumar, T. K., 17, 137, 298
Kurz, M., 86
Kuznets, S., 13, 85

Lancaster, K., 27, 28, 86, 217, 221
Lange, O., 22, 56, 81, 87
Lave, R. E., 26
Layard, P. R. G., 40
Lee, S. M., 69, 179
Leontief, W. W., 13, 16
Lerner, A. P., 85, 86, 90, 127
LeVasseur, P. M., 38, 40, 41
Levine, H. S., 190
Lind, G., 207
Lindsay, F. H. I., 207
Lipsey, R. G., 27, 28, 86, 217, 221
Lipták, T., 17, 29, 90, 110, 113, 114, 119, 156, 171, 172, 191
Little, I. M. D., 90
Luce, R. D., 161, 203

MacDonald, J. S., 45
Madansky, A., 203
Mahalanobis, P. C., 40
Malinvaud, E., 94, 131, 190
Manne, A. S., 75
March, J. G., 161, 239
Marschak, J., 116
Marschak, T., 200
May, K., 193
McCamley, F. P., 69, 239, 344
McKean, R. N., 230, 239
McManus, M., 217, 221
Meade, J. E., 151, 210, 211, 217
Melichar, E., 17, 314, 315
Mesarovic, M., 94
Miller, L. S., 62
Mincer, J., 23, 44, 57

# AUTHOR INDEX

Mirrlees, J. A., 211
Mond, B., 137
Montias, J. M., 21, 22
Mood, A. M., 71, 73
Morgenstern, O., 116
Morishima, M., 80, 136, 149
Morris, W. T., 146, 150, 205
Moser, C. A., 40, 51, 226
Myers, C. A., 38

Nance, P. K., 252
Naslund, B., 170, 172
Nef, W., 204
Negishi, T., 20, 88, 149, 201, 202
Neumann, J. von, 116
Nikaido, H., 21, 150, 170, 171, 201
Nyblen, G., 203

Oakford, A., 251

Pareto, V., 1, 80
Parnes, H. S., 38
Parsons, T., 261, 342
Passy, V., 216
Pearson, J. D., 94, 139
Pfouts, R. W., 155, 172
Phelps, E. S., 217, 222
Pigou, A. C., 86, 88
Plessner, Y., 9, 49, 68, 118, 140, 151, 152, 172, 232, 238
Poignant, R., 38
Pollack, R. A., 217, 222
Pontryagin, L. S., 139
Portes, R. D., 150

Radner, R., 62, 116, 149
Radstrom, H., 116, 131, 196, 217
Raiffa, H., 161, 203
Rath, G., 226, 252
Redfern, P., 51, 226
Reisman, A., 226, 251
Riew, J., 50
Robinson, J., 113
Robinson, Joan, 86
Roose, K. D., 269
Rosen, J. B., 135
Rosenfeld, J. L., 197
Ryans, D. G., 226

Samuelson, P. A., 81, 217
Sandee, J., 10, 143, 152, 229
Sanders, J. L., 134
Sanyal, B. C., 9, 17, 68, 118, 127
Scarborough, C. W., 257

Schotta, C., 49
Schotta, S. G., 49
Schultz, T. W., 9, 23, 43, 56, 66, 313, 334
Scitovsky, T. A., 84
Sen, A., 75
Sengupta, J. K., 17, 19, 21, 27, 29, 36, 37, 49, 51, 63, 75, 82, 88, 127, 128, 139, 140, 141, 153, 166, 171, 172, 187, 191, 193, 195, 200, 202, 210, 212, 217, 225, 226, 232, 238, 295, 307, 310
Shackle, G. L. S., 161
Shapley, L. S., 196
Shaw, B. T., 292, 293
Shell, K., 46, 55
Sheshinski, E., 46, 55, 217
Shubik, M., 116, 153, 189
Sik, O., 81
Simon, H. A., 71, 82, 155, 171, 238, 258
Smith, B., 52, 227
Smith, C. S., 51, 65, 226
Solow, R. M., 56, 86, 211
Southwick, L., 32, 207
Steiner, P., 23, 24, 90
Stigum, B. P., 149
Stoikov, V., 52, 61, 226
Stoller, D. S., 71
Stone, R., 38, 39, 40, 51, 53, 226, 257
Streeten, P. P., 31
Stubblevine, W. C., 217
Swanson, J. E., 252

Taft, M. I., 251
Tatum, E. L., 293
Taylor, F. M., 87
Theil, H., 10, 26, 45, 50, 62, 63, 76, 118, 154, 193, 195, 308
Thorbecke, E., 88
Tinbergen, Jan, 3, 4, 13, 26, 38, 39, 51, 52, 88, 118, 145, 226
Tintner, G., 51, 191
Tisdell, C. A., 217
Tullock, G., 239
Turvey, R., 211

Uzawa, H., 92, 175

Vaizey, J., 40
Van den Bogaard, P. J. M., 154
Van de Panne, C., 122, 127
Van Eijk, C. J., 10, 143, 152, 229

Walden, L. J., 40
Ward, B., 21, 22
Weathersby, G., 26, 69, 253, 257
Weisbrod, B. A., 23, 31, 40, 43, 57, 66, 73

Whinston, A. B., 28, 81, 122, 127, 156, 173, 217, 218, 220, 221, 222
Wilde, D. J., 216
Williams, A. C., 135
Williams, B. R., 50
Williams, H., 230
Williamson, O. E., 147, 206
Windham, D. M., 31
Wolfe, P., 17, 95, 122, 187, 191, 200

Wolff, P. de, 38

Yaari, M. E., 144

Zemach, R., 26, 244, 257
Zielinski, J. G., 149
Zionts, S., 32
Zoutendijk, G., 146, 205
Zukhovitskiy, S. I., 184

# Subject Index

Activity analysis model, 179; assumptions, 234, 236; matrix determination, 237–38; McCamley's, 239–43—degree activities, 241–43; intermediate product identification, 243; supply function, 240—objective function, 155, 236–37; for resource allocation, 32; usefulness, 179, 232–33
Administered prices, 115
Aggregate demand, 174–75
Aggregate linear programming model, 195–96
Aggregate output measure, 46
Aggregate production function, 43
Aggregation, imputation vector, 196–97; perfect, 195
Aggregative models, classification, 51–52
Aggregative planning, 149–50
Algorithms of computation, linear programming (Dantzig and Wolfe), 110; nonlinear programming, 125–27
Allocation of economic resources, direct costs of various activities, 293–94; history, 80–81; multiproduct firm parallel, 206–7; of scientific effort, 61; without shadow prices, 29–30
Annual expenditures (education), 36
Arrow–Hurwicz formulation, 117
Aspects of stabilization and optimization, 63
Average discounted lifetime earnings stream, 44

Balanced growth, concept, 52–53; von Neumann model, 136

Basic feasible solution, 125, 126–27
Behavior settings (university), 260–61, 294, 310–11, 341–42, 346
Block-diagonal policy model, 7
Boundaries of scientific communities, 312
Brookings quarterly econometric model, 13, 16; condensed flow diagram, 14–15

Capacity, concept of, 75
Centrally planned economy, 32, 87
Central model, 175; agency, 131–32; under aggregation of resources and activities, 197–98; problems of, 149–50
Closing of model, 52, 55–56
Clustering courses and fields, complementarity, 314; principles for, 313–14
Cobweb model, 62, 63
Collective goods, 23
Commodity, linear decision model, 180–81
Community college, 297, 307
Comparisons of, departments within a discipline, 281–83; entire universities, 283–84; graduate programs, effectiveness, 280–81; heterogeneous groups of departments, 272–74; quality of graduate faculty, 277, 279–80; science departments, 269–72
Competitive equilibrium, Arrow's analysis, 85; model, 117
Competitive model, 19–20; Arrow–Debreu type interpretation, 149
Competitive pricing, mechanism, 150; theory, 210–11
Component analysis, definition, 63

371

Composite resources, 33
Computer, use for resource allocation, 81
Computer models, economies of size, 218
Consistency model, 153; activity mix, 335; coverage, 323; for departmental planning, 323–36; input-output coefficients, 326; inputs, 330–33; intermediate goods, 327; matrix, 334–35; outputs, 328–30
Constraints, 9, 27, 96, 97–98; in modeling educational systems, 45–46; and transfer cost, 172
Consumption, theory of, 307–8
Consumption bundles, 20
Convex set theory (concave programming), 85; integer convexity criterion, 214–15; logarithmic convexity criterion, 215–16; use, 213
Correlates of quality, graduate education, 320–22
Cost-benefit analysis, 43
Cost of training, 53

Dantzig–Wolfe rule, 127
Decentralization, resource allocation under, 143–44. *See also* Decomposition
Decentralized decisionmaking, logic of, 109
Decentralized resource allocation mechanism, 143
Decision analysis and goal programming, 45
Decisionmaker, university, 206, 233–34
Decisionmaking, decentralized, 94–95, 109; internal in a university, 33
Decision models, constraints, 180; linear, 179–80; for university system, 229–31
Decomposition, active approach of, 78; Dantzig–Wolfe method of, 106–8; game theory approach, 203, 205; guiding rules of price adjustment, 192; infeasibility, 202; need for subprograms, 187–88; organizational slack, 202; penalty cost function approach, 202–3; problems of aggregation and disaggregation, 193; transfer pricing, 203
Decomposition algorithms, 29; of Dantzig and Wolfe, 110; DW, RL, AL, 191, 193; problems, 204–5
Decomposition techniques, 82; decentralization of decisions, 92; limitations, 145–47; transfer price, 188–89
Demand function, 63, 64
Demand sector model, 245–47
Double decomposition method, 139

Dual control problem, 137
Dummy activities, usefulness, 77
Dynamic planning approach, planning horizon, 58
Dynamic systems, 12–13; models, importance, 135–36

Econometric models, advantages, 207–9; in land grant university context, 209; linking with optimizing, 209–10
Economic optimum (Pareto), 80
Economic policy, theory of, 308
Education, modeling systems, 38–41, 50–51; as public good, 25
Educational systems, 340; aggregate models, 51–52; as part of nonmarket system, 30–31, 83; as quasi-public good, 31; role, 36–37, 340
Efficiency concept, competitive pricing, 210
Efficiency indicators, 8
Enrollment expansion, 265–67
Equilibrium, in systems model, 48
Equilibrium demand price, 64, 65
Evaluation, of faculty performance, 284–85, 287; use of worksheets, 285–86
Extension service, 296–97; boundaries, outer and inner, 297; need for objective function, 306; objective function, 297–99, 306; outputs, 329
Extension settings, 306
External benefits, effect on university, 57
Externality, from technology, 217–18
Extra education, price of, 63–64
Extremum (optimum), 8

Faculty allocation, 35
Faculty grades, assignments and salaries, 263–64
FEA. *See* Functional economic area
Feasible points, 123
Finite planning horizon, 61–62
Firm production possibility sets, 20
First-best policy, 27–28; Pareto-optimality conditions, 28
Forecasting approach, defined, 38
Functional economic area (FEA), 296, 298–99, 307; and community colleges, 307
Functions, specification of objective, 9–10

GAME (global accounts for manpower and education model), 41

# SUBJECT INDEX

Game strategy, polyhedral game, 113–14
Game theory approach to decomposition and aggregation, 202, 205
General systems approach, 227–29
Global optimum, 85
Goal programming, fixed goals, 185; minimum goals, 183–84
Goals, setting of, 72–73
Gross benefits, 333
Gross social product (GSP), 18, 32–33, 72, 342, 345
Growth problem, probabilistic aspects, 76
Growth programming model, assumptions, 79
GSP. *See* Gross social product

Hass algorithm (decomposition), 128–31
Homogenous inputs, aggregate labor and capital, 43
Household indifference maps, 20
Human capital investment, in schools, 43, 49

Identity matrix, 54, 56
Implicit imputed prices, 80. *See also* Shadow prices
Implicit optimization, 26; in systems model for university, 47–48
Imputation, 122; benefit-cost analysis for public goods, 150, 152–55; functions, 178; used for quantification, 143
Imputation vector, 196–97
Imputed prices, 153–59
Income redistributive role of education, 32; negative income tax, 32
Indivisible resource, imputation as shadow prices, 170; treatment, 150
Indivisibility problem, 211–13
Input-output analysis usefulness and limitations, 40–41, 43; small college model, 258–59
Integer convexity criterion, uses, 214–15
Interior maximum, 85
Intermediate goods, 327
Internal administrative organization, purpose, 311
Internal rate of return, educational investment, 64
Intertemporal allocation, 74
Iteration, 99, 106, 108
Iterative method (Hass algorithm), 129–31
Iterative methods, second level of decomposition, 139

Jensen's inequality, 223

K-divisional linear programming models, 200
Kuhn–Tucker theorem, 88, 121, 124, 125, 219

Lagrange multipliers, 19, 124; column vector of, 11, 19; linear programming, 82; nonlinear programming, 93; in partial equilibrium, 94; in second-best policy, 27, 28, 29
Lange–Lerner model, assumption, 88
Limited indivisibility, 213
Linear activity analysis, limitation, 118
Linear activity analysis model, constraints, goal vector, 181–92; goal programming, 183–84; optimal allocation of resources, 140–41
Linear decomposition model (Dantzig and Wolfe), 134–35
Linear fractional functional (LFF) programs, 171
Linear programming (LP) models, 127–28, 157–60; decomposition methods and shadow prices, 190–92; use for optimization models, 46
Linear programming solution, Tchebycheff method of approximation, 203–4
Logarithmic convexity, 215–16
Long-range planning, 35
LP model. *See* Linear programming model

Manhours (input), reading publications, 331–33
Marginal rate of substitution, competitive economy, 84
Market adjustment, Marshallian output adjustment, 92, 93; Walrasian *tâtonnement*, 92, 93
Market failure, characteristics, 24
Market systems analysis (postulates), 19
Market *tâtonnement*, 19, 22
Matrix, input-output, 157
Maximization, 11
Measurement of student performance, ego ideal, 264–65; mastery of subjects, 250–51, 261–63
Measures of performance, multiple regression analysis, 262–63; problem background, 260–62
Microanalysis, microeconomic decision unit, 67
Mixed framework, 22

Monotonic procedure, defined, 132
Monte Carlo methods, 252–53
Multiproduct model, 156–57; objective function, 119; similarities to university, 66–67, 70, 119–20, 154, 173
Multistage stochastic process, 65

Near-profit maximization theorem, 214
Noncompetitive rules of resource allocation, 21
Nonlinear duality theorem, 120–22
Nonlinearity, aspects of, 117–19
Nonlinear programming, problem of feasibility, 190
Nonmarket institution, 2–3
Nonmarket system (framework), defined, 3, 81–82
Non*tâtonnement*, process, 201–2; rules of exchange, 20
$N$-person cooperative game, 116; theory, 197

Objective functions, 9, 13, 45; normalization factors and specification, 155; ordinal vs. cardinal, 10; quadratic, 10; target variables, 9
OCI. *See* Overall central information problem
Optimal control problem, 65
Optimal control theory, applications, 175–76
Optimal growth of economy, 45; inputs, 178; objective functions, 75, 76; theory, 72, 74–76, 178
Optimal solution, 60
Optimal tolls, 91–92
Optimization approach, 74
Optimization models, application, 342–44; at college and university levels, 307, 344–45; and gross social product, 308–10; McCamley's, 344
Optimizing policy model, 26–27
Ordinal function vs. cardinal function, 10–12
Organizational model, described, 20
Organizational slack, 170, 202
Overall central information problem (OCI), 110–14
Overhead cost allocation problem, 171, 172

Pareto-equilibrium conditions, criticisms, 84
Pareto model, assumptions, 83–84
Pareto-optimal allocation, 20

Pareto optimality, conditions, 28, 29, 32, 84–85, 86; marginal conditions, 71; standard for comparison, 70
Pareto-optimal system, effects of constraints, 221–22
Pareto optimum, 27, 28
Partial equilibrium, 93–94
Peak load pricing, 90
Penalty costs, 154; penalty cost function approach, 202–3
Perfect aggregation, 195
Perfect competition, 1
Pigouvian welfare optimization model, 88–89
Planning, educational system, 50–51
Planning horizon, 58, 59; resources, fixed and variable, 76–77
Policy approach, defined, 38
Policymaker, planning calculations, 78–79, 136, 140; problem of resource allocation, 152; role, 2, 26, 62, 93, 181–83; satisficing behavior, 68
Policy model, academic department, 68–69
Potential output, education, 33
Price adjustment mechanisms, centrally planned systems, 87
Price-guided allocation rules, 29
Price imputation, 174
Price vectors, equilibrium with other fields, 320; salary differentials in scientific fields, 219–20
Pricing rules for resources, 37
Pricing theory, multiproduct firms, 71
Primal method, 133
Probabilistic models, optimal supply, 65; expected costs, equation, 66
Problem of increasing school size, 265–67
Procedures, defined, 132
Production function, any university department, 178
Production possibilities frontier, 2
Production sector model, 247–49
Program planning and budgeting (PPB), 226
Prospective indices, 131–32
Prospects of future goods and services, 149
Pseudo-objective function, imputed prices, 153
Public allocation, pathological situations, 89–90
Publications, estimating quality, 291–92; publication index, 288; publication units, 328; Shaw's system of ranking,

## SUBJECT INDEX

292–93; volume and quality considerations, 287–88, 289, 291–93
Public goods, definition, 23, 24; education as, 25; in two-part model, 220; university as supplier, 143–44
Public sector, monopoly elements, 90

Quadratic cost function, 69
Quantitative models, approaches of, 226–27; constraints (small college), 259–60
Quasi market, 81–82; model, 20
Quasi-public good, 31

Rate of return approach, criticisms, 44–45
Rating of, graduate faculties (Cartter), 277–80; graduate program, 280–81
Ratio of marginal utilities, theory of economic policy (Theil), 308
Reallocation, convergence process, 200–1
Recursive policy model, correspondingly consecutive, 6
Redistributive role of education, 60
Regression analysis, science departments, 269–71
Relocation cost function, 172
Resource aggregates, 198, 199
Resource allocation, 22–23; in educational systems, 30–31; need for pricing systems, 341; noncompetitive rules, 21; by policymakers, 49; problem of quantification, 46; Public Policy Research Organization, 73; relative fixity, 190; salaries of personnel, 293–94; theory of public goods, 143–44; use of two-good model, 219–20
Resource-directive method (decomposition), 133, 135
Rule of anonymity (universality) of prices, 19–20

Saddle point theorem. *See* Kuhn–Tucker theorem
Salaries, multiple regression analysis, 314–16, 318; age, 316; degree held, 315–16; interpretation of deviations, 318–19; related to grades, 263–64; relationship to resource allocation, 293–94
Satisficing behavior, 27, 68; suboptimal solutions, 75
Scalar function, objective, specification, 75; of target variables, 8
Scheduling model, sequencing, 250–51
Schultz–Becker theory (human capital), 72

Science programs, compared, 269–74
Scientific communities, boundaries, 312
Second-best policies, 70; problems, 222; sources, 217; usefulness, 216–17
Sector programming problems, two-level planning, 112–13
Separability, 28–29
Sequencing, measuring mastery of subjects, 250–51
Sequential process of computation, 82. *See also* Decomposition technique
Shadow prices, 25, 29, 59–60, 134, 174, 179, 190; vs. market prices, 221–22; nonnegative, 46; output of public sector, 91; of resources, 200–1. *See also* Lagrange multiplier
Short-run decision model, goal programming, 183–84
Short term (year-to-year) model, 336–39; activities, inputs and outputs, 336–38; dollar output estimates, X department, 339
Simplex multiplier (Dantzig and Wolfe), 98, 99, 106
Simulation, of competitive market mechanism, 22; vs. optimization, 25–26
Simulation model, 252–53, 257; Monte Carlo technique, 252–53
Simulation techniques, use of, 229
Slack variables, 121
Slater condition, 120
Small-scale models, 343
Standard coefficients, used for workload estimates, 286–87
State-space approach, definition of static and dynamic model, 243–44
State-space model, advantages and limitations, 249–50; cost of production units, 248; input-output model of production sector (equations), 247–48; updating model, 248–49; vector equations, 245–48
Stock of students, 54
Structural relations, 5
Structural variables, 73
Structure of knowledge, concept, 312–13
Suboptimal (second-best) policies, 27–29, 216–17
Suboptimization, 48
System analysis approach, 73–74, 229–30, 238–39; use of decisionmaking model, 229–30, 238–39
Systems model (Brink), use of flow diagram, 230–31

*Tâtonnement* process, 29, 142–43, 144, 201, 206
Tchebycheff method of approximation, linear programming, 203–4
Teaching budget allocation, equation, 268–69
Teaching performance, evaluation, 287. *See also* Evaluation
Team-decision problems, 116
Theory of consumption, 307–8; the divisionalized firm, 115–16; the second-best, defined, 86
Tinbergen-type policy model, 3–7; matrices, 5–7; summary, 4
Trade-offs, short-run equilibrium model, 177
Transfer activities, 172–73
Transfer pricing, 199; in decomposition algorithms, 146, 206
Transformation function, 85
Two-good model (Davis and Whinston), 218–19
Two-level planning (Kornai–Lipták), 110–13; compared to Dantzig–Wolfe method, 114–15; using quota mechanism, 110

Two-part division of costs, advantages, 173–74
Two-sector interdependence, 151–52

University cost simulation model, cost categories, 253; estimation of outputs and costs, 255, 257
Utility function, university president, 309

Vector objective functions, competitive equilibrium model, 93
Vector optimization, 47
Vectors, linear activity analysis model, 181

Walrasian adjustment, 87
Walrasian *tâtonnement* process, 93, 201
Welfare economics, as basis for educational planning, 71; Pigouvian welfare optimization problem, 88–89
Workloads, collection and use of data, 282–83; other components, 275–76; estimates, using standard coefficients, 286–87; student credit hours and salaries, 274–75; worksheets, 285


THE JOHNS HOPKINS UNIVERSITY PRESS

Composed in Modern text and News Gothic display
by Monotype Composition Company

Printed on 60-lb. Sebago and
Bound in Holliston Roxite Vellum
by The Maple Press Company